F
1231   Cohen, Martin A.
C32C63
               The martyr

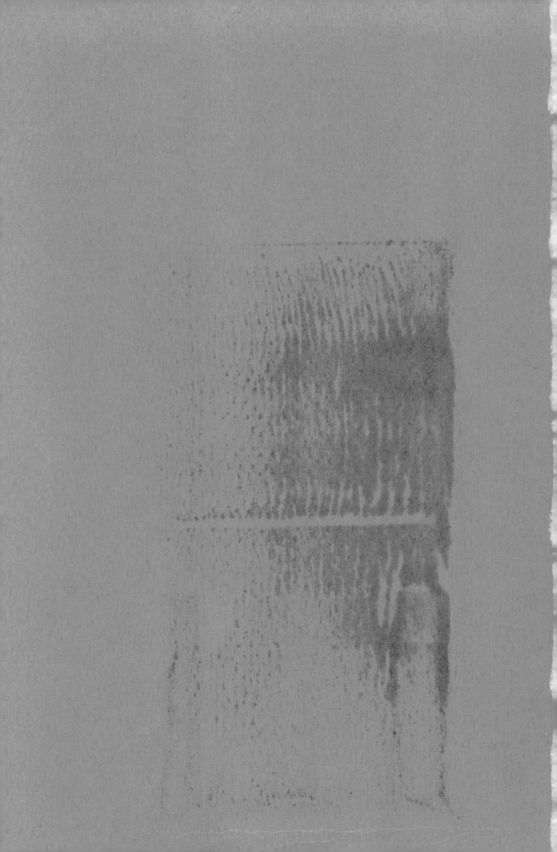

THE MARTYR

THE

Martin A. Cohen

MARTYR

The Story of a Secret Jew
and the Mexican Inquisition
in the Sixteenth Century

The Jewish Publication Society of America
Philadelphia   5733-1973

ACKNOWLEDGMENTS

Gratitude is herewith expressed to Dr. J. Ignacio Rubio Mañé and the
Archivo General de La Nación in Mexico City for permission to reproduce
pages from inquisitorial documents and other materials belonging to the
Archivo General de la Nación;

to the American Jewish Historical Society for permission to reproduce
parts of inquisitorial documents and other material under its jurisdiction;

to the Henry E. Huntington Library for permission to quote from inquisitorial documents in its possession;

to the University of California Press for permission to reproduce the
illustrations found on pages 52, 75, and 76 from Philip W. Powell's Soldiers,
Indians and Silver (1952), and the quotation on page 109 from Lesley Byrd
Simpson's Many Mexicos (1966) (originally published by the University of
California Press; reprinted by permission of the Regents of the University of
California);

to the Cambridge University Press, American Branch, for permission
to reproduce the map found on page 119 from P.J. Bakewell's Silver Mining
and Society in Colonial Mexico (1971);

to Ingeniero Ángela Alessio Robles, for permission to reproduce maps
from Vito Alessio Robles, Coahuila y Texas en la época colonial; and to
Lic. Guillermo de la Mora G., for permission to reproduce illustrations
from Alfonso Toro, La familia Carvajal.

To my wife

SHELBY RUTH

Contents

Illustrations

Preface

One of the lessons that history teaches is that fact is often stranger than fiction. The records of history contain indisputable facts that novelists would seldom invent.

The story told here is a web of such facts. It is a tale of adventure and heroism, set four hundred years ago in the land then called New Spain. With the passing of the centuries the ideas that stirred its characters have lost their passionate immediacy. The characters themselves have been largely forgotten, except by a handful of scholars burrowing through archival manuscripts. Yet the emotions that galvanized their actions, their ideals, and their struggles continue to ring relevantly for modern man.

The Martyr is the story of a man regarded by one contemporary Mexican author as "the most . . . exciting personage in New Spain" (F. Benítez, *Los primeros mexicanos* [*La vida criolla en el siglo XVI*], p. 132). It is the saga of a man who wanted to live for an ideal but found himself compelled to die for it. It is also the story of his family, his people, and his era, an era where men like him became martyrs not because they were doctrinaire fanatics but rather because they were placed in circumstances that left them little choice.

Our protagonist, most of his family, and many of his friends struggled to maintain their freedom of conscience in an increasingly stifling and oppressive society. In his brief life he was a student, merchant, conquistador, scholar, teacher, inspired writer, and one of the towering figures in the religious life of New Spain. He belonged to a group of people whose beneficent influence on the development of Mexican society has not as yet been sufficiently delineated.

The book is entirely factual. Every detail, description, and transcribed conversation is found in the trial records of the Inquisition or other unimpeachable primary or secondary sources. When the picture drawn by the facts is not complete, the text uses adverbs like possibly, probably, apparently, seemingly, certainly, depending upon the extent of evidence available. Since the inquisitorial records transcribed the testimony of all witnesses in the third person, it has been necessary to change their direct statements back to the first person when they were quoted, but otherwise the quotations have not been violated. The chief violations to the literalness of the original text have been my attempts to translate some of the Spanish poetry into equivalent English verse. In addition I have used both "Thou" and "You" and their corresponding forms for addresses to the Deity, the first in liturgical pieces, the second for all other cases.

Because many of the facts may appear stranger than fiction, it was decided to provide full and precise documentation for every detail. This was by no means an easy procedure in the case of the inquisitorial records, since these originally bore no page or folio numbers, and those subsequently placed on the manuscript folios proved to be incomplete and often incorrect. As a result it was decided to cite all evidence from the trial records by listing the name of the witness giving the testimony, the italicized name of the defendant in the case, and the date of the testimony. An italicized name alone, followed by a date, indicates the testimony to be that of the defendant himself. The names of witnesses other than the defendant remain unitalicized whether or not their testimony appears in the trial records of their own cases. Thus *MNC II*, May 30, 1600, refers to testimony given by Mariana Núñez Carvajal in her second trial on the date indicated, while DDN, Jan. 18, 1600 (in *JA III*) refers to the depositions of Diego Díez Nieto in the third dossier dealing with Jorge de Almeida. A full identification of the trial records and other manuscript material used in the study will be found in the Appendix. Where a printed text is available, the Notes list the appropriate page number in parentheses.

At the same time the number of individual details from which the story is woven is so large that to indicate the source of each separately would have increased the Notes to an unwieldy size. Since many of the facts derive from the depositions at a single hearing, or dovetailing accounts, either by the same individual or different persons in separate cases, it was decided to provide all the pertinent sources for a given section under one note at the end wherever possible. Thus, for example, the description of the brothers at the beginning of chapter one is derived from three sources mentioned in note one, as indicated at the end of the second paragraph of the narrative.

The story behind the composition of this book begins in the spring of 1955, when Professor Jacob Rader Marcus, the Milton and Hattie Kutz Distinguished Service Professor of American Jewish History at the Hebrew Union College–Jewish Institute of Religion, suggested that I prepare an English translation of the transcript of the memoirs of Luis de Carvajal the Younger, published in an appendix to Alfonso Toro's *La familia Carvajal*. My work on the translation was sufficient to kindle my interest in the Carvajals. Though occupied with other studies and research in the succeeding decade, I returned periodically to the subject and eventually prepared a translation of Carvajal's letters and his last will and testament. These were published in the *Quarterly* of the American Jewish Historical Society in the March and June issues of 1966.

By 1966 I was already several years deep in the research that was to lead to this volume. The research had begun with a study of the records of the two trials of Luis de Carvajal the Younger. I soon realized that a complete picture of the man would be possible only after a study of the trials of all the members of the family and most of the Carvajals' friends, and that almost all these records were still in manuscript in Mexico City and in libraries in the United States.

Only one previous work dealing with the Carvajals, that of Alfonso Toro, was based on extensive research of the manuscript material. An invaluable effort, it suffers from extensive padding and fictionalization, confusion of facts (even to the point of confusing Almeida's wife with the wife of Díaz de Cáceres), frequent and perhaps unwitting expressions of anti-Jewish bias, unexpected in an antagonist of the Inquisition, and a lack of knowledge of Judaism sufficiently profound to have induced the author to include a photograph of a page in Gujarati script and call it a page of the Hebrew Torah (vol. 2, p. 94). On the other hand, Pablo Martínez del Río's *Alumbrado* was, by the author's own admission (p. xxiv), a popular work, not written for the historian, and containing "not . . . a single line proceeding from the study of unpublished material." Arnold Wizniter's "Crypto-Jews in Mexico during the Sixteenth Century," though devoting thirty-four excellent pages to the two men named Luis de Carvajal, likewise is not based on a deep study of the manuscripts and relies primarily on printed records. Earlier sketches, such as those of Vicente Riva Palacio (in *El libro rojo* and *México a través de los siglos*), are partial and confused (he confuses the two Luis de Carvajals as well as occasional dates and details).

All this spurred me to continue the project. In the course of my work, it was my good fortune to have the vast manuscript collection of the Archivo General de la Nación, in Mexico City, made available to me. Through the graciousness of its director, Dr. J. Ignacio Rubio Mañé, and his accommodating staff, I was able to consult these documents in situ and to have many of them microfilmed. Since that time I have enjoyed the privledge of regular communication with Dr. Rubio Mañé and the advantage of his frequent advice.

Additional manuscripts were made available to me through the American Jewish Historical Society and the Henry E. Huntington Library.

I also wish to express my thanks

—to the librarians and archivists who gave generously of their time in providing me with additional materials that I needed: to Dr. I. Edward Kiev, librarian of the New York School of the Hebrew Union College–Jewish Institute of Religion, and his staff, Mrs. Susan Tabor, Mrs. Catherine A. Markush, and Mr. Israel Diesenhaus; to Dr. Herbert C. Zafren, director of the libraries of the Hebrew Union College–Jewish Institute of Religion and his staff; to Dr. Marcus and his associate, Dr. Stanley F. Chyet, and their staff at the American Jewish Archives; to Mr. Bernard Wax, director of the American Jewish Historical Society, to Dr. Isidore S. Meyer, editor emeritus of the society's journal, *The American Jewish Historical Quarterly*, and the society's librarian, Dr. Nathan M. Kaganoff, now the editor of its *Quarterly* as well; to Miss Shirley Victor of the Hispanic Society of America; to the staff of the New York Public Library Research Division, particularly the staff in American history; and to the staff of the Queensboro Public Library in Flushing, New York; to Dr. Erroll Rhodes of the American Bible Society for his help in the identification of the Gujarati document; to Father Ladislas M. Orsy, S. J., professor of theology at Fordham University, and to Sister Mary Alethea Brennan, professor at the College of Mount Saint Vincent, for their assistance with matters of Catholic theology; to the librarians of the Library of Congress, Harvard University, and the University of Pennsylvania, for their provision of numerous materials.

—to Dr. Marcus, Dr. Chyet, Dr. Meyer, Dr. Herman P. Salomon, editor of *The American Sephardi*, and my wife, Dr. Shelby Ruth Cohen, for reading the manuscript and the invaluable suggestions they offered for its improvement;

—to Dr. Chaim Potok, editor of The Jewish Publication Society of America and my copy editor, Mrs. Kay Powell, for their suggestions and guidance of the manuscript of this work through publication;

—to Dr. Rochelle Weinstein, of the City University of New York, for her technical assistance with the photographs;

—to Mr. Richard J. Scheuer, for his friendship and encouragement of this project;

—to Mrs. Lillian Morgan, who has been typing and retyping the manuscript of this work for five years, with amazing accuracy, unflagging patience, and an uncanny ability to decipher my enigmatic scrawl;

—to Mrs. Virginia T. de Rosenblueth, of Mexico City, and to Miss Elizabeth Osher, of Mexico City and New York, for their help in obtaining permissions to reproduce materials under Mexican copyright; and

—to Mr. Robert Jacobs, for helping in the reading of proof and providing the index for the book.

The encouragement, friendship, and inspiration I have received from all who have helped me in this work are for me priceless and enduring gifts.

Martin A. Cohen

THE MARTYR

"This is the road to the glory of paradise . . . and there is none other.
And the journey is better than the one to Castile."

Luis de Carvajal the Younger,
letter to his sisters
in the inquisitorial prison, May 1595

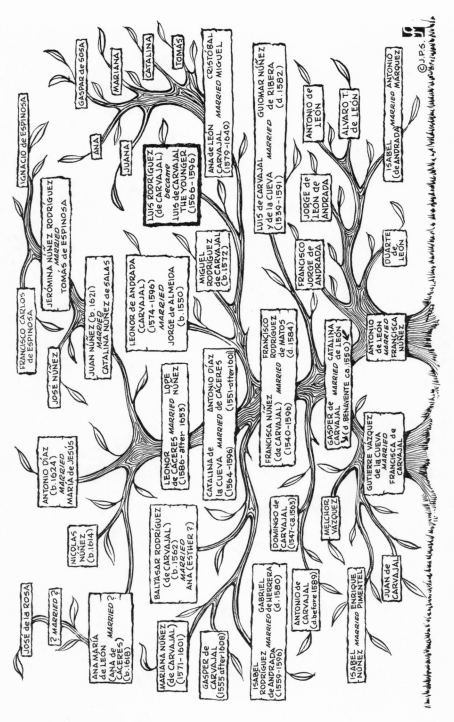

The Genealogy of the Carvajals

1 The Fugitive

Early in May 1589 Luis de Carvajal the Younger, wearing a doublet and breeches of blue and greenish denim, returned to his home in the Valley of Mexico.

Young Carvajal was a Spaniard, part of the small caste of less than a hundred thousand who claimed the homage of millions of Indians in the land they called New Spain. He was not yet twenty-three years old. He was of average height, with dark hair and skin that was white and clear. A Roman nose was prominent on his long, oval face. The down of a sluggish beard covered his chin, but failed to give him a boyish appearance. In fact, one of his cousins thought that he looked the same age as his fair-bearded brother Baltasar, four years his senior. Cultured and articulate, he might have been taken for a member of the Spanish nobility, though he possessed aristocratic status through neither birth nor achievement. If his name conjured up the noble exploits of the conquistadors, it was because it was also borne by his uncle, pacifier of the sprawling region to the north of the Valley of Mexico known officially as the New Kingdom of León.[1]

For young Luis de Carvajal the Valley of Mexico marked the end of an arduous journey begun more than two hundred miles away at the sultry coastal town of Veracruz. The trip from Veracruz through Las Ventas and Puebla was exhausting, a rugged climb from the coastal lowlands to the crest of the cordilleras cradling the valley. The tortuous mountain paths, stamped by the hooves of horses and mules, offered the traveler few consolations besides the welcome dry breezes of the temperate mesas and the colorful variations of landscape. But perhaps the greatest relief came at the end of the journey when he caught his first glimpse of the Valley of Mexico.

The valley was a sprawling oval some two hundred miles in circumference, nestled a mile and a half above sea level. Luxuriant streams, golden fields, stately forests, and picturesque towns of white stucco and the reddish volcanic *tezontle* gave it a captivating beauty.[2] Gigantic snow-capped mountains girded with porphyry enclosed the valley. Many had once been volcanoes, but by now the passions of all had subsided, except for two that stood alongside each other at the valley's southeastern rim. These were Popocatépetl, the "smoking mountain," nearly eighteen thousand feet tall, and its majestic consort, almost its equal in size, known as the "white lady," Ixtaccíhuatl. The Indians had long venerated the mountains as tutelary deities. Most often Popocatépetl and Ixtaccíhuatl appeared benign and protective. But capricious like gods, they might momentarily burst out in fitful anger, belching smoke and lava from their cavernous maws.[3]

Seventy years before, Hernán Cortés and his minuscule forces had traversed the same general route to the hills dominating the Valley of Mexico. When they beheld its coruscating splendor, they instinctively conjured up visions of the enchanted places described in the *Amadis of Gaul* and other famous novels of chivalry that were being read voraciously in Spain. Cortés later told his sovereign, Charles V, that the sights of the valley "are so amazing that they will hardly seem credible. We who behold them with our own eyes find it difficult to believe them."[4] For the conquistadors the valley came to symbolize the enchantment and boundless wealth of the New World. And New Spain as a whole came to be regarded as a land "indisputably superior to all the nations of the world in the fertility of its soil, the variety of its products, the extension of its pastures, and the abundance of its opportunities for enterprise."[5] Lured by the valley and the surrounding land, people from all walks of life flocked to New Spain, impatiently anticipating the actualization of the accumulated fantasies of their lives.[6]

Luis knew the Valley of Mexico well. He had frequently traversed its length and breadth in the eight and a half years that had elapsed since his arrival in the New World. Its mottled terrain and strange peoples had gradually blended into the pattern of his familiar associations. And the exotic appellations of its Indian towns, like Texcoco, Azcapotzalco, Chalco, and Ixtapalapán, once certainly a jumble of cacophanies, now doubtless rang as naturally in his ears as the Romanic names of the towns in his native Spain.

Luis now made his home in the valley. He lived in the Spaniards' city of Mexico, the "very noble, notable, and loyal city," as the Emperor Charles had dubbed it by imperial decree in 1549.[7] Built on Lake

Title Pages of Records of Inquisitorial Trials

left top: Governor Luis de
Carvajal y de la Cueva (1589)

left bottom: Luis de Carvajal
the Younger, First Trial (1589)
below: Luis de Carvajal the
Younger, Second Trial (1595)

Texcoco and ribboned with beautiful canals, it was more popularly called by the Spaniards the "Venice of the New World." Once, under the name Tenochtitlán, it had served as the capital of the Aztec empire. Around its Great Square had clustered all the buildings of Emperor Moctezuma II, who met Cortés on his arrival at the valley— the palace, the harem, the zoo, and the dens of human monsters kept for the emperor's sport. In its center, behind an eight-foot-high wall of stone and lime, stood numerous shrines, or teocallis, and precious objects, including a fifty-ton porphyry calendar stone that reckoned time with uncanny accuracy. The principal attraction was the Great Teocalli, an imposing edifice constructed of pieces of solid marble. From its base four tiers of stairs gently sloped to a platform holding twin towers. Here were housed the most precious objects of the Aztec cult: icons of gods and urns containing the ashes of Aztec princes. In the towers also stood a large convex block of jasper, where human bodies were regularly stretched out for sacrifice to Huitzilopochtli, the awesome, flaming sun god of the Aztecs, insatiably athirst for human blood.[8]

Luis's people had almost entirely destroyed the wondrous, barbaric splendor of the former Aztec capital. In the heady flush of their conquest of the city in mid-August 1521, they had wantonly broken the treasured structures of Tenochtitlán. They then impressed the vanquished Indians into service to convert the city into the capital of New Spain, using the slabs of their demolished buildings as the foundation. A contemporary Spaniard was to write: "The Indians do the work and provide the material at their own expense. They pay the stonecutters and the carpenters and starve if they fail to bring their own food along."[9] With Indian labor the Spaniards widened the streets, filled many of the canals, and erected sturdy edifices in European style. A few years after the conquest, convents and monasteries dotted the Great Square; on the site of the Great Teocalli, and constructed with its slabs, rose a simple, wooden-roofed church. By 1589 the construction of a sumptuous cathedral, dedicated to Saint Francis, was under way. When finally completed in the second decade of the nineteenth century, it was the largest church in the Western Hemisphere, an imposing blend of the Gothic, baroque, and churrigueresque.[10]

Living evidence of the old metropolis still abounded everywhere. The population of Mexico City, well over a hundred thousand, remained predominantly Indian, with an increasing number of mestizos, born of Spanish fathers and Indian mothers, and mulattos, the product of the union of Spaniards with black slaves brought from Africa.[11] The natives fortunate enough not to be consigned to brutalizing service near their homes or away at the mines continued for the most part to live as they had in the days before the coming of Cortés. They still inhabited their rude dwellings and slept on pillows of wood or stone softened with reeds or palm leaves. They still ate on the floor, retaining their frugal diets of vegetables, fruit, and tortillas. Though wax and grease were plentiful, they still lighted their homes with candlewood or other resinous bark. The common men wore their *moxtlis,* or loincloths, though the friars insisted that they also put on trousers, while the women continued to adorn themselves with their elaborately embroidered *kuipils.*

The Indians' swift canoes still plied the waters of the lakes and lagoons—or what was left of them now that the negligent Spaniards used them as garbage disposals. On market days especially, countless canoes could be seen bearing food and building materials from afar. Other Indians served as masons and carpenters, silversmiths and stonecutters, merchants, farmers, and fishermen.[12]

Sadness cloaked Luis's first memories of the city. He had accompanied his father on a business trip to the capital late in the summer of 1583. In February of the next year, Don Francisco became desperately ill. Luis remained in the city for six months, devotedly nursing his father and helplessly watching the irreversible ebb of his strength. When Don Francisco died in the home of their cousins, Catalina de León and Gonzalo Pérez Ferro, Luis buried him on the grounds of the Dominican monastery in Mexico City.[13]

Now, except for his brother Baltasar, whom he left at Veracruz, the entire family was in Mexico City. Gaspar, his oldest brother, was a Dominican priest, serving in the Mexico City monastery as a preacher and teacher of novitiates. Their two married sisters, Catalina and Leonor, lived in their own homes. Catalina was a woman of twenty-five but Leonor was only fifteen. Gaspar said she still looked at life as a children's game.[14] Luis's unmarried siblings, Ana, affectionately called Anica, Miguel, and Mariana made their home with their mother, Doña Francisca de Carvajal. Ana was nine years old, Miguel eleven, and Mariana seventeen. Miguel was studying in a Jesuit school. Mariana had been enrolled at Mexico City's School for Girls (Colegio de las niñas) established by the Fleming Peter of Ghent for girls from noble families of modest means.[15]

Luis's oldest sister, the brilliant and devout Isabel, who "from childhood on was always very fond of reading and praying," now thirty and widowed, also lived in Mexico City, but tragically separated from her kin. On Monday evening, March 13, 1589, she had been suddenly

Peter of Ghent, Founder of the School for Girls (Colegio de las niñas) in Mexico City

arrested by the Inquisition and spirited off to its makeshift prison, not far from Gaspar's monastery. Since that day the family had had no contact with her, and no one had been permitted to see her. She had been swallowed up alive, as it were, by Flat House, as the Inquisition's jail was popularly called.[16]

Isabel's arrest had set off the chain of events that led to Luis's journey from Veracruz to the Valley of Mexico. The Inquisition's indictment of Isabel had been based upon the most serious charge in its arsenal. According to its claim, Isabel was a heretic. She was accused of betraying the church by the clandestine practice of another faith. Though born and raised a Roman Catholic, Isabel had been discovered to be living secretly as a Jewess. Luis knew that the charge was not unfounded. Nearly everyone else in his family, though officially and publicly Catholic, were secret Jews—his parents, his sisters, his brother Baltasar, and numerous cousins who had emigrated with them from Spain in the summer of 1580. And so was he. Even his uncle, arrested earlier in the year for political reasons, had been quietly whisked away to the inquisitorial prison, an almost certain sign that he too was suspected of having betrayed his Catholic faith.[17] As he returned to the Valley of Mexico, Luis had no reason to doubt that the Inquisition had prepared a warrant for his own arrest.

This had, in effect, occurred. A formal indictment against him had been handed down on Tuesday, April 18, by Dr. Lobo Guerrero, "the prosecutor for the Inquisition of Mexico City, the states and provinces of New Spain," and the warrant had been issued two days later.[18] An indictment against Baltasar was also issued, along with a description of the two fugitives and instructions for their apprehension and return to Mexico City.[19] Failing in its initial efforts to apprehend Luis, on April 22 the Inquisition dispatched a certain Rodrigo de Ávila, characterized as a "man of caution and circumspection," to the mining region of Taxco, where Luis was known to conduct much of his business as a merchant and tradesman. Armed with "special instruction for the most effective execution of his duties," Ávila lost little time in getting down to Taxco. But his mission proved futile.

When he returned to Mexico City, he submitted a disheartened report in which he advised that he had diligently searched "for the said Luis de Carvajal in the mines of Taxco, Sultepec, Temazcaltepec, Zacualpa, and Pachuca," but that he had "failed to find him . . . or any trace of him . . . in these places or in this city of Mexico."[20] On May 6, after a second effort, he was again compelled to report that despite the diligence and care with which he followed instructions he had been unable to gather any information about Luis or Baltasar except that they had been in Taxco two months before and in Sultepec two months earlier.[21]

But being at large could hardly console a man like Luis, who knew how difficult it was to elude the Inquisition's grasp.

Luis knew what lay in store for him if he were to be arrested by the Inquisition. His possessions would be sequestered. He would be thrown into its prison to wait for his case to be brought to trial. The trial might begin within a reasonable time, but then again months or years might elapse. Once begun, it might drag on endlessly. Even in the unlikely event that he were proven innocent, he would have to bear the full expense of both the incarceration and the trial. Until the final verdict he would be presumed guilty. The Inquisition would confront him with the testimony of accusers but would adamantly refuse to disclose their identity. It might send spies to his cell for information to seal its case against him or incriminate others. It might even resort to torture to extract details it suspected him of concealing.

If he repented and abjectly renounced his Judaism, he would be sentenced to undergo the usual onerous penance. Attired in a sleeveless, knee-length yellow penitential cloak known as a *sambenito*, or "holy sack," he would be marched from the inquisitorial prison to the cathedral for the ceremony of sentencing, piously called an auto-da-fé, or act of faith. There he would doubtless hear a tripartite sentence imposed upon him. It would include a fine involving a considerable percentage of his residual estate after the cost of the imprisonment and the trial. It would entail a spiritual penalty, such as marching in religious processions barefoot and in his penitential garb. And almost certainly all this would be accompanied or preceded by a period of labor, perhaps even at the galleys.

Yet even after consummating his atonement, he would remain a marked man. The Inquisition would keep him under careful surveillance, ready to rearrest him at the first sign of a reversion to Judaism. It would then consider him a relapsed heretic and automatically condemn him to death at the stake. He would be burned alive unless he again repented. If he did he would be mercifully garroted before his body was consigned to the flames.

Technically the Inquisition, claiming to be devoted solely to life and salvation, could not impose the death penalty. It would therefore release, or as it said "relax," a convicted relapsed heretic to what it called the "secular arm." The secular authorities could not review the Inquisition's findings and had no alternative but to impose the required sentence. The sentencing and burning regularly took place at the conclusion of the auto-da-fé.

The Coat of Arms of the Inquisition of New Spain

The Seal of the Inquisition of New Spain

Luis knew that even if he sedulously avoided a relapse into heresy his life would be a nightmare. He would be barred by law from the professions and positions of public service. He would be forbidden to wear finery or display any sign of affluence. His neighbors and friends would shun him, fearing guilt by association. And these and other impediments would fall as well upon his children and their descendants.[22]

But worst ignominy of all, the distinctive cloak of humiliation that he would wear on the day of his sentencing would be hung permanently in the cathedral so that all might recall his infidelity to the faith and sneer patronizingly at his family. Twenty-two such heretical garments had been ceremoniously nailed to the cathedral walls in August 1574, and in the subsequent years fifteen more had been added. All had been worn by men convicted of the heinous crime of heresy. Although the Inquisition tried people for bigamy, sodomy, concubinage, and solicitation in the confessional, it did not regard these malefactions as sufficiently serious to warrant eternal recollection. Ironically, many of the garments hung in 1574 had been worn by members of a group of English pirates captured by Luis's own uncle, Governor Carvajal. Accompanying each one was a legend revealing the wearer's name, occupation, birthplace, domicile, and offense.[23] The legend for the garb most recently placed read: "Gaspar Pereyra, Portuguese, hosier, native of the city of Porto [Portugal], resident of Oaxaca, convicted as a heretic for practicing Protestantism. Reconciled to the church, year 1574." With

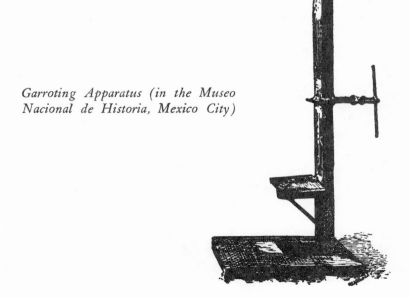

Garroting Apparatus (in the Museo Nacional de Historia, Mexico City)

the first penitential garb came the legend "Hernando Alonso, farrier, native of the county of Niebla [Spain], resident of Mexico City, a Judaizing heretic. Burned at the stake, year 1528." He had also been a conquistador and friend of Hernán Cortés.[24]

Only a minimum of effort was needed for young Luis to imagine his garment adorning the cathedral, its legend beginning "Luis de Carvajal, merchant, native of the county of Benavente [Spain], resident of Mexico City, a Judaizing heretic." It might have been somewhat more difficult for him to imagine its conclusion: a statement that Luis de Carvajal the Younger had been brought back in repentance to the bosom of the church, or an announcement that as an impenitent he had been burned at the stake.

Ironically, in sixteenth-century Mexico the Holy Office of the Inquisition could indict only Europeans and their descendants for the crime of heresy. Before the coming of this Inquisition, other church agencies, empowered to preserve the purity of the faith, had often arrested Indians for divergence of practice and belief. But a decree of Charles V in 1538, reissued and amplified by his son and successor, Philip II, in 1571 and again in 1575 had specifically exempted them from such investigation by the Inquisition. A xenophobic myth, popular among the Spaniards and the Creoles, held that these decrees stemmed from the Indians' alleged inferiority and their incapacity to grasp the tenets of the Christian faith.[25] One Spanish resident of the capital did not hesitate to remark that "if you lived in Mexico,[26] you would miss only the soil of the land of your birth, the abundance of your people, and, if we may speak frankly, the superior intelligence of the Spaniards."[27] Many other Spaniards, like the famous Dominican, Bartolomé de las Casas, repeatedly condemned such opinions. The exemption probably resulted from the authorities' fear that the Indians might shrink from a speedy acceptance of Christianity if the threat of the Inquisition dangled over their heads. Deeply rooted in their own traditions, the Indians were, therefore, at least for the time being, permitted to deviate with impunity from their captors' faith.[28]

And deviate they did. The Indians found the Christian religion strange and even irrelevant to their accustomed ways of life. When they did accept it, they not infrequently blended it with their own hallowed rites. To the consternation of the Christian clerics, large numbers of Indian converts, particularly in the provinces, continued to serve their atavic gods, bringing them their traditional offerings of food, flowers, and scented copal. Within the bonds of Catholic licitness, the Indians retained many of their ancient practices. Often they would be seen wearing their feathered headdress, carrying their wreaths of votive flowers, and performing their guitar-led dances in honor of a Catholic saint or even the Virgin Mary. For many of the Indians, the patron saints were nothing more than Christian masks for surviving Indian deities. They had adored the cross as the emblem of the god of rain. And the mother of Jesus was none other than Tonantzin, the bearer of the gods.[29]

But such freedom in religious practice was barred to Spaniards and their European descendants. For them the authorities provided no exceptions and extended no sympathy. In their case deviation was regarded as a brazen expression of heresy, and hence a criminal offense. And no less criminality was imputed to anyone sheltering a heretic or failing to report the slightest suspicion of divergence from the recognized norms of Catholic behavior and practice—even within his own family. When the Inquisition was introduced in New Spain late in November 1571, the faithful were solemnly admonished, under threat of anathema, to pursue all heretics and suspected heretics "like wolves and ravenous dogs who infect Christian souls and destroy the holy spouse of the Lord, which is the Catholic Church."[30] Since the Inquisition never moved without evidence, anyone arrested for heresy or failure to report it had ample reason to despair.

The inquisitors' inability to discover Luis in the mines around Taxco did not stem from poor judgment. The Taxco region was one of the most natural places to look for Luis when he was away from Mexico City. He and Baltasar often went there as itinerant merchants traveling from mine to mine and selling silverware, clothing, confections, and household articles, like curtains and beds.[31] What the authorities did not realize was that the brothers had learned of the Inquisition's activities and were studiously avoiding their usual haunts. Even more, they were planning an escape from New Spain.

Luis and Baltasar had sensed the increasing danger of the Inquisition before Isabel's arrest. They realized that the bold practice of Judaism by the entire family could not go undetected for long. They had therefore laid careful plans to remove their family from New Spain before the Inquisition struck. They had determined unobtrusively to shepherd them at the right moment to the eastern coast, where they would purchase a vessel and attach themselves to one of the fleets that left semiannually for Europe. They would follow the fleet to Spain and then escape to the Ottoman Empire, southwestern France, or one of the Italian cities, like Pisa, Genoa, Venice, or Florence, where they could live openly as Jews.[32]

For some time the brothers had been carefully preparing for this

THE MARTYR | 14

eventuality by collecting debts and converting their merchandise to cash. They were on such a trip in the vicinity of the town of Pachuca when Isabel was arrested. With them was their brother Miguel. They had apparently taken him along to divert suspicion from their activities by giving the impression that they were on a routine, unhurried trip.[33]

When Isabel was arrested, Luis's family recognized the urgency of informing the brothers in order to give them a chance to put their cash reserves out of the Inquisition's reach. Doña Francisca therefore asked Francisco Díaz, a former servant of her son-in-law, Jorge de Almeida, to deliver the message to her sons, but Díaz demurred, stating that he was on his way to Spain.[34] Jorge de Almeida then prevailed upon a family friend, the merchant Manuel Alvarez, to send his son Jorge with the sad news.[35]

Jorge Álvarez was not known to be a paragon of reliability except in his addiction to women and gaming, but he did carry the message to Pachuca. When he arrived he immediately went to the house the brothers had taken. Baltasar was at home, but not Luis. Luis had gone off to the nearby mines of Zimapán to collect a debt of two thousand silver pesos. Álvarez delivered his message, rested awhile, had a goblet of wine and two caramels, and returned immediately to Mexico City.[36]

When Álvarez broke the stunning news, Baltasar, fearing that the Inquisition was on its way, immediately took steps to divert it. He gave his home to two fish vendors, took his silver, and went into hiding with Miguel at the home of his close friend, the merchant Manuel de Lucena. Lucena, a native of São Vicente in Portugal, lived in the mining town of Tlahuililpa, near the city of Pachuca. At Lucena's home Baltasar tried to estimate the time of Luis's return to their old dwelling in order to intercept him.[37] But Luis returned before Baltasar.

Surprised at the transformation that had occurred, Luis was trying to learn his brothers' whereabouts when Baltasar arrived. "I was beginning to worry that lightning had struck twice in the same place and that the Indians had killed you," said Baltasar surprisingly, for it was he who had been delayed and not Luis. He then proceeded to tell his brother about the disaster that had befallen them with the arrest of Isabel.

His eyes welling with tears, Luis followed Baltasar to Lucena's house, where Lucena, his wife, Catalina Enríquez, his mother-in-law, Beatriz Enríquez, and trusted friends like Antonio López comforted them. Antonio López piously proposed that God punished those He loved. Doña Beatriz, less given to cerebral consolations, brought the brothers a plate of raisins, embraced Luis maternally, and told him not to worry anymore. The group also suggested that perhaps nothing would come of Isabel's arrest, implying that she had not been incarcerated on a charge of Judaism or else that the Inquisition might not have sufficient evidence against her.

The brothers knew, of course, that they could not stake their future on such unlikely possibilities. When they had overcome their initial shock they tied their silver into bundles and left Pachuca for Jorge de Almeida's house in Mexico City.[38]

Luis and Baltasar remained in the capital for ten days, commiserating with their family. Their mother advised them not to take any rash steps but to go about their activities in a confident manner as if they had done nothing wrong. Isabel, she pointed out, had been instructed to volunteer no information that would incriminate her family, regardless of the price she might have to pay. Luis's other brother-in-law, Antonio Díaz de Cáceres, had told the family shortly after Isabel's arrest that his mother and brother, arrested by the Inquisition in Lisbon on a charge of Judaizing, had both been set free after adamantly and persistently denying any wrongdoing. Perhaps, Francisca suggested, the Inquisition would at least not touch the rest of the family.[39]

Despite such advice, the brothers decided to proceed immediately with their plans for escape. On April 3 Luis went down to the mines of Taxco to collect an account from his friend Tomás de Fonseca. He remained there a week and then began his return trip to Mexico City. On the way, near the village of Xalatlaco, he met Juan Rodríguez de Silva, another servant of Jorge de Almeida. Rodríguez de Silva told Luis the disconcerting news that his uncle, Governor Luis de Carvajal, had been arrested by the Inquisition on the night of April 13.[40]

This information changed the urgency of the brothers' plans to desperation. With the governor's arrest the possibility loomed larger than ever that the Inquisition was carefully watching everyone in the Carvajal clan.

Stunned, Luis hurried back to the capital, where he and Baltasar went into hiding in Manuel Gómez's house, behind the Tumor Hospital. For three days the brothers ruminated on their plans and sought advice from trusted friends on how best to remove their family from the Inquisition's eye. They now determined to accompany the fleet to its stop at Campeche or Havana and there await the disposition of the governor's case. The ships regularly remained in Havana for several weeks, until they were joined by the fleet from Terra Firma, as the northern coast of South America was called. If they went to Havana they would have ample opportunity to revise their plans. As things turned out, the fleet, captained by Pérez de Olozábal, was not to leave Havana until around the tenth of September.[41]

Their minds made up, Luis and Baltasar took Miguel, stole out of Mexico City, and headed for Veracruz. There they met a cousin of their mother's, Diego Márquez de Andrada, who had come to Veracruz to buy and ship some wines. Diego cautioned them to give no signs of fright. He also advised them against fleeing, but Luis and Baltasar declined to heed these words. They took lodging in the inn belonging to a mulatto widow named Isabel de la Cruz, where Diego was staying, and began laying plans for their escape.[42] But when they were ready to, they could not leave. Throughout their feverish preparations they were bedeviled by the thought that what they were doing was tantamount to abandoning their family. This thought was strong enough to destroy all the rationalizations they had mustered to justify leaving New Spain.

It was not that they were suddenly overwhelmed by a surge of maudlin emotion. To be sure, their love for their family was powerful, but it was cool reason that led to their decision. Doubtless amidst a farrago of guilt and anxiety over the family's fate, a painful comprehension appears to have dawned on Luis and Baltasar. It was the simple realization that if they left New Spain, they could rely on no one to look after their family's welfare. Even their wealthy brothers-in-law, with all their contacts, were subject to inquisitorial arrest. Their departure would thus leave their family helpless precisely when they were in greatest need. Whatever they could do for their kin from abroad would be futile if there was no one to protect and comfort them at home.[43]

Luis and Baltasar therefore again revised their plans and threw themselves into their new project with their accustomed zeal. The first step, they agreed, would be a trip to Mexico City. It would be a kind of fact-finding mission in the lions' den itself.

Prudently, the brothers agreed not to return together. Luis chose to undertake the journey alone. Baltasar would eventually join him if the danger was not too great. Should Luis be arrested by the Inquisition or find himself in inextricable difficulty, Baltasar would have an opportunity to escape. In Mexico City, Luis would contact friends and collect money. He would visit his mother's house and glean every shred of available information about his family's position.[44]

Thus, Luis began his trek to the Valley of Mexico late in April 1589, not proud and swaggering like the conquistadors, but with the covertness and apprehension of a fugitive. Baltasar promised to remain at the coast with Miguel to await the arrival of trusted messengers sent by Luis with the latest news on the family's fortunes. He would stay either at the inn of Isabel de la Cruz or at a rural hostel several miles from the city.

Luis left early in the morning, while Baltasar was still sleeping, as if to create the impression that no one knew his destination. He told Isabel de la Cruz that Baltasar would pay the bill, and the innkeeper agreed to this arrangement.[45]

By Saturday, May 6, Luis was back in the Valley of Mexico. On the following day he was ensconced in a secret lodging in the quarter of Santiago, or Saint James, where the Spanish population lived in substantial houses of wood and stone. He delayed visiting his family, afraid perhaps to contact his kin until he could feel certain that his whereabouts were unknown to the authorities and that he could elude any ambush around his mother's house. Or he may have first planned to contact friends and learn of relevant events in the city during his absence. One of the people he saw was the merchant Cristóbal Gómez, from whom he demanded seven hundred pesos the brothers had lent to him, though repayment was not yet due.[46] He also learned that during his absence from the city the Inquisition had arrested his brother Gaspar.

Finally on Tuesday, May 9, Luis prepared to hazard the short trip to his mother's house, located at the Canal Gate (el Portal de la Acequia), southeast of the Great Square, not far from the cathedral and the School for Girls.

He waited for nightfall, perhaps even for the curfew to toll, as it did between nine and half past nine, before slinking out of his covert. Since the city had no street lighting, night brought a protective sheath of darkness. Luis had arrived in the Valley of Mexico at the time of the new moon and knew well in advance that its first sliver would be insufficient to betray him, regardless of how clear that Tuesday night was.[47] To be sure, travel within Mexico City was neither pleasant nor safe by night. The streets were poorly paved, and footing was made more precarious by heaps of dirt and debris strewn along them, awash with the miry waters that oozed from luxuriant streams. In addition, the anxious passerby was in danger of being pelted with buckets of garbage and feculent slops, which might at any moment be tossed with supreme nonchalance from the upper window or balcony of some Spaniard's two-story home. Even worse, he might be struck by robbers or assassins lurking behind some building or beside one of the city's many makeshift bridges.

Yet undoubtedly Luis regarded none of these as his primary danger. For him the enemy of the moment was light, the occasional flicker of a lamp in someone's home or the arc of a lazily swinging lantern in the hands of the agents of the peace who felinely threaded their way through the streets.[48]

Luis managed to avoid these hazards. He traversed the short distance without incident, moving past the alleys and houses he had come to know so well. Finally, after what must have seemed an eternity, he found himself before the two-story stone structure whose upper floor constituted his family's home. Luis climbed up and exchanged greetings.

Another of his mother's cousins, Antonio Díaz Márquez, had paid the family a visit that day. In March, after Isabel's arrest, he had come to console Doña Francisca. At that time he revealed to her and Mariana that he was a secret Jew, though he was unable to perform any of the rites or ceremonies of Judaism at home because his wife was a staunch Catholic. Now, in the presence of Doña Francisca, Mariana, Leonor, and Luis he reaffirmed his allegiance to Judaism.[49]

As the family prepared for the late evening meal, there was an ominous knock at the door. Everyone seemed to know intuitively who was calling. When the family's shock gave way to an acceptance of the inevitable, someone went down to open the door and admit the bailiffs, constables, and notaries of the Mexican Inquisition. At their head stood Pedro de los Ríos, the Inquisition's secretary and its chief constable, Pedro de Villegas y Peralta.

They had come to make at least one arrest, the primary object of their search apparently being Luis's fifty-year-old mother. Earlier that day the inquisitors, Licentiates Bonilla and Santos García, had issued an order to Pedro de Villegas y Peralta "to arrest Doña Francisca de Carvajal, widow of Francisco Rodríguez de Matos, resident of this city, living in the house of her son-in-law, Jorge de Almeida, removing her, if necessary, from any church or other sacred, protected, or privileged place where she may be."[50]

The agents seized Doña Francisca and began to lead her away. Though disgraced by the arrest and toppled from her pedestal as the matriarch of the Carvajals, Doña Francisca, ever the lady, accepted her fate with resignation and dignity. The only words she uttered were an expression of sincere gratitude to God for sending her her trials.[51]

But Luis's sisters, reacting differently, were convulsed with horror at their mother's ordeal. "Where are they taking her?" they screamed hysterically, though they knew full well that her destination was the building that had swallowed Isabel not quite two months before. Doña Francisca, though able to accept her own plight, felt unbearable grief at her daughters' hopeless agony.[52]

The Inquisition's agents might also have come to apprehend Luis. Alerted to search for him in every corner of the city, they were not likely to have overlooked the possibility of eventually finding him at his mother's house. For all Luis knew, they may even have been aware of his hiding place and, despite his precautions, trailed him to his rendezvous with his family.

When he heard the Inquisition's knock, Luis instinctively scampered for refuge. To his misfortune, there was little time to find it and no secure place in his immediate surroundings. The best he could do was to run behind the kitchen door and entertain the naive hope that he could thus escape his enemies' gaze.

It was not long before the agents of the Inquisition discovered the cowering Luis and placed him under arrest. Unlike his mother, Luis grappled with the agents and their guards, but was finally subdued and carried away. Vanquished, Luis cried out, "O God, reveal the truth."[53]

On June 14, the warden of the Inquisition, Gaspar de los Reyes Plata, paid Rodrigo de Ávila thirty pesos for his efforts to find Luis de Carvajal and his brother Baltasar. The money came from the funds belonging to Luis, which the Inquisition had already managed to confiscate.[54]

2 Bar Mitzvah

A mere decade earlier, in 1579, Luis would hardly have believed that such a bizarre series of events could occur. He was living at the time in the northwestern region of his native Spain, in Medina del Campo, an old and charming town that had fallen on evil days. Its misfortune derived from the precipitate decline that had overtaken its entire economy. Through a good part of the century, it had been a prosperous ganglion of finance and commerce on one of the two routes used by mule convoys that carried goods for trade to northern Europe. It had also served as a major center for the manufacture of cloth and one of its principal depots for the transatlantic trade. But gradually trade had begun to shift to the populous region around Seville, the gateway to the New World, and people from the north drifted southward in increasing numbers.[1]

When Luis's parents moved there in 1577, Medina del Campo was already in the stupor of a depression. Its population had dwindled to considerably below the twenty-one thousand persons it had numbered a mere half century before, and its renowned fairs, among the most prominent in Castile since the Middle Ages, had been suspended for two years. Why the family moved from Benavente, Luis's birthplace, is nowhere told. Luis's father, a merchant, perhaps hoping that prosperity would soon return to Medina del Campo, may have made the move as a calculated gamble for a more prosperous existence. To be sure, the fairs were reopened in 1578, though on a more modest basis than before, but it was still too early to tell whether they would ever reclaim their former greatness. In any case, the establishment of the family shop on Salamanca Street certainly could not have been motivated by any urge to make an eventual journey to the New World.[2]

Yet, like other twelve-year-old boys, young Luis may have dreamed of that world. He may have heard of the treasure ships returning to Castile laden with gold and silver taken from seemingly inexhaustible stores. He may have listened with rapt attention to returning adventurers' stories about barbaric rites and exotic gods and red-skinned natives living in aureate and argentine cities filled with plunderable wealth.[3]

Bright and hyperimaginative, he may even have pictured himself as someday taking the long voyage to the enticing lands beyond the sea. He might have dreamed of fighting corsairs and Indians, and carving out a pocket empire in the name of his king, Philip II of Spain. But whatever young Luis's fantasies, and however strange they may have seemed, the thought that he might someday be intimately associated with Jews and Judaism in New Spain could hardly have entered his mind.

For from the moment of his birth, in the summer of 1566, through the spring and summer of 1579, young Luis had had no contact with Jews. His knowledge of Judaism was minimal, confined to hearsay and personal deductions reached from his own superficial exposure to the Bible. Like everyone else in Spain in the middle of the sixteenth century, Luis was a Christian. The Jews had been expelled by a rescript issued by the Catholic Sovereigns, Ferdinand and Isabella, in 1492, six and a half months before Columbus discovered America. Ten years later, a similar edict summarily removed the remaining Moors from Spanish soil. Spain was left a Christian nation. And when its leadership stifled the frequent and often cogent voices of Protestantism resounding within its borders through the early decades of the sixteenth century, Spain became a nation in which every man, woman, and child belonged to the Church of Rome.[4]

Luis was born a Catholic, the son of Francisco Rodríguez de Matos and Francisca de Carvajal, both respected members of the church. The boy's name originally had been Luis Rodríguez; or, following the Spanish custom of using both the patronymic and matronymic, Luis Rodríguez Carvajal. This was later to be changed to Luis de Carvajal.

Luis Rodríguez Carvajal was baptized and scrupulously reared in the Catholic faith.[5] His home and upbringing left him not the slightest room to doubt his parents' unswerving Catholic piety and devotion. In the comfort of his home in Benavente, Luis received his elementary education, "learning . . . reading, writing, and arithmetic," as he rather unoriginally summed it up. Like his brothers and sisters, he was certainly also adequately exposed to the rudimentary responsibilities of belief and practice imposed by the church, learning the Lord's Prayer,

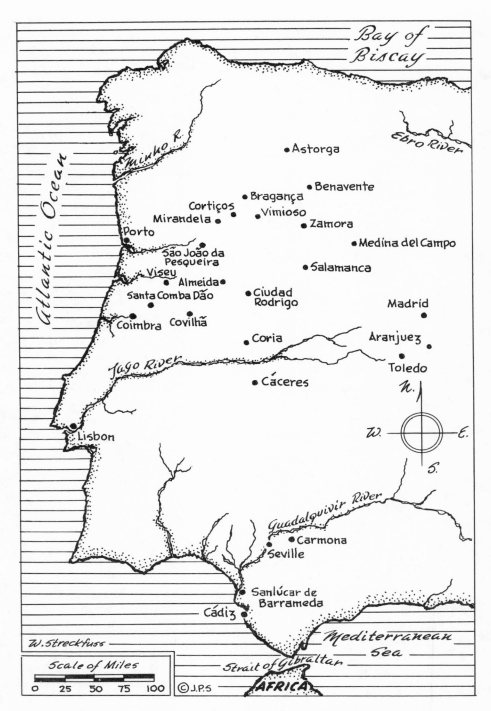

Map of Spain and Portugal Showing Major Cities and Towns Mentioned in This Book.

the credo, the Hail Mary, the Hail Holy Queen, and the general confession in Latin.[6] Not until his family moved to Medina del Campo did he change from tutorial to more formal education, and this change too appeared to bespeak his parents' Catholic zeal. Shortly after their arrival in Medina del Campo, they enrolled their son in the Jesuit school of that city. There young Luis went through at least two of the grades of traditional Jesuitic study, the first concentrating on Latin grammar and the second on rhetoric, or, as it was sometimes called, "humanities," with readings from Virgil, Cicero, and other Latin writers. There is no mention of his having proceeded further to the study of dialectics, aimed at opening a student's mind to opposing arguments and helping him resolve them by the use of medieval scholastic techniques.[7]

Only an accident of history linked Luis Rodríguez Carvajal to Judaism and the Jews. It was simply the fact, as yet unknown to him, that his ancestors had included Jews. And to Spanish Catholics in the middle of the sixteenth century the question of whether or not they had Jewish ancestors made all the difference in the world.

If one could discern no Jewish ancestors at all on his family tree—or if he could successfully conceal any who might be lurking there—he might claim that he was an Old Christian. But if any Jewish ancestors, however inconspicuous, however few or far removed, hung from one of its branches, he might some day be compelled to acknowledge that he was "a New Christian, descended from Jews."

The distinction between New Christians and Old was not academic. The New Christians were considered an inferior race, contaminated by Jewish blood. And though countless New Christians were paragons of Catholic piety, the New Christians as a group were considered to be pulled irresistibly, as if by blind atavic forces, toward a propensity to Judaism. The New Christian syndrome, it was believed, included an ineradicable scorn of Catholic practice and belief and a compulsion to the clandestine practice of Judaism. Conversely, the Old Christians, even those in the ruck of Spanish society, knowing their Catholic pedigree to be free of Jewish intrusions, strutted proudly with the claim that their stock was pure and their faithfulness to the church beyond reproach.[8]

Although this doctrine was accepted and preached by many clerics in Spain, the Church of Rome never acquiesced in its perverse distinction between Christians, based on unfounded and untrue concepts of race. Canon law unequivocally extended full equality, regardless of ancestry, religion, or race, to all who embraced the mother church.[9]

But church doctrine was utterly powerless to overcome the stark realities of sixteenth-century Spain, resulting from problems deeply rooted in the social structure of the Iberian Peninsula.

The term New Christians first applied to those who accepted Christianity in the wake of the massacres of Jews that swept Spain in 1391 and the waves of disabling legislation and compelling conversionist activity by the churchmen in the ensuing decades. Jews had converted to Christianity in Spain in prior years, but never before in such spectacular numbers. By conservative estimate, over fifty thousand Jews had become Christians by 1470. To designate these converts, the terms "New Christian" and "converso" had been coined. At first, they carried no pejorative connotation whatever.[10]

Practical considerations more than religious zeal had fostered both the intensive persecution of the Jews and their stampeding conversion to Christianity. Spain in the fourteenth century had tossed impotently in the throes of economic and social turbulence. Its two kingdoms, Castile and Aragon, perennially stood on the brink of open conflict. England, France, and Portugal relished such struggles and were planning vulturine swoops upon the warring states. At the same time, Castile and Aragon both rankled with internal strife, bringing nearer the possibility of revolution. The persecution of the Jews in these states may well have represented a valetudinarian effort on the part of the leadership to maintain their own position by diverting from themselves the hatred of the multitude.

For centuries the Jews had faithfully and creditably served the ruling classes in Christian Spain and had attained a wealth and status superior to that of any other Jewish community in the history of Christian Europe.[11] Though they faced numerous irritants, including the jealousy of petty nobles and churchmen and the odium of the mob, their lot was essentially secure as long as society maintained its stability and the ruling classes lent their support. But now these very forces had turned against them, permitting outbursts that otherwise would have been impossible. The most powerful voice among the instigators of the massacre of 1391 was Fray (Brother) Ferrán Martínez, archdeacon of Ecija and confessor to the queen. Despite all kinds of opposition, including orders from the archbishop of Seville to be silent, he was able to continue spewing out his venom. The persecutions of subsequent decades were similarly led by persons on the highest rungs in government and the church. All this was hardly a coincidence.[12]

Hounded on the pretext of religion, Jews by the thousands chose to save their lives and preserve their status by converting to the Christian faith. Both Christian doctrine and the experience of previous Jewish converts in Spain led them to believe that once they embraced Christianity, their disabilities would evaporate. They would be fully integrated into Christian society and nothing further would be heard of them as Jews.

Their expectations were not unwarranted. The New Christians were fully accepted into Spanish society. Learned, able, and enterprising, they speedily attained coveted positions, including government posts, university chairs, and even church preferments. Old Christian families hankered for marriage alliances with them, and within a short time New Christians belonged to the most distinguished Spanish houses. By the middle of the fifteenth century, the seed of Abraham was believed to have married into almost all the noble families of Aragon. The daughter of one of these houses, the Henríquez, was destined to become the great-grandmother of King Ferdinand of Aragon, the king who later expelled the Jews from Spain.

As is apparent from their meteoric rise and facile acceptance into the highest echelons of Spanish society, including the church, the New Christians were treated as the equals of the Old and regarded as exhibiting proper behavior in religious matters. Stray individuals among them, tortured by guilt for their conversion, may have sought release in the clandestine practice of their ancestral faith, but this was not true of the group as a whole.

However, the problems that the ruling classes had sought to avert by a systematic reduction of the Jews were left unresolved and reappeared ominously throughout the early years of the fifteenth century. Again, a scapegoat had to be sought, and this time none better could be found than the New Christians. Their prominence had made them the envy of both the masses and the aristocratic Old Christians who had not allied with them.

Beginning with the middle of the fifteenth century, rumors began to spread to the effect that New Christians as a class were hypocrites. It was bruited that their Christianity was merely a façade, that at heart they were all fervent Jews, that many even secretly practiced their forebears' faith.[13] For the first time libels against Jews, such as that they poisoned wells, desecrated the host, murdered Christians, and used the blood of Christian children for religious rituals, came to be promulgated in Spain, receiving official sanction from the highest sources. They were intended at least as much for use against New Christians as for their unconverted Jewish brethren. Around 1460, Alfonso de Spina, the compiler of the first collection of such libels patently intended for pulpit use in Spain, went so far as to call for organized action against the religious waywardness of the New Christians.[14] The heresies of these New Christians—these Marranos, or pigs, as they came to be called[15]—must be extirpated, he declared, and the best way to do this was to introduce an Inquisition into Spain. What Spina and other agitators wanted was not the episcopal inquisition or board of inquiry that traditionally looked into matters of heresy for the church. They wanted an extraordinary organization, such as the one established under the Dominicans to extirpate the Albigensian and Waldensian heresies from Provence two centuries before.[16]

The suggestion of such an Inquisition racked the New Christians with fright, not only because they suspected the severity of the measures it would take to crush all heresy, but also because they knew that the charges against them were patently false. Many Old Christians rallied to their defense, denouncing the preposterousness of the blanket indictment. And the New Christians themselves took all possible measures to avert the introduction of an Inquisition. Their efforts may have helped delay its coming, but they were powerless to prevent it completely. In September 1480 the first Inquisition was established in Seville, and soon others were instituted throughout Castile and Aragon. Before long New Christians, leading and respectable citizens among them, were being indicted for heresy, stripped of their wealth and honor, and given stiff sentences, including death at the stake.

Ironically, the Inquisition's record itself appears to have disproved the innuendos and charges in its propaganda. Though the New Christians as a class were accused of Judaizing, the total number of people arrested and punished by the Inquisition by the most generous of reasonable estimates could not have exceeded one-tenth of the total population of New Christians in Spain in the sixteenth century. Of those punished, more than 90 percent were reconciled to the church, never to be arrested for heresy again.[17]

The majority of the New Christians, both those who could and those who could not conceal their Jewish ancestry, thus remained sufficiently good Catholics to avert prosecution, or at least its repetition by the Holy Office. Some, perhaps prompted by the portent of imminent arrest, returned wholeheartedly to Judaism. Though they comprehended how their country's problems had come to be laid at their doorstep, they could find no adequate answer to the visceral question "Why?" Why were they being made to suffer for a situation they had not created? Even more, why were they, so eager for acceptance into Christian society, rejected in the name of the very faith they were sincerely trying to uphold? Their new, Christian faith could provide no answer, but Judaism did. It declared that the New Christians, having brazenly and maliciously defected from Judaism, were now being punished for their reckless apostasy. Many dispirited New Christians, desperately searching for meaning in life, accepted this explanation. They returned secretly to the practice of Judaism, even though from the perspective of the church they were committing heresy, since officially they remained Catholic. Often these Judaizers even sought instruction from unconverted Jews.[18] In this way the sinister canards against them became self-fulfilling prophecies. The Inquisition, once it got started, did not have to strain to find evidence. The evidence it needed was soon present in abundance.[19]

In 1492 the majority of Jews remaining in Spain chose expulsion and exile over the opportunity to remain as Christians in their homeland. To a large extent this decision was motivated by a deep love for their faith, but entering into it also must have been the recognition that as Christians, Spain would offer them no guarantee of security. They concluded that only by remaining Jews would they always be free from the inquisitors' scourge.

They left Spain for Moslem lands and for other Christian countries in Europe where Jews were free to practice their religion. The majority, however, preferred to cross the border into neighboring Portugal, swelling the formerly small Jewish community there to over a hundred thousand persons. The Portuguese monarchs tried vainly to convert them. Finally King Manuel, pressured by the Catholic Sovereigns of Spain to rid his land of Jews, had them all converted by force and fiat rather than permit them to leave his borders.

Thus began the romantic history of the Portuguese New Christians, or Marranos, as they also came to be called. In many ways it duplicated the tragic history of the Marranos in Spain. Like their Spanish counterparts, the Portuguese New Christians rose quickly to the heights of success. They too found themselves confronted by crescendoing cries for the introduction of an Inquisition. They too fought vigorously against its introduction, aided by Old Christians at home and abroad, even in the curia at Rome. Their battle also ended in defeat when the Inquisition was established in Lisbon in 1536.[20]

While some conversos in Portugal decided to live as faithful Christians, others determined to remain loyal to Judaism and face the risks involved in its clandestine practice. Many chose to depart from Portugal for places where they could live freely as Jews. The allegiance to Judaism by Portuguese New Christians became notorious. By the end of the sixteenth century "Portuguese" was synonymous in many circles outside of Portugal with "New Christian" and even "Jew." All Portuguese were therefore scrutinized with suspicion by Christians concerned with the purity of their faith.[21]

Born and raised in Spain, close to the border of Portugal, Luis could not have failed to know the plight of the New Christians, especially the Portuguese. Yet, sensitive and perceptive though Luis was, there is every reason to doubt his ever having entertained suspicions that he was a Portuguese New Christian descended from Jews.

He was aware, to be sure, that his ancestry stemmed largely from Portugal. His father, Francisco Rodríguez, had a surname used frequently by New Christians in Portugal as well as Spain. Yet this fact was insufficient to impel anyone to the conclusion that he had Jewish forebears. His father's matronymic, de Matos, was unquestionably Portuguese.

Luis had never seen any of his paternal relatives. Some of them, including his father's parents, were not even known to him by name. Of two brothers of his father, he could say only that he had been told that one uncle, Diego Rodríguez, was living somewhere in Portugal and the other, Hernán Rodríguez, had died in the town of Puebla, in New Spain.

Even Luis's maternal grandfather, Don Gaspar de Carvajal, though possibly born at Salamanca, in northwestern Spain, was of Portuguese descent. Don Gaspar's parents came from Mogadouro, a small town with a total population of less than a thousand in its center and environs, located in the province of Trás-os-Montes, near the Spanish border.[22] Don Gaspar owned an estate in Benavente, and was married there to the widow Doña Catalina de León. Not long after his marriage, he moved back with his wife to his family home in Portugal. Luis did not know his grandfather's profession, but his mother believed that Don Gaspar had served for some time as a judge.

Doña Catalina had a sister named Isabel, who lived in Medina del Campo with her second husband, Antonio Márquez. She could also boast of four distinguished brothers. One, the late Duarte de León, served the king of Portugal as chief factor in the Guineas. According to Luis's mother, Don Duarte "was very rich and had a daughter named Isabel who was married to Commander Rodrigo de Castro." Another brother, Francisco Jorge, also in the service of the king of Portugal was, so Doña Francisca said, "a very rich and powerful man in that country, who had only one daughter and married her to the

Portuguese nobleman Rodrigo de Meneses and thereafter to another important nobleman." Francisco Jorge also served in Guinea as factor and captain general. Later, in New Spain, he became an Augustinian monk and was known as Fray Francisco de Andrada. A third brother, Alvaro de León, was a wealthy merchant who lived and died in Medina del Campo. The fourth, Antonio, had lost his life at the hands of French corsairs as he was returning from India to Spain, according to Luis's mother. Of a fifth brother, Jorge de León de Andrada, nothing is known except that he lived in Cortiços, "between Mirandela and Mogadouro" according to Luis de Carvajal's namesake-uncle; but it was actually only some twelve miles northeast of Mirandela.[23]

Equally distinguished were Doña Catalina's sons, Luis's maternal uncles. Domingo de Carvajal was a Jesuit. Antonio de Carvajal had migrated to the New World and died in New Spain, "around Oaxaca or beyond." And then of course there was Don Luis de Carvajal y de la Cueva, the most successful and renowned member of the family. Though no more than forty years old, he had already served as treasurer and comptroller of the Cape Verde Islands for the king of Portugal. He was now a conquistador in the far-off land of New Spain, valiantly subduing Indians and securing their obeisance to the crown and the church.[24]

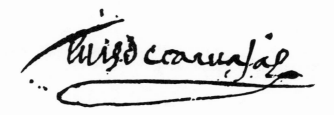

Signature of Governor Luis de Carvajal y de la Cueva

If young Luis required assurance of his Old Christian descent, the record of his relatives would have sufficed. It would have been difficult to believe that anyone other than Old Christians could now rise so high in society. And in view of the laws specifically prohibiting descendants of Jews from traveling to the New World, it must have been almost impossible to believe that men who became famous there could be of impure lineage. There was thus every reason for Luis to be free from the anxieties gnawing at the New Christians and to look forward with equanimity to a life of service to his society.

Rarely in its history had Spain had a greater need for skilled and able men than it did in the late 1570s. In 1579 its dour and energetic King Philip, though on the threshold of realizing the crown's perennial dream of annexing Portugal, was striving mightily to keep his own nation strong and his vast empire together. At home he was beset with seemingly insolvable problems: increasing vagabondage and crime, mounting inflation, and a soaring national debt (by the end of his reign it would be five times the already staggering deficit of twenty million ducats that he had inherited from his father).

Abroad he faced enemies on all sides, particularly the hated Protestant peoples, led by the United Provinces of the Netherlands and Elizabethan England. Early in 1579 the United Provinces, signatories to the Treaty of Utrecht, had bolted oppressive Spanish rule and now looked upon their former masters with anger and contempt. And England was as usual scheming to outmaneuver her Spanish rival. For some time now she had been working on Spain's former archenemy, the Turks. The Turks had been quiescent since their smashing defeat at Lepanto at the hands of Philip's half brother, Don Juan of Austria, eight years before. They were presently locked in a one-year treaty of peace with Philip and were giving indications of a willingness to renew it. Queen Elizabeth I and her government were attempting to entice the Turks into an entente against Spain.

Besides its needs at home and on the familiar continents of the Old World, the crown also required able men who would serve in its American possessions. It needed colonizers, administrators, soldiers to subdue the native Indians, and sailors to defend the ships bringing the treasures of the New World to Spain from the English and French corsairs.

And of course one could serve by entering the church, as so many noble youths had chosen to do.[25]

Challenges and opportunities like these belonged primarily to families of Old Christian descent or to those who could pass themselves off as Old Christians with impunity. As he grew into adolescence, Luis, believing himself to be of Old Christian stock, could dream of a free choice of vocation.

He could, that is, until a certain Thursday at the beginning of the fall of 1579, when something occurred to shatter his youthful vision of life.

That Thursday happened to be the tenth day of September and the first day of fall, according to the Julian calendar still in use in Spain. The day had begun unexceptionally for Luis, marked only by the fact that one of his cousins was in town for a visit. His sister Isabel had also come to visit. She had been living in the town of Astorga, about a hundred miles northwest of Medina del Campo, since her marriage to a merchant, Gabriel de Herrera, around 1574. But at one moment during the day, when Luis was standing near his cousin, his mother, and his sister Isabel, an unforgettable event occurred. His brother Baltasar took him aside and revealed a fact that would radically transform Luis's entire life. With stunning simplicity, Baltasar told Luis that he was not a Brahman but a pariah. He was not an Old but a New Christian, descended from Jews.[26]

It may have taken a while for Luis to grasp the full implication of Baltasar's words, but once he did they drew a thousand pictures. It was clear, of course, that Baltasar himself was a Judaizer; otherwise why would he have informed his younger brother of their ancestry? Others in the family, his parents included, must also have regarded themselves as Jews, for if they did not, they would have spared no effort to conceal their origin from Baltasar, and they would not have been represented at this crucial moment by witnesses like his mother and his oldest sister. Gabriel de Herrera, too, must therefore be a Judaizer, for the New Christian Judaizers were careful to marry only among themselves.

There was a reason why Luis had had to wait until that moment to discover the vital role that Judaism played in his family's life.

The practicing of Judaism was fraught with the greatest danger for the New Christians. At the slightest suspicion of their Judaizing, the Inquisition might begin to shadow them, amassing evidence that could spell doom not only for them, but also for their families and friends as well. The safety of the Judaizers therefore depended upon a mature awareness of their mutual responsibility to maintain the tightest secrecy about their activities and meetings. Realizing that a childish slip might embroil them in inextricable difficulty with the Inquisition, whenever possible the New Christian Judaizers scrupulously concealed every intimation of their clandestine religion from their children until they thought them ready to understand its significance and its dangers. Sometimes an overzealous relative indoctrinated them into the faith prematurely, as Beatriz Núñez, Don Francisco's paternal aunt, had done with her great-niece, Luis's sister Catalina.[27] Mariana, too, was indoctrinated into Judaism by her parents before she was ten years old, under circumstances that are not altogether clear.[28]

But Luis came to that momentous September day without ever seeing his parents engaged in any of the practices Judaizers were reputed to observe; or if he did see any, he did not recognize them as Jewish. His parents might have followed a number of the practices current among the Judaizers of Spain and Portugal. They may have refrained from eating pork and other Pentateuchally forbidden meats. To the extent that they could, they may have observed the Jewish holidays and the Sabbath. In honor of the Sabbath, they may have donned their finery, changed household linens, and abstained from work. And though they did not, like some Judaizers, circumcise their sons, they may have practiced Jewish burial and mourning procedures and followed other customs in the life cycle of the Jew. And, as Luis was learning that very morning, they observed the occasion of their son's attainment of religious maturity, at the end of his thirteenth year, not by the rituals of bar mitzvah customary among Jews elsewhere in the world, but by a simple ceremony intended to make an equally indelible impact upon the boy's spirit.

Jewish tradition holds that a boy of thirteen, around the age of puberty, attains responsibility for the fulfillment of Judaism's commandments. The New Christian Judaizers often waited until the time of puberty to inform their sons and daughters of their heritage and obligations as Jews.[29]

The Judaizers regarded this distinctive induction of a child into the faith as a religious responsibility. Though the responsibility naturally devolved upon the parents, they occasionally delegated it to an older son or daughter, perhaps trying in this way to minimize the child's shock at learning of his true identity and to offer him the opportunity of asking his sibling the sharp questions he might not venture to pose to his parents. In this way the parents could also learn from the child's reaction whether he could be safely exposed to the full gamut of the family's religious activities. If he could, the parents could proceed to teach him more about Judaism. If not, they could shield him from the Judaizing practices of the family. Should it become necessary, they could even disavow the entire incident of his initial indoctrination— or at least explain it innocuously away.

Baltasar was the sibling chosen to tell Luis about his origins. In light of Luis's personality, the decision had to be most carefully made. To judge from the record of his entire life, Luis was not the kind of boy to whom one could confidently entrust a secret. He was emotional, hypersensitive, visionary, doctrinaire, and mercurial. Though he coupled these qualities with a natural vigor and dynamism of character that stamped him as a potential leader, his parents could not have failed to realize that the stuff of leadership breeds villains as well as heroes. Don Francisco and his spouse might have envisioned their son becoming one of the great paladins of New Christian Judaizing in the future. But they could not close their eyes to the fact that Luis's admixture of attributes might just as easily turn him virulently against his own people and even his own kin. There was ample precedent for such betrayal. Many New Christians with similar endowments had become the most bitter enemies of the Jews, spewing venom toward them with pen and tongue.

Of all his brothers and sisters, Luis always felt closest to Baltasar. Doubtless his parents believed that even if Luis recoiled at the suggestion that he Judaize, he would say nothing further about it out of his love for Baltasar. Judging from the content of Baltasar's conversation with Luis, it is likely that his parents had instructed him to stay away, at least initially, from the subject of their own religious practice.

After his startling revelation, Baltasar went on to inform his brother that the day of his induction into Judaism had not been randomly chosen. It was a very special day. It was the holiest day of the Jewish year. That September 10 happened to be the "Day of Pardon," as Baltasar called it, "the day when we are cleansed of our sins." It was the Day of Atonement, Yom Kippur, which the family had appropriately chosen as the day to inform their son of his ancestral origins.[30]

For the New Christian Judaizers, the Day of Atonement was laden with awesome significance. On that day, according to Jewish custom, they strove to expiate the ordinary sins they had been accumulating during the previous year. They sought as well to lift the heavier burden they felt for their participation in the practices of another faith, even though their practice of Christianity was a protective formality to divert suspicion from them. At the same time they tried compulsively to wash off the ineradicable stain of inherited guilt they irrationally felt for their forebears' conversion, regardless of whether it had been voluntary or forced.[31]

After Baltasar had made his disturbing disclosure, he proceeded to indoctrinate his brother in the rudiments of Jewish observance. He spoke to Luis of the Sabbath, the holidays, and the dietary laws. Above all he emphasized the cardinal requirement of absolute secrecy. Secrecy was essential for the safety of loved ones and the continuation of the Judaizers' own service to the will of the God they called Adonay.

After listening to Baltasar, Luis reacted as the family had hoped. He decided then and there to accept his brother's instruction and become a Jew, or, as the New Christian Judaizers usually called themselves, a keeper of "the Law of God," or as it was more frequently called "the Law of Moses."

Thus on that Day of Atonement a new existence began for Luis. It was to be a life of public conformity to the demands of the church and at the same time one of deep inward commitment to what he understood to be the requirements of Judaism. Ironically, his continued stay at the Jesuit school was to provide him with a unique opportunity to learn as much about his Jewish roots as was possible for a young Judaizer in late sixteenth-century Spain or Portugal.

Since the cessation of corporate Jewish life in these two countries there naturally had been no schools of Jewish learning, and the private or clandestine study of rabbinic books, especially by persons of Jewish descent, was an open invitation to seizure by the Inquisition. The Judaizers' only licit contact with Judaism came by way of the Bible; but study of the Bible was not permitted to the ordinary citizen, being limited to priests and scholars in their schools. It was therefore not uncommon for a New Christian family eager to learn everything possible about biblical Judaism to send one of its sons, preferably its oldest, to study for the priesthood. While some of these young men became ardent Catholics, others were fervent Judaizers and wore their priestly habits as a disguise.[32]

Luis's own brother Gaspar had become a priest, after surmounting numerous difficulties that might well have been related to his New Christian descent. Like Luis, Gaspar had received his primary education at home. At the age of thirteen he left for the University of Salamanca, where he studied law for two years, and then entered a Dominican monastery, Saint Stephen, in Salamanca. He was dismissed from Saint Stephen for reasons never disclosed, though Gaspar was to insist, at least in public, that they had nothing to do with suspicions about his family's origins. From Salamanca he moved to Medina del Campo, where he again entered a monastery, this time the Seraph of Assisi, belonging to the Franciscans, the Dominicans' traditional rivals. Here too he ran into bad luck, leaving after two months for reasons nowhere revealed.[33] He then accompanied his sister Isabel to the town of Astorga for her marriage to the merchant Gabriel de Herrera, who sold linen and notions. Herrera had studied theology at the University of Salamanca in preparation for the priesthood. After he changed his mind about his vocation he gave his books to an Augustinian friar named Diego de Velasco, a relative of the marquise of Astorga. Gabriel de Herrera became a merchant and a fervent Judaizer. He even fasted on Mondays and Thursdays, the traditional Jewish fast days.[34]

After the wedding, Gaspar went to serve his granduncle Duarte de León at Lisbon. He remained with Don Duarte for a year and a half before leaving him and going to the New World. There he met with his uncle Don Luis de Carvajal y de la Cueva and entreated him to help him enter the Augustinian monastery. The governor recommended Gaspar to the inquisitor Ávalos, who took him as his page. After several months in Ávalos's service, Gaspar succeeded in entering the Dominican monastery, where after some two years of diligent study, he was ordained "in all orders, minor and major" by the archbishop of Mexico.[35] At the moment, no one in the family knew for sure what Gaspar's attitudes toward Christianity and Judaism were. It was certainly possible that at heart Gaspar was a Judaizer.[36]

No account of Luis's first year as a Judaizer remains. He doubtless met scores of secret Jews and learned with fresh surprise in each instance that friends and acquaintances of the family regarded as pillars of the Catholic community were simultaneously important in the circles of the Judaizers. He may have discovered that it was his uncle Diego Rodríguez who had indoctrinated his father into Judaism. It had happened when Don Diego and his two sons, Antonio and Miguel Rodríguez, both itinerant merchants, came from São João da Pesqueira for a visit to Medina del Campo. During the visit Catalina observed her father discussing Judaism with his brother and nephews.[37] Don Diego had since migrated to southwestern France, which served as a refuge for notorious Judaizers from across the Pyrenees.[38]

Luis may also have learned that both his parents came from Jewish stock. His sister Mariana once overheard her mother saying that her mother and father had fled from Portugal in order to escape arrest by the Inquisition on the charge of Judaizing. Even Doña Francisca's uncles, including Fray Francisco de Andrada, were Jews at heart. It may also have been in Medina del Campo that Luis learned that his father's brother, Hernán Rodríguez de Matos, was a fervent Judaizer. His son Diego, who later came to the New World, was also a Judaizer.[39]

Doña Francisca claimed that despite her husband's pleas, she refused to Judaize until she contracted a serious illness. Don Francisco, away on one of his business trips, traveled posthaste from the city of Valladolid to be with her. He then urged her to Judaize but was able to overcome her scruples only when he proved to her that her grandaunt, Beatriz Núñez, was also a secret Jewess.[40]

Like Mariana and Catalina, Luis also doubtless came to know the circle of Judaizers among his relatives in Benavente. They included Leonor Rodríguez and her daughter-in-law, Beatriz Núñez, Luis's grandaunt. Some, like his mother's cousin, Gonzalo Pérez Ferro, revealed themselves directly to him as secret Jews.

He doubtless also became aware of some of the Judaizers among the family's friends in Medina del Campo, like the physician Dr. Manrique, his wife, his daughter, Marquesa Enríquez, and his sister, Isabel Enríquez, or the widow Catalina López, her son Luis López, and her son-in-law, Fernando, also surnamed López, or the widow Leonor Rodríguez and her son, Francisco, or Antonio Álvarez Trancoso, his wife, and two daughters. The Carvajals even had tenants who Judaized. In their home lived a certain María Núñez and her daughter, Isabel. Mariana frequently saw them engaged in the prayers of the secret Judaizers, and years later could still recall the one that began: "Greater is Thy mercy to send us salvation/Than the power of our sins to bring us damnation."[41]

Luis doubtless also learned that the famous physician, Licentiate Manuel de Morales, a dear friend of the family's, was also one of the most learned among the secret Jews. Luis's parents regularly sought him out for religious counsel and instruction and transmitted his teachings to their children.[42]

That year was also certainly one of insecurity and anxiety. Luis knew that the threat of the Inquisition, only recently so remote, would now haunt him day and night, and that the only surprises the future could be expected to bring would be unpleasant. Such anticipations were the lot of the keepers of the Law of Moses. But they were also the necessary price for the precious salvation they were certain it offered.

Yet early the next year, when a surprise did come, it was a pleasant one, so pleasant indeed that it seemed to offer a panacea for all the problems confronting Luis and his family.

In the spring of 1580 the older Luis de Carvajal suddenly appeared in Medina del Campo. The major purpose of his appearance was to urge his sister and brother-in-law to emigrate with their family to the land of New Spain.[43]

3 The Governor

Don Luis de Carvajal y de la Cueva returned to Spain distinguished with achievement. In the turbulent decade he had spent in the New World he had repeatedly proved his mettle as an enterprising servant of the viceroy in New Spain and his sovereign, King Philip II. At the age of forty Don Luis stood at the pinnacle of a career of spectacular service to Portugal and Spain, going back almost uninterruptedly to the day his father died some thirty years before.

The oldest of the four children that the former Doña Francisca de León bore to Don Gaspar de Carvajal, Luis first saw the light of day in 1539, in his father's family home at Mogadouro. His life passed uneventfully from infancy to childhood and to a schooling consonant with his parents' station. In 1547, when he was eight years old, his father took him to the city of Sahagún to visit an abbot, a relative of theirs, perhaps to have Luis enrolled in the monastery for the continuance of his education. But Luis did not stay long at Sahagún. His father soon became ill, and Luis took care of him in the city of Salamanca. Shortly thereafter Don Gaspar died in his home at Benavente and was buried in the Church of the Holy Sepulcher.[1]

With Don Gaspar's passing a new life opened for his son. Luis's maternal uncle, Duarte de León, the Portuguese crown's factor for the lands of Guinea, came to Benavente and took the boy under his wing. First he took Luis to Lisbon. After three months doubtless devoted to careful planning and preparation, he sent him to the Cape Verde Islands, a tropical archipelago off the West African coast, located on the major Atlantic trade route.[2] The islands, owned by Portugal, formed a vital link in its extensive commercial empire and served as the heart of its slaving network.[3] In Don Duarte's expert eyes, the Cape Verde Islands undoubtedly appeared to offer the best opportunities for Luis's development. They seemed a natural stepping-stone to positions of increasing responsibility in the service of the Portuguese crown. Don Duarte appears to have made an excellent appraisal of both the islands and his nephew. Luis thrived in the islands, where he appears to have acquired the multifarious talents he was to display throughout his life. In time he became the islands' treasurer and comptroller, though he was still a stripling. When he left the archipelago, after a stay of thirteen years, he was all of twenty-two years of age.[4]

The talent and ambition that had impelled Carvajal to success in the islands continued to drive him on his return to the Iberian Peninsula in 1561 or 1562. He went first to Lisbon. After a brief stay there he moved to Seville, the whirling hub of Spanish trade with the New World. Carvajal settled in Seville and became a wholesale merchant, very likely cocking a longing eye at the lucrative commerce passing through the city's harbor on its way to and from the New World.

In Seville he met Miguel Núñez, a wealthy and aristocratic New Christian from Lisbon. At the time Núñez was in the enviable position of holding the asientos, or slaving contracts, granted by the kings of both Portugal and Spain. Though the evidence is scant, Luis appears to have entered into a business arrangement with Don Miguel lasting for well over a decade, until Núñez's death around the year 1577.[5] It may have been in the service of Miguel Núñez that Carvajal's nautical skills came to the attention of the court. We soon find Carvajal captaining ships in a spectacular if brief career as a naval warrior in Europe. Within the next six years Carvajal was even given command of an armada in the waters off Flanders.[6]

Through his association with Miguel Núñez, Carvajal also acquired a bride. He met Núñez's daughter Guiomar, known as Guiomar de Ribera, doubtless after her mother's maiden name. Guiomar's family wealth and status gave her all the qualifications that a young man sitting atop success and driven by ambition could possibly desire. Don Luis and Doña Guiomar were married around 1566.[7]

By this time Don Luis had certainly absorbed the shock that overcame all noble young men who suddenly learned that they were not Old Christians.

Like many another comfortable and proud Iberian of converso pedigree, Luis had grown up believing that he derived from Old Christian stock. His family's entrée into the highest circles of society and the important positions held by his father and uncles no doubt reinforced this belief.

Besides, as far back as Luis's recollection reached, his parents had zealously clung to the church, never giving him reason to doubt their Old Christian descent. Of course, Luis was never really in a position to determine whether his family's Christian piety was a façade, concealing an intense devotion to Judaism, as it did among other New Christians. His father's tragic death had uprooted Luis from his home before he had reached the age when any such dichotomies were usually permitted to reach a youngster's attention. As a result, any secretive Judaizing his parents might have indulged became irrelevant for Luis's future life. He left Mogadouro faithful to the church.

His faithfulness continued throughout his stay in the Cape Verde Islands. If any of his mentors there secretly Judaized, they did not see fit to risk self-exposure for the sake of saving the boy's soul for Judaism. Luis consequently moved through adolescence investing the faith of his upbringing with the same fervent zeal and the same uncompromising idealism that he brought to every other endeavor he believed worthwhile. Had a different constellation of circumstances driven him into the camp of the Judaizers, the imagination and intrepidity he was to display throughout his life might have propelled him to a position of leadership among them. As things were and in the context of the only faith he knew, the same qualities turned the adult Luis into a staunch champion of the church, impatient with anyone disparaging it or deviating in the slightest from its mandates.

On this undivertible zeal hinged the difficulties that soon sprang up between Luis and Doña Guiomar. Guiomar was, like her husband, a New Christian and was similarly endowed with a brimming reserve of religious strength. But unlike her husband, Guiomar unabashedly discharged her energies in the clandestine practice of Judaism.[8]

Carvajal could not have failed to know that Guiomar Núñez de Ribera was a New Christian. He may even have found this fact to be magnetically attractive in his choice of a mate. Eager to hide his identity for the sake of his career, he may have felt more secure with a noble wife similarly encumbered than with one who belonged to the aristocracy of unblended Old Christian blood. Such a wife might scorn him if she learned of his origins. She might even brandish the threat of revealing it in order to attain her ends. Other New Christians are known to have avoided such marriages for similar reasons. One of these was the very learned Sevillian, Pedro de San Lúcar, who had studied in Bologna and Russia as well as the great Spanish University of Salamanca. He refused to marry a certain woman precisely because she was of Old Christian descent and, as a result, later found himself haled before the Inquisition.[9]

But whether or not Carvajal discriminated between Old and New Christians in his quest for a mate, the one quality she had to possess, judging from the record of his life, was an uncompromising devotion to the church. How he could have failed to learn of Doña Guiomar's penchant for Judaism early in his association with her must therefore remain a mystery. Perhaps he did know of it, but rather than lose so noble a bride, he may have entertained the hope of converting her to a wholehearted Catholicism after marriage. If he entered marriage unaware of his bride's secret passion, it could not have taken him long to discover it.

But even more painful than the fact of Guiomar's Judaizing, whenever learned, was Carvajal's postnuptial realization that it would be impossible to change his wife's mind. This disturbing conclusion, coupled with a disastrous business reversal involving a large shipment of wheat, drove Carvajal to a decision that he had apparently been contemplating for some time. Shortly after his business fiasco, he made up his mind to emigrate to New Spain.[10]

For a man of Carvajal's ability and determination New Spain offered a cornucopia of opportunities. To begin with, the authorities wanted to subjugate numerous bellicose Indian tribes. In the official cant this was called pacification. They also wanted to have vast stretches of the land explored and surveyed. If, as there was every reason to hope, these lands resembled others already under effective Spanish control, they would be suitable for farming and cattle-raising and might even be heavy with silver and gold.

The Indians provided the huge labor force required for the Spaniards' ambitious projects. The Spaniards, particularly the nobles among them, had an almost pathological aversion to manual labor and could hope to succeed only by the exploitation of others. When they subdued Indians, they regularly impressed them into virtual serfdom— no worse perhaps than what many had experienced under the Aztecs, but at the same time hardly any better. Often they were parceled out like slaves in repartimientos, or forced labor allotments, or distributed in encomiendas, or estates, of various sizes under the feudal jurisdiction of a conquistador. The conquistador levied tribute and in return provided, or at least was supposed to provide, the Indians with protection and education.

The Indians were made to work under brutalizing conditions in hot fields or squalid mines, and were often compelled to be away from their family for months.[11] Some Spanish clerics, like Bartolomé de las Casas, himself the holder of an encomienda, and the Franciscan Gerónimo de Mendieta, intrepidly assailed their countrymen's abuse of the Indians, and their voices did secure the passage of some mitigating legislation. But they were powerless to uproot the system that provided Spanish leadership with its lavish wealth.[12] For, to paraphrase the apt words of Bernal Díaz, the chronicler of Cortés's conquest of Mexico, the first Spaniards came to the New World not only "to serve God and His Majesty," and not only through Christianity "to give light to those in darkness," but "also to get rich."[13] The Spaniards who followed were cut from the same cloth, and Carvajal was a paragon of the model.

Evidently Spanish officialdom, King Philip included, thought so too. To judge from the honors and responsibilities they heaped upon him when he left, they were hardly indifferent to Carvajal's migration to the New World, and may well have pressed him to undertake the voyage. Carvajal left Spain for the Americas not as an ordinary passenger aboard an emigrant ship, but as an admiral[14] in a fleet of eleven vessels—nine bound for New Spain and the other two for Santo Domingo—that sailed under the command of Captain General Francisco de Luján and his deputy, Juan de Ubilla.[15] The fleet left Seville at the end of June or the beginning of July 1568 with an abundance of precious cargo, including 873 quintals of mercury, the indispensable ingredient that had but recently been put to use in the beneficiation of silver ore.[16]

Carvajal's ships carried a heavy load of wine, to be sold with other goods by agents in Veracruz, Mexico City, and the bustling mining center of Zacatecas. The fleet also carried a host of important officials. Foremost among these was the honorable Martín Enríquez de Almansa, recently appointed the fourth viceroy of New Spain.[17] And when Carvajal set foot on the American mainland, he was not an ordinary citizen, but the local judge or magistrate of the port city of Tampico.[18]

But before landing in New Spain, the twenty-nine-year-old admiral was called upon to display the qualities of leadership that had inspired the crown's confidence. As his ship, following royal instructions, approached the island of Jamaica, Carvajal descried a number of pirate vessels brazenly anchored along the coast. It was obvious that the pirates were on a raid and were not expecting maritime visitors. Halting the ships under his command, Carvajal divided his men into two groups. He ordered one group to remain with the ships and dispatched the other in small boats to the mainland with instructions to pursue the raiders.

No evidence remains of these sailors' foray or of any battles or feats of heroism that may have taken place. What is known speaks honorably of the Spaniards and of Admiral Carvajal. When the expedition was over, the Spaniards had captured three pirate vessels, which turned out to be English ships carrying stolen hides. Carvajal promptly delivered the ships and their cargo to the governor of Jamaica and nobly refused to accept any reward for himself or his men. His business in the island completed, Carvajal rejoined the ships of the main fleet destined for New Spain.[19]

Unknown to Carvajal, Luján, or the viceroy, at that very time the notorious English privateer John Hawkins was sailing off the waters of New Spain, heading directly for Veracruz. With the approval of his queen, Elizabeth, who had given him two of her own ships, including his flagship, the seven-hundred-ton *Jesus of Lubeck,* Hawkins was nearing the end of his third slaving and trading voyage in the Caribbean. On August 8, 1568, still carrying numerous unsold slaves and a cargo that included hides, sugar, pearls, and precious metals obtained in exchange for the balance of his human merchandise, he had begun his homeward voyage to England. In the first few weeks of sailing he met with one severe tropical storm after another, but managed to overcome them all. Early in September, however, he ran into a violent hurricane, which lashed his fleet relentlessly for four successive days, capsizing one ship, tossing another far out to sea, and damaging the rest of the fleet. The separated vessel, the *William and John,* managed to return without escort to England. The *Jesus of Lubeck* was left helmless and adrift and in danger of immediate sinking.

Hawkins first limped to the Florida mainland, scouring the coast in a fruitless search for a place to anchor and repair his battered vessels. At the end of two weeks he realized that if he wanted to survive and eventually return to England, he had no recourse but to turn south and westward toward New Spain and put himself and his ships at the mercy of its inhabitants.

Accordingly Hawkins decided to head directly for New Spain's chief port, on the island of San Juan de Ulúa, off the coast of Veracruz. On the way to San Juan de Ulúa, Hawkins captured three Spanish vessels. On learning from their captains that the Spanish fleet was momentarily expected at Veracruz, he ordered the captured vessels to travel at the head of his fleet.

When the lookouts at Veracruz saw the distant sails of the Spanish ships leading Hawkins's vessels on the morning on September 16, they not unnaturally concluded that they were witnessing the arrival of Admiral Luján's fleet and Don Martín Enríquez de Almansa. The

John Hawkins

The Jesus of Lubeck

Spaniards on the mainland ordered the firing of a salute to the new viceroy and soon heard a salvo of response, which Hawkins, briefed by his captive Spanish pilots, had executed "as is customarily done on the ships of Spain." But when the Spanish officials eagerly sailed out into the harbor to greet their leader, they were stunned to find themselves in the company of a pirate.

After diplomatically explaining his predicament, Hawkins proceeded to assume command of the harbor. He then sent word to the authorities in Mexico City, informing them that he wished to careen his ships and to buy food and supplies, "which we hope will be granted to us, after due payment, since we are friends of King Don Philip."

The same night the advance section of the Spanish fleet approached the mainland.

The next morning, when the long-awaited fleet was seen, the distressed Spaniards sent word to the viceroy, apprising him of Hawkins's presence. Enríquez immediately summoned his captains and shipmasters, Carvajal necessarily among them, into an emergency conference. The conference decided that it would be best to make a peaceable entrance into the port.

In the meantime Hawkins sent a message to Enríquez offering an olive branch. But while the message was being delivered by Antonio Delgadillo, captain and inspector for the port of San Juan de Ulúa, Hawkins proceeded to make himself master of the port and fortify it for possible battle.

The conditions in which Hawkins's olive branch was wrapped soon ignited the viceroy's displeasure. Hawkins threatened to block Luján's entry into the port unless the viceroy offered certain guarantees to the pirate. Hawkins demanded the right to buy provisions for a fair price, time to repair his damaged ships and an opportunity to trade with the inhabitants of New Spain. Any agreement was to include an exchange of hostages. On Saturday, September 18, Don Martín Enríquez acquiesced in the drawing up of such a pact, ratified it with hand and seal—and planned to break it at the earliest opportunity.[20]

The appropriate moment came with fair weather on the following Thursday morning, September 23. The viceroy's ships, carefully prepared for battle, attacked Hawkins's fleet and dropped soldiers to fight Hawkins's men on the land. The battle lasted for hours, highlighted by a series of spectacular naval encounters. When the cannonading and fires were over, the viceroy had gained a complete victory. The Spaniards had sunk or capsized all but three of Hawkins's ships. Of these the *Jesus of Lubeck* was so badly damaged that Hawkins was soon compelled to abandon it outside the port. A second ship, the *Judith,* deserted Hawkins and headed directly for England under its young commander, Francis Drake. Except for a tender, Hawkins was left with only the H.M.S. *Minion*, his second largest ship; although it weighed over three hundred tons, it was hardly spacious enough to accommodate all the survivors of the disastrous battle.

Hawkins packed most of the survivors aboard the *Minion* and then somehow managed to slip away through wind, storm, and Spanish surveillance to the Isle of Sacrifices.

He remained there for two days, harried by the possibility of imminent Spanish attacks, the near-exhaustion of his supplies of food and water, and the terrible dissensions among his men, who realized that unless they could find a way of replenishing their stores, they could not all survive the voyage back to England. After two days Hawkins re-established order, got his men back to the ships, and, with the calming of the ferocious north winds, set out to sea again. Soon Hawkins realized that he had no way of getting new supplies. He therefore decided to leave behind half his sailors, a hundred or more, to fend for themselves in the wilds of New Spain, while he tried to make it back to England with the rest of the crew. Some say that the men Hawkins left behind were volunteers and that he promised to return and rescue them eventually. Others insist that Hawkins himself decided who should stay and who should go and that the men left on the shores of New Spain were regarded by him as the more expendable.

In either case Hawkins left New Spain on October 8 and sailed through the Straits of Florida. After an amazing journey that brought him to the coasts of the Iberian Peninsula, he eventually reached Plymouth, England; by this time his crew was further weakened by death and disease. Astonishingly, in spite of all his troubles and losses, a good part of Hawkins's profits, including some forty thousand out of the sixty thousand ducats proceeding from his sales, remained intact.[21]

We do not know what part Luis de Carvajal may have played in the rout of John Hawkins's fleet or the capture of some thirty-five prisoners off Veracruz. But he was to exercise a major role in the lives of the sailors abandoned on the coast of New Spain.

These men decided to find their way to the nearest Spanish settlement in the hope of seizing food and supplies. The morning of October 9 found them inching their way inland through the thicket. Their quest, however, was unsuccessful. Enervated by hunger, drenched by rain, and attacked by noxious insects, they soon fell into the hands of the Indians. The Indians killed eight men and despoiled the rest of every visible sign of wealth.

Then, as suddenly as they had attacked, the Indians changed their attitude. They took compassion on the survivors and offered to provide them with guides who could lead them to Tampico, the nearest Spanish town. What motivated the Indians to change is not known. It might have been a touch of human kindness, alloyed perhaps with a desire to do anything that might injure the Spaniards.

One group of Englishmen, headed by a sailor named John Hooper, decided not to go toward Tampico but to venture northward. There they ran into other Indians, who were not as hospitable. Many of the men, Hooper himself among them, died in battles with the Indians. Only three of the group survived and eventually were able to get back to England.

The other group, under Anthony Goddard, decided to march to Tampico. After numerous hardships, they reached the bank of the Pánuco River on October 14.

Their arrival did not come entirely as a surprise to the Spaniards. As early as October 8, the day when Hawkins abandoned his men on the shore, the authorities in Mexico City seem to have been aware of their presence. They lost little time in notifying all provinces in their general vicinity to be on guard against the possible appearance of the fugitives.

The Spaniards in Tampico did not react courageously to the news. The report that English pirates were roaming in their vicinity sent them into a panic, and they began to talk of abandoning the neighborhood. But Don Luis de Carvajal refused to cry craven, though he had no way of knowing the size and strength of the pirates' forces. On the contrary, he emphatically insisted that everyone stay and fight.

On October 15 two Negro slaves, Álvaro and Antón, came to inform Don Luis that they had seen the English fugitives. Carvajal found it difficult to get men to fight against them, and his exhortations succeeded in enlisting only a total of some twenty men. Dividing these into three patrols under the captaincy of Cristóbal de Frías, Diego Ramírez, and Antonio Villadiego, he sent this force to capture the intruders.

Not until October 15 could Carvajal have realized that the pirates were not at the peak of their strength and morale. This fact greatly diminished the numerical disadvantage of his men and made their victory over the invaders much less heroic. Yet by any standard their action was worthy of note. The patrols captured seventy-eight pirates: seventy-three of them English, four French, and one Portuguese. The Portuguese, Antonio de Teixeira, was leading the group at the time of its capture, doubtless because of his familiarity with the language and culture of the Spaniards.

The captives were brought before Judge Carvajal. They were stripped of jewels and gold, amounting to 209 pesos, which they had miraculously hidden from the Indians, and were compelled to testify about their activities and recent experiences. Teixeria gave Carvajal the amazing report that though Hawkins had lost some twenty thousand ducats in the disaster off San Juan de Ulúa, he had managed to salvage forty thousand ducats and many other valuable possessions.

Carvajal retained the captives in Tampico for three days, then sent them on to Mexico City. Here they were cured of their wounds and allowed to live peacefully for a while. Within a few years, however, they fell into the hands of the Inquisition. One of them, Miles Philips, eventually escaped and wrote a fascinating account of his experiences.[22]

These stupendous events in the fall of 1568 provided an apt conclusion to one of New Spain's most turbulent lustrums. Five years earlier two of the colony's foremost bluebloods, Gil and Alonso González, sons of the indomitable conquistador Don Gil González de Ávila had hatched a plot to take over the government. Many members of New Spain's aristocracy had come to their aid. Prominent among them were the Marqués del Valle and his two mestizo half brothers. All three were sons of Hernán Cortés. In the midst of the conspiracy the aging viceroy, Don Luis de Velasco, "looked up to . . . as a father," as his contemporaries said, died on July 31, 1564, adding to the land's disruptive confusion. Though the conspiracy was aborted and the González brothers were unceremoniously hanged, the embers of the plot continued to glow. When Velasco's successor, Don Gastón de Peralta, cavalierly dismissed reports of the continuing threat posed by the surviving leaders of the conspiracy, he found rumor and innuendo implicating him in an alleged new plot against the crown.

Exasperated by his colony's seemingly incorrigible instability, Philip reacted resolutely, if somewhat precipitately, by establishing a dictatorship in New Spain. The new government, which deposed Peralta and ordered him returned to Spain, was headed by one of Philip's most trustworthy servants, the renowned Spanish jurisconsult, Alonso de Muñoz. An uncompromising and insensitive martinet, Muñoz surrounded himself with servile myrmidons and inaugurated a veritable reign of terror. He arrested scores of people on mere suspicion of disloyalty. He immured commoners and noblemen in the capital's airless prisons. He executed more than a few of New Spain's foremost citizenry, including the popular and beloved Quesada brothers, who had helped to crush the González conspiracy.

Culminating Muñoz's scandalous rule was the arrest of Cortés's mestizo son, the noble Don Martín. For withholding information he was alleged to possess, Don Martín was tortured and sentenced to perpetual banishment from Mexico City. There is reason to believe that this sentence was never carried out. Instead, it was Muñoz who was compelled to leave when his merciless repression created new restiveness. Philip deposed Muñoz, who ironically returned to Spain on the ship bearing the delayed Peralta. In Muñoz's place, Philip dispatched Don Martín Enríquez to attempt the inauguration of a more tranquil era in New Spain.

Enríquez's coming did bring Spaniards and Creoles into greater harmony and permitted the continuation of the leaping prosperity that New Spain had been enjoying with only minor interruptions from the time of its initial conquest by Cortés. But, as Carvajal was to learn almost immediately upon his arrival, the new viceroy was powerless to insure peace for the land as a whole.[23]

Carvajal had hardly had time to recover from his harrowing adventures with the various groups of pirates when the viceroy called him to enter into battle against the Indians of the frontiers. Known by the collective name of Chichimecs, they belonged to scores of different tribes, most of them primitive and savage. "They use [sic] to wear their hair long, even down to their knees," wrote Miles Philips about the Chichimecs in his account of New Spain. "They do also color their faces green, yellow, red, and blue, which maketh them to seem very ugly and terrible to beholde. . . . The weapons that they use are no other but bows and arrows, and their arm [sic] is so good that they very seldom miss to hit any thing they shoot at." The Chichimecs were always restive and always dangerous to the small communities of Europeans in New Spain.[24]

For decades the viceroys had been trying to cope with Indian attacks. Beginning with the administration of Don Luis de Velasco (1550–1564), defensive towns and presidios were established and military reprisals against Indians begun. But these and subsequent measures had not brought dramatic results. The Indian attacks lost little of their intensity. In the subsequent decades they were as frequent and fearless as ever.[25]

In addition to the ultimate goal of bringing eventual pacification to the Indian territories, Martín Enríquez was concerned with the interim objective of putting the Indian wars on a sound financial basis. Prior to his arrival the cost of forays and defense against the Indians had been raised on an ad hoc basis by special pledges to the viceroy. All too often the authorities found it difficult to collect these pledges. On April 20, 1567, it was announced that henceforth such costs would be shared

Viceroys of New Spain

above: Martín Enríquez de Almansa (1568–1580)

left: Lorenzo Suárez de Mendoza (1580–1583)

below left: Álvaro Manrique de Zúñiga (1585–1590)

by the royal treasury, the mineowners, and other parties interested in warding off the Indian threat. More specific regulations along these lines were promulgated by the viceroy in 1570.

Yet Martín Enríquez's wholesome intentions were not destined to be translated into reality. The Indians continued their incessant pressure, and the viceregal coffers remained disappointingly unfilled. Even when Enríquez decided to solve his financial problem by taxation and by the creation in 1576 of a special "fund for the expenses of the Chichimec wars," he still found himself without the necessary means to carry out his program of pacification.[26]

When Carvajal reached Tampico, he learned that groups of Pames Indians, pacified and converted to Catholicism sometime earlier, had rebelled against their Spanish overlords in the region of Xalpa, a hundred miles southwest of Tampico, and were in the process of uprooting the symbols of Spanish rule. They had burned the town of Xalpa, the principal town in the region, and set its monastery on fire. Then they had attacked and depopulated the nearby towns of Gelitla and Chapuluacán. The towns of Acicastla and Meztitlán, the residence of many friars and soldiers, also suffered and were on the verge of becoming depopulated.

In alarm, the viceroy had dispatched one of his military commanders, Captain Francisco de Puga, with some twenty-four soldiers, to quell the disturbance. Shackled by the absurd paucity of his troops, the captain failed to carry out his mission. The viceroy thereupon withdrew Puga and issued a call to Carvajal to assume the repacification of the Indians. Carvajal's task was even more difficult than his predecessor's. Although Puga's failure had done little to dampen the Indians' courage and determination, the viceroy gave Carvajal only ten soldiers and no provisions whatever. Unlike Puga, Carvajal was compelled to furnish all the matériel for his seemingly impossible war.

Yet, as the viceroy surely expected he would be, Carvajal was successful. It took him ten months and endless skirmishes in which his minuscule force, always in danger of instant annihilation, won astonishing victories against incredible odds. But at the end of that period calm returned to the region of Xalpa. The Indians submitted to the obedience of the viceroy and the church, and Carvajal began to rebuild the Spanish settlements. Soon Xalpa and its adjacent towns and hamlets were restored. The main settlement was given a new lime and stone fort, one of the finest in New Spain. Within the fort Carvajal built a new church and monastery at a cost of more than twenty thousand pesos. Unlike other conquistadors, Carvajal refused to subject any of the Indians to assignments of forced labor or to reap any profit from his acts. He personally supervised the process of reconstruction and, with his accustomed nobility, bore its entire expense himself.[27]

Carvajal's victory proved to be unexemplary and ephemeral. Indians in other areas continued to be restive, while those around Xalpa were soon on the warpath again.

It was probably after the completion of his assignment at Xalpa that Carvajal settled down to his administrative duties. He also began to attend to the business of promoting his future. In partnership with Captain Sebastián Rodríguez he purchased a cattle ranch from Lope de Sosa.[28] He also appears to have continued his international merchandising, including the shipment of slaves and cochineal, in concert with his father-in-law.[29] One unusual document, executed in Seville on November 10, 1574, lists Carvajal as assuming responsibility for payment to a certain Juan de los Reyes of a bond involving a female relative of his. Carvajal's relative, named, like his sister, Doña Francisca, had obligated herself to join her husband, Damián Aguirre, in the New World. Carvajal had put up the bond as a surety and forfeited it when Doña Francisca refused to keep her promise.[30]

Despite his numerous business interests, Carvajal continued to play a vital role in Indian affairs. He soon sported the titles of captain and pacifier and—very likely as a reward for his achievements—became the "mayor of the towns of Tamaulipas and its environs."[31] How often the viceroy called upon him we do not know. But one of the most important summonses came on December 15, 1575. It ordered the mayor of the towns of Tamaulipas to protect prospectors against Indian raids. Around the same time the frontier Indians in the nearby region of Huaxteca had attacked the Spaniards. The viceroy, "desirous of spreading the faith, and seeing the great damage that the . . . Indians were visiting," as we read in the old chronicle by Alonso de León, decided to take action. He ordered Carvajal "to enter the war territory, punish and pacify the restive peoples." Carvajal "being . . . of an incredibly valorous spirit," as the chronicler goes on to say, launched his expedition and accomplished the mission with his accustomed dispatch. As usual, he bore the full expense of the pacification.[32]

Carvajal's valor brought him the fear and respect of countless Indians and the esteem of the viceroy. Though many border Indians within the province of Pánuco, from the towns of Tampasquín, Tanmotela, and San Miguel to Xalpa and Xichú (Carvajal called it Suchú), continued restive, even after the ravages of the epidemic of 1576, when New Spain lost 40 to 50 percent of its Indians,[33] the viceroy came to

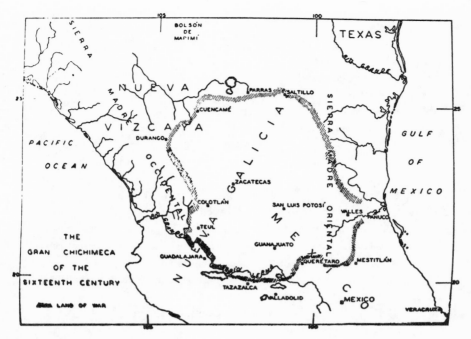

The Gran Chichimeca Area of New Spain

*The Northern Indian
Nations in New Spain*

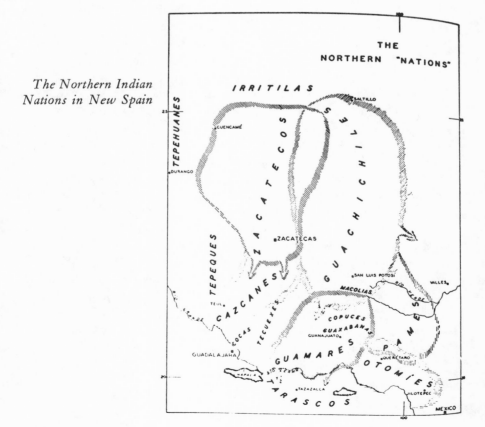

regard Carvajal as almost indispensable for imposing peace on the native population. On leaving his position in 1580, Don Martín Enríquez made laudatory mention of the services of Luis de Carvajal in the report to his successor, Don Lorenzo Suárez de Mendoza, count of Coruña.[34] In his final report, dated September 25, 1580, the retiring viceroy, after bemoaning the continual uprisings by the Indians and the difficulties and costs of keeping the roads of New Spain safe and passable, urges his successor to carry on his program of protecting the roads with troops. He writes:

And I advise Your Excellency that Luis de Carvajal . . . is the person who in my estimation is best qualified to be of service in this regard. Since he has had considerable experience living amidst these Indians and possesses an intimate acquaintance with their ways and knows most of their leaders, as they know him, he has made considerable progress toward the attainment of our needed goal, which is living with them in peace.

He goes on about Carvajal's relations with the Indians: "And since he has been inclined to this goal rather than to the shedding of their blood, I have always called upon him and believe you would do well to do the same."[35]

Ten years of devoted service had catapulted Carvajal into the ranks of New Spain's most illustrious citizens. Carvajal's work, however, was not performed entirely out of selfless motives. The magistrate, captain, and pacifier doubtless regarded his activities and expenditures as solid investments that would sooner or later yield dividends. By 1578 he had a clear idea of where these dividends might come from.

His struggles against the Indians had brought Carvajal northward beyond the mines of Mazapil and westward all the way to the border of the province of New Galicia. Around him and before him lay a vast territory of stunning beauty and stark contrasts, familiar to only a few of the Spaniards and for the most part unexplored.[36]

It was a land of vast plateaus and mountain chains. Toward the Pacific one could see the majestic peaks of the Sierra Madre Occidental, while toward the Atlantic rose the more familiar hills of the Sierra Madre Oriental, "so steep and rugged that it delights the eye," as the chronicler was to say.

It was a land of rich soil and desert, of extreme temperatures that made the winters too cold and the summers too hot. "The dog days are extremely hot, and it seldom rains," the chronicler reported. "It freezes well in November, even better in February and March. It snows in

December and January, often so copiously that the trees droop to the ground for an entire day, and the gush of the waters in some mountain areas lasts for more than two months."

The territory as a whole was rich in natural wealth and favored with numerous rivers, streams, and fertile fields. It could boast trees of brazilwood and lignum vitae, known as the holy wood, as well as oak, laurel, and ebony. In its midst grew herbs yielding indigo and lifesaving drugs, and clusters of nopal (the prickly pear cactus), from whose insect parasites could be squeezed the precious dye cochineal. In its woods roamed armadillos, rabbits, wild boar, and species of mountain fowl. Its many freshwater streams "colorless, tasteless, and odorless, as the philosophers say it should be," the pedantic chronicler declared, teemed with trout, bagres, and more exotic varieties of fish.

The drier regions between the eastern and western sierras could not support a large population, and the Indians living there were fated to eke out a paltry existence from the soil. But elsewhere, particularly in the often isolated intramontane valleys, the land was fertile, "with many pastures, almost always green." It was capable of yielding large stores of grains and fruits and sustaining large populations of sheep and cattle. The region was dotted with an abundance of mines. If they were not as rich as the celebrated mines of Zacatecas, they were nevertheless laden with enough silver, lead, and copper to yield many a generous fortune. "All that is lacking," the chronicler bemoaned, "and I cannot say this without great sorrow," he added parenthetically, "are diligent and industrious men. As a result there is only a little of everything, though there can be such an abundance that life could be very pleasant there."

The chronicler did not forget to mention that the territory was peopled by some of the most savage Indians in New Spain. They belonged to a multitude of tribes and spoke a babble of tongues, but they were united in their hatred of the Spaniards.

Carvajal, "desirous of seeing new lands and making discoveries," according to the chronicler, penetrated this territory and surveyed the possibilities for its exploitation. Following the pattern of other conquistadors, he began to wonder why this land could not someday be his. As other conquistadors were accustomed to do, Carvajal soon began to consider requesting permission to pacify the new territory and hold it as a kind of fief from the crown. In the spring of 1578 he translated his thoughts into action. He decided to return to Spain to present his petition for the territory at the court personally.[37] Doubtless contributing heavily to his decision was the death of Miguel Núñez and the consequent disruption of Carvajal's international business ties.[38]

Luis de Carvajal left Veracruz with the fleet under the command of Captain General Diego Maldonado.[39] He could hardly have left at a more opportune time. In 1580 a flood inundated the capital of New Spain and caused Viceroy Enríquez untold difficulties.[40] One can only imagine what miracles the viceroy would have called upon the redoubtable Carvajal to perform had he been present in New Spain.

The fleet arrived at Sanlúcar de Barrameda, Seville's port at the mouth of the Guadalquivir River, on July 10, 1578, but took two weeks to cross the difficult bar at Sanlúcar and make its way up the tortuous stream to the metropolis, some fifty miles away.[41] When Carvajal at last debarked, he went to the Magdalene (La Magdalena) district of Seville for a reunion with his wife at her family's sumptuous estate, La Pajería (The Straw-loft). During the time Carvajal remained at Seville, he undoubtedly attended to aspects of his late father-in-law's affairs.

At La Pajería, Carvajal met a young relative of his wife's, an eighteen-year-old lad named Felipe Núñez. He became fast friends with Núñez and asked him to be his companion on the travels he had planned to various parts of the Iberian Peninsula. When the two left Seville, they went first to Salamanca to visit a relative of Don Luis's named Gerónimo de Carvajal. From Salamanca they proceeded to Medina del Campo for Carvajal's momentous invitation to his sister and brother-in-law to return with him to New Spain. His invitation was in all likelihood gilded with enticing descriptions of the wealth and bounty of the New World and, from what can be gathered, some glowing but vague promises to help them attain it.

After a week at Medina del Campo, Carvajal left his brother and sister-in-law to mull over his proposals. Accompanied by Núñez, he proceeded to Toledo for the presentation of his claim at court.[42]

Arriving at court late in 1578, Carvajal spent a half year pressing his claims before his efforts met with success. He received a charter from the king signed at Aranjuez on May 31, 1579, which recognized his "desire to be of service to our Lord and ourselves . . . that our holy Catholic faith and evangelical law may be exalted and our crown, its income and patrimony may be increased." The detailed document named Carvajal governor of the entire expanse of land he had traversed, which henceforth was to be known as "The New Kingdom of Léon"; the charter gave him the privilege, frequent in grants to conquistadors, of passing his holdings on to a son or other heir of his own designation. In addition, it authorized him to take a hundred people of his choice from the Iberian Peninsula to the New World.[43]

A second royal decree, issued two weeks later, on June 14, 1579, confirmed the provisions of Carvajal's charter, added some details, and made an amazing concession: it specifically exempted everyone traveling in Carvajal's entourage from the mandatory investigation of their family origins. This form of investigation had been instituted to prevent the descendants of Moslems or Jews from emigrating to the New World.[44]

Although New Christians had been very much in evidence in the discovery of America, the Catholic sovereigns, Ferdinand and Isabel, soon denied Jews, Moors, and their descendants permission to settle in the New World. An exception was made in 1509 in the case of New Christians who wanted to trade in the Americas. They were permitted to emigrate on the condition that they stay no more than two years on each excursion. After Ferdinand's death, Emperor Charles V confirmed this decision, but reversed himself in 1518, when he closed the New World to the children and grandchildren of conversos and convicted prisoners of the Inquisition. His change of mind was occasioned at least in part by complaints about the influx of New Christians into America, such as the one registered by the Jeronymite monks in January of the preceding year. The gravamen of their charge was that their territory was becoming a haven for fugitives from the Inquisition. The New Christians railed unrelentingly against the restriction, and it was finally lifted in 1526.

But the respite did not last for long. In 1537 King Philip II obtained a papal bull instructing colonial bishops to expel from their domains any New Christian descended from Jews or Moors who might come to the New World. The old restrictions were repeated in September 1539. Four years later, in August 1543, the king ordered his deputies in the New World to conduct a meticulous probe for unauthorized New Christians still within their domains and to dispatch them to Spain on the first available ship.[45]

Despite such laws and precautions, it was difficult to keep New Christians away from the Americas and next to impossible to find and send back all those who had already settled there. But the fact is that the discriminatory legislation remained in force, and this made Carvajal's privilege all the more remarkable.

Carvajal's success in obtaining this clause in his charter may yield an insight into the primary motive behind his desire to see his family. Whatever else this motive might have been, it certainly could not have been love or longing. He had not lived with his wife in over a decade, and his failure to induce her to accompany him to the New World could not have strengthened the tenuous bond that existed between them. His two brothers had died, Domingo, the Jesuit, in Medina del

Campo and Antonio in the New World. And as for his sister, Francisca Rodríguez de Carvajal, or, as she was more commonly called, Francisca Núñez, Carvajal and she had not been so close as to prevent his leaving Spain ten years before. In fact, the two had been separated since the death of their father, when Don Luis, age eight, left for Lisbon and Francisca, only three, went to live at the home of her aunt, some eight leagues from Mogadouro, not to return to Benavente until her marriage ten years later.

Of his nephews and nieces Carvajal knew only Gaspar, who had come to the New World and had sought his help in getting back on the road to the priesthood. When Don Luis left Spain in 1568, Leonor, Anica, and little Miguel had not yet been born. The others were children. Isabel was nine, Baltasar four, Catalina no more than three, and Luis an infant of one.

Carvajal may have felt a tug of love for his family and even a longing for a son to inherit his lands. Perhaps he wanted his family near him to mitigate the loneliness he might have felt in New Spain, or to fill important positions that might be his to dispense. Whatever worthy plans and emotions Carvajal may have harbored, beneath them undoubtedly lay a recognition of how desperately he needed his family near him for the advancement of his career.

Carvajal could not have failed to realize that as he reached higher and higher levels of success the greater and more powerful his enemies would be and the more determined would be their efforts to discover his Achilles' heel. His greatest liability lay, of course, in his Jewish ancestry. Heretofore he had managed to avoid any close scrutiny of his family's origins. But whether he could continue to do so depended in no small measure upon Guiomar, Francisca, and others close to them.

Doña Guiomar's Judaizing posed a continuous threat. Were she to come to the attention of the Inquisition, Don Luis would likely be subjected to a thorough interrogation, and such grilling would almost certainly reveal his New Christian descent. Besides, Doña Guiomar's continued separation from her husband, hardly an asset to his career, could only breed suspicion—and suspicion spelled danger for them both.

We cannot be sure whether Don Luis, before his return to Spain, had any notion that Doña Francisca or her husband were Judaizers. But he was aware of their New Christian background and their exposure to other New Christians in the family, some of whom he surely must have suspected. It is therefore unlikely that he dismissed the possibility of their Judaizing out of hand. He did know that the revelation of the ancestry of Francisca or any of her brood, whether in connection with Jewish practice or for any other reason, would lead to the utter demolition of his claim to Old Christian descent.

The same was no less true of other relatives, particularly those in regular contact with the family. It was true as well of some of the family's closest New Christian friends.

Thus there is every reason to believe that Don Luis returned to Spain intent upon persuading his family and even many of his friends to return with him to the New World. His wife's presence by his side would remove the embarrassment of their separation and any pernicious queries as to its cause. Doña Guiomar, even if still adamant in her Judaizing, might consent to delimit the scope of her activities, or at least to indulge in them with more than the Judaizers' customary circumspection, out of consideration for the precariousness of her husband's lofty position. Having the rest of his family and his friends with him in an isolated region where his power was all but supreme would give him two further advantages: it would reduce the chances for the discovery of their Judaizing practice, and it would give him repeated opportunities to bridle such practice. But if anyone in his entourage did become involved with the Inquisition, Don Luis would certainly be in a better position to protect himself in the New World than in the Old.

Besides, the threat of the Inquisition was as yet not nearly as strong in the Americas as it was on the Iberian Peninsula. It was not until January 1569, four months after Don Luis's first arrival in Tampico, that King Philip established the Inquisition in America, "seeing that those who . . . pertinaciously cling to their errors and heresies, always strive to divert or seduce the other faithful Christians from our holy Catholic faith." The royal decree went on to explain that his action was being taken in order "to obviate and prevent so great an offense to the faith and religion of Christianity in these regions, where the inhabitants, our subjects, have been providing such a good example of Christian devotion, and those who have recently come to the recognition of the faith comport themselves with such docility to be instructed and educated in Christian doctrine."[46]

To judge from the early years of the Inquisition's activity in New Spain, the seducers were Protestants rather than Jews. Their danger could hardly have been regarded as alarming in all quarters, for a full year was to pass after Philip's decree before the Inquisition was actually established on American soil. The viceroyalty of Peru received its Inquisition in January 1570. New Spain had to wait almost two more years before the Inquisition was instituted there in November 1571.[47]

Actually, the Holy Office of the Inquisition at first posed no more of a threat to Judaizers than the episcopal investigations or inquisitions into matters of faith that had preceded it in New Spain. Judging from the number of cases preserved in the incomplete lists deriving from this period, the earlier inquisitors assiduously discharged their obligation of preserving religious purity. One inventory lists over six hundred cases involving crimes against the faith prior to 1571, a large proportion of them between the years 1527 and 1543, when New Spain's first bishop and archbishop, the stern and overly zealous Juan de Zumárraga, also served as inquisitor. Most of the defendants in this inventory were charged with crimes like witchcraft, concubinage, bigamy, defilement of sacred objects, and blasphemy—a term which covered a wide variety of offenses. Only thirteen people suspected of Judaizing were haled as defendants before the Inquisition prior to 1570 and only sixteen prior to 1574, and not all of these were actually denounced as secret Jews.[48]

Nor did the hunt for Judaizers appear to become intensified when the Holy Office began its work, though the new Inquisition was hardly inactive. As early as May 1572 it had already gathered the testimony of at least four hundred people who had committed religious infidelity. These first six months of its activity found it indicting thirty-nine men and women and issuing warrants for the arrest of sixteen others.[49] It was not long before this Inquisition rounded up the hapless survivors of John Hawkins's abandoned crewmen captured by Carvajal and now dispersed throughout the land. It arrested them and brought them to trial on the charge of being Protestant heretics, or, as it called them, "faithful observers and ministers of the sect of Luther." It even arranged for posthumous trials for several of the sailors who had died. At the first auto-da-fé held in New Spain, on the first Sunday of Lent, February 28, 1574, many of the men heard themselves sentenced. All together, thirty-six of Hawkins's crew were tried and punished. Two were garroted and burned at the stake. The others received varying penalties, generally including two hundred or more lashes and up to ten years in the galleys.[50]

On March 6, 1575, thirty additional prisoners were sentenced, none on a charge of Judaizing, though two were known to be of Jewish descent. No punishment for Judaizing was meted out until December 1577. At that time a man named Hernando Álvarez Pliego was fined five hundred pesos "for matters and ceremonies of the Law of Moses."

Another New Christian, Pedro Núñez de Montalbán, whose mother had been burned at the stake in Seville on a charge of Judaizing, was given a mild sentence for wearing gold and silk, carrying arms, and riding horseback, in defiance of the sumptuary regulations imposed upon the descendants of the Inquisition's prisoners.

The first Judaizer to be burned at the stake in New Spain after the advent of the Holy Office was a seventy-year-old man named Garci González Bermeguero, the father of an Augustinian monk. His sentence resulted not so much from his Judaizing practices as from his stubborn refusal to disclose particulars about his activity or to reveal the names of his associates in religion. Bermeguero's sentence was

The First Auto-da-fé in Mexico City, February 28, 1574

carried out on October 11, 1579, after Luis de Carvajal had left Tampico for Spain.[51]

The Inquisition's apparent neglect of Judaizers may be explained by the infrequency of known Judaizers in New Spain. Whatever the explanation, it would have been reasonable for Carvajal, especially after the grant of immunity from investigation given his family and friends, to expect the Inquisition not to deviate substantially from its course.

The privilege did not come too early for the newly appointed governor. While at court he received a letter from Francisco Rodríguez de Matos announcing that since he was poor, he was contemplating moving his family to France. Francisco was planning to join his brother Diego there "if the position or business the governor promised him turned out to be unacceptable." The letter was a bit of undisguised blackmail. In the very midst of Carvajal's profitable negotiations, his brother-in-law was threatening to take a step that could instantaneously overthrow the ziggurat of his achievements. Francisco was obliquely demanding substantial concessions from Carvajal, obviously greater than any he may hitherto have made, as the price of his family's assent in migrating to the New World.[52]

Whether Carvajal wrote a reply is not known. What is known is that upon concluding his business at court, the new governor, still accompanied by his faithful Núñez, went directly to Medina del Campo and succeeded in placating Don Francisco. From the fact that his brother-in-law acquiesced in accompanying him to the New World we may conjecture that Don Luis acceded to at least some of his demands. In all probability, the family believed that in the New World they could practice their Judaism unnoticed. Even if detected, they doubtless expected their religious irregularities to be overlooked out of consideration for Governor Carvajal.

Before the family left Spain, the governor named Baltasar as his treasurer and young Luis as his heir and successor. Like Francisco Rodríguez de Matos, Carvajal regarded young Luis as more richly endowed for leadership than his brother Baltasar.

In addition, at the governor's behest various members of the family dropped the name Rodríguez and regularly used the surname Carvajal. The young heir to the New Kingdom of León thus became known by the name of his uncle, Luis de Carvajal.[53]

Carvajal then left his sister and brother-in-law to settle their affairs and prepare for the journey to Seville, where the emigrants were to assemble. He traveled to Astorga to visit his niece Isabel, for whom he appears to have had a particular fondness. The purpose of his visit appears to have been to persuade her and her husband to liquidate their business and join the rest of the family in emigration. Gabriel de Herrera did not take kindly to the idea; he insisted on remaining in Spain. After a fruitless week, Carvajal and Núñez left Astorga and crossed the border into Portugal. There they visited various towns, among them Braganza, Cortiços, Carvajal's birthplace of Mogadouro, and Mirandela. Then, coming back to Spain, they traveled to Ciudad Rodrigo, Coria, and finally to Seville. The purpose of the journey, though nowhere stated, seems patently to have been to round up as many of the people Carvajal wanted to take along to the New World as possible.[54]

In addition to Francisco Rodríguez de Matos and his family, Carvajal's passenger roster was to list several of his cousins. Among them were Catalina de León, and her husband, Gonzalo Pérez Ferro, whom the governor's namesake called "uncle" and with whom he had Judaized at Medina del Campo. Then there were Catalina's bachelor brothers, Diego, known as Diego Márquez, and Jorge de León, who was eventually to be designated as the governor's treasurer, in all likelihood replacing Baltasar, and their widowed sister, Doña Ginebra. From Guiomar's side came her bastard half sister, Francisca Núñez Viciosa, and her husband, the notary Alonso del Aguila, and of course, Felipe Núñez, who was slated to serve as Carvajal's adjutant in the New Kingdom of León. Also on the list were various artisans, including the skilled mason Rodrigo de. la Barreda, from Burgos, the bellmaker, Diego Martínez de Valladares, from the small town of Yola, also in the diocese of Burgos, and the carpenter Juan de Saucedo Espinosa, originally from the town of Guadalupe, who was bringing his wife and child.

The total number of Carvajal's passengers may have exceeded the authorized limit of a hundred and may even have gone twice as high. Among the passengers were two distinguished gentlemen. One was Dr. Manuel de Morales, who had come over from Málaga with his wife, brother, sister-in-law, and several of his sisters to join Carvajal for the Atlantic crossing. The other, accompanied by two servants, was Diego Enríquez, the son of Martín Enríquez de Almansa.

The name of the governor's wife was conspicuously absent from this roster. Don Luis had been eminently successful with his sister and others, but he could not persuade his wife to join him in New Spain. Though the Spanish authorities regularly placed obstacles in the way of married men, especially of the highest echelons, who wished to emigrate alone to the New World, Carvajal's right to do so was no-where questioned.[55]

If the realization that they might be forever separated brought disappointment to the governor and his wife, it certainly brought no rancor. Doña Guiomar offered her home and hospitality to the departing emigrants, and Don Luis and his kin appear to have continued to keep in touch with Guiomar and her family after their arrival in the New World.[56]

The records reveal that in addition to assembling his passengers, Carvajal was also busy with other matters vitally related to his interests. Some involved the settling of his father-in-law's estate. He had his mother-in-law, Doña Blanca Rodríguez, named executrix to collect debts due the estate. He paid the sum of three hundred ducats to Martín Fernández de Olivos, constable of the Audiencia (the royal court) in Seville, for various items of merchandise, including slaves. He closed an account with Francisco de Nova in Seville, receiving a substantial sum for the sale of cochineal. On January 10, 1580, after a Seville cobbler named Gonzalo de Morales had defaulted on a loan he had guaranteed, Carvajal paid the sum in question to a man named Agustín Rodríguez.

Other matters were more directly allied to Carvajal's projects in New León. He delegated power to a man named Alonso Rodríguez to contract married farmers for the New Kingdom of León. He gave similar authority to a Diego Ruiz de Ribera, possibly a relative of Guiomar's, naming him captain, governor, and loyal executor of the town of Jimena. On March 3, 1580, he gave power of attorney for all his affairs to Cristóbal Ortiz of Seville. Two months earlier, on January 2, he had acquired possession of a ship anchored off Gibraltar and promisingly named *Our Lady of Light* (*Nuestra Señora de la Luz*). He also patently acquired permission from the House of Trade in Seville, the powerful agency regulating all aspects of commerce with the Americas, to join his ship to the fleet scheduled to leave for New Spain late in the spring of that year. On May 21, 1580, a mere two weeks before the departure date of the fleet, he purchased twenty-seven quintals of hardtack for the price of eleven hundred reals, as part of the provisions for his passengers.[57]

In the meantime the emigrants were converging on Seville. After a two-week trip from Medina del Campo and a brief stop at the inn on the highway from the town of Carmona, some twenty-seven miles away, Don Francisco and his family reached the outskirts of the city around the middle of May and proceeded directly to Doña Guiomar's house. There they met the governor's wife for the first time and were introduced to various members of Guiomar's family. These included Guiomar's mother, her brother, Núño Álvarez de Ribera, her sister, Isabel, and her half sister, Francisca Núñez Viciosa.[58] Don Francisco and his wife were also reunited with their daughter Isabel, who had decided to accept her uncle's invitation. Shortly after the governor's visit to Astorga, Gabriel de Herrera had died. Isabel, despondent and groping for security, thought of entering a convent. She had gone so far as to cut her hair preparatory to taking the veil when Don Francisco intervened and persuaded her to join the family in Seville.[59]

Don Francisco and his family remained in Guiomar's house for at least several days prior to their departure for the New World. According to the later recollection of some members of the family, they remained there longer. On one occasion Isabel said they stayed at Guiomar's house a week, while on another she stated that they were there for some two months.[60] However, everyone agreed that during the family's sojourn there the tasks were many and the pace of activity frantic. "There was hardly enough time to sit down and relax," the governor was to recall. The burdens of the family increased when Doña Francisca was felled by a severe attack of kidney stones. Isabel claimed that her father also became ill.[61]

During this period the governor was perhaps busier than anyone else in the family, for he had to cope with the myriad of last-minute details that always preceded a ship's departure for the New World. In addition to all other problems demanding resolution, he had to run his ship through the customary gantlet of three inspections, or *visitas*, by officers of the House of Trade, before it could be cleared for departure. The first, carried out while the vessel was still empty and anchored at Sanlúcar or farther up the Guadalquivir, determined the vessel's seaworthiness and pledged the captain to take aboard only personnel authorized by the House of Trade. The second, occurring after loading, checked the cargo as well as compliance with instructions given in the earlier *visita*. The final inspection, conducted at Sanlúcar by high officers of the House of Trade immediately before departure, focused largely on the search for unauthorized cargo and personnel. If the examiners found everything to be in order, they affixed a certificate of clearance to the ship's register.[62]

His involvement left the governor little time to be with his family. He was practically never at home, and when he was, many matters preoccupied him. Not the least of these was the fact that the voyage would cost him the staggering sum of more than twelve thousand pesos or well over a hundred thousand contemporary American dollars.[63]

Under the circumstances he could hardly have found out that his wife, Guiomar, and her brother, Núño Álvarez de Ribera, had revealed themselves as Jews to Doña Francisca and her husband, and that his sister had confided to Guiomar that Catalina, Mariana, Baltasar, and Luis were also secret Jews. They apparently did not yet know that Isabel had already been indoctrinated into Judaism by her husband. Nor could the governor have learned that Guiomar had extracted from Isabel a promise to do something to unravel all his well-laid plans and precipitate his eventual downfall.

Guiomar found herself attracted to her niece. She doubtless found it difficult to understand why this bright and intelligent young lady had not been taken into the family's confidence. She did observe her niece frequently reciting her Catholic devotions and may have curiously wondered whether their iteration was not a compensatory façade for a hidden faith. She decided to broach the subject to her sister-in-law. She remarked to Doña Francisca that "Isabel prays a great deal" and then proceeded to ask her whether Isabel "knew what was good." Francisca answered no, because she did not dare to bring up the subject of Judaizing in Isabel's presence, apparently because Isabel had been ready to discard her secret Judaism in favor of the veil.[64]

Guiomar did not resign herself to the possibility of Isabel's remaining a Catholic. She was soon able to bring up the subject of Judaism with Isabel and to persuade her to become a secret Jewess. Isabel did not tell Guiomar that she was already indoctrinated. Instead, she gave her aunt the satisfaction of feeling that she was doing the converting.

Her bonds with Isabel thus strengthened, Doña Guiomar felt she could ask her niece for a special favor. Adjuring her to secrecy, she begged Isabel, on reaching the New World, to attempt to convert her governor-uncle to Judaism.[65] Guiomar knew that this would not be easy. In fact, when she asked her sister-in-law whether Don Luis knew that the rest of the family was Judaizing, Doña Francisca answered, with apparent dread, "Please do not let the thought of telling him pass through your mind."[66]

Isabel agreed to do as Guiomar requested. Her aunt told her that she must convince the governor that "if he wanted to succeed in his endeavors, he should cleave to the Law of Moses, for not to do so would lead him to failure." At the same time Doña Guiomar explained that she did not dare to broach the subject to her husband, fearing that Don Luis might fly into a murderous rage if she tried. She asked Isabel to write her informing her of the governor's reaction to her words. If his reaction was favorable, Doña Guiomar promised she would come over to the New World. Guiomar also asked Isabel to try to convert Felipe Núñez.[67]

Like all other merchantmen, *Our Lady of Light* was required to travel in a convoy for protection against the ubiquitous pirates who combed the waters of the Atlantic. Official Spanish regulations, most recently modified in 1564, called for the assemblage of two annual fleets at Sanlúcar, one in the late spring, the other in late summer. The first group of vessels, which came to be known as "the fleet" (*la flota*), had the port of San Juan de Ulúa as its ultimate destination. On the way some ships regularly dropped off at places like the Greater Antilles, Honduras, and Santo Domingo. The destination of the second group, known as "the galleons" (*los galeones*), was the Isthmus of Panama, with some ships withdrawing earlier for various ports on the South American mainland. In King Philip's time the vessels in the fleets were convoyed by a fighting galleon carrying thirty-six guns, and later by two fighting ships, for whose expenses a tax, or *avería,* was assessed on the merchantmen.[68] Pirates, as well as wars with the Netherlands and England, reduced to eleven the number of Spanish fleets arriving at Veracruz in the last twenty years of the sixteenth century. *Our Lady of Light* was in one of the fortunate eleven.[69]

At the beginning of June 1580 the entire family, except for the governor, boarded *Our Lady of Light* at Seville and sailed down the Guadalquivir to the town of Bonanza, two leagues distant from San-lúcar. They remained there for four days as guests of the local vicar, waiting for the governor to finish his business and join them.[70] When the governor arrived, the ship was laden with its human cargo and proceeded to Sanlúcar, where it was certified for departure. It traveled with the other ships to pick up their escort off the city of Cádiz. Al-together there were twenty merchantmen in the convoy, ranging in weight from 150 to 800 tons. Thirteen ships were destined for New Spain, the rest for the islands and the South American mainland. Many of the ships carried a cargo of precious mercury. The convoy was under the direction of Captain General (Admiral) Francisco de Luján.[71]

On June 10, the convoy, with *la capitana*, the ship carrying the royal banner and the insignias of the captain general leading the pro-cession, and *la almiranta* (the so-called vice-admiral's ship) scanning the waters to the rear, sailed from Cádiz harbor and headed out to sea.[72]

4 Conversations

The voyage from Europe to the New World in the closing decades of the sixteenth century could hardly be called a pleasure trip. The wooden ships, though constructed with increasing care and science, were with disheartening frequency still clumsily assembled. Often they "were planned to be small," a contemporary wryly observed, "but turned out large, while others planned large came out small."[1] On the ocean the ships were spiritless slaves to the elements: the calm stranded them; the zephyrs pushed them languidly; the gales tossed them about; and all the while they were roasted mercilessly by the rays of the summer sun. Shipwreck and attack by pirates were constant dangers, but not nearly as certain as the debilitating nausea brought on by the ships' incessant roll and tumble.[2]

The vessels lacked even the most basic comforts. Their quarters, horribly cramped and dirty, were infested with vermin and rodents, and the decks, used for table and bed as well as for promenade, offered no appreciable contrast. Passengers and crew regularly brought along a small number of live sheep, pigs, and fowl to be slaughtered on the voyage, and there was usually olive oil and wine to grace the feast. But such banquets were the exception and not the rule. The usual rations, even if sustaining, were spare and drab. There were staples like hardtack, beans, chick-peas, olives, hazelnuts, and dried dates and figs. To these were added small quantities of moldering cheeses and meats covered with salt to retard spoilage. The salt, combined with the unbearable summer heat, inevitably fired scorching thirsts, and these could not be slaked by the small rations of potable water doled out to each hapless voyager.[3]

Diversions aboard ship were few. There were structured activities such as gatherings for worship and occasional songfests, often to the tune of a guitar. There were games of cards and dice and occasionally cockfights and even simulated bullfights. The less gregarious among the passengers could engage in incidental conversation, watch the sea, or read.

Usually the passengers brought a great variety of reading matter aboard a transatlantic ship, including books of devotion, sacred and profane histories, epic and amorous poetry, and the ever-popular novels of chivalry. All these genres were well represented on the ships sailing with Captain General Luján. Among the books available to the passengers were a life of Charlemagne and a history of the Caesars, various copies of the Italian Lodovico Ariosto's *Orlando Furioso*, apparently in Spanish translation, and a number of copies of the *Amadis of Gaul* and other Spanish novels of chivalry. The books also included parts one and two of Alonso de Ercilla's *La Araucana*, the moving and historically faithful epic about an Indian insurrection in South America. The second part of *La Araucana* had just come out in 1578, nine years after the first, and the concluding section was not to appear until 1590. Yet the work was already a favorite among Spain's Atlantic passengers.

In addition, the fleet carried the *Pontifical and Catholic History*, another perennial delight of voyagers, and various books of devotion in Latin and Spanish. These included the work entitled *Contemptus Mundi* (Contempt of the World), *Flos Sanctorum* (The Saints' Anthology) by Alfonso de Villegas, and a work or two by the sensitive preacher and apologist Fray Luis de Granada. One of Luis de Granada's works, *Introducción al símbolo de la fe* (Introduction to the Symbol of the Faith), a tour de force in Catholic apologetics written for the layman, with ample quotations from the Hebrew Scriptures, was ironically to become, almost from the moment of its publication in 1582, one of the chief sources used by the Judaizers to learn of the Jewish biblical tradition.[4]

But none of these activities could relieve the dull routine or enervating discomforts of the Atlantic passage. And usually the voyage lasted from two and a half to three and a half interminable months.

Admiral Luján's ships followed the usual course taken by the fleet on its westward voyage. Leaving Cádiz, they headed south and west toward the African coast, then veered west toward the Canary Islands, arriving at the island of Gómera on June 19. In the Canary Islands, Spanish ships regularly replenished their stores and made necessary adjustments and repairs. The ships left Gómera on June 23 and headed southwest toward the sixteenth parallel, then due west once more toward the Lesser Antilles. On July 15 they reached the island of Désirade. Then they set sail for Ocoa, another supply depot and the terminal point for the vessels assigned to remain in the Indies. On July 27, after two days at Ocoa, the thirteen ships destined for New Spain left the island. Four weeks and a day later, on August 25, they reached the port of San Juan de Ulúa, off the mainland at Veracruz.[5]

The long voyage certainly gave Governor Carvajal ample time to ponder the extent and prospects of the territory he had been granted.[6]

The charter of May 31, 1569, seemed to be specific enough when it described this land as extending "from the port of Tampico on the Pánuco River and the mines of Mazapil to the borders of New Galicia [Nueva Galicia] and New Biscay [Nueva Vizcaya], and thence northward, whatever can be discovered from sea to sea, provided that the territory does not exceed two hundred leagues in latitude and two hundred in longitude."[7] The territory embraced all of the contemporary Mexican states of Nuevo León and Tamaulipas, almost all of Coahuila, and part of San Luis Potosí. But because the boundaries of New Galicia and New Biscay were not firmly fixed, the deed was to lead to controversies at the northern border of New Biscay around the town of Saltillo. It also created problems in the border areas of New Galicia around the present states of Durango and Chihuahua.

Like all conquistadors given a territory to exploit, Carvajal had to shoulder a considerable number of weighty obligations. His charter was a derivative of the crown's *Ordinances for Founders,* published in Spain in 1563, and various regulations in New Spain dating from 1573. Developed from earlier Spanish experience in the Western Hemisphere, the regulations covered such matters as the colonization of an area, the planning of towns, the appointment of administrative and judicial officers, the utilization of Indian labor, and various other aspects relating to the conquest and settlement of a region.[8]

Carvajal's charter detailed such responsibilities. Within a period of five years he was to make incursions of discovery into his territory for a distance of at least two hundred leagues. He was to pacify the region and insure obedience to crown and church by its Indians. As he pushed forward he was to form a chain of colonies, in strategic locations, all the way to the border of Spain's Florida Territory, his northeastern frontier, "so that the said Territory of Florida might communicate with your territory and with the provinces of New Spain and New Galicia and might bring from them the provisions, cattle, and other items it may need." He was also instructed to establish colonies in the

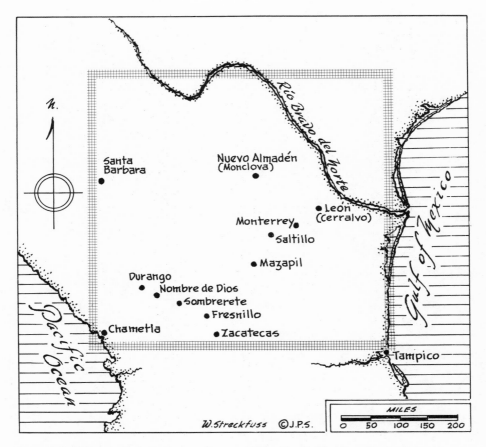

Carvajal's "Tragic Square," according to Vito Alessio Robles, *Coahuila y Texas en la época colonial*

ports that fell under his jurisdiction "from Tampico to the Saint Joseph Bay," at the border of the Florida Territory. Since Carvajal had discovered concentrations of nopal on his earlier travels in the region, he was ordered to establish settlements for the extraction of cochineal. He was also expected to develop agriculture in his territory and to bring in sheep and cattle for the occupation and sustenance of the settlements he would found.

In addition, Carvajal had to assume the obligation of defending his entire territory. The charter required him to build a fort at the mouth of the Pánuco River "for the security of the port of Tampico and the defense of the land, and to prevent the damage that could be wrought by corsairs who might attack it." He also assumed the obligation of pacifying the seething areas around the towns of Tampasquín, Tanmotela, San Miguel, Xalpa, and Xichú within a period of eight years. To protect the embattled town of Tamaulipas, Carvajal was ordered to erect a fort at the nearby nebulous boundary between what the Spaniards called "the lands of war and peace."

Carvajal had to be prepared to bear the full expense of all these activities. In addition, on arriving in New Spain he would have to put up eight thousand ducats as security that he would scrupulously fulfill all the provisions of his charter. The money was to be kept in the capital in the "triple-locked safe."[9]

The records do not indicate to what extent Carvajal was preoccupied with his future responsibilities during the voyage, or how he withstood the rigors of the sea. But they do reveal that violent sickness felled numerous passengers on *Our Lady of Light*, including Dr. Morales's sister, who died at sea, and his wife, Isabel, who was fortunate enough to survive her ordeal. When word of Mrs. Morales's indisposition reached the governor's sister, Doña Francisca de Carvajal, she immediately rushed to offer her help. Later, when illness overcame nearly everyone in Francisca's family, the good doctor reciprocated her kindness by personally taking charge of the entire family's cure.[10] Francisca and her daughter Catalina often spent the entire day from sunrise to sunset fasting and "praying to God that just as He had removed and freed the children of Israel from the Red Sea and set them on their path, so might He now guide and free them from the greater danger through which they were passing."[11]

Dr. Morales's most difficult case appears to have been that of young Luis de Carvajal. The boy remained ill for the balance of the voyage.

Their sickness and mutual help brought the Carvajals and the Moraleses much closer to one another—so much so, in fact, that one day in an intimate conversation the physician's sister-in-law, Doña Blanca de Morales, wife of the doctor's Judaizing brother, summoned enough courage to verbalize the question that every good Judaizer sooner or later felt compelled to pose to his cherished friends. She asked Doña Francisca what her real religion was. If Francisca had ever wondered whether every member of the Morales family was a secret Jew these doubts were dispelled when she observed them dressing in their finery on the Sabbath and abstaining from pork during the journey. To Blanca's great joy Francisca replied that she too was a fervent Judaizer. According to Francisca, she and the Moraleses took solemn oaths in the name of the Lord never to reveal each other's secret. From that time on the Carvajals and the Moraleses, including the doctor and his wife, his sister-in-law, and his four maiden sisters, were knit in indissoluble friendship.

(The bond was to be broken only by the doctor's departure from New Spain. Although he had many friends and followers, Dr. Morales became disillusioned with the New World and tired of having to practice his Judaism clandestinely.[12] He therefore took his family and slipped out of New Spain in May 1584 aboard the huge fleet returning to the mother country. He left with twenty thousand pesos, at least some of them doubtless earned in the New World. Shortly after his arrival on the Iberian Peninsula in August of that year, Morales disappeared. His friends in the New World later heard that he had spirited his family to one of the many cities in Europe where Jews and New Christians who reverted to Judaism were able to practice their faith openly. An Italian sailor named Giovanni di Messina, once cured by Dr. Morales, said that he heard from a sailor friend that the Moraleses were living in Venice.[13])

Their friendship with the Moraleses was one of the factors that eased the discomfort of the Atlantic crossing for the Carvajals. Another was the hope, kindled by the governor's promises, that once they arrived in the New World, their material lot would improve meteorically. But this hope began to dissipate almost the moment the family set foot on American soil.

Our Lady of Light docked at the port of Tampico, at the mouth of the Pánuco River, some six miles inland. Young Luis, still ailing, had to be carried off the ship.[14] Those who debarked under their own power might have felt a recurrence of vertigo on coming to grips with the stark realities of the life that awaited them.

Except for the presence of Indians, the town of Tampico bore little resemblance to the fabled cities described by adventurers returning to the Old World from the New. It was a cluster of wooden and adobe shacks, surrounded by orchards of transplanted European fruit trees and dominated by a fortress and simple thatch-roofed church, all jutting out incongruously from a swampy clearing in a thick and tropical jungle. A hot, damp heat clung to the town. Rains poured torrentially from the skies during the wet season from spring to fall, and the rivers periodically overflowed their banks. Snakes and lizards challenged the human inhabitants' control of the ground, and the ubiquitous mosquitoes, of the air. The Spaniards at Tampico did not exceed two hundred. Together with their Negro slaves the entire community could hardly have amounted to more than five hundred persons. Nor were the Indians as harmless as they might have seemed from the transoceanic perspective of Spain. Seething with violent hatred for the decades of Spanish brutality, they were a constant threat to the hopelessly outnumbered European community. Life in the town of Tampico was thus neither peaceful nor tranquilizing for Spaniard or Creole.

By no stretch of the imagination could the region have been called rich. It did possess mines, but they were mines of salt rather than gold, and salt-mining and fishing were the townspeople's principal occupations. There was room for some crafts and handiwork and a modicum of trading, but all in all the life that faced newcomers like the Carvajals was primitive and difficult, and through it all shone not a single shaft of realistic hope for future amelioration.[15]

Symbolically, the Carvajals' hardships in Tampico began with a hurricane. When they arrived at Tampico, the family lodged in a house belonging to Alonso or Antonio de Torres and stored the wares they had brought from Castile in one of the town's stronger buildings. Luis and Baltasar were spending a night in this building. They had gone to bed and were fast asleep when they were aroused by a thunderous crack the likes of which they had never heard before. In rapid succession the noise recurred again and again, preceded by strident howls. The brothers cowered at the eerie noises and impulsively threw their bedclothes over their heads. Suddenly recovering their composure, they climbed out of bed and trained their ears on the direction of the sound. They soon realized that the noise was coming from gigantic winds that were uprooting trees, leveling flimsy houses, and threatening even the sturdiest structures. The winds were already ripping beams from the roof of the warehouse and battering furiously against the door.

Deciding to abandon the building, Luis and Baltasar skittered toward the door. Normally the door opened outward, but the relentless pressure of the winds prevented them from budging it. Desperate, Luis and Baltasar decided to break the door's hinges and rely on the wind to push it inward. This strategy worked. They succeeded in prying the door loose sufficiently to squeeze through the opening and escape unharmed. When the building collapsed minutes later, the brothers were already on the way to their family's home. Their parents, who had despaired of ever seeing them alive again, regarded their return as a miracle.[16]

The governor, too, faced unexpected difficulties when he disembarked. The lands under his jurisdiction were in even greater turmoil than when he had left New Spain to claim them at King Philip's court. The Chichimecs had been furiously attacking Spanish settlements and were wreaking havoc within the very town of Tampico.

They had already killed fifty people in the city and its environs and appeared to be concentrating their rage upon disembarking immigrants. In two raids they had already massacred over four hundred newcomers. Other towns, like the mining settlement of Mazapil, with a mere hundred Spaniards, found themselves cut off by the warfare. Roads became impassable, especially those beyond Zacatecas leading to the northern frontier. The Spaniards were terrorized and began to talk of abandoning the region.

In consternation the new viceroy erected four presidios in the beleaguered regions: three within the territory assigned to Carvajal and one on a riverbank apparently contiguous to his land. He also dispatched fresh companies of soldiers to put a stop to the Indian assaults, but his efforts met with failure.[17] As had happened so often in the previous decade, the viceroy's office again called on Carvajal to pacify the insurgents. As before, Don Luis was given no funds and few if any troops, though the troubles went beyond the area of Carvajal's jurisdiction and responsibility. The governor was thus again compelled to underwrite the entire expedition with his own money and to equip it with his own men and matériel. With these he went in pursuit of the Indians, intrepidly engaging their superior numbers and inflicting heavy casualties in battle after battle. In an incredibly short time the war was over. The majority of the restive Indians had been killed or captured and their surviving leaders condignly punished. The rest of the Indians, utterly drained by their overwhelming defeat, complaisantly submitted to Carvajal's will. Near the end of the decade, in 1589, Carvajal was able to report proudly: "The land has remained secure and peaceful for nine years now. No man is killed, as used to happen daily before, and the few Indians who have remained say that they do not want to kill anyone, because I have commanded them not to do so. Thus if they capture someone, they release him for ransom and do not kill him."[18]

Carvajal's claims were confirmed by the chronicler Alonso de León, who said that the governor came to be "obeyed in lands so far away by so many people and loved and cherished by so many Spaniards."[19]

One of Carvajal's earliest acts was to try to remove the viceroy's four presidios. He planned instead to maintain surveillance over the region with roving patrols. He appears to have failed, but his efforts may have gone far in establishing an atmosphere of respect and trust among the Indians.[20]

As usual Carvajal's spectacular success made it possible for the royal exchequer to save huge sums of money. Again Carvajal received no tangible rewards.

Carvajal's huge outlays in unexpected services of this nature could not have failed to strike hard at his resources. Another unanticipated blow came when he lost *Our Lady of Light,* anchored in Tampico Bay.[21] These losses, and the heavy expenditures he had to make for the voyage and the posting of his eight-thousand-ducat bond, added up to what was doubtless a staggering sum. In prospect, Carvajal knew that before he could hope to reap substantial material benefit from his territory, he would have to have enough capital on hand to cover all the contingencies related to their pacification and colonization. Judging from the restiveness of the Indians during the early 1580s, these expenses too were almost surely heavier than originally envisioned.

To increase the new governor's vexations, there was soon a dispute or a series of disputes with the viceroy. The difficulties stemmed from judisdictional squabbles over territorial boundaries,[22] though Carvajal's attempt to remove the presidios was doubtless a contributing factor.

The Highways to the North of Mexico City

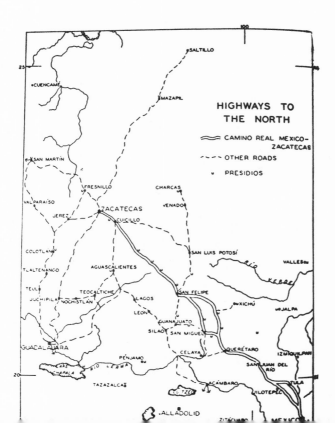

Encumbered by all these difficulties, Carvajal neglected his sister and her family, failing to provide them with the concern and the material advantages he had apparently led them to expect.

Toward the end of 1580 or the beginning of the following year, the governor set out on his first major expedition to the interior of his vast domain. His objective was to explore parts of his territory, establish settlements, and begin the exploitation of the land's resources. Whether because of his tangled problems or his feelings of guilt over his treatment of his family, the governor found it impossible to return to Tampico and extremely difficult to keep in touch by letter.

While Doña Francisca and her husband may have understood the complexity of the governor's dilemmas, they could not forgive him for his neglect. In their first four or five years in New Spain, the family was to receive from the governor only small amounts of money and merchandise amounting to no more than three thousand pesos.[23]

With the meager sums doled out by Don Luis, his brother-in-law, Don Francisco Rodríguez de Matos had to content himself with becoming an itinerant peddler, carrying items like blankets, linen, confections, and sometimes furniture to and from the mining regions and between the capital and the coast.

Presidios and Towns of New Spain

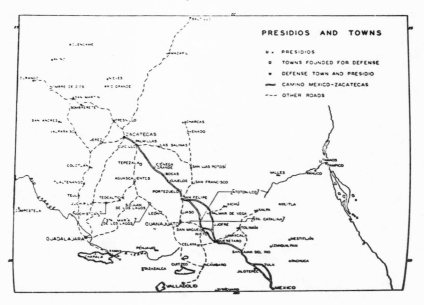

Nor did the governor give money and merchandise outright to the family. He considered the three thousand pesos as a loan to be repaid eventually. In the meantime he cleverly exacted a heavy interest, impressing his brother-in-law and nephews into his service as suppliers for the Spaniards' advance positions. In addition to Baltasar, the comptroller of the New Kingdom of León, and Luis de Carvajal the Younger, the heir presumptive to the territory, Don Francisco often took the priest Gaspar along. Besides handling more routine merchandise, Don Francisco, certainly at the governor's behest, seems to have trafficked in Indian slaves.[24] Apparently the lucrative profits of the slave trade went directly to the governor, for Don Francisco and his sons had little to show for all their enterprise. Despite their diligence they just managed to eke out a paltry existence.

As a result the Carvajals lived at the edge of poverty in Tampico and chafed at what they regarded to be the governor's deceit. Life was particularly hard on the women of the family. Confined to Pánuco's stifling isolation—young Luis was to call it "a disconsoling place of exile filled with many mosquitos and heat"—and burdened with the drudgery of their ceaseless chores, they passed their days in unmitigated boredom.[25]

One ray of sustaining brightness managed to pierce the family's deep gloom. It was the secure conviction that, however difficult their lot, their implicit trust in the Law of Moses would not fail of reward. In the religiously charged atmosphere of the Hispanic world in the sixteenth century, the family firmly believed that a miracle could momentarily occur to vindicate their trust and turn their troubles into joy. But even if a miracle did not come during their lifetime, Don Francisco, his wife, and his Judaizing children were certain that adherence to the Law of Moses would assure them eternal life in the world to come. It alone, they believed, would give them the salvation that they, like their non-Jewish countrymen, regarded as the supreme goal of terrestrial life.

Don Francisco and his wife zealously continued their clandestine practice of Judaism. They were often joined by other Judaizers, such as Francisca's cousin, Catalina de León, wife of Gonzalo Pérez Ferro.[26] As long as Dr. Morales lived in New Spain, they availed themselves of his presence to obtain further instruction in Judaism. Their older children, including Luis and Mariana, appear to have been present at most of these meetings.[27] As a result of Dr. Morales's teaching, the family learned that its previous practice of Judaism was imperfect and assiduously went about correcting its mistakes.

Among the teachings of Licentiate Morales were various liturgical hymns and poems. Some had been composed by other Judaizers. Among these was an unusual piece written by Morales's father-in-law, an eminent Judaizer burned at the stake in Seville at the conclusion of an auto-da-fé. Addressing New Christians favorably disposed toward Judaism but reluctant to begin the secret practice of the faith, he wrote:

Now let others dare exclaim
"This is no time for righteous striving."
Yet if we can no merit claim,
How can we at all proclaim
That such time will be arriving?

I think it a gross heresy
To let one's mind retreat
To such a crass conceit;
For he who trusts such fallacy
Assures his own defeat.

For the wish to gather oil
Not tending the olive shoot
Can yield but evil fruit.
Can milk, without cattle and toil,
Be a hope that has a root?

So he who does no seeding
Yet dares to strip the vine
Can expect no end benign,
For he who lives from thieving
From the gibbet will incline.

And he who will not sow
Or in sweat plant earth he's hurled
Yet demands its gifts unfurled
Will justly be laid low
By the Planter of the world.

How arrant the intention—
A mock of God's omnipotence—
For man to seek admission
Within His holy mansion
Unless he shows obedience.[28]

Other pieces were written by Morales himself. For years the family was to remember one of his longer compositions. It was an eloquent expression of the Judaizers' deep feelings of guilt and their longing for a miraculous redemption. The poem began:

> O Lord, receive my fast as penitence
> For every ill
> I have committed.
>
> Do not withhold your clemency
> For You see the pain
> With which I plead it.
>
> I shall exalt Your grand omnipotence,
> Your name through me
> Will be enhanced.
>
> Give not as I deserve, O Lord,
> For this very thought
> Makes me shiver in a trance.
>
> If I have gravely offended You
> It was because I did not understand.[29]

In addition, Dr. Morales prepared a booklet containing the Ten Commandments and various of the Judaizers' precepts and prayers. The booklet was to circulate in New Spain long after the doctor's departure.[30]

Don Francisco and his wife also continued their private discussion and practice of Judaism with their children, except for the infant Anica, Miguel, and their firstborn son, the priest Gaspar.[31]

In all probability Gaspar had been indoctrinated into Judaism at Benavente before he was permitted to prepare for the priesthood. For the first two years that he and his family were together in the New World he failed to give them any hint that he was a secret Jew. Finally, in 1582, Don Francisco was ready to risk broaching the subject to his son with the secret Judaizers' usual discretion.

One day when they were on the way from the province of Pánuco to see the governor in his quarters at Temapache, Don Francisco and Fray Gaspar found themselves alone in an Indian community. Apparently believing that they were in no danger of being overheard or understood, Don Francisco turned to his son and posed an innocent question. "Why do people observe Sunday as the Sabbath instead of Saturday?" he asked.

The question was innocent enough. Yet it was just this kind of question that New Christians asked in order to give their interlocutors an opportunity to reveal themselves as secret Jews.

Gaspar, seemingly aware of the nature of the question, did not lunge at the bait.

"Because Sunday is the day when our Lord Jesus Christ was resurrected," he answered academically. Then, as if to make his own position clear, he added, "and this resurrection has brought us such great benefit."

This conversation did not suffice to convince Don Francisco that his son was a devout Catholic. The next day he gave Gaspar another opportunity to emerge as a Judaizer by offering to share a confidence with him. He told Gaspar that for some time he had been confused about the significance of some of the figures of speech in the Old Testament, especially since they were so diversely interpreted by different preachers. To illustrate, Don Francisco pointed to a verse in the Book of Psalms which reads: "O Israel, hope in the Lord; . . ./And He will redeem Israel/From all his iniquities."

Don Francisco might have expected to hear his son suggest that the only correct explanation of the verse was a literal one. This would, of course, imply ͡od's continuing relationship with the Jews and the consequent worth and validity of the Jewish faith. But these were not the words that Gaspar uttered. Instead, the priest spoke with unequivocal Catholic orthodoxy, saying that "in accordance with Saint Augustine, any concept could be accepted provided that it did not contradict the Catholic faith."

Don Francisco still refused to accept the obvious conclusion that Gaspar wanted no part of Judaism. On the contrary, he decided to become even bolder in his leading questions. When he had a new opportunity to be alone with his son he asked bluntly why it was that the pope permitted Jewish communities to exist in Rome. Gaspar could hardly have failed to appreciate the thrust of the question, and once more he gave his father no satisfaction. He replied with succinct propriety that the church does not exercise compulsion upon anyone who is unbaptized.

Don Francisco also asked Gaspar "why God abandoned the Jewish people, since they were His favored and chosen people and why He chose the gentiles instead." Gaspar answered "that God had not abandoned it, but rather was punishing it like a wicked miscreant who had placed his hands on His son."

Don Francisco then said, "That's some reason! I have heard a better one, namely, that since God is omnipotent, He could do whatever He wanted." Then he added, "But the Jews say that the Messiah has not come," and he smiled as he said this. Gaspar returned the smile but said nothing further.

Refusing to abandon the hope of bringing Gaspar into the Judaizers' camp, Don Francisco decided to strike at his son's insecurity. Alluding to Gaspar's New Christian origins and the widespread tendency to exclude New Christians from the clergy, he asked him why he had decided to become a priest, "knowing that he could not be." Gaspar caught the none too subtle hint. To his father's chagrin, he proceeded to reply with unequivocal clarity that "the reason such people are not received" into the priesthood, "is because of the fear that they might return to the race and breed from which they are descended." But he, said Gaspar, "would not return." Don Francisco replied, "That's what they all think," and would have said more had not the approach of another man put an abrupt end to their conversation.[32]

Henceforth Don Francisco, apparently convinced of his son's Catholic devotion, never again spoke to Gaspar about matters of faith. For his part, Gaspar, despite the impeccable expression of his faithfulness, now found himself bound to display another sign of devotion. On hearing what amounted to Don Francisco's confession of his Judaizing, Gaspar automatically incurred the obligation of denouncing his father as a suspected heretic before the Inquisition. He now found himself between the hammer and the anvil. If he made the denunciation, he would ruin his father, impoverish his family, and at the same time focus attention on his own New Christian roots. If he chose to do nothing, he might someday be accused of abetting heresy. Under such circumstances he might find refuge in the fact that on the surface his father's statements were innocent and did not explicitly point to belief in or practice of secret Judaism.[33]

Gaspar chose the way of silence. His choice proved to be one of the cardinal factors in his eventual downfall.

If Don Francisco sulked gloomily over the fact that his oldest son appeared lost to the cause of the secret Jews, he received at least some compensatory solace from his oldest daughter, Isabel. Isabel had come a long way since the days of her husband's death, when depression and confusion had led her to dally with the thought of taking the veil. She was now a fervent and even fanatical Judaizer. Aboard ship on her way to the New World she was able to persuade Gonzalo Pérez Ferro, Jr., namesake and natural son of the husband of Doña Francisca's cousin, to become a secret Jew. The boy was singing some verses dealing with the Messiah when Isabel broached the subject. When she had won him over she made him take an oath to preserve the strictest secrecy about their conversations.[34]

Nor did she forget her religious vow to Doña Guiomar. The goal of converting her uncle and Felipe Núñez, far from being overlooked, appears to have become a compelling obsession. Her desire to bring the governor and his adjutant to Judaism was further stoked by the encouragement of her parents, who eagerly shared Doña Guiomar's hopes.

In Tampico, Isabel laid careful plans for the conversion of the two men, but their long absence from the city made it impossible for her to carry them out. The family even found it impossible to contact Don Luis when it received word that Guiomar had died.[35] Almost a year elapsed before the governor learned that he had been widowed. When he returned to the province of Pánuco in mourning, Isabel's first opportunity to work on him was at hand.

One afternoon the governor, attired in mourning, sat absorbed in prayer on a porch in his sister's house. He was in the midst of his vespers, reciting his psalms fervently, and, like a true son of the church, dutifully concluding them with the refrain "In the name of the Father, the Son, and the Holy Ghost, Amen." During his prayers Isabel had unobtrusively slipped into the room and she quietly stood there patiently waiting for Don Luis to bring his devotions to a close.

When the governor arose to put his book away, Isabel called him and asked whether she might speak with him. Acquiescing, he followed Isabel into a nearby room. There she told her uncle that she had a favor to request, and solemnly adjured him to keep everything she was about to say in strictest confidence. The governor agreed.

The conversation that followed lasted only a few electrifying seconds but was to prove to be a cardinal event in the family's history. Speaking in her own name, in accordance with Guiomar's wishes, Isabel began by asking abruptly: "Why don't you look after the health of your soul?"

"But I am," answered the governor, patently taken aback.

"Not really," his niece retorted, adding, "If you are so wise, why are you traveling along the wrong road of the law of Jesus rather than that of the Law of Moses? Because you are not observing the Law of Moses, nothing is going your way. You have no material wealth in this world, and you will have no salvation in the world to come. If you believe your religion and die in it, you will go straight to hell."

The governor, his temper flaring, cried out, "But I want to follow Christ."

"You should believe in the one almighty God," Isabel interrupted. Then she added categorically, "There is no Christ, and there is no Virgin Mary either."

Incandescent with rage at such temerity, the governor struck his niece across the mouth. The force of the blow was so great that Isabel was thrown to the floor. The governor rushed toward her and stood menacingly over her slumped body, ready to strike again, "to kick her or kill her," as he himself later confessed. He pulled angrily at his beard, murmuring the wish that he had never been born or that he had been fated to a life as a collier rather than to have been cursed with such a relative. He called Isabel a traitor and an enemy of God and His saints. "You can say something like this?" he cried out in rhetorical rebuke. He demanded to know who had first introduced her to Judaism, and when she blurted out that it was her late husband, Gabriel de Herrera, he angrily cried out, "Well, he's probably burning in hell right now."

When Isabel began to recover her composure, she wanted to give her uncle a word of explanation, but he would not listen. He covered his ears, declaring that her brazen words were a disgrace to the entire family. He demanded that she return to "God and Our Lady" and take an oath to say nothing further against the Christian faith. He swore that if she did not, he would again hit her in the mouth so hard that she would never recover. With this warning he stormed out of the room.[36]

Unfortunately for the governor, almost everyone in the family was home when this incident occurred. Baltasar and Luis were in a nearby room. Catalina and Mariana were in the kitchen, preparing dinner. All could hear the sounds of the argument, and at least Catalina and Mariana could make out parts of the conversation. Catalina impulsively decided to go into the room with her uncle and Isabel on the pretext of using it as a corridor to a contiguous chamber. When she did, she was furiously ejected by the governor, but not before she heard a few more words of the exchange. Luis too rushed into the room and got a similar reception.[37]

Doña Francisca and Baltasar came on the scene as the governor was rushing out of the chamber "like a lion," according to Francisca's later recollection. Turning angrily to his sister, Don Luis shouted, "You should kill or drown that daughter of yours."

"Why?" asked Francisca.

"Because," said Don Luis, "she said something terrible to me. She told me that I am in error because I am living as a Christian."

Francisca sororally suggested that her brother calm down. Baltasar also tried to placate the governor. Then, referring to Isabel's advice, Francisca explained, "She said it for your own good." On hearing this the governor again pulled his beard and cried out angrily that "no greater ill could have come to him in this world than to have had her say what she just did."[38]

Don Francisco had also come on the scene, but he did not stop to talk with his brother-in-law. He headed straight for the room where Isabel had been left. He emerged, angry, just as the governor was completing a scornful denunciation of Isabel with the words, "She is a Jewess." At this point Don Francisco released a question that he had apparently been saving for such an occasion. Turning to the governor, he asked devastatingly, "And what makes you think that your mother was any different?"

"My mother was a good Christian," snapped the governor, "and whoever said anything different was lying."[39]

Doña Francisca soon left the room, but her husband, undivertible from his desire to turn New Christians into faithful Judaizers, tried to persuade the governor that in speaking to him Isabel had had his best interests at heart. But he "could find no way to make the governor believe," Don Francisco later explained to his wife with more than a touch of understatement. Don Francisco and Doña Francisca then regretted that Isabel had spoken to her uncle. They even reprimanded their daughter, undoubtedly in Don Luis's presence, apparently in an effort to neutralize some of the governor's animosity.

That evening the governor, a little more composed, appeared before his family to continue the dramatic conversations of the afternoon. The younger children were not present. Neither were Isabel or Luis. Mariana, Catalina, and Baltasar were there, as well as the governor's sister and brother-in-law.

Returning to Isabel's words, the governor sternly lectured his family on the significance and truth of the Catholic faith. He began with the articles of faith and the mystery of the Trinity. He went on to say that if he needed proof to believe all this, "the cleanness, sweetness, and goodness of the church" would have dispelled his every doubt. Had this not sufficed to persuade him he would have been convinced by the realization that Christian princes and kings, cardinals and popes, theologians and church councils cherished this faith, certain that it would lead them to salvation. Why, then, he said, should anyone accept the anti-Christian deceits of misguided tailors and shoemakers—by which he meant New Christian Judaizers or Jews. Calling them base and vile, he railed against the "Jews who wished to create stupidities and new laws and make use of them."

Don Francisco, far more circumspect than he had been in the afternoon, tried to placate the governor by calling Isabel mad and irresponsible. It was a futile gesture. If the governor's suspicions that his sister and brother-in-law Judaized had been ebbing, they were fully renewed by the events of that afternoon.[40]

To protect herself, Isabel later decided to tell one of her confessors, Fray Pedro de Luganas, something about the practices of her mother and her late husband. Or so at least, she later claimed. She said that her confessor absolved her from guilt and assigned many penances to her. She admitted that she told him nothing of her own Judaizing.[41]

The governor left his sister's house the next morning, though he was later to state that he stayed on for two or three days after the encounter with Isabel, expounding Catholic doctrine to his family. Assembling the soldiers he had brought with him to Tampico, he left for the town of Temapache, determined never to return to his sister's house.[42]

Don Luis must have traveled wrapped in a cloud of preoccupation, for, like Gaspar, he had now incurred the obligation of making a denunciation before the Inquisition. This might open a Pandora's box of troubles for his own career. If he informed the Inquisition, it almost certainly meant revealing his own background and jeopardizing his position as governor of the New Kingdom of León. On the other hand, if he failed to denounce his niece, he risked arrest by the Inquisition on the charge of abetting heresy by concealment.[43]

The governor finally conceived a stratagem to avoid both horns of his dilemma. If he could get someone in the family to persuade Isabel to return to Christianity, the entire incident—and with it his obligation to report his niece—would be conveniently forgotten. The natural person for the governor to turn to was his nephew Fray Gaspar.

One day, on his long-delayed first visit to his parents in Tampico, Gaspar was seated with his family around the dinner table when a messenger arrived with a confidential letter from the governor. The language of the note was cautious and veiled. It apprised the priest that his sister had committed a serious offense against the faith and that he would do well to reprimand her. The letter did not specify the nature of the offense.

Though puzzled by the slippery wording of the message, Gaspar could not have failed to perceive its underlying cause. He passed the letter around the table in an apparent quest for enlightenment on the nature of Isabel's fault, doubtless hoping that someone would reassure him that nothing serious was involved. Gaspar did not want the responsibility of denouncing Isabel to the Inquisition. At the same time, no one at the table wanted to impose the obligation upon him, for to do so implicitly involved the recognition of a similar obligation upon the other members of the family.

Baltasar read the letter first, then passed it to the women of the household. As if to voice the entire family's opinion, Doña Francisca spoke up and said that she had no idea of what her brother was hinting at. But she did venture an explanation for the cryptic note. The governor and the family had not been getting along too well, she explained somewhat superfluously. The family was angry at the governor because he had brought them to the New World on false pretenses and callously abandoned them to poverty. As Doña Francisca saw it, the governor's letter stemmed from a spiteful desire to sow discord in the family.

This answer seemed to mollify Gaspar, who was doubtless eager to accept any explanation that would relieve him of the responsibility of denouncing his own sister and enmeshing himself in the Inquisition's web. Still, after hearing his mother's explanation, Gasper turned inquiringly to Isabel. Refusing to volunteer any substantive details, Isabel offered her brother a proverb that referred to a frail vessel. Her use of the proverb implied that she was aware of her frailty and was in the process of attending to it.[44]

Nothing further had to be said. Gaspar had fulfilled his duty. Though he had learned nothing specific about Isabel's problem, he could pretend that it was inconsequential. He might have reasoned that it was, after all, his family's obligation to disclose to him any breach of religious practice serious enough to warrant a report to the Inquisition. From the fact that they had not done so, Gaspar could rationalize that he had no need for further concern.

To make sure that he would not involve himself more deeply, Gaspar twice refused to take confession in Tampico from his sister Isabel and his brother Baltasar.[45]

If the conversations with his father had not given the young priest reason to suspect that secret Judaism was rife within his family, his brief stay in the province of Pánuco would have been sufficient.

In addition to the letter from his uncle, Gaspar had another cause to be concerned about Isabel. During his visit he had been surprised to see that Isabel was in possession of an old and worn book, which turned out to be a Bible. "Considering this bad," Gaspar later said (doubtless because the Bible was not supposed to be read by the laity), he "took it along to Mexico City on the pretext of repairing it." He saw nothing else that was strange. Baltasar, Isabel, and Mariana were all versed in Latin and in Scripture. They even knew many psalms and prayers by heart. Since in their recitations they piously concluded the psalms with the approved refrain, "In the name of the Father, the Son, and the Holy Ghost, Amen," Gaspar saw nothing unusual in this.[46]

But then he overheard a strange conversation between his mother and his cousin, Jorge de León de Andrada, in the presence of his sister Mariana. Doña Francisca and Don Jorge were admiring some human figures printed on leather. One of the figures represented a hero of the Hebrew Bible, perhaps King David himself. Pointing to the figure, Francisca said, "Mariana, do you see King David?"

At this juncture Don Jorge interrupted, saying, "Be careful, madam," implying that she should not mention such things at all or that she should not mention them where she might be overheard by unreliable people like Gaspar.

Unaffected, Francisca responded, "What's wrong with it? Let Mariana here be proud to see this figure." And she proceeded to show it to her daughter.

The presence of the Bible and the general atmosphere in his parents' home disturbed Gaspar. Perhaps to ease his conscience, he left a prayer book for Isabel and a book of hours for Mariana on his departure from Tampico.[47]

But the matter of Isabel's wrongdoing soon cropped up to plague the young priest once more. Shortly after leaving his family, Gaspar went to one of the frontier towns, Xilitla, Acatlán, or Cuzcatlán, to see his uncle, possibly on a business trip. There the governor took him aside to the portal of a church and shot an unexpected question at him. "Don't you remember having told me that Gabriel de Herrera, your sister Isabel's husband, was an Old Christian?"

The question appears clearly to have been intended to lead Gaspar into a discussion of Isabel's Judaizing. But once again the governor failed to achieve his objective. Gaspar responded that he acknowledged Gabriel de Herrera to be an Old Christian and always considered him as such.

If the governor had now chosen to express his doubts about Herrera he might have had to bare his misgivings about Isabel, and thereby expose his responsibility for bringing her to the attention of the Inquisition.

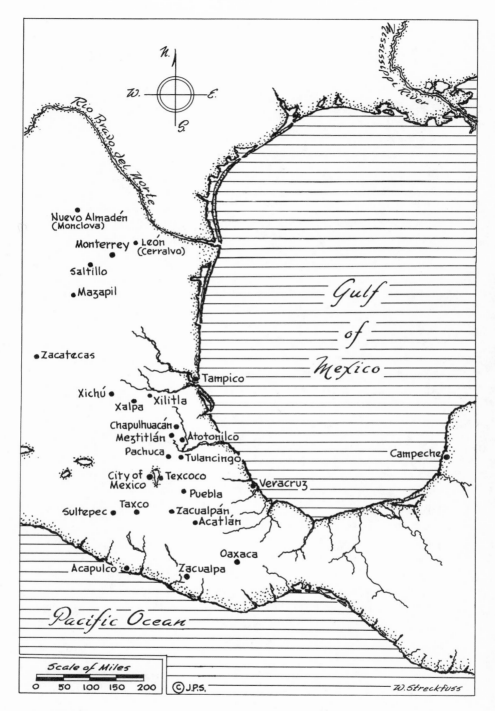

Some Towns of New Spain in the Life of the Carvajals

Don Luis tried another tack instead. He asked his nephew whether he had reprimanded Isabel, as the letter had requested him to do, and whether Isabel had disclosed the reason for her uncle's anger.

Again Gaspar answered discreetly and correctly. Yes, he said, he had reprimanded his sister, but she had not been explicit as to the details of her wrongdoing.

It was most probably at this point that the governor, desperate in his attempt to involve Gaspar in his problem, confessed that his own mother had died in the state of Isabel's current sinfulness. Still refusing to be more explicit he said, "They tell me my mother died in that condition." And he added, "If that is so, she is not my mother and I am not her son."

Gaspar heard the governor, but he apparently avoided any entangling response.

Frustrated again, the governor turned solemnly to his nephew and, after making the sign of the cross, told him that he wished to communicate something to him in the strictest of confidence. He adjured the priest to reveal nothing of their conversation, for "revealing it," the governor explained with pathetic gratuitousness, "would make the secret public." Still refusing to be explicit, he told Gaspar that the problem in his family was a serious one. He said that the entire family was "blind," a word clearly connoting its purblindness in matters of faith. Indeed, said the governor, the problem was so serious that it could be surmounted only by "contending with God through fasts, mortification, and prayers, by which God might be induced to send a remedy." The governor intimated that not only Isabel but her father and mother and even Baltasar might be implicated in the offense, and he therefore asked Gaspar to correct the wrongdoing. The governor could not do so, he said, for since he was a layman, no one would heed him. He would of course keep in touch with Gaspar, writing to him in Mexico City "at the right time and with the proper remedy."[48]

As a priest Gaspar could not very well refuse to accept responsibility for the correction of a religious error. He returned to his monastery, wondering uneasily whether he should inform the Inquisition of his conversation with his uncle, but once more he rationalized that he lacked definite evidence to bring before the Holy Office. He therefore decided, not without benefit to himself, to say nothing about the whole affair.

But the governor found it difficult to lay the matter to rest. He brooded over Isabel's Judaizing to such an extent that he finally decided to reveal the incident with his niece in full detail to Gaspar. When he and Gaspar were together in the province of Pánuco the governor launched into his confession. Since this was one confession that Gaspar was not eager to hear, he avoided it the only way he could: he put his hands to his ears as his uncle was speaking. Ironically, one of the governor's soldiers, a relative of the family's named Luis de Pimentel, happened to pass by as the governor was talking to Gaspar. He took in the scene as well as some of the governor's remarks and later reported it all to Isabel.[49]

Unable to contain his problem, the governor confided it to his cousin, Jorge de León. But, understandably, he still could not bring himself to disclose it to the authorities of the Inquisition.

The incident with Isabel served to sharpen Don Luis's awareness of the widening religious gulf between himself and his sister's family. He realized that there was little he could do to bring Isabel, his sister, or his brother-in-law back to the church, though once, in Cuzcatlán or Temapache, while instructing some apostate Indians in the presence of his brother-in-law, he said some things about the church that he hoped would have a salutary effect on Don Francisco.[50] With Francisco, Francisca, and Isabel already lost, the governor had reason to wonder whether any other nieces or nephews of his had been indoctrinated into Judaism and, if not, how long it would take before they were swept into its vortical current.

For his own sake at least as much as for the sake of the church, the governor set his sights on keeping his nephews within the Christian fold. He did not have to concern himself with the priest or with Miguel, who at nine in all likelihood had not yet been exposed to Judaism. He chose instead to concentrate his energies on Baltasar and Luis, in whose brightness, acumen, and diverse abilities he could not have failed to see an extension of himself. At every opportune moment the governor plied Baltasar and Luis with admonitions to cleave to "the doctrines and teachings of the holy mother church of Rome," and believe "in one true God: Father, Son, and Holy Ghost." The governor's closeness to his nephews, and doubtless his dependence upon them, were such that he could not help but share with them the growing bitterness and animus he felt toward the rest of the family. Once, in a blast of anger against their parents and siblings, he exclaimed that "the others in the family should kiss the ground he trod in gratitude for his having brought them to this land and prevented their father from taking them to France."[51]

It was not long, however, before Baltasar fell into disfavor with the governor. Baltasar had no intention of relinquishing his Judaism. On the contrary, when the governor departed from his parents' home at Pánuco, Baltasar picked up where Isabel left off and determined to convert his uncle. One day when he and the governor were bound for the area of Tamaulipas, Baltasar confided to him that he entertained certain doubts about the correctness of Christian doctrine. He found it difficult to believe, he said, that the body of the Christ actually resided in the host.

As was usual in such conversionist conversations, Baltasar was not seeking explanations. He was attempting to involve his uncle in a discussion of religion in the hope of gradually winning him over to his own beliefs. But Don Luis would have nothing to do with this kind of talk. He apparently gave Baltasar an evasive answer, and when his nephew pressed on and asked with seeming pious concern, "What should I do?" the governor responded that he should turn himself in to the Inquisition.[52]

After this conversation, the relationship between the governor and Baltasar deteriorated rapidly. It appeared to reach its nadir when the governor removed Baltasar from his position as comptroller of his territory of the New Kingdom of León and replaced him with his cousin, Jorge de León.[53]

At the same time, the governor could not help but worry whether the contagion of the family's apostasy had spread as well to his nephew Luis, the cynosure of all his hopes and aspirations for the perpetuation of his name. The older Don Luis determined to find out. One day as he and his nephew were traveling in the province of Pánuco, on the road from Temapache or Cuzcatlán, Governor Carvajal got on the subject of Isabel. In the course of the conversation he asked young Luis cautiously, "Have you ever had any suspicions about your sister?"

Young Luis, understanding perfectly what his uncle meant, began to weep. His only words were a protest that he was living like a good Christian. And these words apparently rang with such sincerity that, as young Luis later recalled, "that was all he had to say."

Luis's reaction reassured his uncle, at least temporarily. But the governor soon felt anxious again and decided to put his nephew to another test. One day when young Luis was accompanying the governor and some of his soldiers from Cuzcatlán to the hacienda of one of the governor's friends, Diego de Torres, the governor sent his troops ahead and then, when he was alone with his nephew, he asked him bluntly, "Do you know that your father has lived as a Jew?"

Young Luis, his eyes filling with tears, responded, "It's awful."

Touched by his nephew's emotion, the governor countered, "That is why I love you more than all your brothers and sisters." Then he said, "Do you know that your father tried to cozen me into converting to the Law of Moses?" And as if to counteract any Judaizing tendencies sown within him by his father, Don Luis went on solicitously to advise his nephew, "Remember that the Christian faith given by Jesus Christ is the correct one. Just look at the popes, kings, and wise men of the world who have clung to it. And everyone else wants to save his soul as much as they did."[54]

With these words they arrived at the Torres estate, the governor joyously confident that his young nephew would remain a Christian and a friend.

5 Commitment

But any such trust on the governor's part was woefully misplaced. Young Luis de Carvajal had not forsworn his Judaism, although he seemed to evince some signs of ambivalence toward it. One such sign was his continuing relationship with his uncle, in whose presence he had to be more circumspect than usual about his secret religious activities. Another was his patently continuing aspirations to succeed the older Carvajal. As long as his uncle was alive, Luis knew that he would tolerate no deviation from Catholic practice and belief in any of his followers, and would become at least as angry as he had with Isabel should he learn of any Judaizing by his namesake and heir apparent. And once the governor was dead, young Luis would be in a position of sufficient public exposure to force him to curtail his Judaizing activities considerably, if not to abandon them altogether. Secret Judaism was simply not compatible with survival in the governorship of the New Kingdom of León.

In selecting young Luis as his heir, Governor Carvajal had demonstrated his conviction that his namesake possessed superior capacity for leadership. The same capacity must have been very much apparent to young Luis's father. Don Francisco Rodríguez de Matos could hardly have been oblivious to his son's manifold talents and the many benefits they might bring to the circles of secret Jews in New Spain. If he demurred from any attempts to prepare his son for a position of leadership among the secret Jews of New Spain, it was undoubtedly because he had reason to wonder whether he could trust the boy's reaction.

But early in 1584, in Mexico City, circumstances appear to have compelled Don Francisco to broach the subject to his son. The two had arrived there from Tampico late in the previous summer to engage in various business enterprises, including the traffic in Indian slaves. For several months they lived at the home of one of Don Francisco's cousins, a man named De Chaves; but around the beginning of 1584 they moved to the house of Gonzalo Pérez Ferro, Sr., and his wife, Catalina de León, the cousin of Luis's mother. It was there that Don Francisco became ill, revealing symptoms of an incurable malignancy of the intestinal tract. Six months after the onset of the illness Don Francisco was dead.[1]

As his condition deteriorated, Don Francisco realized that he could no longer postpone a decision on whether to hold a serious discussion with his son. He apparently soon decided that he would, obviously in the hope that Luis would spend his life as a leader among the secret Jews. Late in June or early in July 1584 Don Francisco began to review with Luis all that he knew about his cherished faith.

Like other New Christians on the Iberian Peninsula and in the Americas, Francisco Rodríguez de Matos was convinced that the religion he was now systematically teaching his son was the authentic Judaism practiced throughout the ages. But he and all others like him were utterly mistaken. Don Francisco's spiritual legacy, though transmitted with unexceptionable devotion, was a pathetically atrophied form of Judaism. It was a shadowy caricature of the tradition of Judaism as it was being practiced in Constantinople, Salonika, Safed, Ferrara, and the great centers of Jewish life in Ashkenazic Europe in the sixteenth century.

The Judaism of the late sixteenth-century New Christians was a precipitate created by isolation and persecution. The massive expulsion of the Spanish Jews in 1492 and the forced conversion of the Jews in Portugal half a decade later had ended the official toleration of Judaism on the Iberian Peninsula. With these events both rabbinic texts and houses of Jewish learning became superfluous on the Iberian Peninsula, and the use of either was peremptorily forbidden.

To be sure, many New Christians in Spain and Portugal continued to cherish Judaism, and throughout the peninsula it survived as an underground religion. The forced converts to Catholicism who categorically rejected their new faith from the moment of their baptism and the many willing ones who experienced a change of heart spared neither effort nor imagination to keep the customs and learning of their ancestral faith unattenuatedly alive. They performed every possible Jewish ritual. They zealously preserved every possible rabbinic book. They met clandestinely in secret conventicles for prayer and study and assiduously indoctrinated their children into the traditions of the past. As long as these clandestine Jews had books and teachers who had studied Judaism before the catastrophes in Spain and Portugal, they could preserve an authentic form of their faith. But books and teachers dwindled with the passing decades, and Iberian Judaism began to change. There are stories of young men escaping from Spain and Portugal to study in academies of Jewish learning elsewhere in Europe and the Near East. But such men did not as a rule return to the danger of an arrest by the Inquisition. The New Christian Judaizers on the Iberian Peninsula were thus abandoned to their own memories of Jewish knowledge and practice, and with time their memories blurred.

Increasingly deprived of rabbinical texts, they found their only continuing literary contact with Judaism to be the Bible. This contact was possible because the Bible in its Latin version, which also included the New Testament and the Apocrypha, was venerated and studied as the source of the faith of the surrounding Catholic society. Unfortunately for the New Christians, the Bible was generally restricted to the clergy. Laymen, especially those already suspect and those with considerable knowledge of the Old Testament, courted trouble by owning or reading a Bible. The knowledge of Judaism among the New Christians shrank to such an extent that men like Dr. Morales, who had merely a superficial acquaintance with some Jewish practices and beliefs and a familiarity with some of the details and traditions of the Bible, could be regarded as one of the most learned teachers of Judaism on the Iberian Peninsula. By the same token, Francisco Rodríguez de Matos, possessing only a fraction of Dr. Morales's knowledge, was also regarded as a learned Judaizer. In its eagerness to condemn them, the Inquisition described such men as "rabbis and dogmatizers." The Inquisition's ordination, however, certifies their zeal rather than their knowledge.

The best way for a Judaizing family to retain a knowledge of the Bible often proved to be to enroll one of its sons in a course of study leading to the priesthood. Such families hoped that even if the boy became a priest, he might also be a secret Jew and serve as a clandestine teacher of the Judaizers. Francisco Rodríguez de Matos almost certainly had such a goal in mind for Gaspar when he permitted him to begin the studies leading to ordination as a priest. Gaspar's invincible loyalty to Catholicism could not have failed to hurt his father deeply. It was only after the disappointment resulting from his conversations with Gaspar that Francisco appears to have decided to complete Luis's indoctrination and doubtless to invest him as a leader of the Judaizers.

Though Don Francisco had been schooled in Latin, he had no

knowledge of Hebrew. From Dr. Morales he had apparently learned to recite in Hebrew the profession of faith, the *Shema' Yisrael Adonay Elohenu Adonay Ehad* ("Hear, O Israel, the Lord, our God, the Lord is One"), and its liturgical response, *Barukh Shem Kevod Malkhuto leOlam Vaed* ("Praised be His Name whose glorious kingdom is forever and ever"). Yet there is some question as to whether he understood the meaning of the individual words in these affirmations. Even if he did, it is reasonably certain that his comprehension of Hebrew went no further. For that matter, there is no evidence that any of his precursors or contemporaries in New Spain, including Dr. Morales, knew another word of Hebrew.

Don Francisco gives no evidence of acquaintance with the traditional prayer book. His entire liturgy appears to have been confined to two sources. One was the Bible, especially the Psalter, and within it the psalms used frequently in Catholic services. The other was the repertoire of original compositions collected by the Judaizers, many of them enshrining the sentiments and echoing the practices of traditional Judaism.

Nor did Don Francisco reveal any direct contact with the extensive heritage of rabbinic Jewish writings. The Talmud was unknown to him. So were the collections of midrash, commentaries, responsa, codes, and mystical writings. Outside of what was recorded in the Vulgate, he was totally innocent of the history of the Jews.

The Judaizers observed four sacred occasions. According to Luis, his father taught him only three. One was the weekly Sabbath, which Don Francisco instructed him to observe "neither more nor less than the Christians observe Sunday." The Sabbath, Don Francisco explained, was a memorial to God's creative work and His rest on the seventh day. It was to be observed from sundown Friday to sunset Saturday by donning clean clothing, abstaining from work, and lauding God with psalms of praise. Since the kindling of fire was prohibited, on the Sabbath Judaizers could only eat food prepared the preceding day, although it might be kept warm in an oven lit before the Sabbath began.

The second occasion was the fast of the Great Day, also called the *Quipur* (*Kippur*) and Day of Pardon, "the day when God especially judges souls."

The third was the Passover. It was to be observed, said Don Francisco, echoing the Bible, "in memory of the time when God took the children of Israel out of Egypt and brought them across the desert to the promised land." It was to be kept for seven days, Don Francisco reminded Luis, with the first and the last days to be regarded as major occasions. Its main observances included the eating of unleavened bread and bitter herbs and the reenactment of the Exodus meal. Unaware of the haggadah service, Don Francisco, following the custom of the other Judaizers, instructed his son that on Passover he was "to take a small white lamb and slaughter it, and smear the thresholds of the doors with its blood, for so had God commanded the children of Israel when He brought them out of Egypt." Then, meticulously following the biblical example, the Judaizers "were to roast it [the lamb] whole, without breaking a single bone and eat it, while on foot, like someone about to embark on a journey, with their loins girded and staves in their hands." They were to eat the entire lamb. Nothing was to remain. The Bible said that if anything did remain beyond midnight, it was to be burned. Curiously, the impoverished Francisco, possibly following the practice of other Judaizers, told his son to give any leftovers to a neighbor.

In addition to these holy days, Don Francisco and the other Judaizers knew and observed the sacred Fast of Esther "in memory of the kindness which God showed to Esther and Mordecai in freeing their people from the hands of Haman." They kept this fast not for one day, the day before Purim, or the fourteenth day of the month of Adar, as it is observed in the world of normative Judaism. They inflated the Fast of Esther to three days around the middle of the month of March. Purim as such was no longer celebrated.

Each one of these sacred occasions held a special significance for the New Christian Judaizers. Each was intimately connected with one or another of their overriding concerns. Observance of the Sabbath quickly became one of the major symbols of the Judaizers' identity, serving as a kind of weekly demonstration of allegiance to their ancestral faith. The Day of Pardon gave them an opportunity to cleanse themselves of the sense of guilt they felt for their own apostasy or their forebears' and to pray for deliverance from a God who, according to the Ten Commandments, punished the descendants of even the third and fourth generation of those that hated Him. The extended Fast of Esther reinforced this theme. The Judaizers identified with the Jews in the story of Esther as told in the Bible and the Apocrypha. They saw the Jews of ancient Persia, who lived in a foreign environment under constant threat of arrest and death, as a reflection of themselves. They adored Queen Esther and saw in her story an example of how God miraculously intervened to turn a people's seemingly irremediable sorrow into sudden unbounded joy. The honor bestowed upon Queen Esther may have been at least in part a reaction by the Judaizers to their Catholic environment, with its exaltation of the Virgin Mary.

The Passover was the grand holiday testifying to the possibility of

God's miraculous redemption. The Judaizers prayed fervently for this redemption, hoping that God would redeem them not merely by bringing them out of their present Egypt but leading them back to the Holy Land. They saw all this tied to the coming of the Messiah, and they fervently believed that God would send the Messiah soon.

The Judaizers did not celebrate their sacred occasions according to the traditional Jewish calendar. The details of this calendar had slipped from their recollection in direct proportion to the rest of their knowledge of Judaism. Recalling that the first month of the Jewish calendar began approximately at the time of the first new moon of spring, the new communities of Judaizers developed a calendar that commenced with the new moon occurring during the month of March. Because they lacked the traditional Jewish calendar, they had no way of knowing that the first month often began with a new moon in April, and even in March the month might begin a day or two away from the day the Judaizers chose to accept as the New Moon. Nor did the Judaizers know that the traditional Jewish calendar was so adjusted as to make it impossible for such holidays as the New Year (Rosh Hashanah), the Passover, and consequently others as well to fall on certain days of the week. As a result, the holidays of the Judaizers were often, if not always, celebrated on different days from those in the normative Jewish world.

The calendar of the Judaizers in New Spain at the time of Francisco Rodríguez de Matos appears to have diverged even more sharply from that of traditional Judaism. These Judaizers appear to have begun the first month of their religious calendar, not with the March new moon, but with the first day of March in the general calendar. Thus Passover, which falls on the fifteenth day of the first month of the religious year, was celebrated on March 15, the Great Day of Pardon on September 10, and the Fast of Esther in the middle of February.

Like most of the Judaizers, Don Francisco did not observe Rosh Hashanah, and his family apparently did not celebrate Hanukkah until long after his death. Nor did he observe the New Moon or any of the commemorative fasts. The family did engage in weekly fasts, sometimes on the traditional Jewish fast days of Monday and Thursday, but just as often on other weekdays.

In addition to the observance of the holidays, Francisco Rodríguez de Matos impressed his son with the need for the meticulous fulfillment of the dietary laws. The dietary laws were limited to those found in the Bible. Don Francisco told his son to shun bacon and other food derived from the pig and to eat only animals that chewed their cud and fishes with scales. He seems to have forgotten that the dietary laws of the Bible declared as permissible only cud-chewing animals that had cloven hoofs and scaled fish that had fins.

To these laws Don Francisco added regulations covering the preparation of meat. They were reminiscent of the laws of normative rabbinic Judaism but were hardly identical with them. Among other things, Don Francisco told his son that birds and land animals could be eaten only after they had been decapitated, completely bled, and stripped of all suet and fat, "for thus it was ordered in the Law of Moses."

Don Francisco may also have reviewed the well-known mortuary rituals of the Judaizers. These included washing the corpse, cutting its nails and hair, wrapping it with a shroud, and placing a gold piece upon it, doubtless as a viaticum for its lengthy journey.[2]

Don Francisco also reviewed with his son four of the basic beliefs of the Judaizers. The first was a literal interpretation of the unity of God. The second was that observers of the Law of Moses "were God's chosen people and descendants of the Israelites and that all . . . descended from Abraham, Isaac, and Jacob." The third was the conviction that the Messiah had not yet come, that when he did come he would be heralded by the "prophets Elijah and Enoch" and would bring vindication to all Jews. The fourth was that salvation could be obtained only through the Law of Moses, "which must be believed because it was given by God Himself and written with His finger on the tablets He gave Moses when He descended from heaven."

These principles were in large measure formulated in response to the beliefs prevalent in the Judaizers' Catholic environment. The belief in God's unity was often expressed in the context of the rejection of the Trinity. The affirmation that the Jews were the chosen people challenged the Christians' belief that they constituted the true Israel. The expectation of a Messiah in the future—and many Judaizers of the sixteenth century, including Francisco Rodríguez de Matos and his family, believed it would be the near future—rejected the Christians' belief in the messiahship of Jesus. And the stress on the divinity of the Law of Moses and its efficacy for salvation, a term the Judaizers understood in its Catholic connotation, disavowed the Christians' belief of the suspension and supersedure of the Hebrew Law by the New Testament.

Like other Judaizers, Francisco Rodríguez de Matos and his son repudiated the adoration of images, and thereby provided the rationale for the rejection of the icons of Jesus, the Virgin Mary, and the saints that confronted them at every turn. At the same time, under the influence of their environment, they did not hesitate to confer the title saint upon Hebrew worthies. The records show that young Luis spoke of Saint Moses and Saint Susanna and possibly also of Saint Abraham, Saint Job, and Saint Jeremiah.

Like their Catholic neighbors, the New Christian Judaizers trusted in resurrection, retribution, and revelation; unlike their Jewish coreligionists, they had no idea of Oral Law, mitzvah, halakhah, chain of tradition, or other concepts integral to rabbinic Judaism.[3]

Meager though it was, such was the content of Rodríguez de Matos's Judaism. But so diminished had the knowledge of Judaism become among the New Christian Judaizers that by the time his father had finished with him, young Luis was unquestionably one of the most learned among them.

On a Saturday shortly before his death, Don Francisco was visited by a Portuguese New Christian named Pelayo Álvarez, a native of Governor Carvajal's hometown of Mogadouro. Pelayo Álvarez was a Judaizer and so declared himself to Don Francisco. Don Francisco entered into a conversation with Pelayo Álvarez on the meaning of the Sabbath. He told his guest that whereas God had created an abundance of food for the body, there was only one nutriment for the soul. This consisted in offering blessings and praises to God. And, concluded Don Francisco, in order to enable man to do this, God had created the Sabbath.

Another Sabbath visitor to his father's bedside was the Mexico City merchant Cristóbal Gómez, who was to remain a dear friend of the entire family's. Cristóbal Gómez came "as a Jew who kept the Law of Moses," said Luis, and he regularly brought presents to Don Francisco.[4]

One of the first religious acts Luis was to perform after the completion of his indoctrination was the ritual cleansing of his father's corpse. Don Francisco died a horrid death. During his last agonizing days fetid discharges oozed from his body. As death approached Don Francisco requested and received the last rites of the church. He did so to avert all possible suspicion that he was a secret Jew. For the same reason he told his son to go to confession and take communion.[5] But since Don Francisco was desirous of being buried in accordance with the Judaizers' rites and customs, he turned to Luis and said, "My son, when I die, wash my body, that it might not be lowered to the grave in its present dirty condition."[6]

Like many other statements of the Judaizers, Don Francisco's request seemed innocent enough. It seemed that all he wanted was to have his body washed to preserve its dignity and to give no offense to those participating in the funerary rites. But Luis understood what his father meant. He knew that Don Francisco was using his noisome malady to screen his request for a ritual cleansing.

Luis was at his father's side when he died. Among those present, Luis later recalled, were a number of other Judaizers: Gonzalo Pérez Ferro's wife, Catalina de León, Doña Guiomar's half sister, Francisca Núñez Viciosa, widow of Alonso del Aguila, and Ana Muñoz, wife of Juan de Nava, a tailor who had also come over to the New World in *Our Lady of Light*. Present as well was Don Antonio Díaz de Cáceres, a wealthy merchant and a friend of the entire Carvajal family's. The only non-Judaizer present was a Negro servant.[7]

When Don Francisco breathed his last, Luis told the servant to wash his father's body with cold water. He cut his father's nails and hair and then wrapped the body in a shroud sewn by Francisca Núñez Viciosa. He did not place a gold coin on his father's corpse because none was available. Don Francisco's friends, among them Antonio Díaz de Cáceres, served as pallbearers at his funeral.[8]

After the burial young Luis returned to Tampico. He revealed his conversations with his father to Doña Francisca and assured her that he had been buried in accordance with the usual practice of the Judaizers.[9]

At one of the discussions about his father's death, Gaspar was present, along with Doña Francisca, Isabel, and Baltasar. The priest was interested to know whether his father had asked to be given last rites before he died and whether he had received them and even whether he had a cross at the headboard of his bed. The questions were asked with such curious interest that Luis could not help but feel that his brother suspected their father of being a secret Jew.[10]

When Gaspar was not around, Luis also reaffirmed his devotion to Judaism in the presence of the rest of his family and reiterated his determination to dedicate himself unreservedly to the Judaizers faith.[11]

He realized that he would be a better Judaizer if he had a Bible at his disposal. Since he was a layman, his desire seemed impossible of fulfillment. Yet shortly after arriving at Tampico, Luis succeeded in persuading the local vicar, Juan Rodríguez Moreno, to sell him his copy of the Vulgate for six pesos.[12]

No sooner did Luis have the Bible in his hands than he began to read it with insatiable voracity. Luis's curriculum at the Jesuit school in Medina del Campo had evidently paid little attention to biblical passages dealing with the Jews, for what he read in the vicar's Bible was new to him.

It was in this Bible, for example, that he learned for the first time of the existence of the holiday of Succoth. In his reading, he recalled, he came across "another festival, called the Feast of Tabernacles, which falls in the month of September and is to be celebrated by having all participants leave their houses and dwell for the entire week in the fields, solely in the recollection and praise of God for having given the promised land to the children of Israel."[13]

Luis also turned avidly to the books of the prophets, particularly Isaiah and Ezekiel, and eagerly searched in them for passages to determine whether the Messiah had really arrived, as the Christians claimed. To his satisfaction he found ample evidence to sustain his conviction that the Messiah had not yet arrived and that God's covenant with the Jews had never been broken or altered. He regarded the Book of Ezekiel as his most cogent proof. Ezekiel had prophesied that the Temple would be rebuilt with the messianic coming. Since the Temple had not been rebuilt, it was evident, thought Luis, that the Messiah could not yet have arrived.[14]

One day when Luis was sitting in a hallway of his house perusing the Book of Genesis, his eyes happened to alight on the seventeenth chapter and its account of Abraham's circumcision at the age of ninety-nine. Luis began to read the account with his usual absorption, but when he reached the verse that warns against the neglect of the commandment of circumcision and in God's name threatens that "the uncircumcised person shall be cut off from his people because he has broken My covenant," he was thunderstruck. For although some secret Judaizers circumcised their sons, Don Francisco had not circumcised Luis.

Impetuously Luis set out to remedy his flaw. Without even taking the time to close the Bible, he jumped up from his seat, found a pair of shears, and as quickly as his legs could carry him, ran down to a tree by the bank of the Pánuco River to perform the sacred rite upon himself. Though the operation was painful and clumsily executed, Luis's anxieties turned to felicity once he had fulfilled the divine precept. Thereafter he always believed that the circumcision provided a powerful restraint to his lust.[15]

With his increasing devotion to the Bible and the practices of the Judaizers reviewed by his father, it seemed that Luis was on the verge of abandoning the brilliant political and military career that his uncle was preparing for him. Yet a short two weeks after arriving at Tampico, Luis left his family and the relatively safe opportunities for Judaizing provided by his home and returned to his uncle's side in the wilds of the New Kingdom of León.[16]

By this time the governor had already explored and pacified much of the territory under his jurisdiction. After gathering many of the people he had brought with him from Spain and Portugal and recruiting a number of adventurers from Mexico City, he had pushed northward late in 1581, into the territory now belonging to the Mexican states of Tamaulipas and Nuevo León.[17] When he reached the region known as La Ciénega (The Marsh), he turned to the nearby San Gregorio Mountains, where lodes of silver had recently been discovered. There Carvajal founded the town of León, called Cerralvo today.[18] He next moved southwest to the town of Saltillo, one of the Spaniards' advance outposts at the border of the *tierra de guerra,* the zone of warfare with the Indians. Saltillo had been founded around 1575 by a handful of soldier-settlers from the province of New Biscay (Nueva Vizcaya) under the captaincy of the adventurous twenty-eight-year-old Alberto del Canto. In 1582 a group of Franciscan friars, led by Lorenzo de Gavira, established the Monastery of Saint Stephen there after preaching the gospel in various parts of the province of New León.[19]

Although Saltillo was under the authority of New Biscay, Carvajal claimed that according to his grant it fell under his jurisdiction. He proceeded to exert his authority by replacing the officers of the town with his own appointees. He also founded some small settlements north and northeast of the town to serve as a buffer against Indian attacks.[20] Then, calling upon "his diplomacy and finesse," as the chronicler delicately put it, he induced some of the leading citizens of Saltillo, among them Diego de Montemayor, Diego Rodríguez, Alonso González, Juan Pérez, Francisco Martínez, and a Rodrigo Pérez or Flores, to join him on a pioneering expedition. The group traveled northeast across the mountain barrier toward the springs of Monterrey, or Santa Lucía, as they were then called. On the northern side of the springs, in the shadow of El Cierro de la Silla (Saddle Hill), the governor founded the town of San Luis, or La Cueva, the precursor of the present city of Monterrey, established in 1596.[21] He named as its mayor one of his captains, Gaspar Castaño de Sosa, owner of the farm called La Encantada (The Enchanted Lady). Castaño de Sosa was of Portuguese descent and may have been a New Christian. At least he had a relative named Manuel de Herrera who was of Portuguese descent and a Judaizer. Young Luis de Carvajal once came upon

Manuel de Herrera in his uncle's territory and learned that he had relatives in Saltillo. When he saw Herrera slaughtering a rooster in accordance with the ritual of the Judaizers, he engaged him in conversation and soon learned that he was a secret Jew.

At his own expense Governor Carvajal built a church in the town of La Cueva and paid the vicar's salary of two thousand pesos. In the area between Léon and La Cueva he claimed to have pacified more than four thousand Indians.[22]

The founding of San Luis took place sometime in 1582 or early in 1583. The oldest extant document signed by Carvajal as governor of the New Kingdom of León is connected with the region around San Luis. Dated March 1, 1583, the document reveals that Governor Carvajal made a grant of land in the area southeast of the town to a man named Manuel de Mederos, who had earlier been one of the founders of Saltillo. A property bearing the name Mederos is still known in the region.[23]

Castaño de Sosa remained in the area to found and populate the mining colony of San Francisco. At the same time the governor returned to the town of León to organize slaving raids on the Indians. The aim of the raids was to capture "people who sold well," at a time when a healthy Chichimec male could bring at least eight gold pesos in the markets around Mexico City and a young female up to a hundred.[24] The desire to share in the profits inherent in this enterprise attracted many a volunteer to Carvajal's forces.

Around 1583 Governor Carvajal decided to undertake the formidable task of conquering the province of Coahuila. He named Captain Castaño de Sosa, "a person of importance," as his lieutenant governor and as captain general over the lands he would be exploring. Using Saltillo as his base, he gathered a sizable group of prospective settlers who took their families, livestock, and other belongings with them on the northward trek.

Yet despite the efforts of these hardy settlers and help from able officers like Captains Palomo and Agustín de la Zarza, and despite Carvajal's uncanny knack to cozen Indians into peaceability, the effort to conquer Coahuila was to end in failure.[25]

Also under Carvajal's authority, an expedition under Antonio de Espejo left the San Gregorio Mountains and headed northward to the discovery of "the provinces called New Mexico."[26]

Carvajal then turned his attention to the difficult task of pacifying the Indians of "Temapache, Tampasquín, Tanmotela, San Miguel, and the other settlements of that mountain region."

Sometime between 1583 and 1585 Carvajal founded the city of New Almadén, later called Monclova. Situated in a dry, nitrous region, poorly wooded, and near a stream "of inferior water . . . there being no other,"[27] the area's great attraction was its rich mineral deposits. The name Almadén itself derived from an Arabic word meaning mine.[28] By the end of the decade, when the mines were still in their early yields, Carvajal could boast that the king's fifth of the silver, the portion that went to the crown, already exceeded two thousand pesos per year. The governor confidently predicted that under his continued administration of the mines the king's annual share could soar to over fifty thousand pesos.[29]

Carvajal appointed Diego de Montemayor the Younger as his comptroller in New Almadén and gave the post of factor to Diego Ramírez from the town of Barrio Nuevo.[30]

By the time his nephew joined him the governor was busily engaged in reaping some of the benefits of his conquest. From 1584 on he appears to have devoted less attention to the discovery of new lands and more and more time to the development of his mining operations.

It was at the mines of San Gregorio that young Luis was reunited with his uncle. There the older Don Luis began an association with his nephew that seems clearly to have been devoted to preparing the younger man for eventual assumption of the governorship of the New Kingdom of León.[31]

Working in the frontier areas required both ability and courage, and Luis de Carvajal the Younger soon revealed an ample endowment of both. He later recalled that "he was in constant danger because the savage Chichimec enemies surrounding him . . . were many and the soldiers he had with him were few."[32] With his military and administrative skill young Luis de Carvajal quickly made a name for himself among both the Spaniards and the Indians. The Spaniards regarded him as indispensable for the maintenance and development of Spanish life in the region, while the Indians doubtless viewed him with an uneasy admixture of dread and contempt. Luis made his share of mistakes. Once, angered at the disobedience of the Indians of Santa Lucía, young Luis ordered their entire town destroyed, to the consternation of his uncle, who believed that understanding rather than force was the way to bend subdued Indians to the Spaniards' will. It was the effectiveness of this policy of the governor's that prompted the chronicler of New León to say that the "barbarous people . . . loved and obeyed him, with great respect."[33] Luis had apparently failed to grasp this lesson; yet he was learning fast and well enough to be able to continue as his uncle's chief lieutenant.

Luis's courage and coolness in the face of danger were exemplified by an incident that occurred a year after he had rejoined his uncle.

One September day Luis's packhorse broke away from him while he was inside or near one of the Spaniards' mining towns. Mounting a brawny horse, he began to pursue it into a hilly and pathless terrain. Several miles outside of town, his horse tired, stopped, and refused to budge. Luis realized that he was in the midst of a danger area, for the savage Indian groups known as the Guachachiles roamed in that region. They were known to have killed Spanish soldiers even within sight of the Spaniards' homes.

When he was unable to get his horse to move, Luis had no alternative but to dismount and return to town on foot. His only defenses were a sword, a lance, and a harquebus, the usual arms of the frontiersmen of the day, and perhaps a buckskin armor.[34]

To Luis's misfortune, night fell before he could orient himself. He realized that he had to remain where he was and pray that no Indian would discover him. Hunger and thirst added to his discomfort, for he had had nothing to eat or drink all day. Frenzied with thirst, he took his dagger, cut some of the sharp, moist leaves of the nopal, and drank their refreshing liquid. He took too many of the leaves, and as a result his mouth was sore for a week.

Luis's failure to return caused grave concern in the town. His uncle, thinking that he might have decided to stay in a nearby settlement, sent a soldier there. When the soldier returned with the information that Luis had not gone there, Governor Carvajal and the entire town began to fear that Luis had been killed by the Indians. The governor immediately organized a search party of ten men and a captain. The men were divided into two groups, each provided with a trumpet and each instructed to move in a different direction. In the meantime the townspeople, eager to help in every possible way, even tried stringing a lantern on a tall tree. It was a gratuitous gesture, for the terrain was mountainous and blocked the light of the lantern. The

A Harquebus such as Those Used in Sixteenth-Century New Spain

only result of the lantern-stringing incident was an added misfortune. The man who had climbed up to hang the lantern fell and broke his legs.

In the meantime, Luis, shivering and praying in the pitch darkness, heard the blasts of a trumpet echoing through the valley and realized that a search party was looking for him. He prostrated himself in thanksgiving to God for his unexpected good fortune. Then, arising buoyantly, he listened for the sounds and began to move toward them. In a little while he heard the trumpet of the second group, but he continued walking toward the source of the original sounds, and soon could discern the voices of his friends. He called to them joyously. They stopped their horses, dismounted, and repeatedly embraced him. They put him on a horse and fired their guns triumphantly to signal the accomplishment of their mission. They then brought Luis back to their settlement for a happy reunion with his uncle and the rest of the townspeople.[35]

Luis remained with his uncle for a year and a half of uninterrupted service. When he left, it was entirely his own decision, one that was not easy for him to reach.

The time Luis spent with Governor Carvajal was certainly one of great personal growth, to say nothing of military and administrative achievements. At least part of the growth resulted from an intense soul-searching and a trenchant reappraisal of his life.

Though he had voluntarily removed himself from his family and the other Judaizers living in the more settled regions of New Spain, and had placed himself in an environment where he had no alternative but to suppress the secret faith Baltasar and his father had taught him, Luis was still drawn to Judaism.

When he had left Tampico to accompany his uncle, Luis did not bring along the Bible he had purchased from Vicar Rodríguez, perhaps because it was too large to be kept constantly hidden or perhaps because he wanted to leave it for Baltasar and Isabel. But he did take along a transcription of the pseudepigraphical apocalypse known as the Fourth Book of Ezra, and he devoted much of his leisure time in the wilds of his uncle's territory to pondering the book's answers to the basic questions that the Judaizers were raising: Why had Israel been delivered into the hands of the heathen? When would its suffering end? When would the Messiah come?

His readings of Fourth Ezra shaped several ideas in Luis's mind. He concluded that God's ways are in their totality inscrutable and that they would be fully known only with the coming of the end of history. He could not therefore explain why Israel suffered. Of one thing he was certain, however—that Israel remained God's chosen people and that its suffering, though enduring, represented merely a transitional state. Israel would be fully compensated by the certain glory that awaited it in the future. When the Messiah came, he would vindicate the Jews, rebuild Zion, and there gather in the Jewish exiles from the four corners of the earth. If Don Francisco's teachings had not sufficed, Luis's reading of the Fourth Book of Ezra persuaded him that the messianic coming would take place soon.[36]

Such reflections, doubtless coupled with a deep emotional attachment to both his family and his secret faith, convinced Luis that his future lay in the service not of the governor but of the God of the Law of Moses. Only in God's service could he be assured of salvation in the world to come or hope to attain the felicity of satisfaction on earth.

At the same time, it must have been evident to Luis that his chances of succeeding to his uncle's position were becoming increasingly slim. The governor and the viceroy were engaged in controversy —and the match was hardly one between equals.

The controversy between the two men formed part of a protracted if sporadic struggle between the conquistadors and the office of the viceroy, a struggle that had been in process since the days of Cortés. The crown's policy, almost from the moment of the discovery of America, had been to induce private adventurers to undertake the risks of exploration and conquest. Once their tasks were on the road to completion, it would begin reducing their authority and even replacing them through the appointment of bureaucratic servants, dependent on the court and therefore more easily controlled. The intent of the crown clearly was to prevent the rise of a semi-independent, feudal-type baronial class and to insure highly structured, centralized control in the New World.[37]

The policy of delimiting the conquistadors' power began in the wake of the capture of Tenochtitlán, with the undermining of the massive strength acquired by Cortés and his associates. Until 1524 the government of New Spain consisted of a tenuous alliance of the nearly omnipotent Cortés, the municipal corporations he had established, and the crown's fiscal agents. But soon New Spain had an Audiencia under the aegis of the crown. The Audiencia, a supreme court consisting of four justices and a president, was empowered with a blend of executive, legislative, and judicial functions. This Audiencia instituted a reign of terror. Its rigid censorship, wholesale confiscations, indiscriminate incarcerations, and summary executions drove the country to the brink of internecine war. The Second Audiencia, taking over in 1530, was able to restore order to New Spain and propel it more peacefully along the road leading to the crown's greater control.

The Second Audiencia was superseded by the viceroy, whose task it was to further the work of defeudalizing New Spain. Under the first viceroy, Don Antonio de Mendoza, who came to Mexico City in 1535, the crown promulgated the controversial legal code known as "The New Laws of the Indies for the Good Treatment and Preservation of the Indians." Declaring the Indians to be free vassals of the crown who were not to be enslaved or exploited for private gain, the New Laws decreed the abolition of the chattel slavery of the Indians and ordered the encomiendas to revert to the crown at the death of their incumbents.

Humanitarianism was not the only, or, possibly, the most important motive of the Council of the Indies in promulgating the New Laws [a modern historian incisively writes]. They were designed to be an effective weapon in the reconquest of the New World from the conquistadors. They were part of the vast centralizing movement that was going on all over western Europe. They were meant to remove the feudal privileges of the Spanish settlers and reduce them to the status of pensioners of the Crown. The Crown, in a word, intended to be the only *encomendero*.[38]

The New Laws were soon to be modified, and some of the stringencies imposed on the encomenderos mitigated. One of the changes gave encomenderos the right to pass their holdings on to an heir, with the encomiendas going to the crown after the death of the heir. Such provision was incorporated in the royal capitulation won at court by Carvajal.

For all their benefits to the conquistador class, the modifications of the New Laws did not restore their old powers. The process of government consolidation and centralization continued apace, and by the year 1560 it had been in the main completed. By then the power of the viceroy and his network of officials was unquestionably established in all parts of New Spain except the marginal areas, principally in the north. In these regions, the crown continued its policy of permitting conquistadors to take the risks and, if successful, to hold supreme power over their conquests until it deemed the moment appropriate to swoop down and take control.

Carvajal was one of this breed of conquistadors. His struggle with the viceroy began once he had commenced to prove his success and once the regime learned of the vast treasures he had discovered. His differences with the viceroys must therefore be viewed as part of the general struggle for centralization on the part of the crown.

The quarrel between the governor and the viceroy's office began as a jurisdictional dispute during the incumbency of Viceroy Lorenzo Suárez de Mendoza (1580–1583). The area in question was located near the borders of New Biscay and may well have involved the city of Saltillo itself. Carvajal claimed that his charter gave him jurisdiction over this region, while the viceroy supported the claims of New Biscay. The controversy flared to such an extent that Carvajal felt constrained to bring the matter to adjudication before the royal court in Mexico City in January 1582. When he presented his charter, the court, on January 18, upheld his claim and gave him full possession of the lands in question.[39]

The viceroy's office had clearly lost this battle, but it was not convinced that it had forfeited the war. The next viceroy, Don Álvaro Manrique de Zúñiga, regarded the court order as only a temporary setback. He determined to wrest Governor Carvajal from his position. To that end he decided to find Carvajal's Achilles' tendon. He managed to enlist the aid of a Franciscan friar from the region of the Huaxteca. The priest was part of the governor's entourage and hence in a position to find out sensitive information. Apparently because he was aware of the suspicious activities of some of the governor's relatives in New Spain, the priest began to doubt his story about his ancestry. He might even have begun to wonder whether he might not be a concealer of heretics or even a secret Jew himself.

The viceroy, apprised of this, kept the information to himself until the moment, early in 1589, when he decided to bring down the ax on the governor's head. At that time the viceroy ordered Carvajal's arrest. The specific charge against the governor is nowhere stated, and was in all probability contrived. The chronicler Alonso de León states that the case seemed to be one of "the big fish swallowing the small." One official document, dated August 8, 1587, alleging Governor Carvajal's inhumane treatment of the Indians, may well have served as the viceroy's pretext for moving against him.

It stated that Carvajal was so eager to reduce the rebellious Indians of the Xalpa region that he lured forty men to volunteer to serve under him on the promise that he would enslave the Indians he captured and distribute half among them. When more than five hundred Indians peaceably surrendered and sought baptism, Carvajal handcuffed them.

After sentencing eight, he proceeded to declare all the rest slaves. Apparently taking half for himself, he distributed the others among his soldiers as promised. In the process he mercilessly separated children from their parents and husbands from their wives. The soldiers hastened to sell the slaves in their possession in various parts of New Spain.

The viceroy sent a judge and a group of soldiers to arrest Carvajal at New Almadén. They bound the governor in chains and took him unceremoniously to the Royal Prison in Mexico City.[40]

Equally instrumental in impelling the younger Luis de Carvajal to his decision was the extraordinary change of his family's fortunes.

After the death of Francisco Rodríguez de Matos, Luis's mother and sisters seem to have sunk into deeper poverty than before. Baltasar continued to work and Luis may have sent some support from the frontierland, but judging from the family's condition, their combined contributions could not have been impressive. The governor did not offer them any additional money. All he was willing to do was to help provide suitable marriage partners for his orphaned nieces, Catalina, Leonor, and, though the records do not explicitly state so, doubtless Mariana as well. The governor's intentions in this regard were not entirely altruistic. The young men he introduced to his nieces were officers and soldiers in his command who were known to be of good Old Christian stock. The governor, still clinging to his claim of Old Christian descent, wanted to give his family an opportunity to do likewise, or at least to place them in a position where they might see the value of being weaned from what he regarded as their intolerable condition. While Francisco Rodríguez de Matos was alive he adamantly refused to consider such matches for his daughters. Now that he was dead, Doña Francisca, faithful to his memory and ideals, effectively obstructed the governor's plan.[41]

Early in 1586 the family's situation did improve through the marriage of Catalina and Leonor. Their husbands were not Old Christians of modest means, but two of the wealthiest New Christians in New Spain. They were "very honorable and suitable men," said Mariana of her brothers-in-law. Enhancing their suitability was the fact that both were secret Jews. One of these was Jorge de Almeida, the other was Antonio Díaz de Cáceres, the trusted friend of both Francisco Rodríguez de Matos and Governor Carvajal.

At the time Jorge de Almeida was a man in his mid-thirties. He was of Portuguese descent, his surname deriving from his hometown of Almeida. His mother, Felipa de Fonseca, was reputed to be a fanatical Judaizer given to ascetic exercises. She was said to fast continually, taking some food only every third day. Almeida's paternal grandfather, Hector Fernández de Abrero, a native of the Portuguese city of Viseu, appears to have been a man of importance in Spain, and to have attained the title of "Knight of the Order of Saint James" (*Caballero del Hábito de Santiago*). Almeida's four sisters had died young. His three brothers, Hector de Fonseca, Francisco Rodríguez, and Miguel Hernández de Almeida, were all living; all were Judaizers. Hector de Fonseca and Miguel Hernández both came to the New World. There Hector de Fonseca married Juana López de la Torre, an Old Christian, or at least a New Christian who was a devout Catholic. The couple had three children: two boys and a girl. Francisco Rodríguez remained in Spain, where he eventually married an Old Christian, a step he regretted after his son was born. He took his son and escaped to Ferrara, where Jorge de Almeida apparently also lived for a time. In Ferrara, Francisco Rodríguez openly espoused Judaism and married a Jewish woman. Miguel Hernández appears to have remained a bachelor.

Of medium height and dark skin, Almeida was anything but prepossessing. An ugly scar cut across his face and uneven patches of baldness blotched his head. But he was a man of great talent and enterprise. In the region of Taxco he owned silver mines and processing plants for the beneficiation of the precious ore.[42]

Antonio Díaz de Cáceres cut a much more dashing and romantic figure than Almeida. He was ten years older than Almeida and also of Portuguese descent. He had been born in the town of Santa Comba Dão, in the bishopric of Coimbra, around 1541, into one of the finer New Christian families of Portugal. His grandfather, also named Antonio, appears to have served as comptroller for the king of Portugal. Around 1550, when young Antonio was ten, his father, Manuel, was named to this position. When Dom Manuel moved his family to the capital, he began to plan for his son's career.

Shortly after arriving at the court, young Antonio was serving as a page of the count of Vimioso. After two years in this position he

Signature of Jorge de Almeida

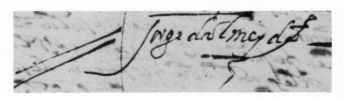

became a valet to a Portuguese prince, thanks to a recommendation by one of the count's relatives. Two years later, he became an assistant to General Gaspar da Cunha, commander of the Portuguese galleys. Two years after that, he served in the company of Admiral García de Toledo. Upon completing this assignment, he spent another year or so at sea with the Portuguese armadas.

Díaz de Cáceres returned to the Iberian Peninsula in 1563. The following year he went again to the New World, this time in the fleet under the command of General Antonio Manrique. He went in the company of Captain García de Cuadras and Lucas de la Gardeña, who was later to become a Franciscan friar. By late 1564 or early 1565 he was back on the Iberian Peninsula, and shortly thereafter was married in Portugal, also to a woman named Juana López. Juana died less than four years later, preceded in death by the couple's infant daughter, Isabel.

Perhaps on the basis of his previous experience in the New World, the young widower decided to pursue a career in transoceanic trade. He bought himself a ship and joined the fleet going to Terra Firma in 1568. Four years later we find him making another voyage to the Americas, this time to the viceroyalty of New Spain, in the fleet under the direction of General Juan de Alcega. Díaz de Cáceres appears to have settled in the viceroyalty of New Spain, most likely in Mexico City.[43] There he appears to have made his fortune, for when we hear of him again, after a lapse of some ten years, he is both wealthy and well connected. Among the people he had cultivated was Governor Carvajal. Doubtless through his dealings with the governor, he had become acquainted with Francisco Rodríguez de Matos and his family.

Not long after Don Francisco's funeral, Don Antonio approached Luis on behalf of himself and Almeida with the offer to marry his sisters. Luis immediately wrote to his mother, enthusiastically encouraging such matches on the grounds that both were men of honor and substance. Very likely he alluded, at least obliquely, to their Portuguese descent and Jewish inclinations. Doña Francisca accepted their proposals without informing Governor Carvajal.[44] The wedding was set for the crypto-Jewish Passover, in the middle of March 1586.

On hearing of the good fortune that had come to his sisters, Gaspar went to Pánuco to solemnize the weddings.[45] From two facts we may infer that Gaspar had learned that both Almeida and Díaz de Cáceres were Judaizers. First, he joined with Luis, Baltasar, and their mother in concealing the arrangements for the marriage and even the wedding itself from Governor Carvajal. As the brothers well knew, the governor would not only be beside himself with grief and anger on learning that his nieces were planning to marry Judaizers; he would do everything within his power to stop the weddings. Second, by this time Gaspar was fully aware that at least the adults in his family were Judaizing and would therefore want in-laws with similar religious inclinations.

If Gaspar needed any reminders of his family's religious activities, his sister Isabel gave him at least two in the weeks preceding the weddings and at least one thereafter.

In the middle of February, Gaspar saw Isabel engaged in a three-day fast. The fast made her so weak that she could hardly speak. To dissimulate what she was doing, Isabel went to the table for meals and pretended to eat. She put food into her mouth but just as quickly removed it and threw it under the table. Gaspar immediately realized that she was observing one of the Jewish fasts. He called it the Fast of Judith, but it was really the Fast of Esther.

Gaspar severely rebuked his sister for her heresy, advising her that it would be better if she had "a nice little altar with some saints and said her rosary, rather than going around trying to follow the Bible." He further told her that if she did observe the fasts that the Bible attributed to Judith she would be excommunicated. Isabel lamely responded that in her own home in Astorga she had statues of saints, but here she did not because she was not in her own house. She finally said she would abandon her belief since her brother, a cleric and preacher of the evangelical law, knew what was best.[46]

On another occasion, after Isabel had spent an entire Sabbath day resting, Gaspar observed her beginning to work around ten o'clock at night. Though he realized what Isabel had done, he decided to ask her why she had waited to begin her work so late and was actually desecrating or about to desecrate the Lord's day. Isabel appears to have correctly guessed the rhetorical nature of the question. She said nothing in reply.[47]

Then, shortly after the wedding, Isabel was serving Gaspar a meal when he noticed something wrong with the bread. It was flat and tasteless. He then realized that Isabel was serving him unleavened bread and was celebrating the Passover. Gaspar knew what it was, but all he said to his sister was that "she probably did not knead the bread well because she was not making good bread." Isabel said nothing in reply. She later said that she was afraid that if Gaspar discovered the truth he might kill her, but this could hardly have been the case. She also said that in order not to be discovered she refrained from eating bitter herbs, but then confessed that another reason for not eating them was "also because there were none around."[48]

In addition to all of this Gaspar was troubled by the disappearance of a Bible of his in his family's home.[49]

If Gaspar approved of his sisters' matches, it may have been because he preferred to have them marry New Christian Judaizers to Old Christians, who might make an issue of their in-laws' origins.

Young Luis was not present at the ceremonies. He was still with his uncle. He therefore had to depend on his family to supply him with the fascinating details of the weddings.

He learned that shortly after the completion of the marriage negotiations, Almeida and Díaz de Cáceres arrived unexpectedly in Tampico, accompanied by a number of friends, among them Gonzalo Pérez Ferro, Miguel Hernández de Almedia, and Fray Gaspar. With them came a number of musicians playing trumpets and other instruments and a large retinue of servants bearing sumptuous gifts for the family, including costly garments for Doña Francisca and her daughters.

When they came to the outskirts of the city, Almeida and Díaz de Cáceres stopped the caravan in order to change their attire. They took off their traveling clothes and donned velvet suits, silver-buckled shoes, and plumed hats. They also hung golden chains around their necks.

Doña Francisca and her family were unaware that Catalina's and Leonor's future husbands were arriving until they heard the playing of oboes and trumpets.

Doña Francisca's neighbors could hardly believe their eyes when they saw the wondrous retinue stop before her door. Several devout ladies, marveling at Doña Francisca's future sons-in-law, asked her what prayer she had uttered to bring such a miracle about. Humbly, "like the saintly Sarah," to use Luis's words, Doña Francisca answered, "God's mercy is hardly proportional to one's merits, which are always few or none." The neighbors also complimented the bridegrooms for extricating their brides from the morass of poverty, or as they said, for "plucking out roses from amidst thorns." They were "roses indeed," Luis later explained, "not so much for their beauty, for this was slight, but for the virtue and chastity which the Lord had given them."[50] At the time of their marriages, Catalina was twenty-one years old and Leonor only twelve.

By this time Luis's fourteen-year-old sister, Mariana, was also being courted. Shortly after the wedding she became engaged. Her fiancé was her mother's cousin, Jorge de Léon, who bore the distinction of having been arrested and then released unscathed by the Inquisition in Lisbon.[51] But unfortunately for Mariana, the marriage between the two was not destined to take place.

After the double wedding, lavish and opulent as befitted the station of the family's new in-laws, Almeida and Díaz de Cáceres could remain in Tampico for only a few days. The spring fleet was in, and the two had numerous weighty business matters to look after. They therefore left for Mexico City, taking with them their wives, their mother-in-law, and their sister-in-law Anica, and rented quarters in the district of San Pablo in a house belonging to Ana de Alcázar. Miguel may have joined the family in Mexico City shortly thereafter, but Isabel and Mariana remained at the coast for another six months. Then Gaspar and Baltasar brought them to Mexico City.[52]

The trip to the capital gave Gaspar another opportunity to observe the Judaizing influences that had worked on the family.

On the way to Mexico City, Gaspar, Isabel, Mariana and Baltasar and the "Indians in their company and service," as Isabel was to say, stopped in the quaint Indian village of Atotonilco. Atotonilco was the home of Doña Guiomar's half sister, Doña Francisca Núñez Viciosa. After the death of her first husband, Alonso del Águila, she had married a man named Juan López.

The travelers planned to spend the night at Doña Francisca's, but at eight o'clock in the evening Gaspar spirited his siblings away to a local inn, apparently without giving a word of explanation. He did not have to. Francisca Núñez Viciosa was a fervent Judaizer who did not care to dissimulate her devotion even in the presence of Gaspar. Isabel saw her performing some Jewish rites in the afternoon—she may have been making Sabbath preparations on a Friday or praying on a Sabbath—and begged her to stop. At the time Gaspar was reciting the divine office with Mariana, who knew it practically by heart. But Gaspar appears to have found out about Doña Francisca quickly enough to remove his sisters and brother from her presence.

He may have found out from Juan López himself. Isabel characterized Doña Francisca's new husband as "a knave of a man and not like her first husband . . . who was affable and a servant of God." By "servant of God," a term connoting saintliness, Isabel meant a dedicated Judaizer.[53]

Young Luis de Carvajal was in the San Gregorio mines when word of his sisters' marriages arrived. He then decided that the time had come for him to leave the New Kingdom of León. He knew that it would not be easy for him to leave. The governor would not accept the idea any more happily than he would the news of the marriages. Besides, his services were very much needed. The mayor of the town, in whose house Luis stayed, even went so far as to say that if he left the region, the town would not survive. Luis therefore realized he would do best to leave quietly, even stealthily, and he began to plan accordingly.

The propitious moment came in a most unusual way. During a lull in the fighting against the Indians, the community leaders decided that it was necessary to send for more supplies, only to find themselves in dire financial straits. At this point Luis offered them a bar of silver if they would facilitate his departure. They accepted with alacrity and Luis left.

A few days later, the Chichimecs mounted a ferocious attack on the settlement and killed many of the Spaniards. Among the casualties was the mayor himself.[54]

By this time Luis was far away from the mining region in the San Gregorio Mountains. His mind was set on beginning a new life, one that he would live unhesitatingly as a Jew.

6 "Servants of God"

Luis headed for Mexico City by way of the towns of Zacatecas and Guadalajara and the territory of Michoacán.[1] How much time he spent in each is not recorded, but the chances are he did not just pass through.

Both Guadalajara and Zacatecas were important foci of Spanish settlement during the sixteenth century. Guadalajara was a beautiful and salubrious town. Founded by Cristóbal de Oñate in 1530 with the name Espíritu Santo and renamed twelve years later, it was a busy center, with a market, cathedral, and court; yet it exuded an air of calmness and dignity. At the time of Luis's visit some seventy Spanish families called it their home, and more than three thousand Indians resided in the nearby hamlets. A year later a terrible pestilence was to decimate the city.[2]

Zacatecas, named after the Zacatec Indians, presented a contrasting picture. It had been established less than forty years before, but had surpassed Guadalajara in commercial activity and was second only to the capital in population. In 1586 the town, squeezed in a canyon, contained more than three thousand Spanish families and countless Indians; Negroes, and half-breeds. The year before Luis's arrival, King Philip II had granted it the status of a city, and in 1588 it was to be honored with the flamboyant appellation of "The Very Noble and Loyal City of Our Lady of the Zacatecs."

The meteoric rise of Zacatecas was built on the seemingly inexhaustible veins of precious metal that had been discovered in its hills. Its thriving mines, dug by Indians and Negro slaves under the most brutalizing conditions, brought incredible opulence to a handful of Spaniards and were to yield the crown twenty-one million pesos in the first century of the city's existence. In addition to honest artisans and craftsmen, the city had attracted adventurers and speculators from England, Flanders, Portugal, Italy, Germany, and Greece.[3]

The nature of these towns gives a possible clue to young Luis de Carvajal's activity there. It seems likely that he went to Zacatecas, Guadalajara, and the surrounding territories to establish business connections. His experience as a merchant and his knowledge of mining and the defense of mining towns, acquired under the tutelage of his uncle, enhanced Luis's value to a community and offered him in return the possibility of profitable enterprise.

It was not until the middle of 1586 that Luis arrived in Mexico City for a memorable reunion with his family. When he had left

Towns and Roads in the Region of Zacatecas and Guadalajara, with Dates of Discoveries of Mines

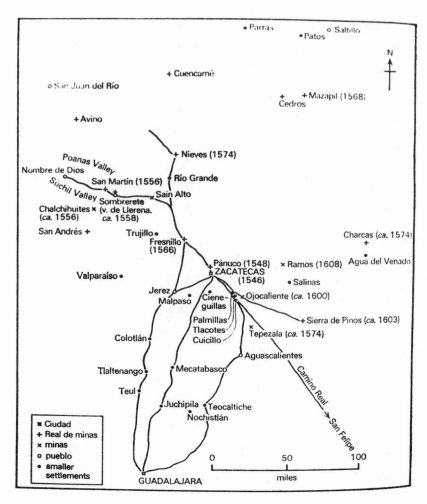

Pánuco, his mother and sisters were languishing in poverty. Now, "under the care and shelter" of his brothers-in-law, as he himself was to put it, they could hold their heads high like the most aristocratic of ladies. Doña Francisca, still mourning for her husband, insisted on wearing black, but Luis's sisters had undergone a marvelous transformation. "Instead of their torn skirts," Luis vividly recalled, he "saw them bedecked in gold and silks and other finery in their husbands' homes."[4]

Since Doña Francisca was poor, Almeida provided the dowry for Leonor, and we may presume that Díaz de Cáceres did the same for Catalina. Through Doña Francisca, Almeida presented his wife with furniture, clothing, and jewelry later appraised at 5,535 pesos. The furniture included various trunks and chests, some with sculptured figures, more than two dozen chairs of various descriptions, a sumptuous bed with a fustian coverlet, a damask quilt, three mattresses of Spanish linen filled with wool, two pillows and sheets of Rouen linen, a secretary from China, a small sewing box, and even a special basket for fruit. Among the clothing were a yellow silk gown and a silken cloak, a mantelet of lustrous black satin, a white jacket with silver lace and gold edging, an upper petticoat of purple velvet and one of white China damask, and slippers of crimson velvet. The jewelry comprised mostly gold and precious stones. It included a headdress and medallion of gold, a large gold perfume box, two gold rings: one with five small emeralds, the other with a large amethyst, a gold necklace with pearls and emeralds, gold earrings inlaid with pearls, and twenty-five gold brooches, each adorned with three or four pearls.

In addition to all this, Jorge de Almeida gave his wife the Spanish husband's traditional gift. In Almeida's case it was a thousand pesos in gold.[5]

On their arrival in Mexico City, the entire family at first lived with the Almeidas. When Díaz de Cáceres found a suitable dwelling, he and Catalina moved out and invited Doña Francisca, Isabel, Mariana, and Miguel to come along. Eventually Doña Francisca rented quarters for herself and her unmarried children "in a place next to Gracián de Balzola." Not long thereafter Miguel was placed in the Jesuit school. At around this time also Mariana was enrolled in the School for Girls, much to the relief of Isabel, who found it difficult to the point of impossibility to get along with her younger sister.[6]

Gonzalo Pérez Ferro did not like the idea of Mariana's being enrolled in the School for Girls. He was aware of the girl's impressionability and feared that she would be irretrievably lost to the secret Jews if she remained under Catholic influence for any length of time.[7]

y en el nombre de dios amen Sepan quantos esta carta Vieren como yo doña
francisca de car vajal biuda muger que fui de Juan de ... de... de ...
mos de la billa de benabente que es en los Reynos de castilla la Vieja Re
sidente al presente en estas minas de tasco de la nueua españa digo que por
quanto a seruicio de dios nro Señor y de su bendita madre se trato y concerto que
doña leonor de andrada mi hija legitima y del dho mi marido difunto casa
se con Jorje de almeyda hijo legitimo de antonio fernandes de almeyda y de ...
pa de fonseca su legitima muger naturales de la ciudad de coimbra en el Rey
no de portugal y al tiempo que se concerto el dho casamiento se prometio en man de
... con la dicha doña leonor mi hija cinco mill quinientos y treynta y
cinco pesos de oro comun de Ciño Reales cada un peso de buena moneda
los quales se quedo de dar y pagar y entregar al dho Jorje de
almeyda ... por que ... y haga scriptura de dote y forma segun derecho de los
... los cinco mill y quis y treynta y cinco pesos los doy y entrego en
la forma y manera siguiente mill ps en Reales de plata y lo de mas en
cumplimiento de los dhos cinco mill y quis y treynta y cinco ps en las joyas
y Joias y bienes muebles de entre casa en la forma siguiente

primeramente Una cadena de oro con Un nauio pendiente
della con el ... del nabio de un benrneo que con su ... y oro   M   ps
fue apreciado en trecientos ps

Iten Un collar de oro con sus perlas y piedras de esmeralda
con diez y seis piecas de oro que con su ... y oro fue apreciado
en trecientos ps   M   ps

Un Rostrillo de oro con treynta y quatro piecas de oro
en cada una una perla a precio de en ciento ...   C   ps

Una miralla de oro con ocho piedras quatro Rubis y
quatro diamantes con su ... y oro y piedras fue apre
ciado en trecientos ps   M   ps

Un como ... guarnecido de oro de forma de medalla grande

---

*First Part of the Inventory of the Dowry Given to Doña Leonor de
Andrada Carvajal*

But as Pérez Ferro well knew, the family had at least one good reason to place Mariana in the school's protective surroundings. They wanted to put her out of reach of Jorge de Almeida and his brother, Hector de Fonseca.[8]

Shortly after Mariana's betrothal to Jorge de León, Almeida announced that he wanted his sister-in-law for himself. He saw nothing wrong in having two wives, he said, since the worthies in the Bible did. He even suggested that if he married Mariana, "it would be in imitation of Jacob, who married two sisters, Leah and Rachel." Besides, he insisted, Mariana could not fulfill her word to marry Jorge de León because he was not really a secret Jew.

Under pressure from Almeida the family compelled Mariana to break her engagement to Jorge de León and become betrothed to her brother-in-law, "with the consent and permission of her sister Leonor."

Since Almeida could not live polygamously in New Spain, he planned to emigrate to one of the Jewish communities of Europe, where he mistakenly believed such arrangements to be common.

No sooner were Almeida's plans formulated than they ran into a barrage of opposition. Gonzalo Pérez Ferro told Doña Francisca, Baltasar, and Luis that he regarded the arrangement as an affront to his brother-in-law, Jorge de León. And as soon as Antonio Díaz de Cáceres heard about it, he expressed his opposition to the match with no less vehemence, insisting that it was no longer customary for Jews to marry two sisters.[9]

On one occasion, probably connected with Almeida's courting of Mariana, Antonio Díaz de Cáceres slapped Almeida's wife, Leonor. On another occasion he stabbed Almeida.[10]

Such opposition was sufficient to get Doña Francisca and her sons to change their minds about Almeida's proposed arrangement. Under their prodding Mariana broke her engagement to Almeida. The reason given by the family for Mariana's change of heart was that if Mariana and Almeida were married, "there would be too much discord and strife between her and her sister Leonor."[11]

Apparently unwilling or unable to renew Mariana's engagement to Jorge de León, the family then decided that she should marry Almeida's thirty-nine-year-old brother, Hector de Fonseca. Fonseca was also a wealthy mineowner. (A decade later he would say that he would not sell one of his mines for a hundred thousand pesos.[12]) Fonseca, too, was married, but he was eager to leave his wife, an Old Christian with whom he lived unhappily, largely because of the differences in their religious beliefs. Fonseca complained that "he lived like a martyr and did not have the opportunity to keep the Law of Moses." As a result, he said, waxing poetical, "he went out into the field among the deer to cry and shout and ask God to pardon him for all his sins."

The family regarded Fonseca's marriage as invalid and agreed that there was nothing wrong in his exchanging an Old Christian wife for a secret Jewess. They even found biblical authority for their position in the Book of Ezra, "where it says that God commanded the children of Israel to leave the wives they had married in their captivity and marry women of the Israelite people."

Again under pressure from the family, Mariana promised to marry Hector de Fonseca. Since there was no divorce in New Spain, it was agreed that Fonseca would take the entire family to a Jewish community in Europe or Asia, where his marriage would be annulled and where he and Mariana could then live openly as man and wife. In the meanwhile he and Mariana went through a type of preliminary marriage ceremony, Mariana "promising to God that he and no other will be her husband," with the understanding that they would not live together until they reached the ghetto, or, as they called it, the *judería*.

Jorge de Almeida was furious when he learned that Mariana had promised to marry his brother. He said that Mariana would be his brother's wife only over his dead body. He even challenged Fonseca to a duel. Fonseca soon decided not to proceed with his plans to take the family to Europe. Whether he regarded his retreat as temporary or permanent is nowhere told.

In the meantime the sensitive Mariana, her emotions drained as a result of all these struggles and frustrations, began to display moods of extreme elation and depression.[13]

Very likely it was at this time that Mariana decided she wanted to become a nun. Isabel dissuaded her, explaining that "there were no nuns in the Mosaic Law."

Under these circumstances it is not surprising that Gonzalo Pérez Ferro complained when the family decided to enroll Mariana in the School for Girls. Mariana, cured of her desire for the veil, later claimed that she remained steadfastly Jewish throughout her stay at the *colegio*.[14] In little more than a decade Jorge de León disappears from the scene. Whether he died of a broken heart is not disclosed.[15]

The priest Gaspar also suffered greatly as an indirect result of the family's attempt to marry off his sister.

As a religious, Gaspar could hardly have been expected to condone the plans of either Jorge de Almeida or Hector de Fonseca, so the family's discussions concerning Mariana were kept from him. But

Gaspar soon had reason to suspect that what was happening had something to do with the Judaizers and their practices.

One day he observed his mother and brother Baltasar engaged in secret and apparently heated conversation with Antonio Díaz de Cáceres and Jorge de Almeida, and expressed his displeasure at being kept out of the conversation. At this point Jorge de Almeida, doubtless upset, took Gaspar into another room and told him that Baltasar had been discussing the fact that Francisco Rodríguez de Matos had died a Jew.

Gaspar, visibly shaken, later recalled that he began to tell Almeida he would denounce them all to the Inquisition; at that moment Baltasar entered the room. On learning what Almeida had told his brother, he said, "I swear to God that this is not so, that I have not said that."

Gaspar, faint with grief, later told his mother that his father was burning in hell, and he was certain she knew what he was referring to. All his mother said, somewhat cryptically, was, "Son, it was done only for your good."

The next day Jorge de Almeida confessed to Gaspar, possibly in front of Baltasar, though Gaspar could not recall clearly, that what he had told him about Francisco Rodríguez de Matos had not been the truth. Gaspar, somewhat relieved at being extricated from the obligation of appearing before the Inquisition, repeatedly begged his mother to forgive him for having said that his father was in hell. His mother, coming to the defense of her late husband, harped on Don Francisco's virtues, especially his charity.[16]

Aside from these problems, all went well with the family in Mexico City. Almeida and Díaz de Cáceres provided munificently for their in-laws. They even supported Baltasar and Luis for an entire year after Luis's arrival in Mexico City.

During the year, in the late winter or early spring of 1587, a daughter, Leonor, was born to Catalina and Antonio Díaz de Cáceres. Proud though Doña Francisca may have been at becoming a grandmother, she was filled with grief when the child was taken to be baptized. Catalina did not care much for the idea either, and determined to make a Jewess out of her daughter at the earliest possible moment.[17]

At the end of the year, however, something occurred to separate Luis and Baltasar from their brothers-in-law. According to Luis, Almeida and Díaz de Cáceres now found themselves in financial straits. The expenditures for their lavish weddings and the huge outlays for the support of such a large family had drained their resources, he explained. His mother and sisters continued to give an appearance of opulence, he admitted, but the outward display belied their growing need. His brothers-in-law, slipping fast down the incline to poverty, unflinchingly continued to provide for Doña Francisca and her unmarried children. But after a year in Mexico City both Almeida and Díaz de Cáceres found that they had to move to Taxco.

They did not think of leaving the family behind. Doña Francisca took Mariana and apparently also Miguel out of their respective schools. Doña Francisca, Isabel, and Miguel prepared to join Jorge de Almeida, while Mariana and Anica were taken by Antonio Díaz de Cáceres.

Almeida and Díaz de Cáceres were also prepared to take Baltasar and Luis to Taxco, but the brothers refused to go. They were embarrassed by their own inactivity and failure to meet the responsibility for supporting their mother and unmarried siblings. They therefore decided to remain in Mexico City and look for jobs, Luis said. We do not know what employment Baltasar found, but Luis accepted a position as a bookkeeper for a merchant. He took this menial job "in order to have a piece of bread with which to sustain himself," he explained.[18]

At least so Luis claimed. But his explanation does not ring true.

A year after Luis's arrival in Mexico City neither Almeida nor Díaz de Cáceres gave the slightest evidence of living on the brink of poverty. They still retained their estates and their businesses intact, including their refining facilities and other property in the Taxco mines. Jorge de Almeida's residence there was not a pauper's abode, though Luis insisted that the entire family lived in only two rooms, one for Almeida and his wife, the other for his in-laws. It was rather a comfortable rustic estate with the melodious name of *Cantarranas*, or Frogs' Song. Antonio Díaz de Cáceres had a similar place a league away at Tenango. Luis's brothers-in-law remained in the Taxco region for a year and a half, and in all that time neither gave any evidence of suffering an appreciable diminution of wealth, prestige, or comfort.[19]

Almeida and Díaz de Cáceres thus appear to have been induced to move to the Taxco region not so much by poverty as by their interests in the Taxco mines.

Late in 1588 Díaz de Cáceres returned to Mexico City, bringing Catalina, Mariana, and Anica along, and in January 1589 Jorge de Almeida followed with the rest of the family. Almeida took quarters near the School for Girls. Doña Francisca soon brought Mariana to

View of a Mining Hacienda in New Spain

The Hacienda of Cantarranas

Almeida's home. Isabel also moved in with the Almeidas and appears to have taken over supervision of their household, since Leonor was only fifteen years old.[20]

In Mexico City as in Taxco there was nothing to suggest any change in the family's total wealth or in their manner of living.

Besides, Luis's work as a bookkeeper could not have absorbed the bulk of his hours. While he was thus ostensibly employed, he was able to find the time to handle an important matter for Díaz de Cáceres before the royal court in Mexico City.[21] Nor could his job have been of long duration, for when Luis reappears in the records, a year or so later, his employer is gone. He and Baltasar are feverishly involved in private business ventures and are reaping substantial profits. By Luis's own admission he and Baltasar earned more than seven thousand pesos between early 1588 and the spring of 1589.[22]

Luis's allegation of idleness and the claim as to his in-laws' precipitate reverses were made after his arrest by the Inquisition. They appear clearly intended to divert the Inquisition from thinking that either he or his family possessed substantial funds. Luis realized that the Inquisition would confiscate his possessions and that its interest in his relatives would be proportional to their wealth. Following a procedure common among people anticipating arrest by the Inquisition, Luis and Baltasar might have left a good part of their property with trusted friends late in 1588 or early 1589.

Likewise, Luis's acceptance of the position with the merchant and Baltasar's move to whatever occupation he undertook may well have been façades to conceal their more significant activities, which were centered in Mexico City. These included not only their budding private business ventures, but also, far more important, their active promotion of Judaism. Although they did not so call themselves, they regarded it as their goal to act as "servants of God." The term was usually applied to devout Christians. The Judaizers used it to refer to the most exemplary secret Jews, as Luis's sister Isabel had done when she applied it to Alonso del Águila, the first husband of her aunt, Francisca Núñez Viciosa.[23]

As they traveled about the mining districts around Temazcaltepec, Sultepec, Pachuca, Taxco, Mixteca, and Oaxaca, selling their wine, clothing, confections, and silver, Luis and Baltasar searched for New Christians who might be secret Jews at heart. On finding one, they would engage him in banter and then would begin posing the ostensibly innocent questions that led Judaizers to reveal themselves to one another. In this manner Luis and Baltasar came to mutual confessions with numerous people. Among these were Domingo López and Juan Rodríguez of Mexico City, both living in a soap factory behind the Indian hospital and formerly members of Dr. Morales's circle of secret Jews;[24] Jorge de Almeida's brother, Hector de Fonseca, with whom Luis declared himself on two occasions, once near the town of Malinalco, and again at Cacahuamilpa, both on the road from Mexico City to Taxco;[25] two men named Tomás de Fonseca, one an uncle and business associate of Jorge de Almeida's from the town of Tlalpujahua,[26] and the other a sensitive student of the Bible and sacred literature who lived in the region of Taxco.[27] There was also a young goldsmith named Jorge Díaz, who had lived in the Jewish community at Venice and promised Luis to escape with him to a similar community after the two had accumulated enough money in New Spain.[28]

But perhaps the most important Judaizer they met was the merchant Manuel de Lucena. Like Luis and Baltasar, Lucena was in his early twenties and resembled the Carvajal brothers in brilliance, knowledge, and devotion to Judaism. This devotion was shared by his wife, Catalina, his brothers-in-law, Diego and Pedro Enríquez, and was, if possible, surpassed by his mother-in-law, Beatriz Enríquez de Payba.

Lucena's home had become a mecca for Judaizers, and Luis and Baltasar went there frequently. Luis later recalled at least eight occasions when he and Baltasar gathered with the family for study and prayer.[29] One of these was the Fast of Esther, 1588, which the brothers celebrated in the company of the family and friends.[30]

The brothers' quest for secret Jews and their sympathizers also brought them into contact with two of the most unusual men in the New Spain of their day.

One of these was a refined and cultured eccentric named Gregorio López, persistently identified by legend with the ill-fated Crown Prince Charles (Carlos), son of King Philip II. The records state that after a long imprisonment the prince was put to death at his father's behest in 1568. López was born around the same time as Charles. López's only biographer insists that Gregorio arrived in Mexico City in 1564. He also records that his subject, who moved comfortably among the highest society, kept a tight-lipped silence about his life and family in Spain.

Shortly after his mysterious arrival in Mexico City, López disappeared, only to be discovered living the life of a hermit amid the barbarous Indians of the hinterlands. He devoted himself wholeheartedly to meditation, study, and service to the poor. One of his mottos was the biblical precept "Thou shalt love the Lord thy God with all thy heart, with all thy soul and with all thy might, and thy neighbor as thyself."

Before long, Europeans coming into contact with López began to question the orthodoxy of his religious practices and beliefs. López refused to wear a rosary or scapular. He was not a member of any religious order, yet he possessed an astonishing knowledge of Bible, particularly of the Old Testament. His hut was conspicuously bare of the likenesses of saints; it did not even have an icon of the Virgin Mary.

Since his dwelling was seven difficult leagues away from the nearest church, he did not attend mass.

Complaints against López finally led to an inquisitorial investigation of his strange practices, but López was cleared of all fault and his Catholic piety was never again questioned. López continued his accustomed way of life, though he did attend mass regularly, especially after illness compelled him to return permanently to civilization. He was eventually beatified. If King Philip IV had had things his way, López would have become one of the saints of the Church.

As he went through life López amassed a vast knowledge of many disciplines and wrote works on medicine, botany, and pharmacology. His knowledge and love of humanity attracted people from all walks of life. López said that he saw the image of God in everything he studied. He saw it in all men as well. He treated everyone with love, making no distinction between rich and poor, Indian and Spaniard, pious Catholic and suspected heretic.

Luis de Carvajal saw López frequently in the late 1580s and early

Gregorio López (oil painting in the Museo Nacional de Historia, Mexico City)

1590s. In late 1587, on a visit to the hospital at Huastepec where López was confined, Luis happened to call his uncle a tyrant because he had taken the family away from its homeland. López told young Luis that he should not have spoken that way. He had spoken poorly, said Don Gregorio, "because men do not know the dispositions of God."

As a result of his association with López, young Carvajal concluded that he was a secret Jew. Not only did López consort with Judaizers, but the hermit's actions coincided with what Luis regarded as distinctively Jewish activities. López, he observed, fasted most of the time. He wore a long beard. He knew the Bible, particularly the Old Testament. He prayed and meditated *without* a head covering, a sure sign of Jewish leanings, according to Luis, who did not realize that Jews wore a head covering during prayer. Gregorio López also prayed and meditated while standing, and this, according to Luis, was "the usual Jewish practice." Above all, Luis felt, López had to be a Jew because he believed in one God, and also because he came from the city of Toledo, "where there are many descendants of the Jews."

Yet López was not a Judaizer. In fact, when he was suspected of heresy, he was charged with acting like a Protestant, not like a Jew. His greatest work, a commentary on the Book of Revelation entitled *The Exposition of the Apocalypse,* points to the true nature of his personality. It reveals him to have been one of the many noble Catholics of the sixteenth century who sought to uphold the church's idea of pure monotheism, derived from the Hebrew tradition, against its increasing concessions to iconolatry. It also shows him to have been one of the many voices clamoring for the equality of all baptized Catholics without regard to color or race. *The Exposition of the Apocalypse* suggests that López eloquently championed the beleaguered New Christian Judaizers and railed against the insidious doctrine of "blood cleanness." His association with them appears to have been a demonstration of supreme protest against attempts to demean them and reduce them to the status of second-class Catholics.[31]

No less interesting a figure was an old invalid, Antonio Machado. Machado had been a tailor in his native Lisbon, and had come to New Spain many years before with his wife and growing brood of children. He had eight daughters and one son, Juan de Machado, an attorney in the royal court in Mexico City.

Soon after his arrival in New Spain, Machado fell victim to a host of infirmities, among them an acute case of gout and a partial paralysis that was to confine him permanently to his room. His physician, Dr. Manuel de Morales, became fast friends with Machado the moment he learned he was a fervent Judaizer. When Morales realized that it would be impossible to restore Machado's physical health, he began attending to his soul. He prepared what he called a "spiritual balm" in the form of a booklet containing various religious poems, some composed by Morales himself, and a translation into Spanish of the entire Book of Deuteronomy.

During Morales's treatment of Machado, the old man's favorite daughter, Isabel, contracted pleurisy, and the doctor immediately undertook her cure. With Isabel, Morales proved successful in both the physical and spiritual realms. To supervise her recovery more closely, he brought the young lady, then in her early thirties, to his home and placed her under the care of his wife. A close friendship developed between the two Isabels. Isabel Machado had an excellent voice and Isabel Morales was eager to improve hers in order to give more melodious renditions of the religious hymns being composed by her husband and other Judaizers in his circle. When Luis and Baltasar met him, Machado was already near ninety. He was living in a single room cluttered with a large desk, a clavichord, two trunks, and sundry boxes, and reeking with the odors of illness and age. His only support, he claimed, came from the largesse of friends. He had been suffering for thirteen years and for the past nine had been miserably crippled and confined to his room.

In a sense the old man's illness provided him with a security he had never had before. For years Machado had done everything possible to repel people he did not wish to cultivate. He had acquired a reputation for being cantankerous, litigious, caustic, and irascible; consequently, his friends were few. Apparently without exception they were Judaizers.

At the same time Machado was respected in public for his Catholic piety. He attended church fastidiously, belonged to various religious fraternities, consorted with renowned priests and monks, and each Christmas displayed a beautiful crèche in front of his home. Machado had thus carefully insulated himself against denunciation to the Inquisition.

His illness enabled Machado to withdraw even further from Christian society unobtrusively. His room became a meeting place for Judaizers interested in prayer and discussions of Bible and other religious books. These included Luis de Granada's *Introduction to the Symbol of the Faith* and a manuscript anthology of religious poetry and prose, including Morales's translation of the Book of Deuteronomy into Spanish.

Such meetings took place with regularity on the Sabbath and holy days and were attended by some of the most renowned citizens of New Spain. The worshipers included Doña Francisca's cousin, Catalina de León, and her husband, Gonzalo Pérez Ferro; Catalina Enríquez and her husband, Manuel de Lucena, and an apparently self-styled Turkish envoy named Alexander Testanera. The merchant Cristóbal Gómez, to whom Luis was to entrust large sums of money before his arrest by the Inquisition, also came frequently, as did Luis's brother-in-law Antonio Díaz de Cáceres.

Whenever the congregation gathered in Machado's room, his daughter Isabel carefully bolted the heavy outside door and announced to all unwanted callers that her father's illness had forced him to retire.[32]

Luis and Baltasar frequently visited Machado. The old man grew so fond of the brothers that he gave them permission to make a copy of the cherished booklet that Dr. Morales had prepared. He also offered Baltasar what he regarded as his most precious possession, the hand of his favorite daughter, Isabel. But Baltasar demurred. At twenty-seven he was not prepared to marry a woman of forty, though Luis said that Baltasar rejected Isabel because of her poverty.[33]

The brothers were fascinated with the Book of Deuteronomy and the poetry found in Dr. Morales's notebook. They called the poetry "flowers culled from the rich garden of Sacred Writ." Amazingly, neither Luis nor Baltasar, for all their previous contact with the Bible, appeared to be very familiar with Deuteronomy. Thus, when they turned to the book's twenty-seventh chapter, dealing with the curses to be visited upon faithless Israel, they were convinced that their difficulties stemmed from their failure to adhere scrupulously to the Mosaic Law. The thought that they were "removed from the true path" struck them with such impact that the two brothers "raised a cry . . . like a compassionate mother over a beloved son lying dead before her."[34]

The sense of guilt doubtless helped induce Baltasar to make a decision he had apparently been contemplating for some time. During one Passover he decided that, like Luis, he had to circumcise himself. He borrowed a barber's razor and proceeded to perform the commandment. In the process he wounded himself severely and required a secluded place in which to recover. On Luis's advice he decided to stay in a house belonging to Governor Carvajal, located in a sparsely inhabited area and, surprisingly, available to him despite the governor's animosity toward the entire family. Baltasar remained there until his recovery, his pain somewhat assuaged by the belief that it "furnished him with no small merit to counterweigh his past sins."

To Baltasar's dismay, the nature of his illness was once almost discovered by the governor. The governor came to his house unexpectedly one day and found bloodstained cloths. "But," Luis explained, "since it was the Lenten season, they distracted him by saying that they had scourged themselves in penitence and brought forth the blood."

When Doña Francisca heard of her son's operation, she chided him for not having come home to recover.[35]

In both Mexico City and Taxco the Carvajal home, under Luis's direction, bustled with Judaizing activity. Every Carvajal participated. Mariana even taught Anica to Judaize though she was only a child, and Catalina and Francisca indoctrinated young Miguel.[36]

Francisca and her daughters diligently prepared for the weekly Sabbath. On Friday afternoon, they cleaned the house, changed linens, prepared a festive meal for the evening, usually a chicken dinner, and put cooked food for the rest of the Sabbath into a warm oven. They then bathed, pared their nails, and donned their finest clothes.[37]

They ushered in the Sabbath by lighting a cruse of oil or a single candle, intended not for the Sabbath Queen, but for the souls of the dead—"so that through it the deceased of Israel might attain glory and rest"—or even for the living. The candlewick, woven by the women themselves, contained numerous strands, each corresponding to a person to be remembered. "I set this one for So-and-so," they would say, mentioning the name, "that God might give him eternal bliss," or, "I set this one for So-and-so, that God might grant him life."[38] Doña Francisca or Isabel usually lit the candle. Mariana did so occasionally, though she later denied it.[39] The lighted candle or lamp was placed "in a room where it could continue to burn until morning," and "would go out by itself."[40]

The family spent the Sabbath praying, feasting, and resting, though the women always kept their sewing handy in case a suspicious person happened by.[41]

The Carvajals also bathed and cut their hair and nails in preparation for the fast of the Great Day of the Lord.[42]

While the fast of the Great Day lasted from sunset to sunset, others were observed only from sunrise to sundown. Dr. Morales urged fasting as a means to benefit the dead.[43] He preferred to fast on Tuesdays and Fridays. Young Luis de Carvajal and his mother's cousin Francisca chose the traditional days of Monday and Thursday. So did Luis's sister Catalina, though her frailty frequently prevented her from carrying out her intentions.[44] Leonor had been fasting since her childhood in Pánuco.[45] Mariana fasted three or four days a week in Pánuco, but in

Mexico City Doña Francisca prevailed upon her to limit her fast days to twice or even once a week. But it was Isabel who acquired the reputation for being "a great faster,"[46] as her brother Gaspar discovered on his visit to Pánuco during the three-day Fast of Esther in 1586. At that time Isabel refused to take the customary evening refreshments during the fast period and completed the seventy-two hour fast despite the fact that she had become so increasingly weak that she could hardly talk.[47]

Occasionally Isabel and her sisters fasted for two consecutive days to commemorate the trials of Judith, the heroine of a story in the Apocrypha. Isabel said that when she observed the Fast of Judith and the Fast of Esther, she prayed to God to make her like these heroines and to give her the grace to continue her fasting. She said that just as Esther and Judith fasted "so that God might free Israel from the indignation of King Ahasuerus and Haman and King Nebuchadnezzar and Holofernes," she too observed them "so that God might free her and some other people from persecutions, difficulties, and afflictions."[48]

The family usually broke its fasts with foods like fish and eggs.[49]

The Carvajals also zealously kept the Passover in spirit even when, as generally happened, they could not fully observe it according to biblical law. They could never indulge in the luxury of a paschal lamb, but in 1588, when they were in the Taxco region, they had a goat instead. One of Jorge de Almeida's servants slaughtered the animal. Doña Francisca took its blood, smeared it on the doorposts of her room, as well as Isabel's and Catalina's, and gathered the family—except Miguel, who was away at school—for a festive meal. An Indian girl named Beatriz prepared the bitter herbs. The family ate standing, staff in hand; they devoured the entire goat and wrapped the animal's bones in a cloth.[50]

Unaware of rabbinic practice, the family developed its own version of the unleavened bread. It was either the flat bread Isabel made in Pánuco, or corn pancakes or tortillas. In Mexico City, Catalina baked her own more traditional unleavened bread "with water and salt and nothing else."[51] But later in the Taxco region the family preferred to eat tortillas.

There is no evidence that Luis or his family observed any of the other holy days of Judaism, including the New Year and the Feast of Tabernacles.

For all their religious zeal, Luis and his family did not gather for daily devotions, though on Sundays, and possibly on other occasions such as fast days, some members of the family were in the habit of reciting the penitential psalms. The family's religious gatherings were reserved for the Sabbath and the handful of other holy occasions honored by the Judaizers.[52]

On these occasions the family and its Judaizing guests joined in the recitation of an artfully improvised liturgy that bore only occasional resemblance to that of traditional Judaism.

The service was conducted in Latin by Luis or Baltasar, or, in their absence, by Isabel or Mariana. The only Hebrew it contained was possibly the *Shema' Yisrael* and its response. Spanish was used for special prayers and explanations of various lections.[53]

The service began with the recitation of Psalms 51:17, "O Lord, open Thou my lips;/And my mouth shall declare Thy praise," which in the traditional Jewish liturgy begins the silent recitation of the set of benedictions known as the Amidah. Similarly familiar notes in strange contexts were sounded throughout the worship.

The reader proceeded, "Comprehend me, O Lord, in Thy help, and forget not to help me," and the family continued, "Lord of the world, I come before Thee to pour forth my soul with a sacrifice of prayers, entreaties, cries, and petitions. I come to pour it forth before Thee for tokens of mercy and to ask Thy compassion."[54] The core of the service came from the psalms, mostly chosen from books of Catholic devotions. The Sabbath worship included Psalm 148: "Hallelujah./Praise ye the Lord from the heavens," Psalm 103 (102 in the Vulgate): "Bless the Lord, O my soul;/And all that is within me, bless His holy name," and the Sabbath psalm (Psalm 92, Vulgate 91): "It is a good thing to give thanks unto the Lord,/And to sing praises unto Thy name, O Most High." One of Isabel's favorites was Psalm 121: "I will lift up mine eyes unto the mountains:/From whence shall my help come?"[55]

To these psalms were added various prayers, constructed mainly from biblical books and original compositions, like Dr. Morales's long penitential poem.[56]

Additionally, the service contained paraphrases from the Bible in Spanish and lections in Latin, often accompanied by explanations in the vernacular.[57]

The Carvajals' liturgy stressed the cardinal ideals of the Judaizers: the oneness of God, the perfection of the Law of Moses and the salvation it offers to believers, the election of the Jewish people, and the belief in the future coming of the prophets Elijah and Enoch to prepare the way for the Messiah. The Carvajals fervently recited the section of Fourth Ezra that spoke of "the signs which the angel Uriel had revealed to the prophet, and how women would bear children after six months, and how they would speak and prophesy things which would happen, and then the Messiah would come."

The Judaizers' service apparently ended with the prayer "Gather us together from all the nations to manifest Thy Law and proclaim Thy name."[58]

On the Great Day, Catalina recited a prayer that began, "Enlighten me, O Lord, and do not hide Thy holy countenance. May I regard myself and recognize Thee. Grant me grace that I may confess my faults and sins. I am a woman, lowly and abject, a worm of earth." The family prayed, "Lord of the world, I come before Thee to pour forth my soul with a sacrifice of prayers, entreaties, cries, and petitions. I come to pour out my soul before Thee for compassion and to ask Thy mercy." And after privately confessing their sins, they entreated, "O Lord, give us decrees of pardon and salvation for our souls."[59] Another prayer, brought over from Europe, began, "Incline Thine eyes, O Lord, and hear me, because I am poor and needy. Preserve my soul, O my God, for to Thee, O Lord, is it offered. Save this Thy servant, O my God, for unto Thee, O Lord is she [or he] offered."[60]

The Judaizers stood facing the east for much or most of their service. They often kneeled, especially on the Great Day.[61] The service had its music, but apparently it was never written down. Prayers were intoned and hymns were sung, occasionally even to the accompaniment of a musical instrument, like Machado's clavichord.

At home the family carefully observed the Judaizers' dietary prescriptions. They ate only permitted foods. They slaughtered their animals in accordance with their hallowed customs and cut away the fat and the veins of the animal's thigh, the *landrecilla*, as they called it. To avoid suspicion, they had lard on hand to use in preparing food for non-Judaizing guests.[62]

The family, Luis included, regularly went to mass and confession to keep up appearances, but in church they tried to avoid every possible expression and gesture at variance with their beliefs. Still, as Catalina said, they had great difficulty repressing their feelings of guilt for attending church. In the confessional the members of the family were deliberately vague.[63] When they recited the psalms in church they affirmed their Jewishness by refraining from concluding with the formula "In the name of the Father, Son, and Holy Ghost, Amen."[64]

Despite their voluntary identification with secret Judaism, Luis's brothers-in-law engaged in few Judaizing practices at home. In public they gave the impression of indomitable opposition to everything the secret Jews stood for. Both Almeida and Díaz de Cáceres worked on most Sabbaths and holidays and conspicuously ate forbidden foods, even at home.[65] To suggest correct observance Isabel once sent Jorge de Almeida a chicken slaughtered according to the ritual of the secret Jews.[66] Yet there were times when the brothers-in-law joined the family for prayer and fasting. Almeida observed the Great Day at least once in Taxco. And on the Great Day of 1588, Antonio Díaz de Cáceres joined Mariana, Catalina, Anica, and Francisco Jorge, who had recently come from Spain, in the observance of the fast.

One person outside the family circle managed to obtain an intimate view of the Carvajals' Judaizing. He was Francisco Díaz, an educated New Christian who came to work for Jorge de Almeida in the Taxco mining region. When Isabel and Luis met Francisco Díaz they were sufficiently impressed to regard him as an excellent prospect for their circle of Judaizers. Luis lent him two books in Spanish. One of them was *The Mirror of Consolation*. The other was apparently a Bible, for Díaz reported that it contained accounts of the Israelite kings and the miracles that God had performed for the Jews.

One day Isabel came to visit Díaz in the mines, bringing along a book of hours that she intended to lend him. She asked whether he would like to have the book, and he said he would, except that he could not read Latin. Isabel said that that did not matter. Turning to a certain page, she handed the book to him and told him that if he would pronounce the words, she would explain their meaning. When Díaz asked what it was that he was about to read, Isabel replied that he was going to read from the psalms of David, for there was no purpose to reading the rest of the material in the book. She counseled him to reread the psalms frequently, because "they were very good," and he would eventually understand them.

Shortly after his conversation with Isabel, Francisco Díaz was promoted to superintendent of the mining works.

Díaz soon had an unusual opportunity to learn of the Carvajals' observance of the Sabbath. One Saturday Jorge de Almeida sent a slave to Díaz for a beating, and the superintendent proceeded to administer it. Hearing the cries of the slave, the Carvajals came running out of their quarters and told Díaz to stop the flogging immediately. When Díaz rejected their demands, explaining that he was following orders, Doña Isabel and her sisters were so angry that they refused to speak to him for several days. Perplexed, Díaz asked little Miguel, then eleven years old, why his sisters had become so excited. Miguel explained that it was because he was meting out the punishment on a Sabbath.

If Díaz still had any doubts that the family was Judaizing, these were completely removed when Baltasar took him aside and reviewed with him the fundamentals of the faith of the secret Jews.

Gradually the relations between Díaz and the Carvajals improved to the point where he was invited to pray with them. The family even gave him a copy of their prayer book written out by Miguel. Díaz had had the prayer book for only a short time when Almeida surprised him one day with the book open and confiscated it after he recognized Miguel's handwriting. Almeida clearly did not approve of his family's proselytization.

Isabel begged Díaz not to tell her brother-in-law anything about his relationship with the rest of the family. She also urged him not to work on the Sabbath. Luis then began a systematic effort to convert Díaz wholly to Judaism by lending him more books and giving him lessons on Jewish history and beliefs. Díaz soon began to participate in a number of the Judaizers' rituals, though later, when haled before the Inquisition, he said that he did so only to deceive the Carvajals and that he remained a good Christian at heart.[67]

By the end of 1588, doubtless before the family returned from the Taxco region, Luis and Baltasar had determined to take them out of New Spain. The family's continuing problems with Governor Carvajal and the rising threat of the Inquisition made New Spain an increasingly undesirable home.

Luis and Baltasar were troubled about the thought of leaving Gaspar behind. It is likely that they were not convinced that he had fully renounced his Jewish identity. Besides, they knew that the family's escape might place Gaspar in an impossible predicament. The priest's reluctance to denounce Isabel or his father to the Inquisition would greatly compromise his position should any word of their Judaizing leak out. So would his failure to report his suspicions about the rest of the family.

Luis and Baltasar therefore decided to test the strength of Gaspar's allegiance to Christianity, with the obvious hope of wooing him into the Judaizers' camp. They communicated their plan to Doña Francisca, in the presence of Catalina, Isabel, and Miguel. Doña Francisca told them to be very careful and "not to enter where there was no exit."[68]

Baltasar decided to take the first step on one of his trips from the Taxco region to Mexico City. He stopped at the Monastery of Santo Domingo to see Gaspar. In the course of the ensuing conversation, he asked Gaspar to take confession from him. Gaspar demurred and offered to have someone else hear him. Baltasar would have no other confessor. He explained "that he had to take confession with him, for with his brother he would dare to say everything that was on his conscience." But, he added, "since he did not wish to take confession from him, he would put his cause in the hands of God, may He be blessed, since he found no help in his own brother."

Gaspar, somewhat taken aback, asked Baltasar what he should do. Baltasar answered that "he would come back to take confession with him, and that then he would see how much he had suffered and gone through in the past four or five years, carrying a hard lump in his stomach that he has been unable to digest." Gaspar, taking the bait, asked him, "What lump is that?" Baltasar answered, "Let me give you an example. Suppose right now a Moor should ask you the reason why one had to believe that the law of Christ was the true law and not his Mohammedan law, what would you answer him?" Gaspar said that he would answer that "one is the Law of God and the other the law of the devil." Then Baltasar retorted, "But the Moor could say the same thing." Gaspar, now realizing what his brother was driving at, exclaimed, "So that's the way you are letting me know your evil intent!" To which Baltasar simply replied, "Why, I haven't said anything here, except that I have a stomachache."

That afternoon the persevering Baltasar came back and again asked his brother to hear his confession. Gaspar refused again, suggesting that it hurt him to do so. "It seems that it does," said Baltasar. "Let's drop it." And he went away.[69]

Shortly thereafter, in December 1588 or January 1589, Baltasar paid another visit to Gaspar. This time he was accompanied by Luis. The brothers sat and chatted in Gaspar's room, illumined by the golden rays of the late sun that streamed through the window. As the conversation developed Luis found an opportune moment to pose a typical leading question. In a tone of innocence he asked the monk whether it was true that God had given the Law to Moses with His own hand. When Gaspar naturally answered yes, Luis responded, "Well, isn't that the Law that we must keep?"

Incensed by the obvious direction of his brother's remarks, the friar sprang up from his seat and said, "No, that's the practice of the devil."

Gaspar proceeded to give a sermonic explanation for his outburst. He offered his brothers the parable of a king who donned a cloak of new coarse cloth and then, after it had become worn, he gave it to a page. It was still a royal cloak, though the king had put it aside and was going to put on a new one. So too the old Mosaic Law had been superseded, he went on to explain. "Though it belonged to God, it had ceased with the law of grace, which was the law of the Gospels."

Baltasar responded in kind. Pointing to the window, he said with inspiration, "This cloak of the heavens and this shining sun, which God created, have they changed, have they perchance grown old?"

"No," replied the priest.

"So," retorted his brother, "there has been even less change in God's incorruptible and holy Law and in His work, and there will be less yet. We hear this affirmed by your own preachers and scholars. And in the Gospels you declare that your crucified one said, 'Do not think that I am come to remove the Law or the prophets, for their prophecies are holy and true.' Rather he said this: 'It is certainly easier for heaven and earth to be lacking than for one jot or tittle of this holy Law to be lacking or change.'"

Gaspar countered with a parable about a silversmith or goldsmith, who begins his work on a piece of metal with coarse instruments and brings it to completion with the most refined. So too had God done, said Gaspar. After giving the Law of Moses he perfected it with the coming of Jesus and the giving of the evangelical law. With this new law, declared Gaspar, the effectiveness of "the rites and ceremonies of the Old Testament had ceased."

"There is no need to discuss your old iron tools," Luis and Baltasar

The Monastery of Santo Domingo, Mexico City

both responded, as if they did not understand what Gaspar was saying.[70]

Apparently at this point Baltasar asked Gaspar a question about the biblical verse "Thou hast ascended on high,/Thou hast led captivity captive," and a second verse stating "God is gone up amidst shouting." Gaspar responded by explaining that these verses referred to "the mystery of the ascension of our Lord Jesus Christ and how by his ascension to heaven the Holy Spirit came upon us." The verses, explained Gaspar, came from the psalms of David. At this point Baltasar gave his brother ample opportunity to deal with one of the cardinal differences between Judaism and Christianity, again with the Judaizers' typical display of innocence. He asked, regarding King David, the author of the psalms, "Do you mean he deals with the Messiah in this psalm?" "Yes," said Gaspar, "and the heavens, the earth, and the sun are good witnesses."[71]

Baltasar appears to have challenged this interpretation. He was cut short by the priest, who said, "Let us not talk about this anymore." He then added, "Blessed be God, who took me out from among you."

His brothers on either side responded with their own blessing, "Be Thou glorified, our God and Lord, who hast not left us in blindness and perdition like this wretch."

Gaspar retorted by saying that he considered his lot happier than theirs. And, clearly referring to the success of Christianity, he quoted the psalm speaking of God's glorious deeds and saying, "He hath not dealt so with any nation."[72]

Then, putting down his Bible, Gaspar picked up a book of epistles by one of the saints of his order—Luis believed it was Saint Vincent—and said, "Let us leave this conversation and read these epistles, which are very devout." Gaspar read from the book until the bells tolled for compline, at which the brothers parted. Gaspar said, "May God pardon us," and Luis answered, "Amen."[73]

Not long afterward, while the unusual conversation in Gaspar's chamber was still fresh in his mind, Luis came up with a daring suggestion that he hoped would bring Gaspar over to the Judaizers' camp. He proposed that after a certain period of study and preparation, Baltasar and Gaspar meet for a private disputation on the merits of their respective faiths, with the one acknowledging defeat to accept the religion of the other. The disputation did not take place. According to Luis, Gaspar at first agreed but then had a change of heart, saying that he could not go through with the debate because he was a cleric, and that his religion forbade him to investigate or discuss principles of faith.[74]

According to Catalina, Baltasar came for the debate, accompanied by Luis, and found Gaspar convulsed with pain and his face all scratched. The priest refused to listen to his brothers. He even angrily told them that "were it not for the love of his mother and, his position as a Dominican he would have done something terrible to them." Baltasar and Luis told Gaspar that their father had died a Jew. To this Gaspar replied, "If I knew that, I would exhume his bones and burn them in this very square."[75]

Gaspar's side of the story is not recorded. What is known is that Baltasar and Luis abandoned their efforts to convert Gaspar and turned all their energies to planning the escape of the rest of the family from New Spain.

Even before Luis and Baltasar had begun planning the conversion of their cleric brother, Isabel, mindful of her promise to Doña Guiomar, had attempted to convert her relative, Governor Carvajal's adjutant, Captain Felipe Núñez.

One day, around Chistmas 1586, the captain visited the Carvajals and had dinner with the family. Isabel took the captain aside and in her own inimitable way asked him what his real religion was. Apparently shocked that anyone should even dare to pose such a question, Captain Núñez proclaimed, with pompous defensiveness, "I hold the faith of Christ our redeemer and plan to die in it as my parents did."

And when Isabel countered by saying that this was not a good faith, the captain indignantly retorted, "What! You are telling me that?"

Isabel, pressing the attack, went on to say that the Christ or Messiah had not yet come, and that she and her family were still expecting the Messiah, "the one the Christians called the Antichrist, to come and save them." She even told Núñez that her father had taught this to the entire family except Fray Gaspar.

Flushed with anger, Núñez replied, "Be careful of what you say, because I believe in Jesus Christ our Lord, who came to the world born of the holy Virgin Mary, died, and was resurrected for our salvation."

Realizing that she could not budge the captain from his beliefs, Isabel began to fear that he might in anger denounce her to the Inquisition. She therefore changed her tune and said, "You believed me, didn't you? Why, I was just joking. I said what I did to see how steadfast your faith was. And I am delighted to see that you feel so strongly about it. But don't say a word about our conversation to anyone."[76]

The captain left the Carvajal home troubled and confused. He was cognizant of his responsibility to denounce Isabel before the Inquisition, but he was certainly also aware of what this might mean to Governor Carvajal's career.

Regardless of how hard he may have tried, Felipe Núñez could not have succeeded in repressing these thoughts for long. When he was recuperating from illness in Mexico City a few months after his conversation with Isabel, Isabel or her mother sent him some chickens, which he recognized as having been ritually slaughtered according to the prescriptions followed by the secret Jews.[77]

Núñez again decided not to denounce the family. He returned to the governor's side without saying a word to the Inquisition.

By the time of the final meeting between Baltasar, Luis, and Gaspar, the viceroy had arrested Governor Carvajal. The family could not have failed to realize how deeply the governor's downfall struck at their own security, if for no other reason than that in anger or in fear he might disclose what he knew about their Judaizing.

In an apparent effort to avoid the effects of the governor's displeasure, the family now attempted to reestablish peaceable relations with him by sending him a gift. The present, consisting of money, preserves, and sweetmeats, was taken to the Royal Prison by Luis and Baltasar. But the governor rejected the olive branch. The other prisoners witnessed a loud argument, which came to an end when the governor ordered his nephews to leave. In a later recollection of the scene, the older Luis implied that if he had not been confined to his cell, he would have thrown his nephews out of the jail bodily.

The governor refused all subsequent offers of help from his sister and her family, though they went so far as to ask to do his laundry. When word reached him that the family was complaining about his refusal of everything they offered, he sent his nephews a letter mentioning the one item he was willing to take. He demanded that they pay him the "two or three thousand pesos for wines and salt that your father and mother pilfered from me."[78]

Word that the governor had been arrested and was in need of help reached Captain Felipe Núñez in the New Kingdom of León in January or February 1589, and soon thereafter the governor's faithful lieutenant appeared in Mexico City to be of service. Before leaving the capital, Núñez decided that it would be best for him to make a full disclosure of his experience with Isabel to the Inquisition. What prompted this decision is not known. It certainly did not help to further the governor's cause, but it did permit Felipe Núñez to retain his freedom.

On the afternoon of March 7, 1589, Felipe Núñez appeared before an inquisitor, Licentiate Santos García, and took depositions "to clear his conscience." After explaining that he was on his way to the civil jail to take some food to the governor, he proceeded to disclose his long acquaintance with Doña Francisca and her family and detailed Isabel's attempts to convert him. He made it a point to assert that "he had always seen the governor living like an exemplary Christian."[79]

Six days later Isabel was arrested.

Isabel's arrest made it dramatically clear that the entire family was in danger. It stunned Gaspar and drove him to visit his uncle in the Royal Prison. His conscience, Gaspar later explained, "was troubling him as to whether, in view of the paucity of possible witnesses, he had the obligation of informing the Inquisition about his suspicions." At the same time he rationalized weakly that "he did not know anything certain that he might say."

Since Gaspar was fully aware that he was under obligation to inform the Inquisition and that Governor Carvajal was in an identical position, the purpose of his visit was likely to lay the primary responsibility for denouncing the family upon his uncle. If arrested, he would then have a plausible alibi for failing to inform on his family: he could blame the governor for withholding the denunciations and then discussing the family's problem with him in terms too vague to be understood.

In the prison Gaspar asked the governor to recall their conversation at the entrance of the church in Xilitla or Acatlán to determine if its substance "was such that it fell under the jurisdiction of the Holy Office." The governor, evasive as ever, replied that he knew what he had to do. Since the governor knew some canon law, he began to argue with Gaspar over the question of whether there was an obligation in disclosing what was secret. When Gaspar insisted that there was, the governor adamantly reiterated that he knew what he had to do. The governor then told Gaspar to go to his mother, Francisca, and inform her on his behalf that everything he had told them in Pánuco was very much the truth. Calling his entire family blind in matters of faith, Don Luis then confessed that if he brought Gaspar's parents from Spain to the New World, "it was because he had understood that his father wanted to move his family to foreign lands, which he took to mean France."[80]

When he left the prison, Gaspar went to his family's home and reported the governor's remarks to his mother. Doña Francisca did not like her brother's statements and said so to Gaspar. In the course of her conversation with Gaspar, his mother insisted that his sisters were simple, pious women. Though Isabel and Mariana knew the psalms, there was nothing wrong with either of them, said Doña Francisca. She believed that both "followed the way of our Lord Jesus Christ." Doña Francisca suggested that Gaspar live in the house awhile to see if there was anything amiss.

Little Ana had apparently come into the room during the conversation. Doña Francisca asked her to leave. Then, turning to Gaspar, Doña Francisca made the kind of confession that the priest never wanted to hear. "I am traveling on as good a road as yours," she said, and then added, "or better." Scandalized, Gaspar repeated, "So you are traveling on a better road than I." Doña Francisca said nothing.

Regaining her composure, Doña Francisca tried to console Gaspar for his sister's arrest. Without attributing it in the slightest to Judaizing, she told him that though the arrest impaired the family's honor, it was only worldly honor that was involved, while the service of God, which presumably Isabel was innocently working for, was the only source of permanent honor. She implied that a trumped-up charge had brought about Isabel's arrest and might just as easily have occasioned her own. In fact, she hinted that she might be arrested in just this way and was ready for it. She then begged her son to hold some money for her in the event of her own arrest, and to use it to support his sisters. Gaspar, aware of what lay behind his mother's pretense of innocence and eager to avoid further involvement with the Inquisition, said that such a precaution would not be necessary.[81]

Two or three days later Gaspar returned to the Royal Prison and again told his uncle to consider whether the matter they had spoken of should be brought to the Inquisition's attention. The governor offered Gaspar a lame explanation, but one sufficient to render further discussion meaningless.[82]

Isabel's arrest drove the entire family into confusion. They, of course, had no idea of the exact charges that led to the incarceration. Nor did they have any way of determining either how much evidence the Inquisition had marshaled against Isabel or what the sources of this evidence were. But Doña Francisca, Luis, and Baltasar placed the blame squarely on Governor Carvajal.

Doña Francisca and the Judaizers among her children began to recite psalms and utter prayers for Isabel's release. Gaspar, visibly saddened, refused to get involved in a discussion of Isabel's arrest. He contented himself with saying piously that if wrongdoing was involved it was the will of God, who did not want human souls to go to perdition, and if there was not, the experience would redound to the sufferer's merit.

Almeida and Díaz de Cáceres were not inclined to express themselves as theologically as the cleric. They pulled their beards in grief. Utterly ignoring their own descent, they even made derogatory references to the family's New Christian origins.[83] Díaz de Cáceres warned the family "to be careful not to implicate him in anything, for if they did blame him, they would be left without their shelter and support." He also advised everyone to say nothing and, if called by the Inquisition, to deny everything. He told Catalina that his mother and his brother, Enrique Díaz, had been arrested by the Inquisition in Lisbon and had managed to escape by unflinchingly protesting their innocence.[84] At the same time, on March 20, a week after Isabel's arrest, Jorge de Almeida took fifty pesos to the Inquisition's prison and established an account "for the food and comfort" of his sister-in-law. In May, Isabel was already receiving such luxuries as orange preserves, almonds, and soap.[85]

Later, after the arrest of other members of the family, Almeida urged Manuel de Lucena's mother-in-law to exert her influence in preventing Judaizers from denouncing each other to the Inquisition. "Madam," he said, "let no one accuse another before the Holy Office. Let each one pay for his own sin."[86]

After Isabel's arrest Almeida put Leonor in charge of the household. He told his young wife to "take care of the house and serve him . . . keeping it clean, cooking his meals, and preparing his shirts." He also told her to be sure to prepare his dishes with ham or bacon.[87] Leonor apparently did not manage very successfully, for Doña Francisca soon moved in with the Almeidas. However, Doña Francisca did not remain very long with her ambivalent son-in-law. Almeida made life so miserable for her that she found it necessary to move to new quarters by Canal Gate, near the Great Square.[88]

On the basis of Isabel's testimony Governor Luis de Carvajal was arrested by the Inquisition on Friday, April 14, and transferred from the Royal Prison to the inquisitorial jail.[89] Earlier that day, at seven o'clock in the morning, the Inquisition had arrested Fray Gaspar on the charge that he was a "cooperator with his . . . sister, and, knowing that she was a Jewess, he did not denounce or reveal her." The arrest had been carried out at that hour by Fray Bartolomé de Nieva, vicar and provincial of the Dominican Order, to minimize the embarrass-

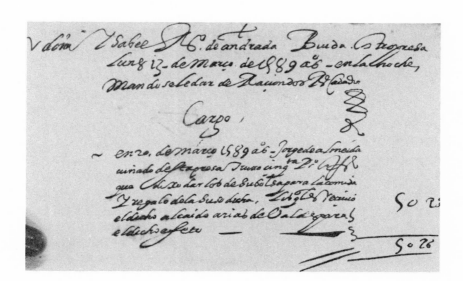

The Inquisition's Record of Jorge de Almeida's Deposit of Fifty Pesos
for His Sister-in-law Isabel

Partial List of Isabel's Special Rations

ment to the Dominicans and the Inquisition that might be caused by the fact that Gaspar was a Dominican friar.[90]

It was less than a month later, on Tuesday, May 9, that Luis de Carvajal the Younger was apprehended, along with his mother, and dragged to the inquisitorial jail.[91]

7 The Holy Office

The Inquisition did not operate on caprice. Stringent regulations governed every step of its procedure, from the gathering of evidence against a suspect to the final disposition of his case. These regulations, called instructions, had been accumulating for over a century. In 1484, Tomás de Torquemada, the notorious first president of the Council of the Holy Office in Spain, promulgated a set of ordinances to be followed by every officer of the Inquisition from the grand inquisitor to his lowliest myrmidons. He revised them the following year and again in 1498. Torquemada's successor, Fray Diego de Deza, prepared a new set of regulations in 1500. In 1561 there was a definitive redaction of the Inquisition's instructions in the form of a meticulously detailed compendium in eighty-one sections "intended for all the kingdoms and dominions of Spain." It left little to chance and the inquisitors' judgment.[1]

The Inquisitions in Latin America were still further encumbered. When they were established, the inquisitor-general, Cardinal Diego de Espinosa, sent them additional instructions. These regulated a diversity of matters, including the maintenance of records, the appointment of subordinate officials, the time of day for audiences, and the referral to Spain of any case the colonial inquisitors might find too difficult to adjudicate.[2]

When he reached Flat House on that fateful May evening of his arrest, Luis de Carvajal the Younger was haled for a brief interview before the inquisitors, Dr. Hernández Bonilla and Santos García, both formerly prosecuting attorneys for the Holy Office. They in turn delivered him to their warden, Arias de Valdés, for confinement down-

The House of the Inquisition, Mexico City

stairs in what were known as the "secret cells." These constituted the maximum security compound reserved for suspected heretics. Luis was stripped and found to be carrying seven and a half reals, and some small pieces of silver, worth eight reals more. Arias de Valdés took this money and credited it to Luis's account.[3] The Holy Office would use the money and any other cash or property belonging to the prisoner that might turn up to pay for his room and board in jail and the expenses of his trial.

Luis described his new home as a "dark and gloomy prison."[4] His cell was heatless and lacked illumination, except for a candle permitted to burn only between seven o'clock in the morning and four in the afternoon. He was allowed no contact with the outside world—no visitors, no mail in or out, no books, not even any writing paper on which to preserve a prayer or poem or just fragments of his thought. If he did not die before, the cell would be his home until the end of his trial. He could leave temporarily only if he went to an audience with the inquisitors or if he was taken into an inner courtyard under heavy guard on the Saturdays when the cells were cleaned and prepared for inspection.[5]

From the Inquisition's perspective, the isolation of the prisoner was eminently practical. It prevented him from receiving advice from friends and relatives on how best to conduct his defense. It blocked him

The Licentiate Santos García

from revealing what was happening to him and what information the Inquisition might have about others. Besides, it served as a powerful psychological device, stimulating a prisoner's anxieties and shattering his defenses.

Lacking any comforting distraction, the prisoner had little alternative but to occupy his time ruminating on his arrest and its implications.

He could reflect on the trial that lay ahead of him. He knew that the inquisitorial court was not renowned for impartiality in meting out justice. Its two judges, the inquisitors, worked in close alliance with the prosecuting attorney, and the prisoner was permitted no effective counsel in the conduct of his defense. In the course of the trial the inquisitors would permit the accused to have a defense attorney, but the attorney would invariably be a member of the inquisitorial staff. He would be permitted no private audiences with his client and would be strictly forbidden to plan his client's defense or even volunteer information on his behalf. He would not even be allowed to take a transcript of the testimony outside the audience chamber. His chief if not sole function was to bring the prisoner to a full disclosure of his malefactions. The inquisitorial instructions on this point could not have been clearer: "The inquisitor or inquisitors will advise the prisoner how important it is for him to tell the truth. Having done so, they will name for his defense the attorney or attorneys who have been designated for this purpose."[6] Attorneys who pursued their clients' defense too zealously might fall into the net of suspicion themselves. Not infrequently defense counsels withdrew from a case the moment they realized they could not wring a confession from their clients.

Most prisoners were prepared for three cardinal events in their trials. The first was the inquisitors' reading of a prisoner's indictment, or, as it was called, his accusation. This did not take place at the beginning of the trial, but only after the inquisitors had exhausted every effort short of torture to make him volunteer the reason for his incarceration and the catalog of his crimes. The second was a trip, or a series of trips, to the torture chamber. This took place if the inquisitors were persuaded that the prisoner, after responding to the accusation and then to the publication of witnesses against him, was withholding pertinent information about himself or others. He could be sentenced to torture *in caput proprium*, to make disclosures about himself, or *in caput alienum*, to reveal information about others. A prisoner could avoid the torture chamber by persuading the inquisitors that his testimony was complete. The third step was the handing down of the sentence against him in a special ceremony known as the "act of (the) faith," the auto-da-fé.[7]

At the very beginning of his trial the prisoner faced a serious dilemma. He had no way of knowing who had denounced him, what information the Inquisition had amassed about him, or which of his friends and relatives were under its surveillance and in danger of arrest. Eventually he might be able to infer the answers to these questions from the accusation and the testimony published against him. Although the Inquisition would conceal the names of all witnesses, alluding to them as "a certain person" or "a certain relative," the context of the charges would reveal their identity in most cases.

But in the early phases of the trial, when the inquisitors would try to wring confessions from him, the prisoner realized that if he volunteered information he might reveal more than the Inquisition knew. He might further incriminate himself or unnecessarily involve others. As a result, most arrested Judaizers decided to remain "negative" until the delivery of the accusation. This meant that they would repeatedly deny any offenses against the Catholic faith and reveal no information that might be of help to the inquisitors.

The Carvajals were no exception.

Luis's first audience took place on the afternoon of May 12, two and a half days after his arrest. As was its custom with all trials, the

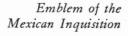

*Emblem of the
Mexican Inquisition*

Inquisition had a scribe in the audience chamber to record every detail of the proceedings of each hearing; the questions, the answers, and any extraordinary occurrence, including a prisoner's sighs and groans were taken down.

Responding to the inquisitors' routine opening questions, Luis accurately stated his name, age, marital status, birth date, occupation, and some facts about his relatives. But he declined to admit that he was of New Christian stock. "As far as I have heard," he said, "I come from Old Christians, without trace of Moors, Jews, or any other group." He also refused to volunteer a reason for his imprisonment, though he did offer a guess. "I imagine that my troubles are due to my uncle Luis de Carvajal," he said, explaining that the governor, "almost a mortal enemy," had brought the family to the New World under false pretenses and had been feuding with them ever since. "If it was not the governor," Luis added, "then some other enemy must have falsely testified against me."[8]

Aware of the nature of Luis's gambit, the inquisitors responded, as expected, with the first of three admonitions customarily given to reticent prisoners before the presentation of the indictment against them. They reminded Luis that "in the Holy Office of the Inquisition it is not customary to arrest anyone without ample evidence of his having done or said, or heard others doing or saying, something, whether pertaining to the old Mosaic Law of the Jews, or to the sects of Mohammed and Luther, which is, or appears to be, opposed to the holy Catholic faith. Since you are arrested," they went on to say, "you should realize that there is an accumulation of this type of incriminating evidence against you. You are therefore admonished to unburden your conscience and disclose the truth. If you do so you will earn an opportunity for the mercy the Holy Office is accustomed to show to those making proper and correct confessions." Then they warned, "If you do not, know that justice will be done to you."

Luis returned a studied reply. "I fully understand what I have been told and admonished," he said, "but I have committed nothing against the holy Catholic faith either in word or in deed, and I cannot confess to having done so." Then, as if in afterthought, he again pinned the blame on his uncle. "It is possible," he said, "due to my great sins, that someone, maybe my uncle in his mortal anger, has falsely testified against me."[9]

Temporarily thwarted in their probe of his heresy, the inquisitors turned to an investigation of Luis's finances, another subject that Luis was not interested in discussing. When the inquisitors asked what resources he possessed, Luis decided to throw them a bone, apparently hoping it might dissuade them from further investigation. He said that he owned nothing: his merchandise belonged to his mother and Baltasar. But he had recently deposited some five hundred pesos with Cristóbal Gómez in Mexico City, the proceeds from the last business trip he and his brother had taken. They had gone to the mines of Pachuca, and he had seen Manuel de Lucena as recently as ten days before.

Luis had doubtless expected Gómez and Lucena to corroborate his alibi. Yet for some unexplained reason, perhaps fear of the Inquisition or failure to get their signals straight, neither did. Called before the inquisitors, Lucena stated that he had not seen Luis in over a month. For his part, Gómez revealed that he owed the Carvajals seven hundred pesos instead of five. This discrepancy would not have been too serious had Gómez not gone on to say that the sum represented the balance that he owed Luis and Baltasar for the purchase of a quantity of silver. The inquisitors ordered Gómez to pay his debt directly to the Holy Office. He brought in four hundred pesos on June 2, 1589, and the balance five months later.[10]

In the course of this interrogation, Luis wrapped another fact in a fabrication. He declared (incorrectly) that his recent absence from the city began as an errand for Almeida and (correctly) that it ended in his flight with Baltasar to Veracruz when they heard of their uncle's arrest.

On hearing that Baltasar was in Veracruz, the inquisitors immediately contacted Francisco López Rebolledo, their commissary there, and his lieutenant, Juan de Villaseca, informing them of the wanted man's presence and ordering his immediate arrest.[11] When López Rebolledo and Villaseca failed to locate Baltasar, the Inquisition concluded that Luis had lied again, and three days later gave him a second admonition.[12]

Except for one brief hearing where he was asked for additional information on his stay with his brother in Veracruz, Luis spent the next month immured in his cell while the inquisitors frantically but vainly searched for Baltasar.[13] They finally despaired of finding him and decided to wrest all possible information from Luis. On June 19 the inquisitors called their prisoner to interview and began plying him with pointed questions, which Luis proceeded to parry with consummate coolness.

"Have you recalled anything pertaining to your case?" the inquisitors asked. "If so, tell the truth. You are under oath."

"No," answered Luis, "and God knows I have nothing to recall and nothing to say. May my innocent suffering serve as remission for my sins."

"Why did you and your brother, Baltasar Rodríguez, absent yourselves from Mexico City when you did?" the inquisitors proceeded.

"For fear of Luis de Carvajal, my uncle," he said, "on account of his notorious hatred for us, especially for my brother." Then he added, "Since my brother had more to fear . . . he decided to remain in Veracruz, while I, with no reason to be afraid, came here to be with my mother."

"Why did this fear grip you after your uncle . . . was arrested by the Inquisition?" the inquisitors wanted to know.

"Because he is our mortal enemy . . . and we were afraid that he would concoct a false charge against us."

"Why should he be more inclined to do this after being arrested by the Inquisition than before?"

"Because he had more reason to do so once he was in the Inquisition."

"What additional reason did he have to bring a false charge against you after he was arrested by the Inquisition?" the inquisitors pressed on.

Refusing to budge, Luis calmly answered, "The fact that he was arrested and desired to see his enemies suffer like him."

The inquisitors tried again. "What in particular were you afraid he would falsely accuse you of?"

And Luis held firm. "We were not afraid of anything except his hatred."

At this point the inquisitors exclaimed bluntly, "Answer to the point, for your answer is obviously unsatisfactory. In view of the hatred you allege, you could have been just as afraid before he was arrested [by the Inquisition]."

Luis replied with equal bluntness. "I have answered what I had to answer," and he added what he knew was an impossible request. "All I want now," he said, "is to see the person who made this charge, so that I could prove my innocence."

The inquisitors, clearly near exasperation, decided to try again. "Since the immediate cause for your flight was the Inquisition's arrest of your uncle, the governor, what were you suddenly afraid of?" they asked.

"Nothing, in God's name," said Luis. "I just took note of it and returned to my mother's house."

"Why do you imagine that your uncle . . . was arrested by the Inquisition?"

"I cannot imagine and I have no idea," said Luis; and then, to keep the inquiry from focusing on the question of Judaism, he added, "though here in Mexico City I did hear my brother Baltasar Rodríguez say that the Inquisition probably arrested him for his own good, to get him out of the hands of the viceroy."

But the inquisitors would not be deterred. "If that is the case, what inspired you with fear that he would present a false charge against you once he was arrested by the Inquisition?"

"It was merely fear of his hatred," said Luis in refrain.

The inquisitors, frustrated, resorted to a threat. "There is a contradiction in your testimony," they warned. "Correct your confession and tell the truth."

"We knew nothing for certain," explained Luis. "We imagined it all. Then, as innocuously as possible he echoed the Inquisition's cant. "We also suspected that he might have been arrested for having done or said something against the faith, or having seen others do or say so, and then, in his affliction, he desired to take vengeance on me and my brother."

This was all the information the inquisitors managed to wring from Luis that day. They therefore gave him his third and final admonition and returned him to the solitude of his cell.[14]

In the meantime the Holy Office had been patiently preparing its case against Luis from testimony given by Isabel, Gaspar, and the governor.

Isabel, bordering on brilliance and instability, was not the easiest prisoner to manage. She began her audiences uneventfully with the usual categorical denial of her guilt, but then she moved to the unexpected. When the first admonition was delivered, she demanded to see the charges against her. She claimed that she was falsely betrayed and added histrionically, "I am a Christian. I do not care about the world, but only about my soul. This is my only concern, and I am not just mouthing this. I mean it."[15] Later that week, after her third admonition, she was even more dramatic. She threw herself at Inquisitor Bonilla's feet and cried that she would not leave the audience chamber until she had received a full pardon. The inquisitors ordered her to her feet. But no sooner did the Inquisition's attendants lift her to her feet than she began to tremble and fainted. It took a quarter of an hour to revive her.[16]

Nevertheless Isabel proved a welcome witness because of her willingness to talk about her brother Gaspar and especially about her uncle. Aware that her arrest jeopardized her mother and Luis, she played

Isabel de Carvajal under Torture (from El Libro Rojo)

down their involvement in Judaism and stressed her uncle's fault. Later, after her mother and Luis had been arrested, she softened her stand against Gaspar and her uncle, emphasizing that they were both good Christians. She even called her uncle "a servant of God."[17]

She did not learn Judaism from her family, said Isabel. She was taught first by her husband, Gabriel de Herrera, and then by her Aunt Guiomar in her home in Seville, where, she insisted, the family stayed for two months. In New Spain, complying with Guiomar's wishes, she had attempted unsuccessfully to convert her uncle and Felipe Núñez. These two and her brother Gaspar were well aware that she Judaized, said Isabel, and it was doubtless they who had denounced her.[18]

From these declarations and others made later by Isabel to resolve contradictions in her testimony, the Inquisition had gathered enough information to order the arrest of the governor and Gaspar.[19]

Gaspar's chief concern was to safeguard his position and prerogatives at all costs, even at the expense of the safety of his family. He lied or hedged only to preserve himself; otherwise he was scrupulously honest. He admitted that he came from New Christian stock, "though," he said in mitigation, "I have seen information suggesting Old Christian origins for my mother."[20] He confessed some of the things that aroused his anxiety—the presence of a Bible in the family home at Pánuco, his sister Isabel's dietary habits, the unusual knowledge of Bible that she and Mariana possessed, the governor's cryptic messages and conversations, Almeida's claim that Francisco Rodríguez de Matos had lived and died a Jew, and the discussions with his brothers in the Dominican monastery. But, contended Gaspar, at no time did he have any more than a vague suspicion that his family was Judaizing. He was consequently not certain whether he was obligated to bring the matter before the Inquisition. One of his confessors, Fray Andrés de Almaguer, said that his doubts did not bind him to denounce his family "because they are neither certain nor clear." He advised Gaspar "that he should be on guard to denounce them once he saw that they were."[21]

The inquisitors reacted adversely to Gaspar's defense, but eagerly accepted the testimony he offered against his family.

The governor adamantly insisted that he was an Old Christian, without "any racial strain of Jews or Moors or any other newly converted sect."[22] His defense was built on two points: the hostility of the members of the family and his own ignorance of the extent of their Judaizing. On April 17, in his initial audience, after receiving the first admonition, he gave his version of the incident with Isabel. Isabel, enraged, had uttered the words "There is no Christ," but nothing else that was objectionable. He had objurgated her accordingly, but was troubled by the thought that he might be obligated to report his niece to the Inquisition. He once shared this concern with a confessor, who told him to go to the Holy Office. And, said the governor, he was planning to do exactly this at the time of his arrest.[23] In the subsequent audience he admitted that because of Isabel, he had reason to suspect nearly everyone else in the family of some connection with Judaism. But, he insisted, he was by no means sure.[24]

The inquisitors were no more impressed by the governor's defense than by Gaspar's. They remanded him to his cell and, except for one audience, kept him there for three months until they were ready to present him with the accusation. The only time they called him, on April 27, they asked him to discuss the fleet in which he left New Spain and the passengers his ship was carrying.[25]

By early July the prosecutor, Dr. Lobo Guerrero, who appears later to have been rewarded for his efforts with the archbishopric of Lima, Peru,[26] was ready to present the Inquisition's formal indictments against the family. Doña Francisca was summoned to hear her accusation on July 5. Isabel, the governor, and Gaspar received theirs between July 20 and 24. Three days later it was Luis's turn. Since Luis was under the statutory age of twenty-five, the Inquisition named one of its attorneys, Gaspar de Valdés, as Luis's guardian. But Luis did not need a guardian to grasp the meaning of the eight-paragraph indictment or to be stunned by the scope of the Inquisition's intelligence against him. The indictment read as follows:

I, Dr. Lobo Guerrero, prosecutor of the Inquisition of Mexico City, the states and provinces of New Spain, by virtue of my position and in fulfillment of all requisite formalities, do criminally accuse Luis de Carvajal, an unmarried youth, merchant, native of Benavente in the realms of Castile, now resident in Mexico City, confined to the secret cells, who is present hereto, the son of Francisco Rodríguez de Matos, deceased, and Francisca Núñez, his wife, both Portuguese, born from New Christian stock descended from Jews:

(1) And I say that although the aforesaid was a Christian, baptized, confirmed, and enjoying the grace, privileges, and exemptions that other Christians are accustomed to and should enjoy, he has, contrary to what he professed in the sacrament of baptism, become a heretic and apostate from our Catholic faith, the evangelical law held, believed, preached, and taught by the holy mother church of Rome. And as a descendant of the Jews, indoctrinated and taught by them, he converted and passed over to

the old Law of Moses and its rites and ceremonies, believing he would find salvation therein, and that they had not ceased with the coming of our redeemer, Jesus Christ, because he was not the promised Messiah whom he was awaiting.

(2) Since washing a corpse before burial is a ceremony of the said Law, a certain person closely related to the said Luis de Carvajal [his father, Francisco Rodríguez de Matos], as a keeper and believer of the said Law, asked him, when he was about to die, to wash his body so that it should not be brought to the earth dirty, this in performance and observance of the said Law.

(3) In order the better to fulfill the obligations of the said Law and its observance, he has devoted himself to reading and is well read in the Old Testament and the Prophets [sic] whom he cites—especially Isaiah— whenever the occasion presents itself; though if he heeded and regarded his prophecies with the proper care and devotion he would clearly see that they have all been fulfilled in our Lord, Jesus Christ, the true Messiah; and the vain and perfidious hopes with which he miserably lives, believing that he has not come, would cease.

(4) And because of their suspicions that he held the said belief in the Law of the Jews, certain close relatives of the said Luis de Carvajal [Gaspar and the governor], either to see whether he was firm in it and its observance or for other reasons known to themselves, spoke to him and instructed him in the mysteries of the holy Trinity and the ascension to heaven of our Lord, Jesus Christ.

(5) With the said suspicions that he had about the said Luis de Carvajal and someone else no less suspicious [Baltasar] whom he brought with him [to the Dominican monastery], one of the said relatives of his household [Gaspar] in particular dealt with them about matters of the faith and the coming of our Lord Jesus Christ. He adduced the example of a silversmith who first works the silver with rough tools and then employs fine tools to perfect it; so too had God done in the synagogue, which He began making with material sacrifices—shadows and representations— and, afterwards, fulfilling the prophecies in Jesus Christ, He perfected them with his coming and death. To this both [Luis and Baltasar] responded, "There is no need to discuss your old iron tools," pretending they did not understand and confirming themselves in their false belief.

(6) Furthermore, on the same occasion and discussion of the coming and ascension of Jesus Christ and the psalms of David that deal with the matter, one of the two [Baltasar] responded—and the other [Luis] approved his response with his presence and authorized it with his consent— "So that psalm deals with the anointed one? The heaven, sun, and earth are witnesses." By this he meant that the said psalm did not speak of the anointed, Jesus Christ, our Lord, that he was not the Messiah, nor had he come, and that the heaven, sun, and earth were good witnesses thereto.

(7) Furthermore, as soon as he learned that his sister, Isabel de

Andrada, had been brought as a prisoner to the Holy Office, the said Luis de Carvajal, fearing arrest, fled and absented himself with Baltasar Rodríguez, his brother, to Veracruz. And to learn and scent how matters were going and to determine whether they should proceed with their flight or not, they returned to Mexico City. And his daring has been such that he has sought to deceive this holy tribunal with lies and deceits, for when he was asked about the said Baltasar Rodríguez, he said that he was in the mines of Pachuca, and when he was persuaded that he was lying he changed his statement and said that he was in Veracruz and that he [Luis] had been sent to Mexico City to inform him of what was going on, though this was not true nor did it happen this way, as it has been determined, for both left Veracruz together and started out for Mexico City.

(8) And he has committed other crimes of which I intend to accuse him during the prosecution of the case.

And although he has been admonished and warned under oath to tell the truth, he has not done so and has perjured himself, hiding the truth about himself and others, dead and alive, known to him to be Judaizers and believers in and observers of the said Law of Moses. Aware of the obligation he had to denounce and reveal them to the Holy Office, he has had dealings with them, though he should have avoided them like the excommunicated [who are] removed from the unity of the church. And like an abettor, receiver, and concealer of Jews, an accomplice and participant in the same crimes as they, he has hidden, favored, and concealed them, to the great hurt of his own conscience and the common good. This alone would have sufficed for him to become persuaded toward the observance and belief in the Law of Moses, if he had not previously been.

Dr. Lobo Guerrero accordingly asked that Luis de Carvajal be declared "a heretic, Judaizer, apostate from our holy Catholic faith" as well as a factor and concealer of Jews, and demanded the death penalty. If necessary, he said, the prisoner should also be put to torture to make him confess the entire truth.[27]

Inquisitorial practice required a prisoner to respond to the accusation immediately upon hearing it, before he could recover from the shock of its revelations and plan a solid defense. Luis's response was an almost endless skein of negations. He denied a deep knowledge of any of the biblical prophets. He denied ever having seen anyone performing Jewish rites. Though he conceded "four or five conversations" with Gaspar, he rejected the charge of missionary intent. He denied, correctly this time, that Baltasar had left Veracruz with him. He admitted washing his father's corpse, but insisted that the cleansing was totally unrelated to Jewish practice.[28]

Four days later Luis was again haled before the inquisitors and asked whether he had remembered anything of pertinence to his case. When he said no, he received a transcript of the testimony against him, and was told to select a defense attorney from two Inquisition lawyers. One of the two attorneys offered to Luis was none other than his guardian, Dr. Gaspar de Valdés. Luis chose him, perhaps as the lesser of the two available evils.[29]

On Wednesday, August 2, in his first formal interview with Luis as his attorney, Valdés duly "admonished him to give the full and complete confession of the truth as a matter of great importance for the unburdening of his conscience and the defense of his cause." Luis, his defiance as impregnable as ever, answered indifferently that "he was a baptized Christian and had nothing to add to what he had declared in his confessions."[30]

The next move appeared to be up to the Inquisition; yet it was Luis who moved first.

On the morning of August 7 Luis was back in the audience chamber, this time at his own request. The Inquisition encouraged the granting of such requests "because prisoners receive consolation from being heard" and "because it often happens that a prisoner with the desire to confess or say something relevant to the determination of his case on one day gets other ideas and makes other plans if his audience is delayed."[31]

Luis's appearance on that Monday morning could not have failed to stun the inquisitors. The proud, recalcitrant Judaizer of five days before had been transformed into a groveling, obsequious penitent, contritely beating his breast as he entered the audience chamber, sinking to his knees as he approached the inquisitors and sobbing, "I have sinned. I have sinned. Have mercy. Have mercy."[32]

When the attendants lifted him to a seat, Luis proceeded to explain the miraculous change. "I may deserve to be condemned for my faults," he said, "but I have seen the light of God." He had indeed lied brazenly in previous interrogations, he confessed, but he could not help himself. The devil held him tightly in his grip and try as he might to express the truth he could not. Only in the last few days had he managed to extricate himself, and now, delivered, he could speak freely.

With this spectacular flourish, Luis began to pour out the information the inquisitors had patiently waited to hear. For five days he was the cynosure of their attention as he revealed the details of his family's practice of Judaism.

He admitted being of Jewish stock and being indoctrinated by his father shortly before his death. He at first balked at accepting Judaism, Luis said, and then wanted to compromise by observing both Judaism and Christianity with equal faithfulness, but his father overcame his scruples. When Don Francisco died, Luis said that he washed his corpse because of its unsightly condition and not in observance of a Jewish rite.

Before his death, Don Francisco had told him about Dr. Morales and disclosed that Baltasar, Isabel, and their mother also Judaized. When he returned to Pánuco after his father's death, Luis revealed himself to the trio as a secret Jew and joined them in their practice. He was forced to interrupt his religious activity during the months he spent with his uncle in the New Kingdom of León, but resumed it on rejoining his family in Mexico City. Catalina, Leonor, and Mariana were never involved in Judaizing, said Luis, and of course, Miguel and Anica were too young. Occasionally the three older girls would surprise the Judaizers in the midst of their worship. But, said Luis, "when they happened to enter, singly or otherwise, and asked what they were talking about . . . they answered that they were discussing nothing." As a result, his sisters "were angry because things were being kept from them."

Aside from Isabel, Baltasar, and his parents, Luis knew of no Judaizers and suspected no one of being a secret Jew. Only one person outside the circle of Judaizers was aware of their activity, and that was his uncle, the governor. Both Isabel and his father had tried to convert him. The governor had been aware that Don Francisco was a secret Jew and had therefore sought to countervail his influence by enhancing Catholicism whenever he saw his nephews.

Gaspar, on the other hand, was unaware of the Judaizing in his family, Luis said. He may have displayed a strange curiosity on hearing that his father's corpse had been washed and he may have engaged in religious discussions with his brothers, but he did not necessarily conclude that Judaism was involved.

Luis declared that all the time they engaged in Jewish practice, Isabel, Baltasar, and their mother went to confession and took communion in order not to arouse suspicion. Luis admitted that "seeing that an entire world and its sages kept the Christian faith," he found it difficult to eradicate a residual belief in the communion and frequently felt stabs of remorse for having withdrawn allegiance from the church.

Luis spoke freely of his family, tracing its moves from Tampico to Mexico City to the mines of Taxco and back to the capital. He rehearsed the plans he and Baltasar had made for their escape. He even revealed the quarrels with Almeida and Díaz de Cáceres that broke out in the wake of Isabel's arrest.[33]

On August 14 Luis formally ratified his confessions. In accordance with inquisitorial practice, he was informed that his testimony would be used by the prosecution in the trials of other prisoners. Foremost among them would be the members of his own family.[34]

The striking change in Luis de Carvajal was not due to instability of character. Nor was it a desperate surrender to fear of what might happen if he continued to be "negative." Like other moves he made, Luis's confession was the product of careful and practical deliberation.

At the beginning of his trial, he had no alternative but to deny every charge against him. When he first heard the accusation against him, he had no choice but to follow his initial plan and continue his negations. But now that he had had an opportunity to ruminate on the charges and gauge how much the Inquisition knew and how much it had failed to ascertain, he faced three possible alternatives. He could continue to be negative, refusing to admit anything of substance despite the obvious evidence the Inquisition was accumulating against him, even though persistence in this approach would certainly bring him to the torture chamber and quite likely as well to death at the stake. Or he could sincerely repent and demonstrate his faithfulness to the church by revealing every detail of his heretical activity and betraying the names of all the secret Judaizers he knew. Or he could choose the perilous road of feigning repentance, disclosing what five days of reflection had assured him the Inquisition knew or could easily learn, but carefully concealing all other incriminatory information.

From the testimony he volunteered to the Inquisition, it is apparent that Luis de Carvajal had once more chosen the difficult path. The Inquisition had already begun cases against the people he named as Judaizers—his parents, Isabel, and Baltasar. His mother and Isabel were under arrest. His father was dead and had left no estate for the Inquisition to confiscate posthumously: Baltasar, he believed, had by now surely escaped from New Spain. Luis did his utmost to spare the rest of his family from involvement. With a fraternal love he never relinquished, though it was seldom reciprocated, he tried to shield Gaspar. His revelation of the arguments with Almeida and Díaz de Cáceres seems to have been calculated to improve their standing as virtuous Catholics in the eyes of the inquisitors.

Outside of his immediate family, Luis refused to implicate anyone as a Judaizer, certain or suspect. By emphatically denying that he washed his father's corpse in fulfillment of a Jewish rite he even strove to extricate those present from the aura of suspicion, even though none of them were readily available for questioning. Some were dead; the whereabouts of the others was unknown.

Nor was Luis meticulously accurate in the description of his relationship to Judaism. In his teens he may have had occasional misgivings about leaving the Catholic faith and may have desultorily reverted to practicing it. But there was no question that he had been wholeheartedly and singlemindedly devoted to Judaism for upwards of two years prior to his arrest. During all this time he never vacillated between Judaism and Christianity. He found no fascination in the sacrament of communion. And in the two and a half months he had spent in jail he never felt himself grappling as a Christian against a demonic force.

On the contrary, Luis's incarceration confirmed him ineradicably in his love for Judaism. When he was in greatest need of encouragement, a series of experiences convinced him more strongly than ever that he had a mission to perform for his family and his people as a teacher and spokesman for Judaism.

His incarceration was not unexpected, and at first Luis appeared to take it in stride. But the solitude of his cell soon began to take its toll, enveloping him in a listlessness and despair that he found next to impossible to dispel. When he finally did break through, he believed he had been aided by miracles sent by God from on high.

They began with the remarkable fulfillment of a reverie. Luis often thought of the consolation he would receive if he had a book of psalms in his cell for his prayers and meditations. He understandably regarded his wish as impossible of fulfillment, for the Inquisition would permit him no book, much less part of a Bible. Yet not long after conceiving the wish, he had a book containing psalms in his room.[35]

It happened on a Saturday toward the end of June or early in July. The inquisitors, on their usual rounds of the cells, stopped to talk to a friar named Francisco Ruiz de Luna, who had been arrested on June 27 for celebrating mass and administering the sacraments of the church on the strength of false dimissory letters he had obtained in Italy. The inquisitors asked Fray Francisco whether he needed anything, and the friar said yes, he could use a breviary to recite the customary divine office. Then they passed on to Luis's cell. When they saw Luis depressed and emaciated, they decided to make Fray Francisco his cellmate, doubtless intending to use the friar as a spy to extract information from Luis now that his resistance was low. Instructing Fray Francisco not to reveal that he wore the cloth, they immediately transferred him to Luis's cell. The two men soon found common grounds of interest and spent the afternoon talking amicably. At nightfall the jailer came with the breviary, and Fray Francisco soon made it available to Luis. Luis now had a book with psalms.[36]

Fray Francisco was not a spy and refused to become one. Eventually he joined Luis in a favorite project of incarcerated Judaizers, that of boring peepholes in the doors of their cells. Lacking tools, Fray Francisco and Luis accomplished their objective by rubbing mutton bones against the bottom of their cell door until they could see through.[37]

Additional unexpected relief came to Luis in two successive dreams. One night when he lay down to sleep, weary and depressed after a day when he had managed to fast and pray, Luis heard a voice in his dreams telling him to "be strong and consoled, for the holy Job and Jeremiah are praying most efficaciously for you."[38]

Buoyed by this dream, he was prepared psychologically for the dream that came to him several nights later. He called it a "divine and true revelation," for it assured him in the clearest terms that God had chosen him, like a prophet, for a high and lofty purpose in life. In this dream, suggested by the call of the biblical prophets, Luis saw a glass vial that was covered with a cloth, tightly stopped, and full of a precious liquid. The liquid was the elixir of divine wisdom, dispensed only in drops and only to the chosen few. Near the vial stood King Solomon, the Bible's paragon of wisdom, and not far away stood God. Luis heard God instructing Solomon to "take a spoon and fill it with this liquid and give it to this boy to drink." Solomon immediately executed the command and placed in Luis's mouth the spoonful of wisdom, with its delightfully sweet taste. No sooner had he imbibed it, Luis recalled, than he felt consoled.[39]

He awoke euphoric, convinced that the dream "was a light that God deigned to give him that he might keep the Law of Moses and understand the meaning of Sacred Writ." He regarded himself as divinely called, not merely like the biblical prophets, but like the patriarchal Joseph, to give sustenance to his family and his entire people. As a result of the vision, Luis adopted a new name, Joseph Lumbroso: "Joseph, the bearer of light."

Henceforth Luis's conviction of the purpose of his Judaizing could not be shaken. The dream had inspired him so much, he later recalled, that he no longer was troubled by the oppression of his imprisonment.[40]

Viewed in this perspective, Luis's address to the inquisitors is seen to be a brave man's response to his captors' demands that he compromise with his conscience or die. Luis de Carvajal was convinced of the truth of his faith. He was persuaded that no human institution had the right to challenge it. His attitudes reveal that he refused to acknowledge the legality of the Inquisition's proceedings or the propriety of its charges against him. In the face of the Inquisition's crafty methods and cynical concept of justice, Luis could only preserve his life and values by a reciprocal resort to deceit. The necessity for this guile hurls greater condemnation on the oppressive atmosphere created by the Inquisition than it does on the character of Luis de Carvajal.[41]

His confessions automatically ended the traumatic part of Luis's trial. He was not brought to torture or extensively grilled again. He was returned to the inquisitors' chambers on several occasions to give testimony needed by the inquisitors for his relatives' trials and to hear the publication of the testimony of witnesses against him.[42] But aside from the scraps of information he could glean from these hearings, he learned little about the progress of his family's trials. On October 20 he concluded his own case by acknowledging the tragic error of his former belief in "the evil Law of Moses" and affirming that "Christianity is the true faith in which he will find salvation."[43]

By mid-August the substantive part of the trial of the other members of Luis's family had hardly begun. His uncle, the governor, had rejected the accusation against him and was still relentlessly pressing for acquittal. In mid-September, after hearing the testimony of witnesses against him, the governor requested and received permission to prepare a written defense. The Inquisition gave him five large folios, carefully recording the transaction,[44] and five days later the prisoner brought back his statement.

It was a cogent and eloquent document. It insisted on the pure origins of Carvajal's family and his own unswerving fidelity to the church. It categorically denied Isabel's claim of a long conversation with him. "I am not, nor can I be regarded as so stupid and feckless," he argued, "that I would stand by patiently for the time required to listen to such false doctrine, which I abhor so much . . . that I regard all its followers to be the most dissolute, base, and dishonorable people in the world."

He denied Isabel's claim that her family spent two months in Seville. They were there only three or four days, he said, and so busy preparing for departure and curing Doña Francisca of her illness that they hardly had time to eat or even sit down.

He contended that his discussions with Gaspar were not an artful ploy to help him evade responsibility for informing the Inquisition. On the contrary, he ingenuously wished to share his knowledge with his nephew and to discuss the canon law involved in order to determine exactly how far his responsibilities went. He talked with Gaspar simply because he himself could not properly evaluate his inchoate suspicions. When he decided that he should go to the Inquisition, he found himself in the hinterlands, far from any inquisitorial officer. He had therefore had no alternative but to wait until he returned to a settled area or to the capital itself before disclosing the matter. When arrested by the viceroy, he planned to inform the Inquisition immediately upon his release, and he shared this intention with his confessor. As a result, pleaded the governor, "not only am I unjustly accused, but I deserve a reward and honor."

Besides, he argued, the Inquisition should reject all testimony given by his nephew because of the younger Luis's hatred for him and should instead go to people like Almeida, Díaz de Cáceres, and others he named. All of these, he stated, would support his contentions.

The governor then delineated his devotion to the church. When confined to the battle-scarred wilderness of the New Kingdom of León, where he and his men often did not know where their next meal would come from, he zealously observed the church's required fasts, even if he had to risk missing meals and going hungry for long periods of time. Of his zeal for the church he said, "No obstacle, or war, or journey has been strong enough to divert it. I have set an example for the men accompanying me and inspired them to follow me with the solicitude that is to be expected from the nature of my office and from a Catholic Christian, for as such am I regarded and considered by all those who have had contact with me, and there is no one who has conceived a contrary opinion."

Shifting effortlessly to the offensive, Don Luis rehearsed the rich details of his more than two decades of service to the crown in New Spain. He omitted nothing of note. Methodically he placed before the inquisitors the catalog of his achievements—the smashing victory over the corsairs, the repeated pacifications of the Indians, the rebuilding of ravaged territory and razed edifices at his own expense, the opening of mines, and the creation of cities. He had even performed the feat of bringing peace to the New Kingdom of León and its environs, he noted. And he reminded the inquisitors with a sardonic stab that as soon as he was bound in chains and carried off as a prisoner to Mexico City, the Indians of the frontier became restive again.

The governor climaxed his defense with an impassioned plea to the inquisitors to "declare me free from all charges against me and absolve me from all." He asked that they acknowledge him to be the faithful Catholic he claimed he was and to restore him to his position and prerogatives. "Do not permit me to be remanded to the Royal Prison," he pleaded, "and order that once freed from this prison, I may go back to my governorship and resume my service. Do not permit my good and loyal services to go unrewarded. Consider the difficulties imposed upon me by my extended confinement from the time I was brought to prison in chains . . . and the many days I have been immured in this jail in a secret cell."[45]

He concluded by requesting and receiving more paper for detailed answers to the testimony of witnesses against him. In his answers he stressed that he had never countenanced any Judaizer. He offered in evidence two of Isabel's own statements, first that Doña Guiomar was afraid to broach the question of Judaizing to the governor, and second, that Isabel herself was afraid to do so on her own behalf and needed the crutch of Doña Guiomar's name. Besides, he said, the testimony of none of the witnesses was legally admissible because they all spoke of events that occurred when they were alone with him. He again insisted that his failure to inform the Inquisition was owing to his involvement on the frontier. And he again named people, including Almeida and Díaz de Cáceres, who he believed would testify to his family's hostility.[46]

With this statement the governor brought his defense to a close. It proved a failure. Neither his spirited language nor the inventory of his benefactions could obscure the fact that he had not reported an unmistakable crime against the faith. In the subsequent determination of his sentence the governor's defense carried little weight.

Nor was the Inquisition's battle against the two women in the family far advanced in the summer of 1589. Determined to save her family at all costs, Doña Francisca had adamantly maintained her negative stance. When it became obvious from the testimony of Gaspar and the governor and even some of Luis's innocuous remarks that Doña Francisca was deliberately withholding information, the inquisitors decided to submit her to torture. Early on Friday morning, November 10, after their admonishment to her to reveal what she knew had brought no response, they led her down to the torture chamber. Ignoring her embarrassment and plaintive cries, they first stripped her to the waist, then bound her arms with cords and twisted them. Neither procedure succeeded in eliciting the desired result. Not until they stretched her body on the rack and tightened the ropes around her arms, thighs, and shins did they succeed in loosening her tongue. Then she confessed her New Christian descent, the Judaism of her husband and daughter, and the teachings of Dr. Morales. A second application of torture led to her implication of Baltasar and Luis, a detailing of some of her family's religious activities, and a discussion of Isabel's attempt to bring the governor to Judaism.[47]

Two and a half weeks later Isabel made the trip to the torture chamber. Endowed with weaker defenses than her mother, Isabel revealed three critical facts hitherto unknown to the Inquisition. First, she said, all her siblings Judaized, including Anica and Miguel. Second, not only Guiomar, but also her own parents urged her to convert the governor. And third, it was in Spain that her father taught Judaism to both herself and her mother. This revelation led to Isabel's full disclosure of the family's religious life in Spain and on the high seas on their way to the New World.[48]

The testimony wrung from Doña Francisca and Doña Isabel failed to ruffle the governor. When its pertinent sections were published against him, he refused to change the tenor of his defense. But it did bring a change in the lives of Luis's sisters. The Inquisition, after long surveillance, now decided to arrest Leonor and Catalina, on December 4. A week later, on December 12, they arrested Mariana, and on January 19, 1590, they called Anica in for questioning. They even began to prepare a case against the fugitive, Miguel.

The girls had all been admirably trained in the art of defensive denial. Ten-year-old Anica, who had been living at the home of her cousin Diego Márquez since the arrest of her sisters, was particularly impressive. She denied that she had ever seen or heard anything against the Catholic faith. "It is all on a false charge," she said of her forced appearance before the inquisitors, "for I know nothing, and I have seen nothing from my mother, sisters, and brother."[49] Eventually, however, the resistance of all the girls broke, and they substantially confirmed most of the confessions of the rest of their family.

The new information also was embarrassing to young Luis's case, for he had failed to declare the extent of the family's Judaizing in Spain and had not acknowledged other facts that were now part of the Inquisition's docket. Yet the inquisitors appear to have been so convinced of the completeness of the information they now had that they did not bother to go through the motions of summoning Luis to a special audience to apprise him of the inadequacies in his testimony. Later, when his mother's testimony was published against him, Luis was compelled to admit that he had taken part in various Jewish rites in Medina del Campo and to explain that he had withheld this information in order to protect his kin.[50] Until then Luis sat in his cell, wondering perhaps about the scenes involving his family and the inquisitors but having no real knowledge about them—except one.

The exception occurred around 8:30 in the morning of November 10, when Luis looked out of his peephole in time to see his mother being led to the torture chambers. He could discern the entire procession—the inquisitors, their notary, the jailer, the guard, and the torturer, euphemistically called the minister, shrouded in white from head to toe. A few moments later he could hear his mother's agonized cries echoing through the corridors of the jail. Each cry stabbed him with unbearable grief. Of all his days in the Inquisition's jail, that Friday was unquestionably the worst.

Numb from shock and anguish, Luis drifted into sleep by the door of his cell. No sooner had he dozed off than he saw another vision. A man he recognized as a paragon of virtue and patience had been sent by God to stand before him. Luis did not say whether it was his own father, Don Francisco, or his father's teacher, Dr. Morales, or perhaps even "the prophet Job," as he called the biblical worthy, but he did disclose the purpose of his visitation.

In his hands the saintly man held a large and beautiful yam, which he proceeded to show Luis. "Look!" he said. "What a handsome and beautiful fruit!"

"Indeed," replied Luis.

The man then gave it to Luis to smell. "It smells good, doesn't it?" he asked.

"Indeed it does," replied Luis.

The man then took the yam from Luis's hands and cut it in half. "Now it smells better," he announced.

This was the end of the saintly man's object lesson. He proceeded to explain.

The yam, he said, represented Luis's mother. "Before she was imprisoned and racked with torture," he continued, "your mother was whole and she smelled sweet. She was a fruit of sweet savor before the Lord. But now," he added, "when she is cut with torture, she exudes the superior fragrance of patience before the Lord."

When Luis awoke from his dream, he felt reassured. He understood that his mother was in God's hands and was fulfilling God's will.[51]

Not long after this sustaining vision Luis participated in another seemingly miraculous event, this time not in the spacious world of his dreams but within the narrow confines of his cell. After months of conversations, Luis finally persuaded Francisco Ruiz de Luna to become a secret Jew. While holding his cross one day Francisco had voiced his first doubts about the strength of his own faith, and as soon as he did Luis began to persuade him to Judaize. The two men proceeded to carry on an intense discussion lasting an entire week, until, as Luis was to put it, "the poor purblind fellow came to a knowledge of the divine truth. He rejoiced and was exceedingly glad and sang hymns and praises to the Lord."

Though he had been a cleric, Francisco knew little about the Hebrew worthies in the Bible and listened with rapt attention as Luis narrated their exploits and achievements. "Soon," said Luis, "God's truth became so impressed upon this good gentile's soul that it seemed as if he had been nurtured on it all his life and taught by believing parents." Francisco soon joined Luis in rejecting the bacon, lard, and pork that were served on various occasions, especially for Friday lunch. It was a dangerous decision, since they could not regularly return this food without risking exposure. Nor could they leave the food in the cell to rot. They therefore decided to bury it beneath their cell floor, a process they called "offering the sacrifice." They believed that by sacrificing these forbidden foods they were complying with God's will. They therefore accompanied the burial with the psalm "Lord, have mercy upon me."[52]

The two men observed Judaism to the extent that was possible for the eight to twelve weeks they remained together in prison.

In the meantime the Inquisition was systematically completing its cases against all the members of Luis's family. As early as November 8, when they decided to put Francisca and Isabel to torture, the officers of the Inquisition were already voting preliminarily on Luis's fate as well as Gaspar's and the governor's.[53] Like everything else done within the Inquisition's precinct, the voting was carried out under the strictest regulations. The senior inquisitor first had to review the testimony of each case in the presence of his junior partner and the other officials. One of these, the prosecuting attorney, had to leave the chamber before the voting took place. Those eligible to vote included the inquisitors, the ordinary, and a number of clerics versed in canon law and theology. These men, called consultors, were representatives of the bishop, without whose participation the Inquisition could not pronounce sentence. The regulations provided for the consultors to express their opinions first and the senior inquisitor last, in order "to allow the consultors to vote with full freedom." This procedure, intended to prevent the lesser officials from being prejudiced by the votes of the inquisitors, was more democratic in theory than in actuality. In the preliminary discussions the inquisitors often found it impossible or undesirable to hide their hand.[54]

By February 13, 1590, final votes had been taken on the cases of all the Carvajals. Needless to say, none was found innocent, and no case was suspended for lack of sufficient information.[55] Two members of the family were adjudged impenitent: Francisco Rodríguez de Matos posthumously and Baltasar Rodríguez de Carvajal in absentia. Both were ordered burned at the stake in effigy. After the reading of the sentence at the auto-da-fé, their effigies, bearing placards with their names and the nature of their crimes, would be paraded through the streets to the execution ground and there burned to ashes. Although there is no record of it, it is likely that the Inquisition, in accordance with custom, ordered the bones of Francisco Rodríguez de Matos exhumed and tossed into the flames along with his effigy.[56]

Since the other indicted members of the family had all ostensibly repented and begged for mercy, the inquisitors prepared to reconcile them to the church. Before reconciliation could take place they would have to hear their sentences and then publicly abjure their crimes, solemnly swearing never again to sin against the faith.

Penitents were sentenced to prison for terms up to life. The Holy Office distinguished between two types of life terms: "perpetual prison," from which there could be parole and "irremissible perpetual prison," from which, theoretically at least, there could not be. In New Spain the designations were largely academic, since the Inquisition had no prison of its own. If it did not send prisoners to the galleys, it customarily assigned them to menial duties in hospitals, monasteries, and convents, under the vigilance of the religious. At times it even returned them to their homes and sent visiting inspectors to teach them and report on their progress.[57]

The inquisitorial canons required the confiscation of all property belonging to the penitent during the period of his offenses. Even property that had legally passed over to others before the time of sentencing was subject to sequestration. Though such property theoretically belonged to the royal fisc, the king as a rule saw less of it than did the Holy Office. Having long been in financial straits, the Inquisition welcomed the opportunity to prosecute Judaizers of means and was not about to let a legality stand in the way of its solvency.[58]

The purely spiritual penances were no less burdensome. Penitents would be required to wear their *sambenitos* in public for the duration

The Sambenito *of a Penitent*

of their sentence. They might have to observe special fasts for weeks or months and accompany them with the recitation of special prayers. Or they might have to appear, candle in hand and barefoot, in a designated number of religious processions. Besides, all would have to undergo careful instruction in the requirements of the Catholic faith.

There were two forms of public abjuration: for light suspicion (*de levi*) in the case of penitents convicted of minor offenses, and for vehement suspicion (*de vehementi*) where serious malefactions were involved. The Carvajals all had to abjure *de vehementi*. A reoccurrence of the crime after such an abjuration irrevocably doomed the malefactor to the stake. The penalty for reincidence after an abjuration *de levi* was left to the discretion of the inquisitorial tribunal.[59]

As was their custom, the inquisitors selected a feast day for the auto-da-fé involving the Carvajals. They chose Saint Matthew's day, Saturday, February 24, 1590. Although autos-da-fé could be private, held within the Inquisition's precincts, the Holy Office preferred a "general public *auto*," particularly when heretics were involved. One apologist for the Inquisition went so far as to say that the public auto-da-fé injected a salutary dread of heresy into the populace by dramatically prefiguring the sentencing of the soul on Judgment Day. Attendance at an auto-da-fé was regarded as a mark of piety. To insure the presence of the populace in considerable numbers, public proclamation was made throughout the capital two weeks in advance of the great event, and an indulgence, generally of forty days, was bestowed upon those in attendance.[60]

Well in advance of Saint Matthew's day, the Inquisition announced that the auto-da-fé would be held inside the Great Cathedral in Mexico City.

Spacious as it was, the cathedral was filled to capacity on Saint Matthew's day. So many people crowded into it that the inquisitors wished they had chosen to hold the auto-da-fé in the huge Great Square outside the cathedral, especially since "the nature of the crimes" in their estimation "was not unworthy" of an even bigger spectacle.[61]

On the day of the auto-da-fé the prisoners, following rule and custom, were marched in solemn procession to places that had been designated for them in the cathedral. For the occasion they wore their *sambenitos* and carried lighted wax tapers that had been colored green.[62]

In addition to the Carvajals, the penitents connected with Judaism included Luis's friend Hernán Rodríguez de Herrera, Luis's cousin, Catalina de León, her husband, Gonzalo Pérez Ferro, and her husband's natural son, Gonzalo Pérez Ferro, Jr. Pérez Ferro had dauntlessly followed a strategy of uncompromising negations throughout all interrogation and torture. Having successfully overcome his ordeal, he could not be presumed wholly guilty according to the religious logic of the time and was therefore only compelled to abjure *de levi*. His son also abjured *de levi* and, in addition to other penalties, received a flogging of a hundred lashes "publicly in the streets nude from the waist up and riding on a beast of burden."[63]

The penitents also included a motley assortment of non-Judaizing malefactors. Among them were four bigamists, a blaspheming soldier, and an embarrassingly insubordinate friar. The blaspheming soldier was a Guatemalan whose crime consisted of taking God's name in vain when he went to put on his shirt and found it wet. The friar was a learned Dominican, Dr. Gregorio Calderón, who scandalized his colleagues in Peru, Guatemala, and New Spain with pronouncements favoring the Lutherans, or perhaps Protestants in general, and opposing the pope. The Inquisition also accused him of resorting to judicial astrology. In addition, Fray Francisco de Luna was to appear for sentencing on his original charge. The Inquisition had not discovered that he was guilty of the more heinous crime of converting to Jewish belief. Fray Francisco was to be sentenced to the galleys for six years, after abjuring *de vehementi* and being stripped of his orders.[64]

Little Ana, never formally indicted, escaped the auto-da-fé. At the conclusion of her testimony on January 19, 1590, she was placed in the custody of the Inquisition's secretary, Pedro de los Ríos, and went to live with his family. On August 31, 1590, the inquisitors decided to continue this arrangement so that Anica might be properly indoctrinated. She remained in Pedro de los Ríos's home for the next year and a half.[65]

Gaspar, too, was permitted to escape the humiliation of the public auto-da-fé, doubtless less for his own sake than for that of the Inquisition and the church. Embarrassed to parade a Dominican friar as a concealer of Judaizers, the inquisitors decided that Gaspar should hear his sentence in a private auto-da-fé.[66]

Also marching into the cathedral was the more joyous procession of ecclesiastical and secular dignitaries. Arrayed in their finery, they were eager to witness the humiliation of the sinners and the glorious triumph of their faith.

In addition to the procession, the crowd at an auto-da-fé could look for three pivotal occasions. The first was the sermon, delivered by a distinguished guest. More often than not it was an orotund discourse flashing with theological erudition and homiletical virtuosity. Its aim was always twofold: to exalt the church and the Holy Office, and to shower the penitents with pitiless insults and abuse.

The second was the oath of faith, administered to the entire assembly by the secretary of the Inquisition. It exacted from all the faithful the solemn promise that they would continue to expose all heresy relentlessly and invoked an entire panoply of heavenly curses upon them should they fail to do so.

The third, the sentencing, was the climax of the auto-da-fé. The secretary of the Inquisition would patiently read the detailed sentence handed down against each prisoner. Before the auto-da-fé the Inquisition gave prisoners no inkling of their fate, except in the case of those condemned to die. These would be informed the night before the auto-da-fé and assigned confessors to minister to their spiritual needs and receive any last-minute information they might be prompted to volunteer. Of course in the case of the auto-da-fé of February 24, 1590, where the condemned were present only in effigy, such advance notice was not necessary.[67]

Luis de Carvajal received a typical inquisitorial sentence. It began with a lengthy preamble, detailing the major events in his life, the myriad of facts, essential and tangential, about his crimes, and the highlights of his trial. Then the inquisitors launched into the sentence proper, announcing that the prosecutor had "fully proved his accusation and complaint" and that Luis de Carvajal was therefore guilty of being "a heretic, Judaizer, apostate, supporter, and concealer of heretics," one who "passed over and converted to the dead Law of Moses and to the rites and ceremonies thereof." As a result he incurred all condign penalties and disabilities, including "the confiscation and loss of all his possessions, which we apply to the chamber and fisc of the king our lord and to his receiver in his name, from the time he began to commit these crimes."

The inquisitors went on to say that "though we could in good conscience condemn him to the penalties set by law for such heretics," meaning death at the stake, they had decided to reconcile him because he "showed signs of contrition and repentance and asked God to pardon his crimes and us for penance with mercy, professing that henceforth he wished to live and die in our holy Catholic faith and that he was prepared to fulfill whatever penance we might impose upon him."

They accordingly proceeded with the penances. These included, of course, appearance at the auto-da-fé, abjuration, disqualification from all dignities and public offices, perpetual prison in a place to be determined, and the wearing of the penitential garb for the duration of his sentence.[68]

Of the Carvajal women, Francisca and Isabel drew the heaviest sentences. Wearing the penitential garb was to be irremissibly perpetual for them. Mariana and Catalina were sentenced to "prison and garb," as the official documents read, for two years and Leonor for only one, out of consideration for her youth.[69]

At the sentencing, Governor Carvajal learned to his dismay that his fervent appeals and persistent denials had accomplished little. The Inquisition found him guilty of abetting and protecting Judaizers. It determined that he had been a factor and concealer of Judaizers and a participant in their crimes. It ordered him to abjure *de vehementi* before reconciling him to the church. It stripped him of his position and condemned him to exile from the Indies for a period of six years, admonishing him to be prepared to leave the country in the first fleet returning to Castile.

The governor had certainly not anticipated so severe a penalty, nor had the consultors wished to impose it upon him. They had voted that he abjure *de levi* and be regarded as innocent of participating in the malefactions of the Judaizers. Nor did they want him expelled from the Indies. They believed that if he was exiled for four years from the capital of New Spain and the area within a five-league radius of it, he would be punished sufficiently.[70] But, as often happened, the consultors could not prevail against the adamant inquisitors.

Gaspar, too, received harsher penalties than he had anticipated, though in comparison with his family's they were surprisingly light. He was enjoined to hear his sentence "in the presence of several important clerics of his order," to abjure his errors *de levi,* and to appear as a penitent, with a wax candle, in the chapel of the Holy Office. There he would hear a mass, and receive a reprimand and be warned about the seriousness of his offense. He was additionally suspended from his orders for a period of six months and confined to his monastery in Mexico City. Here he was to be relieved of participation in deliberations and other activities and assigned "the lowest and last place in the choir and refectory." The sentence, formulated on November 8, was pronounced on February 25, the day after the public auto-da-fé.[71]

Along with Gaspar a number of relatively minor malefactors were exempted from an appearance at the public auto-da-fé. These included several clerics convicted of trying to seduce women in the confessional and another who, when gravely ill to the point of death, defiantly or despondently blurted out, "What harm can God to me?"[72]

In August 1590 Gaspar sought permission to recommence his priestly functions, only to find Dr. Lobo Guerrero opposing him. The Inquisition's prosecutor claimed that Francisco Rodríguez de Matos's conviction as a heretic on February 24, 1590, permanently disqualified his son from the clergy. The inquisitors decided to submit the problem to the Supreme Council of the Inquisition in Madrid and extended Gaspar's suspension pending receipt of the adjudication.

Gaspar had to wait a year for the answer, but the wait proved rewarding, for the council decided in his favor. It communicated the decision to the Inquisition in New Spain in a letter dated March 25, 1591. The letter was not received until August 12 of that year. It took at least several more days for word to reach Gaspar, since he happened to be in the region of Oaxaca at the time.[73]

Like the other members of his family, Luis made his formal abjuration for vehement suspicion at the end of the auto-da-fé. "I . . . by these presents, of my own free will and determination," he solemnly declared, "do abjure, detest, renounce, and remove myself from all and every heresy, especially the one in which charges and witnesses have been brought against me and which I have confessed, regarding the Old Dispensation of Moses and its rites and ceremonies. And with my lips and heart true and pure I do profess the holy Catholic faith, held, preached, followed, and taught by the holy mother church of

Rome. That is the faith I hold and wish to uphold and follow, remaining and dying in it and never swerving from it."

He continued, "And I swear by our Lord God and the four holy Gospels and the sign of the cross that I will in every way subject myself to the obedience of the blessed Saint Peter, prince of the apostles and vicar of our Lord Jesus Christ and to that of our very holy Father Sixtus V [1585–1590], who now rules and governs the church, and his successors after him, and not to swerve from obedience to them through any suasion or heresy, especially this one of which I have been charged and accused, always remaining within the unity and jurisdiction of the holy church, and always defending this holy Catholic faith and pursuing all who might be or come against it, and revealing and exposing them and not joining them or with them or receiving or guiding or visiting or accompanying them, or giving or sending them gifts or favoring them."

And he concluded, "And if I should contravene this oath at any time, then let me become subject to and incur the penalty of impenitent, relapsed heretic and let me be cursed and excommunicated.

"And I [hereby] ask the present secretary [of the Holy Office] for the signed testimony of this, my confession and abjuration, and I beg those present to be witnesses thereto, that I have personally affixed my name to it in their presence."[74]

On Monday February 26, 1590, the governor began his sentence. Adjured to strict secrecy about everything he had seen and heard while a prisoner of the Holy Office, he was returned to the Royal Prison, as the Inquisition had promised when it arrested him. Though presumably he was to await deportation there, he never left New Spain. He died within a matter of months.[75]

The rest of the family, penanced with regular fasts and other salutary exercises, were also sent to their respective places of confinement, though Isabel remained in prison until March 6.[76] Luis's mother and sisters were placed in separate convents for service and indoctrination in the Catholic faith.[77]

Luis was assigned to the Saint Hippolytus Convalescent Hospital (Hospital de los Convalescientes de San Hipólito) in Mexico City, an imposing compound located in a vast open area near an Indian market. Established in 1566 by Bernardino Álvarez, an erstwhile roué and highwayman, and supported by charity, it served as a temporary convalescent home for patients discharged from other hospitals and as a permanent shelter for the elderly and the infirm of body and mind. It even functioned as a hostel for wayfarers, especially those recently arrived in the New World who had as yet not found employment.[78] The inquisitors decreed that in the hospital Luis should "occupy himself in constructive duties and services as determined by the administrator." They designated Brother Matthew García, knight commander of the Order of Mercy, "to take responsibility for his spiritual comfort and to administer the sacraments to him." At the same time the Inquisition appointed Arias de Valdés, official warden of the prisons of the Holy Office, "to visit him frequently and supervise the compliance with his orders."[79]

As far as the inquisitors were concerned, Luis was sent to the Hospital de los Convalescientes to prove himself as a Christian. For Luis, the hospital represented the first step toward eventual freedom and a new life as a Jew.

8 The Unreconciled

The Inquisition's failure to locate Baltasar was due to his impulsive decision to leave Veracruz. Apparently disquieted by the prospect of having to wait for news to trickle down from Mexico City, he had decided to violate his agreement with Luis and follow his brother to the capital. A day or two after Luis, he left Veracruz, taking Miguel along.

By fateful coincidence Baltasar arrived in Mexico City on the evening of May 9. He tried to contact Luis and received the stunning news that both he and their mother had just been arrested. He quickly recovered from the shock "like a servant of the Lord God, prostrating and humbling himself before His divine decree," as Luis was later to say. Yet he remained numb with indecision as to what course of action was now best for him to pursue.

He realized that there was little likelihood that the Inquisition would acquit his mother and siblings. At the same time he doubtless felt that Luis was the only one who stood in danger of being burned at the stake. Knowing Luis's nature, he certainly realized the possibility that he might adamantly deny everything throughout his trial and be sentenced to death as an impenitent. The rest of the family would in all probability be reconciled to the church with a heap of burdensome penalties. From the experience of other New Christian Judaizers, Baltasar knew that he might be of help to his family if he escaped to Spain, where relatives of New World Judaizers, even if sought by the Inquisition, often moved about with impunity and made valuable contacts at court. But when should he attempt the escape? If he succeeded in leaving the New World immediately, he would have to wait patiently in Spain for word of the progress of the trials to reach him. This might mean months or even years of gnawing anxiety. If he remained in New Spain for the duration of the trials, he could follow them closely through underground contacts with his relatives in jail and would learn their outcome no later than the day of the sentencing. But he would have to live in constant danger of apprehension by the Inquisition. His arrest, of course, would utterly demolish any plans he might be making for his family's future.

Baltasar finally made up his mind. Though his friends urged him to flee the country at the earliest moment, he determined to stay in Mexico City and face the risks involved.

His immediate problem was to locate a safe hiding place for himself and Miguel. He needed a dwelling where people would keep his secret and where he would have as little contact as possible with the outside world. This meant that the owner and inhabitants of the house would have to be willing to risk criminal exposure as abettors of a Judaizer.

Baltasar soon found ideal accommodations. His dear friend and fellow Judaizer, Juan Rodríguez de Silva, possibly still in the service of Jorge de Almeida, agreed to assume all risks. Rodríguez de Silva lived alone in a commodious house, perhaps one belonging to Almeida. He invited Baltasar to move in and took steps to shield him from all contact with the outside world. He gave Baltasar a room, regularly brought him his meals, and kept him abreast of the news. At no time did Baltasar have to leave the house. In fact, for the year he remained at Rodríguez de Silva's he seldom left his room.

Baltasar's chamber thus became his "voluntary prison," as Luis later called it, though it was hardly an unpleasant one. In addition to Rodríguez de Silva's solicitude, Baltasar enjoyed the usufruct of his host's excellent library, with its collection of biblical and devotional literature, including at least one book of prayers used by the secret Jews. Baltasar whiled away the days of his self-imposed captivity in the constructive study of these books, gaining consolation and deepening his conviction that Judaism represented the one supreme truth. On Saturday, March 10, 1590, the recently penanced Luis paid a visit to his brother Baltasar. Rodríguez de Silva was there too, and the three men reaffirmed their commitment to Judaism.

In all the time Baltasar stayed at Rodríguez de Silva's house he experienced only one serious brush with the Inquisition. It happened that the Inquisition was looking for a priest charged with concubinage, who was rumored to be hiding in the house next to Rodríguez de Silva's. The authorities sent a bailiff and several men after him. When they failed to find their suspect, they conjectured that he might have jumped over the wall onto Rodríguez de Silva's property. They therefore decided to call on Rodríguez de Silva and ask him to allow an inspection of his house.

Since he harbored a criminal high on the Inquisition's priority list, Rodríguez de Silva was naturally alarmed when its agents appeared on his property. Before coming down to the gate, he desperately tried to persuade the bailiff that the fugitive priest was not in his house, but the bailiff insisted on seeing for himself. Rodríguez de Silva therefore had no alternative but to open the gate. On his way he found a moment to warn Baltasar of the Inquisition's presence. He advised Baltasar to leave his room and hide under a nearby staircase.

The bailiff and his men magisterially surveyed Rodríguez de Silva's house and concluded that the elusive priest had not taken refuge there. They were about to leave when one of the bailiff's men gestured to the area where Baltasar was hiding and said to his chief, "Sir, let us take a look under this staircase."

"No, forget about it," responded the bailiff, to Baltasar's certain relief, "he wouldn't be hiding there."

With this definitive pronouncement the search party left the house. Baltasar emerged from his covert and went to one of the rooms that had just been examined.

A moment later the bailiff and his men were back. The bailiff had ruminated on the uninspected area and now said, "I have a feeling that the man we are looking for is underneath the staircase where I chose not to look before." He then proceeded to examine the area carefully. Finding it empty he left the house fully satisfied with the thoroughness of his search. Baltasar and his host agreed that his narrow escape was nothing short of a miracle.

When the trials of his family were over and their verdicts were announced, Baltasar stole out of Mexico City in the company of Miguel and Rodríguez de Silva. Traveling in "great fear of being apprehended by the Inquisition and determined to die for the Lord if they were," the trio edged their way overland to the Port of Horses (Puerto de los Caballos), in the region that later became Nicaragua. There they found a ship waiting to take them back to the Old World. It was not a fortuitous discovery. The ship's captain, Antonio Nieto, also known as Sebastián Nieto, was a cousin of Rodríguez de Silva's and a fervent Judaizer. Nieto was a slave-trader who brought Negroes from Guinea to the New World and was thoroughly familiar with the ocean. He welcomed the fugitives aboard and set sail for Spain.

Through the Judaizers' underground, Luis had received a report that his brothers and their guide had been arrested by the Inquisition on their way to the port. But a few days later his sorrow turned to joy when he learned that the first news had been erroneous and that the fugitives were about to leave New Spain in safety.[1]

As soon as Baltasar arrived in Madrid he systematically set about procuring the liberty of his family and friends. In traditional Jewish fashion he called the process "the redemption of the captives." He contacted relatives and secured an agent, "a banker in such matters," to penetrate the highest political spheres with attractive bribes in the hope of obtaining substantial favors.[2]

Normally the process leading to the commutation of a perpetual sentence and the removal of the obligation to wear the penitential garb took three or four years. It often involved a considerable exchange of correspondence between Madrid and the local Inquisition, including the sending of "merits" or recommendations on behalf of the penitent.

Finding this procedure unduly lengthy, Baltasar tried to circumvent it. When he learned that his funds were insufficient to buy the immediate freedom of everyone he was working for, he decided to concentrate on obtaining freedom for Luis. He did so not only because "he would take the cloak off his back for his brother," but also because Luis could work and earn a reasonable income for the family. Here again Baltasar failed, although he had gotten to speak to the secretary of the Supreme Council of the Inquisition and the secretary of the Indies. However, they told Baltasar that it would be impossible to grant Luis an extraordinary decree of freedom before obtaining the first letters from the New World. These could not be expected before May 1591.

With this news Baltasar realized that he would have to work for his family's release through ordinary channels, at least for the time being. This meant that he would have to plan to be in Europe for some three to four years. Doubtless because he felt insecure about remaining in Spain for so long a time, he decided to go to Rome, where the papacy, often at odds with the Inquisitions on the Iberian Peninsula and never in control of them, had a history of welcoming Spanish and Portuguese Judaizers.[3] Besides, Rome afforded Baltasar an opportunity to work for the intervention of Vatican officials in behalf of his family. His affairs in Madrid would be left in the hands of his coterie of trusted friends, including the secretary to the cardinal.

On November 15, 1590, the day he left for Italy with Miguel, Baltasar addressed a letter to his family, signing it with the pseudonym Francisco Rodríguez and referring to Miguel as Diego Jiménez. In the letter he assured his family of his undying devotion and strove to inspire them with optimism and patience. "What people prize most in this existence are their lives and fortunes," he said. "I have offered both of mine that our Lord may grant you some relief. . . . You may be certain that neither time nor distance will make me forget.

"Remember," he added, "that our Lord did not send manna to our forefathers until the supply of flour they had brought from Egypt had been depleted. And if there had been a fountain or river of water God would not have brought it forth from the rock. . . . Just realize, I beg you, that I feel happy and triumphant because of the obstacles I have overcome in reaching this land and not because of the favors I have received. The same thing will happen when our Lord extricates you from your troubles. You will feel embarrassed by the little you have really endured. So have patience and fear of God and confidence in His divine majesty, for He will bring a remedy for everything."[4]

The letter gives the family news about Gonzalo Pérez Ferro's brother-in-law, Duarte de León, in Havana. "I left him in Havana," writes Baltasar. "He didn't say anything to me, and I didn't say anything to him."[5] It mentions other relatives and friends living in Europe. It discusses Baltasar's financial affairs, revealing that the trip across the Atlantic had cost him three hundred ducats. And it gives some curious tidbits about the world situation. Baltasar mentions that "the sea is filled with corsairs. Nothing escapes them." He also tells his family that "wars are raging in France and the place is filled with Protestants. Two popes have died within a single month."[6]

But the thrust of Baltasar's letter was to reveal to the family what he had been doing in Spain and whom to communicate with now that he was sailing to Italy. He particularly wanted the family to keep his chief contact in Spain, Antonio Rodríguez de Escarigo, abreast of what was happening to Luis.

While Luis's two brothers were sailing to Europe, his brother-in-law, Antonio Díaz de Cáceres, was fleeing westward to the distant lands of Asia. In November 1589 he had learned through his excellent connections that the Inquisition was about to invade Almeida's household and his own. He therefore immediately decided to take a business trip to the Philippine archipelago, indiscriminately called China by many contemporary Spaniards. In partnership with a Dr. Palacio and a man named Antonio de los Cobos, he acquired a ship known by two names, the *Saint Peter* (*San Pedro*) and *Our Lady of the Immaculate Conception* (*Nuestra Señora de la Concepción*). On December 1, several

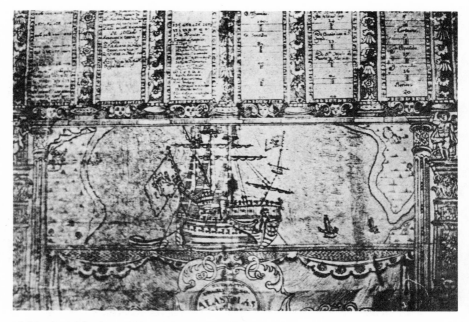

A Typical Mexican Ship Going to the Philippines

days before his wife and Almeida's were arrested, he left Mexico City to meet it at New Spain's western port, the insalubrious and mosquito-infested shantytown of Acapulco.

The ship, equipped and freighted, set sail for the Orient on December 29. It carried twenty-four passengers and a crew of forty-five. One of the passengers was the scandalous Felipe de las Casas, incorrigibly addicted in his youth and early manhood to fighting, gaming, and women, but later in life, as the Franciscan friar Felipe de Jesús, destined to become a martyr and a saint. At the ship's helm was Antonio Díaz de Cáceres himself.[7]

The Philippines were a natural choice for Luis's brother-in-law. Since their discovery by Magellan in 1521, the islands, loosely governed through the viceroyalty of New Spain, had always looked particularly attractive to fugitives of every stamp, as well as to men with a clean past who were smitten with a prurient craving for quick and unscrupulous gains. In the Philippines villains and nonentities from the Americas often rose meteorically to positions of fortune and respect. The "Hernán Cortés of the Philippines," Miguel López de Legazpi, had been the humble secretary of the municipal government in Mexico City before he migrated to the islands. There he rode the wings of fame as conquistador, founder of cities like Cebú and Manila, and ultimately governor of the islands.

Through the gate of the Philippines one also traveled to the fabled lands of China, Japan, India, and the Spice Islands. In the exotic ports of the East the adventurous merchant could stock his ship with the condiments and gems, the perfumes and porcelain, the silks, velvets, and linens, the marble carvings, the bone and jade, and the countless irresistible baubles that could bring him astounding wealth.[8]

When he arrived at Manila, Díaz de Cáceres claimed that he began laying plans to return to New Spain but was prevented from doing so by the authorities. It is probable that Díaz de Cáceres merely stated this for the record, for his family's cases were as yet far from decided. Besides, the Inquisition was moving toward issuing a warrant against him on October 20, 1590. In all probability, Díaz de Cáceres's only concern was to get permission to make a trading voyage to the rich colony of Macao.

The oldest outpost of any European power involved in the China trade, Macao was fast acquiring fame as "one of the noblest cities in the East, on account of its rich and noble traffic in all kinds of wealth to all parts."[9] It had been a mainstay of the Portuguese trading empire since its establishment in 1557. When Portugal was annexed to Spain in 1580, the Portuguese retained de facto control over the colony and its trade routes. Philip II respected this arrangement, but Spanish interlopers did not. They regularly invaded the colony in an effort to capture a share of its lucrative trade.

Thanks to carefully placed gifts and the intervention of an influential attorney named Erber del Corral, Díaz de Cáceres succeeded in obtaining official permission to travel to Macao. Perhaps the hostile governor of the Philippines, Pedro Dasmariñas, derived some sadistic joy in granting the permission, for he may have known that the interloper would not have an easy time once he reached the colony. This is, in fact, what happened. Díaz de Cáceres had hardly set foot on Macao when its authorities put him in chains and sequestered his ship. They then put him on a vessel bound for the East Indies and, probably, the port of Goa, Portugal's colonial headquarters in the Far East. There presumably he would be tried for his piratical acts.

Aware that the punishment awaiting him would prevent him from seeing his family for years, if not forever, Díaz de Cáceres decided to attempt a daring escape from Macao. Before the departure of the ship in which he was being held, he managed to file away his chains and, with the aid of a friend, stow away in the hold of another ship.

As long as this ship was in port, Díaz de Cáceres kept out of sight; his friend periodically brought him food and drink. Not until the vessel was on the high seas did he decide that it was safe to venture on deck. When he did he met with an unexpected reception. On discovering him, the crew, amid verbal and physical abuse, bound him in chains and tagged him for return to Manila.

Despite such mistreatment and the antipathy of the governor of the Philippines, it was not long before Díaz de Cáceres was again the owner of a ship laden with merchandise and this time bound happily for Acapulco. The ship was none other than *Our Lady of the Immaculate Conception*. How the ship got back to the Philippines and how it was restored to Díaz de Cáceres may never be known. Obviously Luis's brother-in-law lacked neither the friends nor the resources to recover quickly from any calamity.[10]

He left Manila around mid-July in 1592 and arrived in Acapulco, ill and enervated from the voyage, on November 24. But his troubles had not ended. The Inquisition had a warrant out for his detention. Two years before, on October 20, 1590, it had issued an order to its representative in Acapulco, Don Alonso Larios, the port officer in charge of the China Chancery, to clamp an embargo on Díaz de Cáceres's ship if and when it returned, and to place its entire cargo in escrow. The purpose of the sequestration by the China chancellor, as he was called, was to collect from Díaz de Cáceres a sum equivalent to what the Inquisition regarded as his wife Catalina's estate. As soon as Díaz de Cáceres entered Acapulco he was accordingly informed that he would be detained.

Almost immediately the chancellor examined the cargo of the *Saint Peter* and the books of both Díaz de Cáceres and Pedro de Solórzano, who served as captain or cocaptain of the vessel. The chief purpose of the examination was to determine whether Díaz de Cáceres was carrying contraband. "I did not find anything for certain," the chancellor wrote his superiors in the capital, "though there are some indications that he was. . . . The register is not clear." In a deposition Díaz de Cáceres admitted carrying three hundred unregistered quintals of iron for his account and that of Antonio de los Cobos, and the chancellor had reason to suspect additional irregularities.

On December 1, 1592, when the inquisitors opened the packet bringing the chancellor's report they also found a letter written by Díaz de Cáceres. In the letter Díaz de Cáceres asked the senior inquisitor to restore all his possessions and begged him to have regard for "a heart afflicted with so many hardships and persecutions."

In addition to the Inquisition, Díaz de Cáceres had to face the wrath of the local authorities in Acapulco. He had hardly set foot in the city when he was accused of dealing in damaged goods and failure to pay his crew. His enemies constantly harassed him and sought to stop his ship from proceeding to Peru. One of them, Jaime García, reviled him intemperately in front of the chancellor and was ready to attack him with his sword. On several occasions the mayor of Acapulco jailed Díaz de Cáceres, but he repeatedly succeeded in getting the chancellor to secure his freedom with an interlocutory decree from the Inquisition. On February 8, 1593, two and a half months after Díaz de Cáceres's arrival, the chancellor felt compelled to write to the inquisitors in Mexico City that

we have had a great deal of trouble with Antonio Díaz de Cáceres because he knows quite a bit. I also understand that he has managed to hide away a good part of his holdings as a result of Your Excellency's embargo, for he seeks to avoid all interrogation, using the embargo as a pretext. . . . The ship's boys and sailors in the ship's service for the past three years have been demanding their pay and he will not give it. Though I have told him to liquidate some property and pay them, he has refused. He keeps getting sent to jail daily by the mayor, and when he makes some payments, he is released at my request. . . . The affairs of this ship are so confused that God's help is necessary.

In March matters were still far from settled. Díaz de Cáceres managed to raise some money by selling his chinaware, but he could find no buyer for his iron, and he apparently could not collect moneys owed him from many sources, including Jorge de Almeida.[11]

Whether as a reaction to Díaz de Cáceres's actions or as part of a prior agreement with him, Jorge de Almeida decided to remain in the New World indefinitely. But if he harbored any illusions that he might escape the fate of his arrested in-laws, they did not last very long. They quickly evanesced when the Inquisition came to call for his wife, Leonor.

Though Almeida may not have been aware of it, the Inquisition had been cocking a watchful eye at him for some time. As early as April 18, 1589, his brother-in-law Gaspar had declared him to be a Judaizer. But through 1589 and the early months of 1590 the Inquisition chose not to trouble him. He went about his business without interference and spared no effort in behalf of the members of his family under arrest. While they were in jail, he contributed money to Isabel's account "for her food and comfort" and had messages and even gifts slipped into his in-laws' cells. In the days following the auto-da-fé he was a source of strength and comfort to them, and almost certainly also provided them with funds.[12]

But by June 1590 the Inquisition had become convinced that Almeida should at least be called for a preliminary investigation. They therefore sent a courier to his home, located near the main post office in Mexico City. When Almeida recognized the messenger at the gate as an emissary of the Holy Office, he ran out another door, mounted his horse, and headed straight for his property in the Taxco mines.[13]

The purpose of his visit to the Taxco region can hardly be mistaken. The Inquisition's call had quickly snuffed out Almeida's hope that he would be able to live unobtrusively in New Spain. Now, like Baltasar, he faced the alternatives of abandoning New Spain or going into hiding. Either move would have to be preceded by a careful disposition of his estate. He would have to collect all debts, including one from a man named Manuel Álvarez in the amount of some three

A Letter From Antonio Díaz de Cáceres Seeking Payment of a Claim against the Estate of Jorge de Almeida

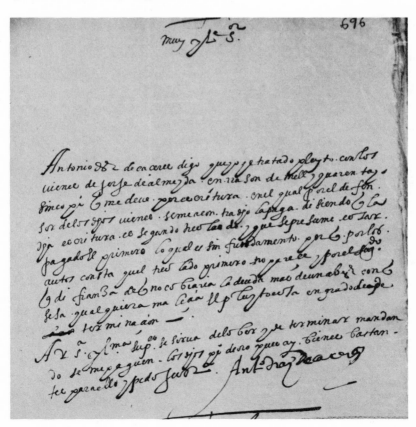

thousand pesos. He would have to determine what to do with the substantial moneys being held for him by a friend, Felipe de Palacios, who had taken over the duties as administrator of Almeida's properties. He would have to sell every possible piece of equipment and real estate under his own name and then take the funds with him or leave them with friends in New Spain. The title of Almeida's large mining hacienda in the Taxco region had already been transferred for this purpose to Tomás de Fonseca of Tlalpujahua.[14]

The inquisitors did not need a report from their emissary to predict the direction of Almeida's escape. They knew very well that fright would propel him directly to his mining properties. Accordingly, on June 13, they sent their scribe, Luis Morván, an inveterate enemy of Almeida's, to Taxco with orders for his arrest. For some unexplained reason, Morván took thirteen days to get from Mexico City to the Taxco mines. But when he did he imperiously flashed his warrant all over and set to work to apprehend his foe.

But Almeida began a game of hide and seek. He kept eluding Morván, slipping in and out of his estate at unexpected hours. In the meantime he attended diligently to the business of putting his affairs in order.

After a week or ten days of fruitless waiting, Morván decided on a more aggressive pursuit, but his efforts were cut short by a freakish accident on Friday, July 13. A bull that had escaped from the arena attacked Morván in front of the government's mining headquarters and wounded him so severely that he died before the animal could be lured away.[15]

Morván's sudden removal from the scene by an act of God gave Almeida the opportunity to slink out of Taxco and go into hiding in Mexico City. He found a covert similar to Baltasar's in a house behind the marketplace of Santiago Tlatelolco. Almeida's hiding place could not have been far from Baltasar's. It may even have been Rodríguez de Silva's home. Almeida was soon joined there by his brother Miguel Hernández.

Though his wife, Leonor, was permitted to move about with some freedom, Almeida did not want her to risk rearrest by using her as his contact with the outside world. The task was therefore assumed by his uncle Tomás de Fonseca of Tlalpujahua.[16]

In the meantime the Inquisition was frantically searching for Almeida. It was also meticulously adding to its store of incriminating information about him. Its principal witness was the sixty-year-old Julián de Castellanos, a Judaizer arrested in the spring of 1590 for celebrating the Passover. In testimony given in May and June of that year, Castellanos declared that Almeida, his brothers, and Antonio Díaz de Cáceres were Judaizers. But on July 14, the day after Morván's death, Castellanos retracted his accusations, stating that when he had testified against Almeida and the others, he believed he was going to die. A few days later he again implicated Almeida and the others, this time offering the explanation that he had cleared them out of fear that one of them might assassinate him.[17]

His own voluntary imprisonment helped Almeida attain two invaluable insights. The first was a recognition of the extent of his pride in his Jewish identity and a determination to maintain it at all costs. The many hours he spent in leisurely study and contemplation helped impel him to this conclusion. Once Luis, who was permitted some freedom in the city, came to pay him a secret visit and brought him a copy of Fray Luis de Granada's *Introduction to the Symbol of the Faith*. The two men studied the text for a while, particularly the sections dealing with the biblical prophets Ezekiel and Jeremiah. Almeida paused at the verse in Ezekiel that Luis remembered as "There will be only one flock and one shepherd, and Israel shall be captive no more." Since Israel had not yet attained unity and freedom, argued Almeida, the verse proved that the Messiah had not yet arrived.[18]

The second realization that dawned upon Almeida was that his continued hiding would serve little useful purpose. For his own sake and his family's he now decided to escape from New Spain. He planned to go to Madrid and then even to Rome to work for the liberty of his in-laws and the clearing of his own name. Accompanied by his brother Miguel Hernández, he rode to Veracruz on horseback and there boarded a ship destined for Spain. His older brother, Hector de Fonseca, remained in New Spain and was eventually arrested as a Judaizer by the Inquisition.[19]

Almeida's mining superintendent, Francisco Díaz, accompanied them as far as Havana. When he learned of Almeida's plans, he had come to Mexico City, contacted Almeida, and asked whether he might come along. Almeida and Hernández agreed to take Díaz, but left him behind in Havana when he failed to come up with a hundred ducats for the transatlantic voyage. Frustrated in his effort to return to the Old World, Díaz managed to get on a ship heading for Peru.[20]

From Havana, Almeida addressed a letter to his wife and at least one, dated February 4, 1591, to Luis and the rest of the family, in which he wrote:

From my letter to Doña Leonor you can follow the course I am taking. I shall merely tell you that I received word here that your brothers have arrived in Spain. After disembarking in Galicia, they went to Sanlúcar in good health and with the intention of going to Rome to seek absolution. May God, for His sake, give them His light and sustain them with His holy hand.

At this port I found Duarte de León, who is on his way to Spain, and Francisco Rodríguez, nephew of Simón Gómez, a silk mercer who has his shop at the entrance to town. I am sending my Leonor a half ounce of very good ambergris and an ounce of civet. I wish I could send her a million presents, for she deserves them all, and I wish all her brothers and sisters would regale her, for she has been such a good sister to all of them and such a good daughter to her mother. Francisco Rodríguez is also taking my dress suit, for I have found no use for it here; and since I am not going to Spain to play the gallant, but only to help Doña Leonor and my mother-in-law and brothers and sisters, I am sending it back so that you can hold it until my safe return, when I shall live happily in your midst. May God Himself give me contentment. Since He took away a greater contentment, He will return it at some other time.

Then he concludes with business:

Hector de Fonseca wrote that I should ask you for a letter with a statement of payment for four thousand pesos I paid to Antonio Díaz [de Cáceres] and some collateral that we gave one another. Please give them to him. And tell Tomás de Fonseca that I am in need of money because what I took out of Mexico City has all gone for ships and expenses. You will also tell Cristóbal Gómez that since he really owes me money he should send me some. . . . Here my debtors tell me they are in such straits that not one of them has a real. Maybe I can collect a few pesos. God be with you.[21]

After reading the letter, Luis, in a gesture of fraternal affection, sent it on to Gaspar in Oaxaca. On August 8, 1591, a week or so before he received word restoring him to his priestly functions, Gaspar perfidiously delivered the letter to the Inquisition. With it he wrote a note of his own, which said:

In a previous letter I sent you asking for mercy regarding the use of my orders, I devoted a section to Jorge de Almeida, whom I regard as a very true Christian and cannot be persuaded otherwise. Nevertheless, having learned after writing the letter that you have been looking for him, I do not want to remain satisfied with what I have written, but send you his own letter, written from Havana and delivered to me from Mexico City, so that if it should serve God and your most holy tribunal to know about him, his whereabouts may be known.

Gaspar de Carvajal's Covering Letter to the Inquisition Regarding Jorge de Almeida's Correspondence with His Family

This letter was sent to me by my brother Luis de Carvajal, to bring me news about my brother-in-law. My brother-in-law gives news about my two brothers, as you will see, in case you should want to make some inquiry to apprehend them.

It was for this reason that I decided to write this note. Please pardon the paper—I have nothing better—and have pity on this poor wretch. And may our Lord guard you with all the favors of heaven. This I ask. Amen.[22]

In Madrid, Almeida met two of his old Ferrara friends, Ruy Díez Nieto and his son Diego. Both were born New Christians on the Iberian Peninsula, but Diego claimed he was born in Ferrara and had never been a Christian. In Ferrara father and son had acquired a modest knowledge of Judaism. They knew much of the traditional Jewish liturgy, and recited the Amidah. They also knew something about the traditional Jewish calendar. They were engaged in various activities, including that of ransoming Jewish captives from the Moslems. Recently they had managed to procure a bull from Pope Clement VIII authorizing them to travel and collect money for this purpose.

When Almeida learned of the plans of Díez Nieto and his son, he secured permission from the court in Madrid for them to travel in the New World. In exchange for this favor, they promised to take along letters for Antonio Díaz de Cáceres, Luis, Doña Francisca, and Almeida's wife and sisters-in-law. They also paid him 100 or 150 ducats.

Shortly before Ruy Díez Nieto and his son sailed from Seville, Almeida delivered these letters to them in a parcel addressed to his brother-in-law Luis. They contained the good news that Baltasar and Miguel were living in Pisa as Jews, that Baltasar had married a Jewess named Ana, and that Miguel was "studying there in a Jewish school where many sages discussed the Law of Moses."

Almeida also had two additional parcels: one apparently containing the funds he had managed to accumulate for the Holy Office, the other with the documents releasing the Carvajals from the obligation of wearing their penitential garments. How instrumental Baltasar's help might have been in obtaining these documents is nowhere delineated. According to Luis, Almeida gave the parcels to the Díez Nietos for delivery in the New World. Luis and his family, however, could not come into possession of the documents until they were fully paid for. Not long after the arrival of the Díez Nietos, Almeida was compelled to write that he had been unable to raise the entire sum required, and that Luis had to find a way to make up the deficit.[23]

Through contacts like the Díez Nietos, Luis was able to keep in touch with his brothers in Europe. His chief contact was the Sevillian merchant Ruy Fernández de Pereyra. Antonio Rodríguez de Escarigo, mentioned in Baltasar's letter, may have been his pseudonym. Under Luis's influence Baltasar changed his name to David and Miguel to Jacob and both assumed the surname Lumbroso.[24]

Almeida had already been of inestimable help to his mother-in-law and sisters-in-law in the months before he was compelled to go into hiding.

Shortly after he heard of the plan to assign the Carvajal women to duties in separate convents, he went to see one of the inquisitors and said to him, "Sir, the action you are contemplating should be carefully weighed before it is put into effect. Do not forget that women are quite curious and impressionable. The damaging influence of these Carvajal women upon the nuns might be very difficult to counteract."

Almeida's words, if not his pressure, influenced the inquisitor to change the contemplated plan. He had Doña Francisca, Isabel, Catalina, Mariana, and Leonor released from the convents where they had been assigned and arranged for them to live together in a house near the Indian market in the district of Santiago Tlatelolco, within easy view of the Franciscan monastery. Almeida assumed responsibility for them.[25] Ana remained with Pedro de los Ríos until February 1592, when she was returned to the family and placed in the custody of her sister Mariana.[26]

Almeida was of no less help to his brother-in-law Luis.

Luis's confinement to the San Hipólito hospital brought him indescribable misery. He lived there in complete isolation from his immediate family. Even his cousin, Gonzalo Pérez Ferro, though free to visit him, did not, and Luis complained about this bitterly to Pérez Ferro's son.[27] He found it impossible to eat the hospital's food, since it invariably included pork, ham, or lard. In addition, Esteban de Herrera, his immediate supervisor, gave Luis two tasks that he found equally depressing. He made Luis an orderly and the custodian of the holy icons in the chapel. As a result of all this Luis felt so distressed that when he had to sweep a room "he did so by first moistening the floor with many tears."

Again Almeida came to the rescue. One day he told the inquisitors that he would have to take a protracted business trip to the Taxco mines. Since Doña Francisca and her daughters would be left without masculine supervision for a longer period than ever before, Almeida wondered whether the inquisitors might consider allowing Luis to stay with them for the duration of his trip. The inquisitors consented, and Luis was temporarily released from his duties at the convalescent hospital.[28] Since there is no record of Almeida's visiting his in-laws or moving about elsewhere in New Spain after this trip, it is likely that it took place sometime during the month of May 1590, just before the Inquisition summoned him for questioning.

By this time Doña Francisca and her daughters were receiving regular visits from a special chaplain and confessor assigned by the Inquisition. He was Fray Pedro de Oroz, a kind, elderly monk and one of the most distinguished members of the Franciscan order. After an early brush with the Inquisition occasioned by his unorthodox thinking, he had carved a brilliant career in the Franciscan hierarchy, crowned by a term as its commissary-general. Now retired, he was serving as the rector of the Colegio de Santa Cruz (the Holy Cross Academy), established for the education of Indians and located in Santiago Tlatelolco.[29]

The assignment of a man of Fray Pedro's caliber to Doña Francisca and her daughters testifies to the high esteem in which the Carvajals were held. It also appears to reveal the prestige and power of Jorge de Almeida.

Fray Pedro soon grew fond of the noble and cultured Carvajals, and before long he saw to it that they were provided with food and money. They were even given permission to employ an Indian maid.

Nor could Fray Pedro have been unimpressed with Luis's knowledge and bearing. When Luis's furlough was about to come to an end and Almeida had not yet returned, Doña Francisca and her daughters asked Fray Pedro whether he could arrange an extension. The monk said he would try. Shortly thereafter he announced an arrangement that could not have failed to strike the family as another miraculous fulfillment of their wishes. Fray Pedro told the family that he would have Luis permanently removed from the convalescent hospital and transferred to the Colegio de Santa Cruz. There Luis would serve as a teacher of the Indians and as Fray Pedro's personal secretary, helping him with his sermons and research. His responsibilities at the *colegio* would be so scheduled as to leave him free to spend nights with his family. Occasionally he would be permitted longer periods away from the academy.[30]

The Colegio de Santa Cruz had been in existence for fifty-four years. Though founded and endowed by the viceroy, Don Antonio de Mendoza, it owed its inspiration to a Franciscan monk named Fray Arnaldo de Basacio, a lifelong teacher of Indian children who wanted

Two Views of the Exterior of the Colegio of Santiago Tlatelolco

them to have a special school of advanced studies in Latin and the sacred texts of the church. Over the years the Colegio de Santa Cruz attracted a distinguished faculty, including the brilliant linguist and scholar Fray Bernardino de Sahagún. Under his leadership, as professor and then as rector, the Colegio de Santa Cruz became a great center for the study of the native culture of New Spain. Fray Bernardino died at an advanced age in February 1590, but when Luis arrived later in the year, his achievements were still very much alive.[31]

For Luis the doors of the *colegio* opened upon a wide and exhilarating world. In the oppressive atmosphere of the convalescent hospital he would never have thought that his life could undergo so radical a transformation. Nor could he have believed it possible that the *colegio* would afford him the fulfillment of another of his extravagant dreams.

When Francisco Ruiz de Luna began to practice Judaism he once told Luis that he wished he were in a monastery library where he could browse at will and study the sacred books.

Luis asked curiously, "Do you mean the libraries are open for all?"

"Yes," replied Francisco, "they are open for the common use and reading of all."

"I wish I could be in one of them," said Luis.[32]

The moment Fray Pedro de Oroz brought him into his private quarters, Luis realized that his dream had been fulfilled. He found himself in a library, amid books that he knew could at least partially slake his burning thirst for a deeper knowledge of his faith.

We do not know whether the books in Pedro de Oroz's quarters constituted the entire library of the *colegio* or just the monk's private collection. In either case it would be a fair conjecture that Luis soon had the entire library at his disposal. "God filled my hands with treasures," Luis jubilantly explained.[33]

The library gave evidence of a panoramic range of tastes and academic interest. It included Aristotle's *Dialectics,* Virgil, Juvenal and Cato, Cicero and Quintilian, Livy and Sallust, Pliny and Prudentius, Plutarch, Marcus Aurelius and Boethius, church fathers like Cyprian, Ambrose, Jerome, and Augustine, the medieval classics of Gerson and Aquinas, and even works of controversial contemporary thinkers like Juan Luis Vives and Erasmus. Bibles and books of devotion were present in abundance, and the *Antiquities* of Josephus was available for enthusiasts of sacred history.[34] In addition, there were numerous grammars, classical and modern, and various dictionaries, including vocabularies of the Indian languages of New Spain.

Even more miraculous than the presence of the library were Fray Pedro's actions facilitating Luis's use of the books.

One of the first things Fray Pedro did was to give Luis a key to his quarters, a privilege he extended to no one else in the monastery. Luis thus had access to the library at all times. He soon got into the habit of going there for private study when the monk and the collegians went to the refectory. In these peaceful moments he pored over the Bible and other sacred books and copied out passages that supported the Judaizers' beliefs.

Then Fray Pedro asked Luis to prepare a collection of illustrative material from the famous sixteenth-century commentary to the Pentateuch written by the Dominican Jerome Oleaster and first published in its entirety in 1569. If Luis was unaware of it before, it did not take him long to grasp that a distinctive feature of this commentary was

The Interior of the Colegio of Santiago Tlatelolco

its reliance on postbiblical Jewish sources. These included Moses Maimonides' Thirteen Articles of the Faith, "unknown and unheard of in lands of captivity," as Luis was to say, referring to the territories where Judaism could not be openly professed. Maimonides' name was not mentioned in connection with the Thirteen Articles in Oleaster's commentary, and Luis never learned their true authorship. Luis naturally found Oleaster to be "suited to his temperament and interests." He happily recognized that "were it not for God's help he could not have obtained it even if he were willing to part with all his blood in return."[35]

Then, within four months after his arrival at the *colegio*, Luis had another distinguished Christian commentary with rabbinic sources at his disposal. It was Nicholas of Lyra's *Glosses,* in a four-volume edition, acquired by Fray Pedro from the estate of another Franciscan monk. When the tomes were delivered, Fray Pedro joyously showed them to Luis and said revealingly, "What precious things we are bringing to our school!"

Although his assigned work brought him constantly into contact with his secret faith, Luis continued to carry on his private program of studies surreptitiously, fearing what might happen should it come to Fray Pedro's attention. On one occasion Luis had a frighteningly close call. He opened the library at mealtime and was about to enter when he had a premonition that Fray Pedro was approaching. Taking no chances, he quickly locked the door and hid in a nearby nook. A moment later the monk came down the corridor and entered his quarters. Luis regarded his presentiment as another of the many miracles being sent his way.[36]

Actually, Luis's fears about his benefactor may have been unfounded, for Fray Pedro's actions seem clearly to have been intended to aid the young Judaizer in the study of his faith. Why Fray Pedro acted as he did is naturally nowhere explained. Perhaps it was his way of squaring a personal account with the Inquisition. Perhaps it was his way of protesting the indignities and humiliations visited upon the New Christians as a group. Perhaps, more simply, it was his way of expressing affection for Luis and his noble family. Though Fray Pedro's motivation may be debated, the unusual opportunity he gave young Luis remains an indisputable fact.

The only other cause for alarm that Luis had during his early years at the *colegio* came when the warden of the Inquisition informed him that Francisco Ruiz de Luna, sentenced to the galleys for his first offense, had been returned to Mexico City and charged with Judaizing.

Luis was certain that the erstwhile friar would reveal the insincerity of his reconciliation to the church and that he would soon again be arrested by the Inquisition.

Around this time Luis's mother dreamed that the inquisitor thrust at Luis with a sheathed sword. The dream appeared to come true, for in reality Luis, though frightened, was unharmed. The inquisitors had discovered that Francisco had been taught Judaism by Luis. But when they asked whether the teaching took place before or after his cellmate's repentance and reconciliation, Francisco saved Luis by saying that it had happened before.[37]

In his hours of private study Luis pored diligently over the biblical books of Isaiah, Jeremiah, Ezekiel, Joel, Zechariah, and Daniel,[38] the books of the Apocrypha, Baruch, Tobit, and the Maccabees,[39] and the pseudepigraphical Fourth Ezra.[40] He also enjoyed sacred books, in Spanish, of later ages, like *The Mirror of Consolation, The Dialogues of the Love of God, The Guide of Sinners,* and, of course, Luis de Granada's *Introduction to the Symbol of the Faith*.[41] Oleaster appears to have intrigued him with his allegorical interpretations as to the meaning of biblical sacrifices.[42]

From the notes on such readings Luis compiled several booklets in Latin and Spanish. He made several copies of one containing the commandments and the Thirteen Articles of the Faith, reserving one for eventual shipment to Baltasar and Miguel in Europe and distributing the others among friends in New Spain. He prepared at least one copy of the psalms in Spanish translation and various collections of prophetic writings. He versified the Ten Commandments in Portuguese with an admixture of Spanish words and selections from Job in Spanish.[43]

He also composed a number of original works, including various liturgical pieces and a tract on "the manner of addressing God." These gave expression to the Judaizers' cardinal beliefs—the unity of God, the immutability of the Mosaic Law, the certainty of salvation for its adherents, the future coming of the Messiah, the "true Christ," as Luis said, and with it the vindication and glory of the Jews.[44]

Luis's creative genius even found some lighter outlets. Among his compositions was a poem composed of the names of forty-five of the leading Judaizers in New Spain.[45]

Conversations with friends occasionally broadened Luis's horizons of knowledge. Ruy Díez Nieto and his son gave him some new insights into the sacrifice of Isaac. Later a Portuguese Judaizer named Domingo Coelho (Cuello) taught Luis some new interpretations of the sale of Joseph by his brothers.[46] Luis identified with both biblical worthies: with Isaac because he was called upon to be a sacrifice for his family and even more with Joseph because he was divinely destined to be the provider for his people.

Having adopted the name of Joseph Lumbroso, Luis proceeded to refer to himself as Joseph in his autobiography.

He began to compose this unusual autobiography around 1591. It was a swift-moving and suspenseful narrative in the third person, in the manner of some fictional memoirs written in Spain. Its purpose was to record for others what Luis regarded as the miraculous events of his life, beginning with the Great Day "when divine mercy gave him the light to recognize it." Captioned "In the name of God, A[donay] S[evaoth], the Lord of hosts," the autobiography reveals Luis in his manifold roles as conquistador and merchant, organizer and leader of the secret Jews, scholar, and poet. It also discloses a man of deep sensitivity and intense religiosity, with a love for life and a respect for human dignity.

At the beginning of his autobiography Luis announced that he would record events "until the twenty-fifth year of his wandering," that is, until 1591. But he kept extending his notes and made his final entry shortly after October 1594.[47] For their protection Luis concealed the names of the many people whose actions are recorded on his pages.

Luis had all the freedom he could wish for in the *colegio*. He could entertain visitors at the school and travel almost at will within a generous radius from Mexico City. Much of this good fortune doubtless resulted from his exemplary deportment at the *colegio*. But at least a little was certainly due to the esteem and affection in which he was held by Fray Pedro de Oroz.

Luis looked upon his privileges as a skein of heavenly miracles. Even when workmen channeled a spring of water into the garden at the direction of the monk in charge, Luis regarded it as a miracle performed in his behalf because he had been looking for a pool or spring in which to bathe.[48]

But the greatest wonder was the way in which, under Luis's guidance, the *colegio* became the underground headquarters for the secret Jews of New Spain. Many of the leading Judaizers of the colony came to visit him there, including his old friends Manuel de Lucena and Antonio Díaz Márquez, and his cousin, Gonzalo Pérez Ferro; and they brought along many other Judaizers for Luis to meet and counsel. They also kept him informed of events in the world outside. On March 25, 1591, for example, Pérez Ferro came to report that he had attended the auto-da-fé that day, seen Francisco Ruiz de Luna sentenced for Judaizing, and enjoyed hearing about all the "heresies" the erstwhile friar had been accused of. Luis grew so fond of Pérez Ferro that he asked him to invest a thousand pesos he had concealed from the Inquisition.[49] Luis later regretted this move, because Pérez Ferro returned only three hundred pesos, pocketing the rest. Isabel said that as a result her brother and Pérez Ferro "were ready to kill one another."[50]

When Luis was given permission to travel freely to and from the *colegio,* he met many new Judaizers and reestablished contact with others, like Antonio López, a former muleteer named Gabriel Enríquez,[51] and Tomás de Fonseca of Tlalpujahua.[52] He frequently saw Jorge de Almeida and his brother Miguel Hernández. Almeida's other brother, Hector de Fonseca, shunned Luis for a while after his reconciliation, but eventually met and even discussed religion with him.[53]

Beginning in 1591 we find Luis frequenting Manuel de Lucena's home in Pachuca, still one of the major foci for the Judaizers outside of Mexico City. In Lucena's home he met important Judaizers like Manuel Díaz, Lucena's cousin, and Francisco Vaez, one of Lucena's servants. At one time Luis was there when Lucena and Catalina Enríquez, his wife, were nursing a sick Judaizer, Manuel Gómez Navarro, back to health. Also present was Gómez Navarro's brother, Domingo. With the help of Luis and Lucena, the invalid tried to convert his brother. Domingo Gómez Navarro not only refused to listen but threatened to report Manuel to the Inquisition. In late 1594 he did. As a result of his testimony the Inquisition apprehended his brother and Manuel de Lucena and almost arrested Luis de Carvajal himself.[54]

Nearly all the Judaizers promised that if arrested by the Inquisition they would not denounce one another "even if they were torn to pieces," as Luis said, and they often took an oath to this effect. They called each other brothers and referred to secret Jews as "good people" or "God-fearers." They also used euphemisms like "going to Portugal" or "going to my land" to indicate a Judaizer's escape to a Jewish community in Europe.[55]

Luis's elation at his new opportunities received a rude jolt when he first returned to his mother's house. To his utter dismay he discovered that Doña Francisca, Isabel, Catalina, Mariana, and Leonor had abandoned Judaism. They had become sincere Catholics. They attended mass regularly and dutifully recited their domestic devotions in a downstairs room converted into a chapel and appointed with religious statues. Their dietary habits gave no evidence of their former ways.

They ate forbidden foods, including ham and pork, without com-
punction.

Luis could not discern whether these changes were the result of
"the great fear imposed upon them by their enemies," the inquisitors,
or "the evil counsel of some friends." Without waiting to find out, he
immediately set about to reconvert his family, arguing that more important than the preservation of their lives was the salvation of their
souls and that this could be achieved only through a reversion to Jewish
practice. He urged his mother and sisters not to fear rearrest by the
Inquisition or death at the stake. He told them "that they would be
fortunate if they died for God, and if arrested he too would die firmly
believing in the Law of Moses."

Luis's persuasiveness proved effective, but not as rapidly as he
later liked to think. It was not until March 1591 that his mother and
sisters "with many tears and reverence . . . returned to their God and
Lord and to their credit cast away their filthy gods," though they
continued attending mass and confession to keep up appearances.
Mariana used to take the communion wafer, put it into a handkerchief,
and throw it away when she left the church. This began about a year
after Luis's transfer to the *colegio*.[56]

The family soon followed all the Jewish rites it had abandoned.
Doña Francisca and her daughters carefully observed the biblical dietary
laws, though they kept a supply of lard on hand with which to prepare
foods for visitors who might become suspicious. They slaughtered
their chickens in the manner traditional among the Judaizers, perhaps
even facing east or west, as some were accustomed to do. They drained
their fowl and meat of all blood and often ate the flesh roasted.[57]

They took pains to prepare for the Sabbath.[58] At sunset on Friday
they ushered in its observance with a lengthy hymn, and later in the
evening, sometimes as late as ten or eleven o'clock, they gathered for
their Sabbath devotions. When non-Judaizers were present on Friday
evening, they postponed their devotions until Saturday morning.[59]
They assembled, not in the little Catholic chapel on the first floor of
their house, but in an unadorned upstairs chamber. Luis carefully bolted
the outside door of the house before ascending to prayer and then locked
the door of the chamber from the inside before the service began.[60]

The service was the familiar one, built on the psalms, original
compositions, and improvisations, but now enriched by Luis's greater
knowledge. It began with the Hebrew profession of faith, *Shema'
Yisrael Adonay Elohenu Adonay Ehad* ("Hear O Israel, the Lord our
God, the Lord is One"), and its liturgical response, *Barukh Shem*

Kevod Malkhuto leOlam Vaed ("Praised be His name whose glorious kingdom is forever and ever"). For several of their prayers only the beginnings are known:

"Blessed be Thou, O Lord, King of the world . . . ,"

"Almighty God, aid of all souls . . . ,"

"Our King, the Mighty One of Jacob . . . ," and

"Our God and God of our Fathers. . . ."

One, of which several phrases remain, is hauntingly reminiscent of the traditional evening prayer: "In the name of the Lord, Adonay. Blessed be the name of the Lord Adonay forever, Amen, who brings the light of the morning to afternoon and from afternoon carries it to evening, and from evening until dawn and from dawn until morning."[61]

During the service Luis read his poetic translations of Job or the Ten Commandments or regaled his family with stories from the patriarchs and prophets that spoke of God's love for Israel and assured the fulfillment of His promises. And, led by Luis, the family recited his compositions:

> I would rather be a sexton
> In the house of the Lord
> Than be an emperor
> Of this entire world, . . .

or the poignant declaration beginning,

> If each day we but took the care
> To lift to God our songs of praise
> That He reveals in sending joy
> And favoring us in all our ways,
> Then our ills would not be persisting
> Our adversity would not long endure
> He would make us all worthy of blessing
> And implant us in His city most pure. . . .[62]

Or they sang them to the accompaniment of the guitar of their friend Manuel Fernández Cardoso's or Manuel de Lucena's harp.[63] Lucena insisted on making the Sabbath a day of dignity and joy. He once rebuked the Judaizer Duarte Gómez for coming to a Sabbath gathering with a dirty shirt, and he even chided the Carvajals for crying while they recited their Sabbath prayers.[64]

The women listened with rapt attention to the recitations and offered their prayers with intense devotion. Isabel and Mariana knew the prayers by heart and were prepared to lead the service in Luis's absence. Even little Anica had memorized much of the service not long after her reunion with the family.[65]

Inspired by Luis, the women often prayed privately during the week. Catalina recited psalms from a book of hours with a parchment cover that looked "as if it was rat-eaten, with some leaves wrinkled like dirty olives and the yellow color of its pages turned red."[66] Leonor, too, often recited her devotions during the week. On fast days she read penitential psalms and other appropriate prayers. Mariana frequently prayed in the solitude of her room. In addition, the women recited special prayers before lying down at night, upon arising in the morning, while dressing, and after eating.[67]

As previously, the Carvajals' liturgy did not vary appreciably from one sacred occasion to another, except for the stress on penitential psalms on fast days and the reading of occasional prayers on holidays like Passover or Shavuot, which they now celebrated for the first time, calling it the Festival of the Firstfruits.[68] For the Great Day, Luis composed an opening prayer, from passages in *Introduction to the Symbol of the Faith* and *Guide of Sinners,* beginning "God Almighty, my soul, afflicted on seeing and understanding the grievous punishment it has incurred because of the wickedness and sins and abominations against Thy precepts and commandments. . . ."

The family's favorite prayers for the Great Day included a prose recitation commencing "O God, true Lord, who dost not withhold Thy favor in the uninhabited deserts," and "Lord God Almighty, for the sake of Thy holy name and this Great Day, which Thou hast established that by our fasting and repentance of our sins Thou mightest pardon us and have mercy upon us." Of these prayers, too, no more is known.[69] They also recited the long poem "Receive my fast in penitence."

In addition to the Great Day the family now fasted with some regularity on Mondays, Wednesdays, and Thursdays.[70] One or two of the women even joined Luis in fasts from sunrise to sunset during the nine days preceding the Day of Pardon, though at times, when in the company of non-Judaizers, they deliberately broke their fast at noon.[71] They often observed extraordinary fasts. Isabel, still "a great faster," continued to observe the three-day Fast of Esther, of which Luis used to say that anyone keeping it "was more an angel than a human being."[72] She also regarded it as a virtue to keep a two-day fast in honor of Judith, as she had always done. She now explained that she liked to do so because when she was a devout Catholic she fasted regularly in honor of the Virgin from noon on Maundy Thursday to the following Saturday morning. She called it the Fast of Anguish "because before she was a Jewess she used to fast it in memory of the anguish of Our Lady, the Virgin Mary."[73]

The Carvajals said their prayers standing and occasionally, especially on fast days, kneeling. They also turned their faces toward the East.[74] On fast days and at times on other occasions they wore cilices to mortify their flesh. Isabel's and Catalina's cilices were six fingerbreadths wide.[75] On pronouncing the word Adonay they often fell to their knees. On reciting the *Shema' Yisrael* they lowered their heads, placing the left hand on the forehead and the right over the heart.[76]

Once the women returned to an earnest observance of Jewish ritual and custom they never thought of leaving Judaism again. Within a short while Manuel de Lucena was able to refer to them as saints, doubtless not only because of the extent of their practice, but also because, at Luis's urging, they tried to bring as many potential secret Judaizers as possible into the fold. Because Luis was so eager to speak of Judaism, even with people about whose loyalties he could not be sure, his family later said that he taught them to Judaize "with less circumspection" than before their reconciliation.[77] Yet in all other respects the family as a whole was as cautious as ever. Mariana was an exception. Tottering on the precipice of madness, she decided to express her Judaism in two perilous ways. She once took the statues from the family chapel and hurled them into the street. They were chipped but apparently not broken. Leonor and Doña Francisca ran out, frantically collected the statues before any scandal occurred, and put them back on the altar. Then Mariana decided to denounce herself to the Inquisition in order to attain a voluntary martyrdom. Doña Francisca, Leonor, and Isabel finally persuaded her not to, for it would have led to the martyrdom of the entire family.[78]

Thus ironically the Carvajal women's perpetual prison, where they were to purge their sins against the church, became a center for Judaism and a refuge for the secret Jews. Though the family was circumspect about its religious practice, the constant stream of former and suspected Judaizers could not have escaped the notice of the Carvajal's mentor and confessor. Yet not a word of protest from Fray Pedro de Oroz is anywhere recorded, though he had taken pride in commending Leonor for her Christian deportment at the end of her sentence in 1591 and doubtless did the same for Catalina and Mariana the following year.[79]

It was at his mother's home that Luis met the beautiful and talented

Justa Méndez, the most alluring of all the secret Jewesses in the history of New Spain. She was the daughter of a seamstress, Clara Enríquez, and the late Francisco Méndez, the sister of the muleteer Gabriel Enríquez, and cousin to the exemplary Judaizers Pedro and Diego Enríquez and to Lucena's good friend Manuel Díaz. She had been born in Seville around 1572 and came to the New World late in 1588 or early in 1589 on a ship belonging to Alonso López de Escamilla. Bright and learned, she was spending some time on the ship reading the section entitled "The Life of the Patriarch Abraham" in a book called *The Ecclesiastical Monarchy* when a young man named Luis Pinto came over to her, engaged her in conversation, and gradually convinced her to become a secret Jewess. At least so Justa Méndez said. Chances are, however, that she had been indoctrinated into Judaism in Spain.[80]

It was Manuel de Lucena who first brought Justa Méndez and her mother to the Carvajal home early in March 1591, shortly after the family had reverted to Judaism. The two women were present, along with Lucena and Tomás de Fonseca of Taxco, when the family observed the Passover on the night of March 14. They joined in the meal of tortillas and fish. At the prayer service they heard Luis explain "the history of this festival, and how it was necessary to celebrate it standing, with loins girded and staff in hand."[81]

Luis and Justa were immediately drawn to one another, and their friendship soon ripened into love. For a while Luis thought of marrying Justa as soon as his penitential garb was redeemed. But then he abandoned the thought, perhaps deciding that he might have to flee New Spain while still under sentence. When he learned that a rich Judaizer named Cardoso from the city of Querétaro had met with Gabriel Enríquez in Michoacán to ask for Justa's hand, he displayed more than a slight trace of jealousy. He advised Clara Enríquez not to consent to the match, asserting that Cardoso would be the gainer, Justa, the loser in such a marriage.[82]

Luis instructed Justa Méndez in Jewish practices and history. He prepared a book of prayers for her and gave her a copy of his book of commandments. Justa guarded these presents vigilantly, lending them only to trusted Judaizers like Manuel de Lucena and Manuel Gómez Navarro so that they might make personal copies. Once she lent it to her cousin Pedro Enríquez for a half hour's cursory reading.[83]

One day the booklet and some sheets of paper containing prayers transcribed by Luis were lying open on a desk within the easy view of anyone chancing to come into the house, when a bailiff unexpectedly entered to attach some mules belonging to Justa Méndez's brother.

Maintaining her calm, Justa Méndez swiftly picked up booklet and papers and hid them in her bosom before the bailiff noticed them. She was so thrilled that she had saved the books and papers—and Luis—that she made Luis a dish of apple fritters in celebration.

Justa and her mother became frequent visitors to the Carvajal home both on weekdays and on Sabbaths. Occasionally they would spend the night there. One Friday night was particularly memorable. Justa Méndez and her mother came for dinner around eight or nine o'clock. After dinner the family gathered for a religious service that lasted until midnight. Justa Méndez, not yet fully acquainted with the service, listened enraptured and nodded assent "in the same way as Christians listening to a preacher preaching the gospel" while Luis sang, read from Oleaster, and explained the last chapter of the Book of Joel.[84]

On weekdays the women would dress plainly, Justa in a woven taffeta and her mother in a blue skirt and black robe of coarse cloth. But on the Sabbath they were elegant, Justa wearing a crimson skirt with multicolored stripes and a mulberry or black taffeta cloak, and Clara Enríquez attired in a woolen robe and freshly laundered head-dress.[85]

The first time they visited the Carvajals on a Sabbath, Clara Enríquez brought her sewing, but was informed that "here nobody works on the Sabbath."[86]

Luis and his sisters reciprocated these visits. Mariana once spent an entire week at Justa's home and Anica, a month.[87]

By the end of 1592 the Carvajals could enjoy a greater serenity than had been possible since long before their arrest. Reunited under one roof, favored by a man of the caliber of Fray Pedro de Oroz, and engaged in the fulfillment of the religion they regarded as the sole expression of God's will, the Carvajals could reflect upon their uncertain future with some measure of equanimity.

Life seemed to lay four alternatives before them. One, voluntary martyrdom, they rejected out of hand when Mariana wished to try it. Another was to wait for the commutation of all their sentences and then remain in the New World as secret Jews. A third was to attempt an immediate escape from New Spain. The fourth was to wait until the commutation of the sentences—after which they would all be permitted to travel—to move unobtrusively to Spain and then to slip out to France, Italy, or the Ottoman Empire, where they could live openly as Jews.

Luis, always practical, sought to secure the survival of his family with the minimum possible risk. Accordingly, he chose the last of these alternatives. He decided to wait until his penitential cloak and those of Isabel and his mother were officially removed and then to follow essentially the same path to Europe taken by his brothers and brother-in-law.[88]

9 The Dream

Squirming out of his difficulties at Acapulco, Antonio Díaz de Cáceres returned to Mexico City, still indisposed and still confronted by a host of problems. The most vexing of these was how to dissipate the cloud of suspicion cast over him by the Carvajals' conviction on the charge of having Judaized.

To insure a public image of supreme fidelity to the church, Díaz de Cáceres resorted to an unassailable, if extreme, stratagem: he refused to live with his wife and child or even to see them. He went instead to the home of his business partner, Antonio de los Cobos and stayed there until he was again arrested, this time apparently on the charge of passing damaged goods. At the time of his release he petitioned to stay on in jail in order to avoid facing the choice of returning to his wife or again rejecting her. Not until the late summer of 1593, nine months after his arrival in Mexico City, did Díaz de Cáceres resume his life with Catalina, and then only at the instance of learned theologians sent by the senior inquisitor.[1]

Yet despite the glaring excesses of his apparent Catholic piety, Díaz de Cáceres at heart remained an impassioned Judaizer. Catalina, herself bordering on the fanatical in her devotion to Judaism, soon said that her husband was such a faithful Judaizer that she was not worthy to take off his shoes.[2]

Almost from the moment of his return, Díaz de Cáceres's home became a vital ganglion of secret Judaism in Mexico City. His mother-in-law and sisters-in-law moved in with him, and friends of the family began to frequent the house. The Sabbath and dietary laws of the Judaizers were carefully observed, and Díaz de Cáceres himself was often present during prayer services and religious discussions led by Luis or other members of the family.[3] Catalina had already begun to indoctrinate her daughter into Judaism, although she was only six years old. She had taught Leonor prayers and hymns and required her to recite them at the appropriate times. Whenever the child balked, Catalina beat her and told her that she would not be fed until she complied.[4] When Leonor was still suckling, Catalina had refused to feed her on the Great Day.[5]

Díaz de Cáceres went about his business on the Sabbath, even refusing to don clean clothes in honor of the day. Though food served in his home was rigorously prepared according to the Judaizers' dietary laws, he always ate forbidden foods outside.[6]

If Díaz de Cáceres concurred with the substance of his family's beliefs, he complained vehemently and often violently about the conspicuousness of their Jewish practice. He did not like the idea that his daughter could recite the Judaizers' prayers. He told her not to do so and instead made her learn prayers like the Lord's Prayer, the Hail Mary, and the Hail Holy Queen.[7] He chided Catalina for not feeding their child on the Great Day.[8] He once took his daughter away from his wife, but when little Leonor began to cry, he changed his mind and returned her.[9] He kept urging his mother-in-law and sisters-in-law to be more circumspect in their observance, reminding them of their certain fate if they were rearrested as secret Jews.[10] He warned Isabel to desist from her customary acts of Jewish penance. Once in a fit of anger he ripped off the wide horsehair cilice she was wearing, tore it to shreds, and threw it into a well, along with her prayer book. He even threatened to denounce Isabel to the Inquisition.[11]

When Ruy and Diego Díez Nieto arrived in Mexico City, Luis took them to dinner at his brother-in-law's. Before dinner the visitors spoke freely about the *judería* in Ferrara, until Díaz de Cáceres, apparently realizing that he had allowed his mask to fall, abruptly ended the conversation by saying, "Let us drop the subject and go have dinner."[12]

By any gauge, Díaz de Cáceres's compulsive concern was legitimate, not only because the family had once been found guilty of Judaizing, but also because a new problem had developed that made their situation even more precarious.

The family's new problems had begun in August 1592, on a Sabbath morning when Luis, Mariana, and Anica were on their way to Justa Méndez's house. Mariana had asked Luis to take her there that day because a Catholic festival was being celebrated in their neighborhood and she did not want to be home when the religious procession passed her house. In order to observe the Sabbath properly Mariana asked Luis for permission to take along her favorite book, a copy of Luis's booklet of prayers, psalms, and other scriptural passages bound in green velvet. Luis agreed and Mariana put it in her bosom.

Luis and his sisters were walking along a main thoroughfare when Mariana realized that the booklet was missing. The trio retraced their steps searching for the booklet, but it was nowhere in sight. Certain that it had been picked up and was already on its way to the inquisitors, they went home to report the tragic loss to the rest of the family. So shocked were his mother and sisters, said Luis, that "they would have taken their own lives in order not to fall into hands as cruel as their enemies' were it not for the fear of damning their souls."

From then on the family lived in helpless terror, expecting an inquisitorial agent whenever they heard a knock on the door. Everything they did revealed their anxiety. When they went shopping they bought only half as much oil and foodstuffs as they used to and worried whether they would be able to finish even this amount. Luis began spending some nights away from the *colegio* in order to dig an escape tunnel beneath his mother's house.

When their Indian maid announced one day that an officer was at the door, the family was petrified. It took them some time to recover their composure and go downstairs to open the door, but when they did they learned to their great relief that the officer had come to give them a present from the mayor's office. The mayor's inspectors had confiscated the bread in a certain bakery because the loaves lacked the required weight, and the mayor was sending the Carvajals two baskets-ful of bread, enough to last for more than a week. The family regarded this good fortune as nothing less than a miracle.[13]

Luis himself had a close call at the *colegio*. The inquisitorial commissary of Veracruz, a Franciscan, came to lodge there for discussions regarding a dispute on protocol between officers of the crown and a constable of the Inquisition at San Juan de Ulúa. The commissary had a brother who was a Dominican, and now that the commissary was at the *colegio*, he asked him for a favor involving Luis. A great preacher of his order had lent him a notebook, and he was eager to have it copied. Having heard of Luis's fame as a calligrapher, he was thinking of engaging Luis for the task, but first he wanted his brother, the commissary, to intercede with the rector of the *colegio* to obtain a sample of Luis's handwriting.

One day Fray Cristóbal, the brother superior at the *colegio*, sent one of the monks for Luis. As Luis approached the place where Cristóbal was standing, he saw a stranger beside him. He asked his escort who the stranger was. The escort replied that he was a commissary of the Inquisition. Luis was troubled. And he quaked when Fray Cristóbal turned to his guest and said, "There he is!" When the commissary took Luis to his room and asked for a sample of his handwriting, Luis was certain that he wanted to compare it with the script in Mariana's lost booklet.

Luis immediately began to plan an escape from the city. But his plans were interrupted by the good news that the commissary wanted his handwriting for a purpose quite different from what he had imagined. He told Luis that his brother was considering asking him to copy the notebook of a great Dominican preacher, and now, having seen his hand, he was prepared to proceed with his request. The commissary's brother sent the notebook on to Fray Pedro de Oroz, and soon Luis was hard at work on it. Once again he regarded himself as the recipient of a miracle.

The only drawback of Luis's new task was that, when added to his other duties, it left him little time for prayer and personal studies, "for the service of the Lord, his God," as he called it. But as Luis himself said, "Even this unbearable situation was converted by the Lord into a means for Joseph's consolation and eventual freedom."[14]

It was around this time that Almeida's friends Ruy and Diego Díez Nieto came to New Spain with the news of the family's conditional liberty, and the need for additional sums of money.[15]

At this point Luis decided to avail himself of the inquisitorial commissary's favorable disposition toward him. He asked the commissary to help him secure permission to travel about the country to raise the required sums, or to seek alms, as the procedure was piously called. Coincidentally, Luis could not have failed to realize that the greater his freedom of movement was, the easier it would be for him to escape should he receive word of pursuit by the Inquisition.

Luis's request was favorably received. He was granted six months' leave, apparently to begin anytime he desired. Luis was eager to start immediately. Since the transcription of the Dominican's notebook was nowhere near completion, he hired four Indian scribes to finish the task at his own expense. The commissary did not seem to mind this arrangement, but Fray Pedro de Oroz surprisingly objected to it. In an unusual mood of pique he told Luis, "It is unfair for you to leave before finishing the inquisitor's notebook. A fine thing it is that now that they have given you liberty you contemn them and abandon your work."

Luis realized that it would require more than a half year for him to finish the project by himself and that this would painfully delay "his going into hiding," as he put it. Yet once again his dilemma evanesced in an extraordinary, and as far as he was concerned miraculous, way.

On the very day that Fray Pedro de Oroz chided Luis for abandoning his task, the brother of the inquisitorial commissary sent two pages to the *colegio* to pick up the notebook. The preacher was leaving the area, and since he needed his notebook, the commissary's brother was obliged to return it even though the transcription had not been completed. Fray Pedro was stunned by the coincidence of this event and Luis's desire to begin his extended leave, and may have viewed it as a sign of God's divine intervention. He again showed himself considerate to Luis and interposed no objection to his plans.

Other seemingly miraculous benefits soon began to flow Luis's way. When the provincial of the Franciscan friars heard that Luis had been granted permission to seek alms, he prepared letters patent to assure him a friendly reception in all the Franciscan monasteries. The provincial of the Augustinian friars drafted a similar letter for the monasteries of his order. The vicar-general of the Franciscans gave Luis fifty commendatory letters of introduction, and the governor of the archbishopric granted him an indefinite extension of his leave. Emboldened by all this good fortune, Luis applied for a letter of recommendation from the viceroy. Here again he met with success, though he had little expectation that his request would be honored. The viceroy placed twenty-five such letters at Luis's disposal.

Armed with these documents, Luis began to travel like a celebrity through New Spain, often without his penitential garb. Wherever he went he was accorded the finest reception, and people presented him with money and food, including cheese, corn, and hens. He deposited these from time to time in his mother's house.

The only recurring problem Luis experienced in his travels came when he was invited to eat in the monasteries. Fearing that he would be served forbidden foods, he declined all invitations, or gave some plausible excuse for not eating if he joined them at their table. "It often happened," Luis later wrote, "when he left the company and board of these men . . . that he went to eat his bread among the beasts, thinking it better to eat among horses in cleanness than in uncleanness at the tables of his well-bred foes."[16]

Among the places Luis visited was the Hospital of Santa Fe at Huastepec. He went there to spend some time with the saintly Gregorio López, who was as concerned as ever with the plight of the

New Christians. He went for a walk in the garden with López and his constant companion, Father Losa. When Losa wandered off for a few moments, López turned to Luis, pointed to his *sambenito,* and said that he should be the one wearing it and not young Carvajal. López told Luis to be happy with his lot, for he was a sheep divinely appointed as a sacrifice for his entire flock and that in consequence he should greatly thank the Lord. Luis left the hospital encouraged by the words of Gregorio López and also more convinced than ever that López was really a secret Jew.[17]

His travels afforded Luis excellent opportunities to see other Judaizers. One of the most colorful was a Señor Carrión, a shoemaker by training and a farmer by occupation. Carrión had been part of Dr. Morales's circle a decade before. Luis met Carrión at Pachuca in the late summer of 1593 at Manuel de Lucena's house, where the shoe-maker-farmer had come to sell some cheese and cream. At the time Luis did not know that Carrión was a Judaizer. But when Carrión learned the identity of Lucena's visitor, he gave Lucena the cream for nothing. At that time or shortly thereafter he invited Luis to dinner.

At Carrión's, early in September, Luis ate in the company of his host, his wife, the mestizo daughter of a Portuguese Judaizer, and a number of other people, apparently workers on Carrión's farm. When the main course, a cabbage stew, was served, Luis told his host that he would not eat it. Carrión then asked his wife to fry some eggs for him. After dinner, Luis explained to Carrión that he had declined to eat the stew because he feared it had been prepared with lard. Carrión, obviously attempting to avoid any suspicion of participating in Jewish rites answered Luis loudly, "Here we eat everything."

Carrión apparently pressed Luis to stay on with him for a while, but Luis refused, saying that he had to go to nearby Pachuca for a few days to collect some debts from Lucena. He promised to return and left his traveling pack with Carrión. But when Carrión saw Luis stopping to bathe at a brook just outside his property, he realized that it was the eve of the Great Day and that Luis was taking a ritual bath. Carrión surmised that in all probability Luis would remain in the area, near some Indian settlements, where his behavior would not be likely to arouse suspicion.

The next day Carrión sent one of his servants on horseback to find Luis. In the saddletree the servant held Carrión's three-year-old son, who carried a basket of roasted eggs, tortillas made with butter, grapes, and possibly some Indian figs for Luis. The servant also relayed a message to the effect that Carrión was piqued at Luis "for having left his house and gone to an Indian settlement," and wanted Luis to return to his home immediately. Luis declined the invitation, repeating that he had to first go on to Pachuca. But once again Luis failed to go, and when Carrión, going about his chores, saw Luis the next day, he chided him personally for leaving his home. Their conversation led Luis and Carrión to a formal declaration of their devotion to secret Judaism.

Luis explained that he had gone off to celebrate the Great Day. He was observing the fast for forty-eight hours instead of twenty-four. This was doubtless due to the confusion caused by the Díez Nietos. They knew that the occurrence of the new moon determined the date of the Great Day but were still not sure which was the correct day of its occurrence in the traditional Jewish calendar.

Luis promised Carrión to come to his home on Friday night, at the conclusion of the fast, and to spend the Sabbath with him. He kept his promise but was disappointed by the meal. The food had been prepared with lard, and the presence of a lieutenant from Octupa deterred him from asking for alternative dishes. Luis was ravished by hunger. When everyone else had gone to bed, he got up and munched on some stale food he had stored in his saddlebags.[18]

Why Luis did not go to Lucena's house to celebrate the Great Day is not known. Many of the most committed Judaizers in New Spain were there, including Justa Méndez and Manuel Gómez Navarro. Perhaps Luis thought that there were too many people there for his safety. Or perhaps the group included some people with whom Luis did not want to become unnecessarily involved.[19]

The following year Luis spent the Great Day in almost identical fashion in the little Indian village of Tilcuantla, less than a league away from Lucena's house. This time he sent an Indian with a message to Lucena asking for bread and candles.[20]

By now, apparently, the question of the correct Jewish calendar was a topic of discussion among a number of Judaizers. A week before this Great Day, Luis, Sebastián de la Peña, Sebastián Rodríguez, Constanza Rodríguez, and Domingo Rodríguez were discussing the necessity of counting the Jewish month from the time of the new moon.[21]

When Luis first returned from his travels to Mexico City he hesitated to proceed directly to his mother's house. Still haunted by fear that the Inquisition might be lying in wait for him, he went to Catalina's house to ask whether all was well. Catalina told him that shortly after he left the city an inquisitorial page had come to call for him at Doña Francisca's, but apparently there was no current danger

Perturbed by Catalina's report, Luis went on to his mother's house, but was soon relieved to learn that the appearance of the page had nothing to do with the object of his fears.[22]

Luis's mother and sisters seem to have moved out of Díaz de Cáceres's home during the fall of 1593. They were still living there at the time of the Great Day and all participated in celebrating it, along with Ruy Díez Nieto. Ruy's son, Diego, was near Pachuca then, but he was back in Mexico City to celebrate the Feast of Tabernacles at Díaz de Cáceres's home five days later.[23]

During the fast Díaz de Cáceres ate at midday and then left the house to go about his business. When the fast was over he refused to join the family for their sacral meal. So said Mariana.[24] Her sister Anica disagreed and said that Díaz de Cáceres fasted with the family all day.[25]

The immediate cause for Doña Francisca's move from her daughter's home appears to have been Doña Mariana. Since losing Luis's book she had slipped back into her manic-depressive cycle. Leonor said that Mariana's madness came on each month "with the waning of the moon."[26] In her manic states Mariana gibbered incessantly, and while much of what she said was unintelligible, she would occasionally utter embarrassing truths or vulgarities in the presence of her family and visitors. These visitors often included monks and nuns.[27] In addition, Mariana would from time to time parade around the house stark naked and tell people to worship her.[28]

Mariana spent the Great Day of 1593 tied to a bed in Díaz de Cáceres's home, despite her protestations that she was lucid. Díaz de Cáceres, who had thus secured her, apparently did not want to take any chances of being embarrassed by her in front of people like the Díez Nietos. It was probably around this time that Díaz de Cáceres, in another of his moments of fury, broke Mariana's arm against a bedpost.[29]

In their own home Doña Francisca, Isabel, and Leonor continued to have a difficult time with Mariana. Contemporary medical practice called for stomach cauteries for illnesses like Mariana's, and when these were applied, the pain provoked Mariana to such rage that she hurled whatever she could lay her hands on at her mother and sisters. According to Luis, only God's mercy prevented her from killing someone. Visiting friends were moved to compassion for the family when they observed Mariana in her rage and bemoaned the family's troubles "as if they were their kith and kin."[30] The family was at the point of asking Fray Pedro de Oroz to have Mariana committed to the Convalescent Hospital. Antonio Díaz de Cáceres summed up the situation perfectly when he said, "The household was going to pieces."[31]

Yet Díaz de Cáceres vehemently opposed the family's attempt to institutionalize Mariana. In taking this stand he was doubtless less concerned about Mariana's welfare than the possibility of her making public mention of his secret Judaism. He therefore argued bitterly with the family over Mariana's fate. In the course of one argument he slapped his mother-in-law and his sister-in-law Leonor.[32] In another he threw Doña Francisca and Leonor down a flight of stairs.

Relations between Díaz de Cáceres and his in-laws grew so strained that when Catalina fell ill and Doña Francisca and her daughters came for a visit, he refused them admittance and shut the door in their faces.[33]

To add to the family's misfortunes, little Ana came down with a throat ailment in the nature of quinsy. The illness lasted more than eight months, and the doctors decided to treat it by lancing her throat. The operation permanently impaired her speech. No one in the family could understand her except Leonor. Anica's heartrending predicament somewhat softened Díaz de Cáceres's hostility toward his in-laws, and he permitted the invalid to spend some time with Catalina.[34]

Luis said that he managed to collect more than 850 pesos in his travels, enough to make up the deficit in the moneys due for the release of the family's certificates of liberty. Apparently the sum included unredeemed pledges, for when the final writ of liberty reached Mexico City on October 10, 1594, Luis had only 420 pesos in cash and found himself constrained to borrow the rest. He paid his final installment on the day the liberty was granted.[35]

In early October the family received another jolting fright when a constable came to summon them to the inquisitors' audience chambers. Once again their fears proved unfounded. The inquisitors had called them to take depositions in the case they were preparing against Miguel. Since the boy was safely out of the Inquisition's reach, the family did not mind volunteering information about him that did not further incriminate those living in New Spain. The family was so relieved by their escape from this Inquisition that on returning home "they joyously celebrated God's merciful deliverance with sacred hymns and songs."[36]

On October 24, 1594, Luis, his mother, and his sisters Catalina and Leonor had their penitential garbs removed. Dr. Lobo Guerrero imposed various spiritual penances on Luis, including prayers and pilgrimages and fasting on Fridays for two years. He admonished Luis to ask "the Holy Spirit to show him favor that he might persevere in the belief of the evangelical law of our Lord Jesus Christ."[37] Lobo Guerrero also took the occasion to ask sarcastically why the Messiah of the Jews, so long awaited, had not yet come. Luis later said that he felt like telling the inquisitor that his theology was all wrong and wanted to conclude by saying, "I shall go to rejoice in paradise, while you, dog, will go to hell."[38]

Once his liberty was attained, Luis involved himself with renewed vigor in the administration of Jorge de Almeida's estate, serving as his brother-in-law's agent. He also began planning to leave New Spain with his family in the spring fleet. Included in the emigrants would be Fray Gaspar, who by now had apparently become convinced that he did not have much of a future in the New World.[39]

Luis also appears to have formulated plans for the safeguarding of his most treasured papers against loss or seizure by the Inquisition. These included his memoirs, the booklet with prayers and scriptural selections intended for his brothers, and some letters, among them very possibly those dealing with Almeida's estate. By the end of January he had placed his memoirs in the ceiling of the attic, where a wooden board had been removed. The prayer book and probably the other papers as well were concealed behind a movable plank in the ceiling of a corridor, near a window next to some large earthen jars.[40] At the same time he sewed a copy of the booklet containing the Ten Commandments into the lining of his hat.[41] In the floor of the attic Luis hid a number of religious sculptures, "among them a Christ and the most holy virgin and Saint Mary Magdalene." These were probably the statues that Mariana had chipped. The likelihood is increased by the fact that Luis was planning to burn these statues. He was clearly determined to leave no evidence that might be used to incriminate his family.[42] Luis was more confident than ever that he was "on the eve of leaving" New Spain, "with the help and favor of God most high and almighty."[43]

On the very day that the penitential garb was removed from Luis, his mother, and two sisters, Domingo Gómez Navarro appeared before the Inquisition to denounce his brother and Manuel de Lucena for trying to convert him to Judaism in Lucena's home a short while before. He also mentioned that there were others in Lucena's house at the time, including Luis de Carvajal.

One day Luis, properly attired in his penitential garb, had come to the home of his friend Manuel Álvarez. Álvarez was not home, having gone off to Veracruz with his son, but Domingo Gómez Navarro was there, along with Justa Méndez and Ana Vaez. Domingo Gómez Navarro thought he recognized Luis and recalled that he had seen him at Manuel de Lucena's house without his *sambenito*. Showing some surprise, he asked Luis, "What is your name?"

Before Luis could answer, Justa Méndez, unaware of the reason for Gómez Navarro's astonishment, turned to him and said, "Why are you surprised? Why do you ask his name? Look at him, he's the nephew of a governor."

But these words merely confirmed Domingo Gómez Navarro's suspicions that this was Luis de Carvajal.

"I am not astonished at seeing him as he presently is," he said. "But I do recall once in Pachuca that this Luis de Carvajal and Manuel de Lucena's wife, Catalina Enríquez, and Francisco Vaez were singing and dancing." And with these words Domingo Gómez Navarro left the house.

Dismayed by this occurrence, Luis proceeded to tell Justa Méndez about the futile attempts by Manuel de Lucena and Manuel Gómez Navarro to convert their visitor. Justa Méndez tried to console Luis by vilifying Domingo Gómez Navarro and saying that molasses candy was not intended for a donkey's mouth. Then, realizing that Luis feared that Domingo Gómez Navarro might report him to the Inquisition, she said, "What were you waiting for? Why didn't you smash him?"

"There is no point to it," said Luis, "I have already seen him twice in the Holy Office."[44]

On the basis of Domingo Gómez Navarro's deposition, the Inquisition proceeded to arrest Lucena and Manuel Gómez Navarro but allowed Luis to remain free. Luis naturally regarded this, too, as a miracle.[45]

A week later the family had another close call. Whatever it was, Luis refused to describe it further, even in his private memoirs. It is likely that it involved an inquisitorial summons to the family to take depositions against Lucena, leading the family to believe that it was in danger of imminent arrest. But within two hours Luis, his mother, and sisters were released.[46]

Whatever his previous plans might have been, Luis now began to think of sending his mother and sisters ahead to Spain with Gaspar while he remained on, in hiding, in New Spain. He could have had only one purpose in mind: to liquidate Almeida's property. Except for

Díaz de Cáceres's possessions, it was the only property of any substance belonging to the family in New Spain. Since an inquiry into the family's religious behavior now loomed as a distinct possibility, Luis realized that if he wanted to preserve Almeida's wealth, he could not risk leaving it behind in the form of real property.

He wrote to Almeida on January 9, 1595, to apprise him of his plans. He enclosed the letter in a packet with several other papers, including a few lines from Leonor, and sent it on to Ruy Fernández de Pereyra in Seville. He also mentioned that under separate cover he was sending Almeida 1,630 pesos, apparently representing the income from some of Almeida's property or proceeds from a sale.

Almeida did not approve of much that Luis wrote. He did not like the way Luis was handling his financial affairs. Nor did he care for the idea of having Gaspar escort Leonor to Spain. By now Almeida must have heard that Gaspar had turned his earlier letter over to the Inquisition. But there was little that Almeida could do about his dis-

A Letter by Luis de Carvajal, as Agent for Jorge de Almeida, on Matters Pertaining to Almeida's Estate

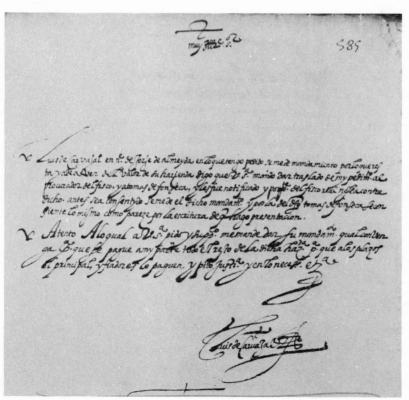

satisfaction, for any response he wrote would not reach Luis before the sailing of the spring fleet from the New World.

Nevertheless, on the possibility that Luis might not have left, Almeida composed a letter to him late in July. In the letter he informs Luis that he has received the packet, but not the money. He blames Luis for this "because you refused to comply with the instructions I had given you not to consign anything to Ruy Fernández."

Almeida explains that he did not send a letter in the fleet leaving Spain for the New World on July 8, 1595, because he expected Luis to be well on his way to Europe by that time. He tells Luis that if there has been a delay he should cancel his plans and await further word from him, because he was thinking of returning to New Spain for the dual purpose of personally attending to his property and escorting his wife to Europe. He apparently now thought he had connections at court sufficiently strong to neutralize any threats that the Inquisition might pose.

Almeida goes on to say that he will send Luis a special note by dispatch boat if he decides to come to New Spain. In the meantime he instructs him to collect some of the moneys due him from various sources, including his estate, which was still in Tomás de Fonseca's hands. He tells Luis to "make no manner of agreement" with Tomás de Fonseca. On the contrary, he tells him to "collect my estate rigorously from him and destroy him. And if he cannot pay what he has stolen from me, ruin him and let him eat lice in jail." Then Almeida adds, "By God, the main reason I want to return is to take vengeance on that crook. I tell you again, make no agreements with him, but proceed with full rigor."

On the personal side Almeida expresses sorrow over the ailments of Anica and Mariana and tells Luis to take care of Leonor, "whose hands I kiss a thousand times." He asks Luis to tell Leonor not to get involved in too much fasting, "for God does not desire more than a person can do." He sends regards to his dear sisters-in-law and also to Fray Gaspar, "even though he has not remembered to write me in four years."

At the same time he explains to Luis that he has not written to his brother in the New World, Hector de Fonseca, "because he does not write to me," but he is sorry to hear of his difficulties. He tells Luis that his other brother, Miguel Hernández, is in Seville "with his indispositions," and informs him that Luis's brothers Baltasar and Miguel are in good health and in Rome.

Almeida's letter did not arrive in Mexico City until May 1596, but the delay did not matter. Even at the time of its composition, in July 1595, it was too late for Luis or any of the other Carvajals to comply with his instructions. Before the end of the spring of 1595, Luis, his mother, and all his sisters except Mariana were back in the Inquisition's jail.[47]

Luis was the first to be rearrested. He was taken into custody on Wednesday night, February 1, 1595, as a result of testimony by Lucena, his wife, Catalina Enríquez, and an erstwhile friend of the family named Susana Galván, who had witnessed many aspects of their Judaizing. He was searched and found to be carrying a leather bag containing three books, bound in black leather, each with a title printed in Latin. One read *Psalms*, the second *Prophets*, and the third, *Genesis*. The books were promptly confiscated. The Inquisition did not think of examining Luis's hat, where he had sewn the booklet containing the Ten Commandments.[48]

Luis was too realistic for the arrest to come as a total surprise. A few days before, while in Taxco, he dreamed of his father, dressed in white and kneeling to God in prayer in the midst of a green field. As Luis approached, his father came toward him with open arms, and the earth on which the two were standing suddenly began to rise toward heaven.[49] Luis was well aware of the possibility of imminent arrest and the certainty of his subsequent fate.

If Luis's arrest shattered his plans it did not shake his faith in Judaism or in the divine guidance of his life. Though he could not understand why he should anticlimactically have been thrown into jail after all the miraculous events of his life seemed to point to his eventual freedom, he accepted the fact as part of God's plan. He knew that, except for the unlikely possibility of a successful escape from the Inquisition's jail, he faced an ineluctable decree of death at the stake. The inquisitors would of course extend him the privilege of being garroted first, provided he repented of his Judaism and asked for a return to the grace of the church. But he was not prepared to do this. Convinced that he was following God's will and that a martyr's death for Judaism would be rewarded by salvation in the world beyond, Luis determined to die in the flames. Like Isaac or the saintly sons of Hannah who suffered torture and fiery deaths rather than relinquish their faith, he was ready to be offered as a holocaust to his God.[50]

On the Sunday night after his arrest Luis again dreamed that he was in paradise. He was robed in white and seated before a large flower-decked table in a spacious banquet hall. His hands held clusters

The Petition for the Second Arrest of Luis de Carvajal the Younger
(February 1, 1595) by the Inquisition's Prosecutor, Dr. Martos de
Bohorques

of roses, and he was distributing these to people entering the room. Most looked dazed and somnolent and held their flowers limply in their hands, fully savoring neither their beauty nor their fragrance. Only two people had their eyes open and all their other faculties alert. These were Antonio Díaz Márquez and Justa Méndez.

Luis had no trouble deciphering the dream. He was Joseph, the provider, or perhaps now Moses, the teacher of his people, and he was distributing the celestial rewards for the faithful among the secret Jews. Justa Méndez, and, amazingly, Antonio Díaz Márquez, being exemplary Judaizers in Luis's eyes, enjoyed the full beauty and fragrance of the roses. Those who Judaized imperfectly or desultorily could attain only a measure of such bliss.[51]

The inquisitors, Dr. Lobo Guerrero and Licentiate Alonso de Peralta, did not call Luis for his first audience until a week after his arrest. In the meantime they were busily preparing an incontestable case against him.

Shortly before two o'clock in the afternoon of the day following his arrest the inquisitors transferred Luis to the cell of a certain Luis Díaz, a priest arrested for celebrating mass without wine and impersonating a commissary of the Holy Office. Luis Díaz had turned inquisitorial spy. Prior to becoming Carvajal's cellmate he had been the companion of Manuel de Lucena, Manuel Gómez Navarro, and Lucena's brother-in-law, Pedro Enríquez, and had extracted substantial information from them.[52]

At two o'clock on February 2, before Díaz had a chance to speak to Luis, he saw his new companion, still wearing his hat and cloak, turn eastward, fall to his knees, and commence a long series of prayers, punctuated by a kissing of the ground whenever he uttered the name Adonay. Díaz recalled that this was precisely the way Manuel de Lucena used to pray in his cell.

When Luis was finished, around five in the afternoon, the two men introduced themselves and became acquainted. To Luis's delight, Díaz revealed that he was a secret Jew—an even better stroke of fortune, it seemed, than had greeted Carvajal during his first incarceration, when he was introduced to Fray Francisco Ruiz de Luna. Overjoyed, Carvajal proudly told Díaz that he regarded himself as a Jew, that he had converted Francisco Ruiz de Luna before the auto-da-fé of 1590, and that he became even more strongly confirmed in his faith in the library of Fray Pedro de Oroz. Now, he said, snapping his fingers in contentment, "God was bringing him to be sacrificed like Isaac and he was delighted that he would be dying in the Law of

The Signature of the Inquisitor Alonso de Peralta

Moses."[53] When Díaz expressed a desire to learn more about Judaism, Carvajal fell to his knees, called upon God in thanksgiving, embraced his companion, and said, "Now I want to die for the Law of the Lord, for I have found someone to teach and declare it to." He promised he would do so the next evening, Friday, in a study-service at around six-thirty or seven o'clock. He showed Díaz his notebook containing the Ten Commandments and explained that his biblical books had been confiscated.[54]

Díaz also observed that Luis fasted all day until nightfall, when he ate a piece of bread and two plantains. Shortly before this meager repast, he took an improvised ritual bath, in the nude, with the drinking water that was given him. It was not long before Díaz learned that Luis prayed frequently, fasted continuously, except on the Sabbath, and was careful to eat no biblically forbidden foods.[55]

During the first few days they shared the cell, Díaz appears to have lent Luis a Bible commentary or some other book of devotion. Luis described it as "a honeycomb with the sweetest honey from the lips of the Most High." Though Luis did not identify the volume, he explained the marvels of its melliferous doctrines. He said that after taking the honeycomb, "I tasted and ate it and my eyes were nearly fully opened. There I saw the explanation of great mysteries that I did not know before, and it brought gladness to my heart." Among these was a beautiful homiletical explanation of the fringes, or *tsitsit*, mentioned in the biblical Book of Numbers.

Díaz also lent Luis his breviary. Luis proceeded to tear it apart, saving the pages that contained the Book of Psalms but destroying all the others.[56]

For a week Luis de Carvajal the Younger freely shared with Luis Díaz some of the most intimate secrets of the secret Jews in New Spain. He told Díaz about the exploits of Manuel de Lucena, Justa Méndez, Pedro Enríquez, Antonio Díaz Márquez, the two men named Tomás de Fonseca, and a host of other Judaizers, among whom he did not hesitate to include Gregorio López. Díaz confided to Luis that he was a relative of Antonio Díaz Márquez's. It was a lie but it endeared the priest all the more to his companion.[57]

Luis also informed his cellmate about the statues of the saints he had left in the attic of his mother's home, and the autobiography and book of prayers and readings as well as the letters that he had hidden. Since Díaz implied that he would soon be released by the Inquisition, Luis asked him to go to his mother's home, pick up the books, wrap them in a package so as to make them appear to be letters, and give them to Antonio Díaz Márquez with instructions that they be sent to Ruy Fernández de Pereyra in Seville. He also asked Díaz to compose a covering letter, in his name, to Ruy Fernández de Pereyra, acknowledging with joy the receipt of a letter from him in the recent fleet.[58]

At the same time he also urged Díaz to make the acquaintance of various Judaizers. One of them was Justa Méndez (who, as it turned out, was being arrested around that very time). All the Judaizers he mentioned, said Luis, would gladly receive Díaz. He asked Díaz to teach the commandments of the faith to Antonio Díaz Márquez.[59]

Encouraged by the presence of such a compatible cellmate, Luis began planning an escape from the jail. By February 9 he had succeeded in removing a slab from his cell wall to show Díaz how easy it would be for both of them to get out. He suggested that the two could flee to the home of Antonio Díaz Márquez. Díaz Márquez would find a suitable refuge for them for six months, apparently to wait for the heat of the Inquisition's initial search to subside. Then they could escape to Europe.[60]

But unfortunately for Luis de Carvajal, Luis Díaz was not like Francisco Ruiz de Luna. The cellmate of Carvajal's first imprisonment showed little desire to be a spy and instead became a friend and eventually a Judaizer. But Díaz was a faithful inquisitorial agent and had proved his mettle in the cells of Judaizers like Lucena, Gómez Navarro and Pedro Enríquez. If his task with Carvajal turned out to be easier than he had a right to anticipate, it was because at the time of his arrest Luis de Carvajal's spirits were in fathomless depression and his guard was down.

As early as February 3 Luis Díaz dutifully began to report to the inquisitors every fact he had learned in his conversations with Luis. He alerted them to Luis's study-service that evening, and before it began, three representatives of the Inquisition—Pedro de Fonseca, the notary for sequestrations, Pedro de Mañozca, the inquisitorial secretary, and the warden, Gaspar de los Reyes Plata—had stationed themselves near the door to Luis's cell. They heard Luis conduct a service of prayer and song, interspersed with explanations of the tenets of Judaism, including his expectation of the momentary arrival of the Messiah. When he came to the recitation of the Ten Commandments, Luis ruefully repeated the story of the confiscation of his biblical books at the time of his arrest, but explained that he was at least grateful that he was able to keep the booklet with the Ten Commandments. "That dog of a warden did not find them when he searched me," he said, "because I had them hidden in my hat." He continued, "If we had light I would show it to you. I shall do so tomorrow."[61]

The spies also heard Díaz ask why it was necessary to kneel when the name Adonay was recited, especially since they were demonstrating their respect by standing throughout the service. Luis responded that kneeling was the form of self-abasement that was due to God and God alone.

When Díaz told the inquisitors about the statues, booklets, and letters in Luis's house they immediately sent someone there to find and confiscate them. Díaz also borrowed the booklet of commandments from Luis and presented it to the inquisitors on February 9, the day Luis began planning his escape. The inquisitors returned the booklet to Díaz the next day with instructions to give it back to Luis as unobtrusively as possible.

When the inquisitors discovered what Luis was doing in his cell, they transferred both him and Díaz and temporarily gave Luis a new cellmate. Why they separated Carvajal and Díaz is not known. Perhaps they suspected Díaz of complicity in the escape plot and wanted to be sure he was not acting as an accomplice before they allowed the two to be together again. Instead they gave Luis a temporary companion, Franco, who as far as they knew was completely innocuous.

But Franco was far from harmless, for he knew that Luis Díaz was a spy. He had overheard a grieved and embittered Manuel de Lucena shouting throughout the compound, "All you prisoners be careful of a priest who has deceived and betrayed me." He also heard Manuel Gómez Navarro cry out words to this effect.

Franco warned Luis about Luis Díaz. Díaz was not called a lure and decoy bird for nothing, he explained. "But see now, Luis," Franco said to him, "if you have told him anything, there is nothing you can do about it. He is bound to reveal you."

On the following day the inquisitors sent Díaz back to Carvajal. When he appeared in the cell, Luis asked why he was chained. Playing his role with the skill of a consummate actor, Díaz told Luis that he had been chained "so that he should not be able to inform other prisoners that Luis de Carvajal had tried to flee and that it was easy to escape from that jail."

To Díaz's surprise Luis said nothing further. An hour passed before Díaz finally broke the silence to tell Luis that he looked disconsolate. Luis then asked for his booklet and, immediately on receiving it, tried to erase the name of Ruy Fernández de Pereyra. When Díaz told him not to do so, Luis snapped, "Please do not do me any more favors, for I have discovered you and I know who you are."

Díaz pleaded that he was not a spy, but Luis would not allow himself to be deceived again. Instead he begged Díaz not to reveal his relatives and friends as Judaizers. As for himself, he said with condescending intent, there was really no need to inform on him either, "because everyone knows that I do not eat bacon or lard and that I fast and bathe and perform all the other ceremonies and rites of the Mosaic Law." Furthermore, he told Díaz, he would ask for a hearing in the "devil's hall," as he called the inquisitors' audience chamber and make full confession on the very next day. He was delighted that the next day was a Saturday.[62]

10 Road to Glory

Luis kept his promise. The next day he was in the inquisitors' audience chambers at his own request. In that audience and in subsequent audiences held over the next few days Luis unraveled the history of his Judaizing, going all the way back to Medina del Campo. He explained in detail the basic Jewish observances and beliefs. He recited the *Shema' Yisrael* and the Ten Commandments, begging permission to do so on his knees, because they contained the name of God. This permission was not granted. According to one of the Inquisition's examiners, it took three familiars to prevent Luis from kneeling.[1] He also recited Maimonides' Thirteen Articles of the Faith, which he had learned from Oleaster's commentary.

While fully accepting the guilt of having Judaized again, Luis de Carvajal was most careful not to implicate anyone else in his crimes, except Manuel de Lucena and Manuel Gómez Navarro, both already under arrest, his brother Baltasar, safely in Italy, and Antonio Machado, long since dead. He said he knew no one else who Judaized and resolutely shielded his family and friends. In order to do so effectively, he denied practicing Judaism in front of anyone else. He avoided any statement or innuendo which might implicate others. He admitted only private practices where no one else was around or where the people present were already under inquisitorial arrest.[2]

In the interview of February 15, the questioning went as follows:

Q. Do your mother and sisters observe the Mosaic Law?

A. No, they have not since they were reconciled in this Holy Office.

Q. What faith do your mother and sisters observe?

A. They observe the faith of Jesus Christ.

Q. How do you know they observe the faith of Jesus Christ?

A. Because they do what the faith of Jesus Christ demands in word and deed.

Q. Since you observe the Law of Moses and persevere in its belief and believe that you will find salvation in it and that no one can be saved through the faith of Jesus Christ, and since you understood, as you do, that they would be damned if they observed the faith of Jesus Christ, how is it that you did not teach your mother and sisters the said Law of Moses?

A. I did not dare because I was very much afraid that one of them might expose me and that I would be arrested by the Holy Office.

Q. This is not credible, because . . . you taught the Law of Moses to strangers, and the Holy Office has sufficient evidence for all of this. You did this because you were driven by the desire for the salvation of the people you taught it to, without regard to the fear that they could denounce you and with unalloyed zeal to spread the Law of Moses and extend its belief. It is clear that if you trusted strangers, you could better trust your mother and sisters, since the love for their own flesh and blood would restrain them from denouncing you to the Holy Office. By the same token you had a greater obligation to look after their salvation and welfare than that of strangers.

A. What I have said is the truth.[3]

Of course it was not, and the inquisitors knew it. Inquisitors Lobo Guerrero and the harsher and more demanding Peralta hammered away relentlessly at Luis's obstinate defense of his family. They finally produced their most potent weapon, Luis's own autobiography, with its transparent references to the family's Judaizing. But Luis kept insisting that all these references were either inadvertent errors or intentional distortions to enhance the status of his mother and sisters in the eyes of the Judaizers who would be reading the memoirs.[4]

It could well have been as punishment for refusing to cooperate that the inquisitors at this point decided to confine Luis for three weeks in a dungeon, where the only light he saw was the flicker of the candle in the hands of the attendant who brought him his meals. He was then transferred, very likely on account of ill health, to a somewhat pleasanter cell with a window facing the courtyard of the building. "I can see the sky day and night," Luis joyfully exclaimed.[5]

Despite his efforts, Luis could not prevent the arrest of his mother and sisters. Doña Francisca, Catalina, Leonor, and Anica were taken into custody early in the spring of 1595, and Isabel was apprehended on June 7 of that year. Because of her illness, Mariana was not arrested but placed in protective custody. When Catalina was seized, Antonio Díaz de Cáceres took their daughter, Leonor, to the home of Agustín de Espindola, where a devout Negro servant named Ana de los Reyes eventually retaught her the prayers of the church. At first Leonor protested, saying, "In my parents' house they don't say these prayers, but others."

To this Ana replied, "Child, don't tell me about it, because my flesh trembles when I hear it."

"Why, isn't it good?" asked Leonor.

"It's so bad," said Ana, "that if they knew about it in the Holy Office, they'd burn you alive."[6]

Luis quickly learned of the arrest of his mother and sisters—though in the early spring he incorrectly believed that Isabel was among them—and he was soon in contact with them. In fruits and in other objects the prisoners were permitted to exchange, Luis and the members of his family sent one another raisins, pins, olive pits, and other objects in various combinations to communicate a variety of information: whether they were alone, who their companions were, and who were the prisoners in the nearby cells.[7]

Luis was not content with such primitive communications. Deterred neither by the Inquisition's regulations nor his own lack of paper or pen, he determined to send letters to his family. On Saturday, May 13, he asked the warden to take a melon to his sister Leonor. Inside the melon, wrapped in a piece of taffeta, was an avocado pit. On it Luis had patiently scratched with a pin such lines as "Have patience like Job," "My darlings, may Adonay, our Lord, visit you," and "I am in chains for my God."

The following day he sent a similar avocado pit wrapped in the peel of a plantain, and he repeated the process on Tuesday, Wednesday, and Thursday. On Friday he sent two notes scratched on pears.[8]

But Luis's messages did not reach their destination. The warden, schooled in suspicion, examined the fruits carefully, discovered their literary content, and immediately delivered them to the inquisitors. The notes contained no incriminating information about Luis or his family, but the inquisitors believed that if Luis could be encouraged to continue his correspondence such information might be forthcoming. On Friday afternoon, May 19, they therefore ordered the warden "to try to leave an inkwell and pen in the cell of the said Luis de Carvajal . . . with the greatest possible dissimulation . . . as if by over-sight," and to "give him some paper with some cherries or other gift wrapped in it," to make it appear that the gift was coming from his mother or sisters and that the paper was incidental.[9]

The warden did as he was instructed. He unobtrusively left pen, ink, and paper in Luis's cell, and Luis immediately addressed a lengthy letter to Isabel and Leonor.

Written with tenderness and pathos, the letter contained two major themes. On the one hand Luis sought to buoy his family with courage and faith. He wanted his mother and sisters to realize that their arrest was God's will, that God had decided not to keep them on earth as wanderers, that He had chosen not to allow them to go to Castile, but to bring them immediately to paradise, where their bliss would compensate for all their terrestrial misfortunes. He heartened them to persevere in their faith and if need be, to face martyrdom with confidence.

At the same time Luis wanted his mother and sisters to cling to the slim possibility of deliverance from the Inquisition. He knew that in the eyes of the inquisitors they were guilty as charged even before their hearings began. But he apparently conjectured that the Inquisition might not have conclusive evidence against them. It might therefore postpone their sentencing and, perhaps with the aid of another miracle, even restore their freedom.

But how could he possibly help his mother and sisters avert the Inquisition's damning scrutiny of their activities? Luis attempted to do so in his letter by telling his mother and sisters that he had confessed his misdeeds, but his alone, that he had defended their innocence, and that they were arrested only on suspicion of wrongdoing. He seemed to be implying clearly that they would do well to deny all guilt, and, if necessary, divert suspicion onto others.

The letter, addressed to Leonor and Isabel, begins:

My precious ones,

By a miracle I was given an inkwell today and a pen, [obviously so] that I might send this note to you, [for you are] the apple of my eye. Whoever should receive it first can very circumspectly wrap it in something and send it on to my other sisters.

I was arrested by the express will and judgment of the Most High and through an accusation [made] by Manuel de Lucena. In order not to implicate anyone else I have confessed the truth about myself alone, expecting God's certain reward, of which I have had substantial and sure promise during my incarceration. My darlings, my angels, my dears, you were arrested on suspicion alone. I [have] defended your innocence; may my soul be similarly defended against Satan and his agents by the holy angel of my Lord, God.

I can tell you that when I was alone [in jail] I spent my time rejoicing. But from the time I was shown my little red book and my letters and learned of your imprisonment, I have been extremely grieved. With hot tears and bended knees I have sighed and cried to my Lord God, asking help—which I very confidently await from His merciful hand—for the salvation of [our] souls. This is what matters most. Dear ones, this [imprisonment] was the will of the Most High, and His lash was less than our sins [required]. Let us accept it wholeheartedly, for God can bring good out of evil [and] water, honey, and oil from hard rocks.

I hear that there may be more than thirty people [in this jail] implicated [as Judaizers] by that poor Manuel de Lucena and others. May our Lord, as the Father of mercy, come to our rescue, even though our faithlessness makes us unworthy. I am [now] in shackles, but neither these nor [the prospect of] burning alive will divert my spirit from [clinging to] the sweetness of the Lord my God. Since I have trust in Him, my Creator has often mercifully revealed Himself here to me.

One day, as my poor mind was sweetly absorbed in petition to my Lord God, I said to Him, "Why, O Lord, would You show so much mercy to a worm like me? And how can it be that I will have a greater crown in Your kingdom than my father?" [Then] this answer was revealed and given to me: "Do you know how this will be? As it was when Joseph stood before his father as prince of Egypt, and the saintly Jacob greatly rejoiced on seeing his son's honor and fame."

Luis then mentions the dream in Taxco when he saw their father in a green field and continues:

My good Lord [now] wishes to turn this dream into reality, my dearest ones, and I will try to do nothing to obstruct His plans. God's truth is witness [to the fact] that I write [these words] not out of vainglory, for I know that I deserve hell because of my sins, but in order to bring joy and solace to your dejected spirits, which have touched my heart [with compassion]. Yet I trust in my good Lord God that since He shows such kindness to a sinner like me, His mercy and comfort will not be lacking for you, my dear ones.

Remember the sacrifice of the saintly Isaac. When he was bound, how obediently he awaited the thrust of the knife! [Remember] the faith of his saintly father, our patriarch, Abraham. [Remember] what the Lord did with Joseph's imprisonment, [or] the dangers confronting the saintly Moses, [or] the wanderings of our holy father, Israel [Jacob], or of David and all the [later] saints.

This [imprisonment given by God] is the road to the glory of paradise, where they are awaiting us, and there is none other [open to us]. And the journey is better than the one to Castile. And since our good God is opening the door for us, let us not obstruct Him. In [times of] temptation, have faith. Have faith like Tobit. Be humble [and] patient like Job. Boldly cry out, cry out to the Lord, who has not changed [in His affection toward us and ask] that He deny us not the mercy with which He raises the dead, heals [the] sick, looses [the] bound, etc. May that mercy help you, my precious ones, my darlings, dear companions of my captivity. Though buckling under afflictions and hardships, I entreat Adonay, my great God, that we may [yet] be bent [in thanksgiving] in the glory of His holy kingdom. Amen. . . .

And what more shall I tell you about God's mercy? For a week there was a honeycomb near me, full of the sweetest honey from the lips of the Most High. I tasted the honey and my eyes have been opened, though not fully. I saw [the meaning of] great and incomparable mysteries and the great joys which await us in paradise. Rejoice! Rejoice! Let sobbing and sighing stop, for great is the joy that will be placed upon our heads through all eternity.

After encouraging his family, he moves to his conclusion with a string of fascinating facts:

Leonor, my dearest—whom I love, as I do all [my sisters], like darling Rachels—since you are nearby, send me signs [to let me know] whether you are alone. The two cloths they gave you yesterday to hem are mine. If they come back [to me] together, I will understand that there is someone with you. If they come back separately I will know that you are alone. May the holy angel who visited Asenath go with you. May he visit you and bless you and me on behalf of God most high. Our dear mother is in one of the rooms near you.

How I wish I could go to see you and greet you [and be with you] for a while. I ask my Lord God for permission to do this; perhaps He will grant it to me. If it cannot be done, I am [at least] consoled [by the fact] that we shall see each other [first, at the stake] before we die, and then, eternally, in the glorious inheritance [which awaits us in paradise] among the surpassingly handsome angels and saints. Oh, what a delicious expectation! You will live! You will survive your death! Hallelujah!

What do you suppose my Lord God has done with our little [sister] Anica and [Mariana,] the poor little lunatic and [our sister Isabel,] the poor widow? Oh, my darling flock, who are so dispersed! "Be consoled, be consoled," says the Lord, "for I will free you from the wolves and in green pastures shall I put you, [the] sheep and [their] mother."

I was near Ana López for a few days and she gave me some news about you. If I am not mistaken, either of you or my [dear sister] Doña Catalina was standing with her daughter in the other court when I sent you my pillowcase. One night [in my dreams] I was shown some tortillas, made of corn flour and the size of shields. And through them I was given to understand the fullness of the joy that awaits us.

[If there is someone else in your cell,] put the first two letters of her name on the cloths [you will be returning to me]. When you pass by my cell, I can tell it is you from the sound of your clogs, and as I kneel, I ask you to help me. I shall always keep a cloth in my little window for you to see when you pass by.

And he concludes philosophically, "As children of Adam we are born to die. Happy is the man who leaves the lingering death of this life to enter into the life truly eternal." And then he adds the equivalent of a postscript: "You sent me a pen and raisins. I understood what you wanted."[10]

Luis gave the letter to Gaspar de los Reyes Plata, and the warden proceeded to deposit it in the inquisitors' chambers.

In the succeeding days Luis found his supply of ink and paper regularly replenished, and he continued his correspondence, stressing the same themes and often embellishing them with consummate sensitivity and literary beauty.

In one of his letters he told his sister Isabel of a dream:

About six nights ago [I,] Joseph, [dreamt] that I was walking in the midst of the ocean without wetting more than my feet. [I] also [saw] hunters trying to kill ducks with harquebuses unsuccessfully, for the ducks were flying [too] high. Then a mighty voice, a revelation from the Most High, said to me: "The sea is this jail, a sea of temptations; the hunters are the unsuccessful inquisitors; the harquebuses are deceits; the ducks are the souls who believe in your God; their flight is the holy prayer [you offer]."[11]

In another he reveals a mature grasp of the psychology of his young sisters, confronted with death after their short and barren lives. To sustain them in their final days Luis tries to compensate for their troubles on earth by painting glowing verbal pictures of the heavenly bliss awaiting them. In paradise, he tells them, they will tread soft fields, luxuriate in scented orchards, and delight to the thrum of the harp and the click of castanets. They will be elegantly attired by the command of God himself. God will summon His angels and say:

Angels, bring My daughters, bring My betrothed some of those rich robes I have told you to make. Exchange their skirts of ordinary cloth for skirts of white satin, their plain jackets for new ones that have seven layers of brocade. Set their hair beautifully and put rich headdresses and garlands on their heads. Leave no finger without a ring, for they have suffered so much on My behalf. And before you dress them, be sure to bathe them in luxurious, scented waters, for they have to eat at My table.

And there in heaven they would be married—to none other than the King of the angels Himself.

In another touching description Luis tells his sisters that when they reach heaven, God, their Father, will rush to greet them with an embrace. Observing their tears, He will take the kerchief of consolations from His pocket and solicitously wipe them away. Nestling His daughters in the security of His lap, He will say to them, "Come, My darling ewes. Show Me, show Me, where did the dog bite you?" And then relishing the joy of that supreme moment of release, they will each cry out with happy tears: "Father, the bite cut to our souls. And [do You know] why [he bit me]—a curse be upon him? He attacked me and bit me a thousand times because I was calling Your name, because I was going to perform Your commandment, [because I was about] to fulfill Your Law."[12]

Luis wrote over twenty letters, and Gaspar de los Reyes Plata delivered them all to the inquisitors, certain that he had entrapped his prisoner into believing that he was carrying on a secret correspondence with his mother and sisters.

Yet if the letters reveal nothing else, they appear to demonstrate that Luis had once again outsmarted his captors.

Two factors, both equally striking, point in this direction. First is the fact that the letters contain not one shred of information that could incriminate anyone except Luis himself. And since Luis had already confessed his guilt, such data had no practical value for the inquisitors.

Second is Luis's repeated insistence on the innocence of his mother and sisters. If anyone was aware of the incorrectness of such an assertion, it was Luis, for he had encouraged his mother and sisters to Judaize and personally had led them in their religious practice in the years preceding their second arrest. Why, then, should he repeatedly insist on their innocence in an intimate correspondence?

It would seem that Luis was aware that the correspondence was not private. Being anything but naive, he could not have failed to realize that some if not all of his letters might fall into the inquisitors' hands. Nor could he have failed to conclude that the inquisitors had

had something to do with the miracle by which he was provided with pen, paper, and ink.

At the same time, Luis could hardly have been oblivious to a more important fact, namely, that by feigning naiveté and unawareness of what was happening to the letters, he might be able to deceive the inquisitors into believing the information he was disclosing in them. If in these ostensibly intimate letters he repeatedly cast doubt upon his family's involvement in Judaism, those that were intercepted might lead the inquisitors to delay the prosecution of his family and even— however remote the possibility—to restore their liberty.

On the morning of June 10, after Luis had again asserted that he had nothing to add to his testimony, the prosecuting attorney, Dr. Martos de Bohorques, presented his accusation against him. A long indictment in twenty-two sections, it scored Luis's religious backsliding and uncouthly compared him to "a dog that returns to its vomit." It detailed the offenses he had committed. And it formally concluded with a request that "he be ordered relaxed and that he be relaxed to the authorities and the secular arm." Paragraph twenty-one of the indictment revealed that the Inquisition was in possession of the notes and letters Luis had written, but judging from Luis's reaction, this did not constitute much of a surprise to him. The shocking revelation had come in the twelfth paragraph, where the Inquisition revealed its knowledge of the entire family's participation in religious rites and ceremonies. It was obvious that someone in the family had confessed. At the time Luis did not know that it had been Leonor. After staunchly maintaining her innocence through two admonitions, she had broken down at the third and revealed the family's Judaizing in the minutest detail.

In his response Luis took umbrage at the Inquisition's derogatory simile. "The term dog," he magisterially protested, "cannot be applied to someone who believes in the Law of God, which promises not only temporal boons but also eternal life." He went on to deny the Inquisition's charges that he had desecrated a statue of Jesus and had called the inquisitors butchers, though he had done both, or at least, so Luis Díaz said.[13] He now said that when he spoke of butchers, he was referring to the executors of secular justice. Echoing the Inquisition's own cant, he said that he knew that "the Holy Office seeks above all else to preserve men's lives."[14] What he did not have to say was that the secular authorities had to put to death anyone the Inquisition "relaxed" to them.

At the same time Luis agreed to every accusation of Judaizing against him. And he had no alternative but to admit the Judaizing of his family. Yet aside from his family and friends like Lucena, who were already under arrest, he refused to implicate any others. He sealed his testimony with the emphatic assertion, "I do not know of any other accomplices except those whom I have named."[15]

But he tried his best to save Anica and Catalina. He claimed that Anica, as a child, did not really know what the family was involved in. She recited hymns and prayers that were mumbo jumbo to her. Besides, whenever Anica was present, said Luis, he would end his psalms by reciting aloud the words "in the name of" to give her the impression that he was uttering the traditional Catholic formula, "In the name of the Father, the Son, and the Holy Ghost, Amen."[16]

Luis insisted that Catalina, who did not live with the family, was so circumspect and reserved that she moved away whenever anything Jewish was mentioned, refusing to hear it, "either because she was afraid of falling into the hands of the Inquisition or because she was a good Christian." Besides, he said correctly, Catalina liked to attend mass and enjoyed the preaching of her priest, Father Reinoso. He might have added that his sister once quarreled with him when he refused to let her see the Procession of the Banner held on Saint Hippolytus day, the anniversary of the conquest of Mexico City by the forces of Cortés. But Luis did try to persuade the inquisitors that when he called Catalina a martyr in his letters he did not conceive of her as a secret Jewess but merely someone destined to die. This argument might have made a greater impression had Leonor not confessed.[17]

The inquisitors, hardly convinced, kept plying Luis with one probing question after another. Yet try as they might, they were unable to extract from him the information they knew he was withholding. With complete self-mastery and condescending defiance he baffled and frustrated his interrogators time and again. He concluded his response to the accusation and the inquisitors' cross-examination by expressing a longing for the day when he would "leave the prisons and chains . . . and go off to the heavens." He wanted to die at the stake, he said, not garroted, "like a wretch on a gibbet," but alive, "in live fire, that I might have the greater reward."

In a prayerful mood he then addressed God imploringly and said, "I beg You, Lord our God, reveal which are the true heresies, and by Your infinite mercy, have compassion on Your creatures and enlighten and guide the purblind sons of Adam."[18]

Luis was given a choice of five attorneys, including Gaspar de Valdés. Although he said he wanted no counsel, Dr. Dionisio de Ribera Flores was appointed. On June 14 Ribera Flores urged Luis to "confess the truth . . . and sincerely repent his sin." His efforts proved futile. "Let the fire come," was Luis's response.[19]

During all this time Luis was kept in fetters. The inquisitors were apparently unwilling to risk another attempt at escape. After the audience of July 3, when Luis once again declined to volunteer information, Pedro de Mañozca, the secretary of the Inquisition, reported that Luis remained in good health. He was not called to audience again until October 5, for the first publication of witnesses' testimony against him.

By the end of October the inquisitors were compelled to face two increasingly embarrassing realities. The first was the fact that their prize prisoner, undaunted by every effort to convert him back to Catholicism, would gain a resounding victory over them if he was burned alive at the stake as a martyr for his faith. The second was the equally patent fact that, despite all threats and cozening, they had extracted little substantive information from Luis de Carvajal that could aid them in their efforts to destroy the wide circle of Judaizers he had created in New Spain.

The inquisitors decided to take remedial action for both situations.

On the morning of October 31 they summoned Luis to an audience that began inauspiciously with questioning on minor details of his testimony. In the midst of the proceedings two inquisitorial examiners, Drs. Hortigosa and Sánchez, both learned Jesuits, entered the room and proceeded to urge Luis to revert to Catholicism. Their efforts were unavailing. Dr. Hortigosa came back alone to spend the entire afternoon with Luis "in a lengthy dialogue," in which Luis steadfastly defended his position. Hortigosa returned the next morning for another futile session, and on the afternoon of November 4 both Hortigosa and Sánchez spent four and a half hours trying to convert Luis by the manipulation of scriptural texts. Luis again adamantly insisted that he wished to remain a Jew.[20]

On December 15, when Dr. Ribera Flores pressed him to convert, Luis responded proudly that his faith was in the Law of Moses "and he would not deny it or leave it even if they promised to make him king of Castile." He then explained, "If in days past I acquiesced in having sage theologians . . . come, it was not that I ever doubted the truths asserted by the Law of.God, because I believe in these more than in my own existence, but rather to confound and convert them." He said he would be glad to affix his signature to this response, and when the document was drawn up and given to him, he signed it "Joseph Lumbroso, slave of the most high A [donay] Sevaoth [the Lord of hosts]."[21]

Though it appeared that they had lost the battle to convert Luis, the inquisitors were as determined as ever to wring out of him all the information about his friends and accomplices they suspected him of concealing. On Tuesday afternoon, February 6, 1596, the inquisitorial board therefore voted unanimously to subject Luis de Carvajal to torture *in caput alienum*.[22]

On February 8, after being duly admonished to reveal what he knew, "especially about people very close to you whom you know to be keeping the Law of Moses," Luis was formally sentenced to torture and subjected to the inquisitors' prayer "that if he die or be maimed in the said torture or if there ensue an effusion of blood or mutilation of limb, let this burden be upon him and not us."[23]

Before the procession started down to the torture chamber, before the activity there began, before Luis was stripped and dressed in his cloth of shame and before he was tied to the frame, he was again admonished to confess, and every time he protested that he had already told all he knew. But when he was tied to the frame Luis broke down and revealed what the Inquisition was most likely to know, namely, that his sister Catalina was a Judaizer. He proceeded to explain Catalina's Judaizing at length, but when he finished he said he had nothing more to confess.

The inquisitorial notary, who had been recording every detail, then made the following entries:

The minister entered [again] and after the prisoner had been admonished to tell the truth, the minister was ordered to give one twist to the rope, and he did, and the prisoner said, "Ay! O Lord, may this help to counteract my abominable transgressions. Pardon me, O Lord, pardon me, have mercy upon me." And he said that he would have told the truth if he had any information about anyone else.

After again being admonished to tell the truth, the minister was ordered to twist the ropes a second time, and the prisoner shouted, "Ay, ay, ay, ay." And he said that his sister Anica observes the Law that God gave to Moses; and sobbing, he said he had told the truth and that the inquisitors should not take vengeance upon him.

After again being admonished to tell the truth, he was given a third twist of the ropes, and he cried aloud, "Lord, God of Israel, I will have to tell a lie. . . . For the sake of the one and only God, please be kind to me.

Woe is me. I shall wretchedly have to tell a lie." And he protested that he had already told the truth.

After he had been admonished to tell the truth, he was given a fourth twist of the rope. He complained bitterly, "Ay, ay, ay, ay, I shall tell the truth, I shall tell it, Mr. Inquisitor, I shall tell the truth." Then the ropes were tightened still more, and he said, "Let the minister leave and I shall tell the truth." The minister left.[24]

Luis's spirit was not yet broken. He confessed that Anica was a Judaizer, since the inquisitors clearly did not accept his alibi for her, but he refused to confess anything more. Thereupon the minister was brought back to apply a fifth turn of the rope, and Luis, realizing that the inquisitors were determined to let him die in pain rather than to allow him to withhold information about even one suspect, expressed his willingness to cooperate and explained that he had regarded it as a sin to incriminate other Judaizers.

Luis's revelations and the inquisitors' interrogations lasted until seven o'clock that evening. Luis was returned for further questioning on the next two days, the sessions on the tenth lasting from 8:30 in the morning to 5 in the afternoon.[25]

On the twelfth, when Luis, somewhat recovered after a day's rest, refused to cooperate any further, he was again stripped, tied to the frame, and given six painful twists of the rope. Once again Luis had no alternative but to speak. But the torture, on top of all his fasting, had brought Luis to such exhaustion that at 11:30 A.M. the inquisitors found it necessary to suspend the questioning until the afternoon. They ordered Luis returned to his cell and canceled his midday meal. They acceded to his request for paper, pen, and ink so that he might write out additional confessions that he had been too weak to deliver orally. Before the end of the afternoon session Luis was given three additional sheets of paper. These were returned on Wednesday the fourteenth with much of the information that he had been withholding. The inquisitorial board then deliberated whether to continue the torture. Three members believed that it should be suspended, three that it should continue, and one that Luis should be kept under threat of torture. The official who wanted the greatest amount of torture applied was the inquisitor Peralta.[26]

The pain of the confessions could not have failed to make Luis feel unmanned. He, the leader and confidant of the secret Judaizers, had exposed the cream of the community. He had been unsuccessful in his attempt to withhold information. He was equally frustrated in his hope that he could satisfy the inquisitors and be relieved from torture by releasing some information and withholding all the rest. He had ended by revealing everything of importance that he knew and giving the Inquisition the wherewithal to strengthen and even seal its cases against his mother and sisters, his brothers-in-law, and countless acquaintances and friends.

Apparently haunted by this realization as he rested from his physical torture, Luis began to plan a double surprise, intended to vitiate the entire testimony he had given in the chamber of horrors.

When called to interview on the afternoon of February 15, Luis was ready to deliver the first surprise. As soon as the inquisitor asked whether he had remembered anything, he said, "Before I was tortured I protested for God's sake that you should not obligate me to utter lies. Thus everything I have said from the time torture began has been a lie. I say this to clear my conscience, for I would rather die in torture than go to hell."[27]

As Luis well knew, such testimony could mean only a resumption of torture. When he was returned to his cell after his brief and startling announcement, it was doubtless obvious that the decision for torture would be the Inquisition's next move.

But around three o'clock, a few moments after Luis had left the audience chamber, the second surprise came. Pedro de Fonseca, the Inquisition's porter, rushed to the inquisitors with the message that Luis de Carvajal had tried to commit suicide. He had amazingly managed to free himself from his guards and had hurled himself from the corridors onto the courtyard a floor below. The inquisitors, alarmed, rushed out to a gallery overlooking the courtyard in time to see the warden and one of his assistants holding Luis by his arms and helping him back to his cell.

The inquisitors then went to the cell area to examine their prisoner. He was not seriously injured. He had a lesion on his right arm and had hurt his feet sufficiently to make it necessary for him to be bedridden for some time. To avoid a recurrence of the suicide attempt the inquisitors ordered Luis handcuffed. In addition, they assigned two prisoners they could trust, Gaspar de Villafranca and Daniel Benítez, to Luis's cell to watch him and report anything worthy of note.[28]

Having failed in his attempt to save his friends, Luis realized that he again faced torture. He therefore did the only prudent thing he could. He prepared to confirm his original confessions. He immediately asked for an audience with the senior inquisitor, Dr. Lobo Guerrero. He begged that Lic. Peralta not be present "because the sight of him and his severity make my flesh tremble." The inquisitors put a note in the margin of Luis's trial record to the effect that Luis's fear derived from Peralta's ability to see through the prisoner's subterfuge. "Despite this," they continued, "he [Peralta] went to see him every visiting day as long as he was in prison, looking after his welfare, to oblige him in every possible way to return to our holy Catholic faith."[29]

Dr. Lobo Guerrero consented. Since Luis was too ill to come to the audience chamber, the inquisitor went down to Luis's cell. There Luis corroborated his confessions and blamed the devil for persuading him to revoke them.

Three further hearings were held in Luis's cell. The last, on March 4, 1596, substantially concluded his case. Luis was not called to audience again until June 27. Thereafter he appeared before the inquisitors only sporadically to add details or resolve differences in his previous testimony. Luis himself requested some of these audiences in an attempt to break the monotony of his cell. In one such audience, held on June 27, he took the opportunity to depose against Gaspar de Villafranca, calling him a blasphemer and sodomite.[30]

In the meantime the rest of the family were completing their confessions. Isabel, "negative" for an entire year, was subjected to torture in the summer of 1596. She withstood the torture for a while, but finally, racked with pain, she decided to confess. On Saturday afternoon, July 13, 1596, she asked for an audience. She was so weak that even with help she could not walk to the audience chamber. Her confessions had to be taken in her cell. In a series of hearings over the next few days she revealed everything she knew about the activities of her family and friends. On August 31 she was too weak to affix her signature of ratification to the transcript of her testimony. On November 12, she revoked her confessions about Anica's Judaizing.[31]

On August 24 the inquisitors again tried to convert Luis. They sent two of their examiners, Pedro de Agurto and Diego de Contreras, both erudite Augustinians, to meet with Luis and discuss matters of faith. After three sessions the theologians gave up. Luis remained as firmly rooted in Judaism as ever.[32]

After two more audiences, held on August 30 and September 9, Luis presented the inquisitors with a paper on September 12 that made the inquisitors realize the utter futility of their attempts to convert him. Though there were further audiences where Luis revealed minor items of information, the presentation of this paper effectively brought his case to an end.

The document, written in a fine, clear hand on both sides of a small

Doña Isabel de Carvajal before the Inquisitors (from El Libro Rojo*)*

sheet of paper, was Luis de Carvajal's final testament. The Inquisition having made it unnecessary for Luis to be concerned with worldly goods, it was entirely a spiritual will, an impassioned defense of its author's desire to live and die in the Jewish faith.[33]

The preamble to Luis's testament was full of faith and pathos:

O most high and sovereign Creator of heaven and earth, not one of Your countless creatures can resist Your will. Without it neither men nor birds nor brutish beasts could live upon the earth. Unless Your desire and will sustained them and ordered the elements [of the world], the heavens would become confused; their natural orbits would vanish; the whole earth would shake; the peaks of lofty hills would tumble; the waters of the sea would cover the land and no living thing would have a chance of surviving. But by Your infinite goodness and mercy You give order and sustenance to all, not that this is necessary for You, but for the sake of the common good and benefit of men.

And since You employ such kindness and boundless mercy with them, I, the poorest and most wretched among them all, ask and beg of You not to abandon me in the perilous entry into death, where I have elected to go for the sake of Your most holy name and true Law. Accept as a sacrifice this poor life which You have given me. Look not at my countless sins, but rather at Your lovingkindness and upon my immortal soul which You have created in Your own likeness for life eternal. I beg You to pardon it and receive it when it has left my mortal frame.

Wherefore, having prepared my last and final will and testament and given it its final form, I write and affix my signature to the religious truths in which I believe and in which I profess to die in Your presence.

Then in ten numbered paragraphs[34] Luis listed and gave arguments in support of his basic beliefs—the omnipotence and unity of God, the validity and centrality of the "sacrament of circumcision," the certainty of the future arrival of the Messiah, the rapid approach of the end of the historical era, and the inauguration of the messianic age.

Perhaps the most memorable words of these paragraphs are contained in Luis's searing indictment of the kings of Spain and Portugal. "These," he said, "have ever been the root of the tree whose branches of Inquisitions and persecutions have spread over the people of God, our Lord, and His holy Law." Luis held them responsible for the death of "the blessed martyrs—the faithful and the true Jews who have died out of allegiance to this Law."

"The princes have persecuted them without cause, calling them Judaizing heretics, unjustly," said Luis, "for the practice of Judaism is not heresy; it is the fulfillment of the will of God our Lord."

The Final Testament of Luis de Carvajal (Joseph Lumbroso)

inst. à q̃ bestia espantosa. vñas fieras, q̃ todo lo perdia con perdicion, y atropellaba con los pies figuro esta 4ª que
naçia a dicha bestia dura. y com̃o caia aquesta es contra de los paganos .... S. Gabriel a diziò S. Daniel ense-
ño el cuerno pequeño con dos ojos, y la boca q̃ dezia grandes blasfemias contra Dios ensalçado que son. Passion de Dios
si es de Dios essa q̃ dize. y ser viendo uno de su q̃ es tres. y q̃ salen de Dios q̃ mueren &c. q̃ el infinito distinto, y eternal etern̄o.
en su esencia. y a si da que será desto el q̃ p.a Aspi. ibi mem. impossible. y muy clara ... y la S. D.D q̃ uid q̃ que hicze es
espiritista. Omnia contra pecatores con firma gẽte. q̃ en si halla Dios no q̃ tã fierza q̃ de seia q̃ en el supuesta Exaltaba el se mismo en este ...
y en su caida justa do con el terrible casi godelcia del sol. promete juzgarlos, y por si se declara el S. mucho diziendo con
a q̃ ue om̃e sienten tal es los q̃ sal q̃ su ti q̃ entrare con ellos en su defuscios en su q̃ higiere a mi pli. y por isai. 49. y 66.
Esaias ibi. q̃ los q̃ y no profundie... por sa me. y el apliq̃ eto todo q̃ Dios veo y a Aborezio. y el tonzes sera q̃ he topado el
...o 4.º y a los santos q̃ es el señor Dios. Aun ibi con tales q̃ eo el su nombre colu... q̃ el... evigno q̃ fable, su ...
figura la ho profecia q̃ la del monte sin manos. e la estatua hecho Nacio no do... caeras. el ymp. se q̃ piso en este q̃
ha a puesto por q̃ so esta ya sobre los pies de barro y de hierro q̃ no nace bu mezcla como se dize en las divisiones
esso. En los es y q̃ si ser franceses. y los q̃ mas se dirian se todos unos mismos pies de la estatua. y ya no hace buena ...
los de esta. Por esta grave caida en de zar. con fatia de Deus 2. ibi dedit se adnes q̃ usq̃ ego retribua. es sent...
pone no distitutaig, res q̃. Y lo de junto creo q̃ aquel rey Anthioco a quien la sagrada script llamo vago es, escado. por ser
persiquid y el spu̅ de Dios. y de su sandales. fue fig. de los reyes se es q̃ y su digital. los cua tes ansi soy. por la rabia q̃ tiene
a nuestra fee y con de los ramos de las ynquisiciones. y persecuciones del spu̅ de Dios 4.º y su santa ley. y de los q̃ vien a ser
de los q̃ moristes los ramos de la fe y q̃ ordena de los judios, q̃ no es heregia, sino ha. q̃ el q̃ manda distrito S. con la ley de los q̃ de su do ...

[...]

y es siervo perpetuo del Altissimo ADON.

y Joseph Lumbroso.

The conclusion of Luis's final testament was full of certainty and triumph:

And thus it is my desire and will to die for God's holy faith and true Law. I look to the Lord for strength, lacking all confidence in my own, for after all I am flesh born of fragile seed. And if, instead of five sisters—in addition to my mother—who are now in danger because of their trust in God's Law, I had a thousand, I would give them all up for my faith in each one of God's holy commandments.

In witness whereof I have written and signed this testament of mine, and with this final deposition, in which I [re]affirm and [re]confirm my faith, I [hereby] conclude the process of my trial.

My God and Lord, give me grace in the eyes of my captors that it may be seen and known in this kingdom and in all kingdoms of the earth that You are our God and that You, O most high and sanctified God, named Adonay, are rightly invoked by Israel and his descendants.

I commend this soul You have given me to Your most holy hands, solemnly declaring that I will not change my faith until I die, nor when I die. I happily bring to end the course of my present life, bearing a living faith in Your divine promise of salvation through Your infinite mercy, and when Your holy will is fulfilled, of resurrection in the company of our saintly patriarchs, Abraham, Isaac, and Jacob, and their faithful children. For the sake of their holiness I very humbly entreat You to admit me to Your love and not to abandon me, and to deign send to my succor and aid that saintly angel, Michael, our prince, with his saintly and angelical soldiery, to help me persevere and die in Your holy faith, and to free me from the Adversary's hands and temptations.

My good God and Lord, have mercy upon the glory of Your name, [Your] Law, and [Your] people, and upon the world which You have created. Fill it with Your light and with the true knowledge of Your name, that heaven and earth may be filled with praise of Your glory. Amen. Amen.

The document was "dated in purgatory," as Luis dared to call the house of the Inquisition, "this fifth month" of August "of the year of our creation, five thousand three hundred and fifty-seven."[35]

11 Death and Transfiguration

Luis de Carvajal the Younger died around seven o'clock in the evening of Saturday, December 8, 1596. He was thirty years and a few months old. His mother and his sisters Isabel and Catalina preceded him in death, and his sister Leonor followed him.[1]

His death climaxed the most elaborate auto-da-fé held in New Spain up to that time. The two prior autos-da-fé, held in March 1591 and May 1593, were drab affairs, with few prisoners and only a handful of Judaizers. Among these were Francisco Ruiz de Luna in 1591 and, in absentia, two years later, Licentiate Manuel de Morales.[2] After 1593 the inquisitors waited patiently until they could assemble a sufficient number of malefactors for a more colorful public presentation. Although arrests were regularly made, few Judaizers appeared in the Inquisition's jail until Manuel de Lucena and Luis de Carvajal began their confessions. As a result of their revelations, the Inquisition was able to conclude cases against forty-five Judaizers by November 1596 and was preparing for an auto-da-fé involving sixty-six malefactors. On November 10 the inquisitors announced this fact to the city fathers and asked for a subvention to enable them to hold the auto-da-fé in the Great Square in Mexico City.[3]

As soon as the date was picked, the inquisitors sent their prosecutor, Dr. Martos de Bohorques, to the viceroy, Don Gaspar de Zúñiga y Azevedo, to invite him formally to the function. At the same time their chief constable was inviting the archbishop of Mexico, Don Alonso Fernández de Bonillo, along with other dignitaries of the capital, ecclesiastical and lay.

The event was announced in a festive procession, led by the inquisitors and accompanied by blaring trumpets and pounding kettle-drums. The procession began and ended at the inquisitorial jail, with stops at key stations along the route. Near the jail the discreet crier made his proclamations in such a way as to be unheard by the prisoners.

In the meantime preparations for the auto-da-fé were already under way. Painters and carpenters, under the supervision of the inquisitorial treasurer, were hard at work constructing stands and platforms. And under the jurisdiction of the Inquisition's familiars, shifts of a large honor guard, comprising leading citizens of the capital, began to watch over the prisoners at night. A holiday air hung over the streets during their vigils. Bonfires were lit, and crowds brought refreshments and sweets for the honorary wardens. The mood in which the auto-da-fé was anticipated was a blend of solemnity and joy. The grand spectacle was to provide an exciting interlude in the monotonous drudgery of the people's lives and a socially acceptable outlet for their accumulated frustrations.

Approximately a week before the auto-da-fé a public announcement was again made in the churches, followed by a lengthy sermon in defense of the Inquisition's cause.

On the eve of the auto-da-fé confessors were assigned to each prisoner sentenced to death. It was their duty to remain with their prisoners to the end, preparing them to meet death and exhorting the recalcitrant to a sincere embrace of the church.[4] Father Medrano was assigned to Luis de Carvajal.[5]

Before seeing their prisoners the confessors assembled to take an oath. They swore that they would absolve of heresy only those who had properly confessed, that they would transmit no messages from one prisoner to another, and that they would maintain the tightest secrecy about everything they saw and heard. They then each received a small green cross to be delivered to their charges in a special ceremony in the jail. The crosses were then tied to the prisoners' hands.

On December 7 the warden and familiars kept an all-night vigil over the prisoners scheduled to participate in the auto-da-fé. Their vigil had a twofold purpose: they would watch every move of the prisoners and would also be available to receive information that any of them might wish to disclose.

At three o'clock in the morning the warden brought tapers to the cells of the participating prisoners and ordered them to dress. After a breakfast consisting of fried honeyed bread and a large glass of wine, they were led to a patio for roll call and the final preparations for their march to the Great Square. Like the other prisoners destined for the stake, the Carvajals were all dressed in *sambenitos* and *corozas,* or miters. The *sambenitos* were adorned in front and back with a Saint Andrew's cross in green cloth and the *corozas* were painted with devils, snakes, and flames. Each prisoner was given his green wax candle to carry in the procession.

The procession began at dawn. In the forefront, escorted by clergy, were the black-draped standards of the parish churches. The funereal colors did not allude to the condemned but to their offenses against the faith. Then came the robed and mitered "criminals," each bearing a placard with his name, birthplace, and offense. The Judaizers to be reconciled preceded those facing relaxation, and these in turn were followed by coffins of the Inquisition's victims sentenced to posthumous incineration. Only one marcher had not been placed with his group. This was Luis de Carvajal. The Inquisition's prisoner extraordinary was given the place of greatest ignominy, at the rear of the criminals' procession. Before the procession had gone very far Luis had to be gagged. He had rejected all efforts to convert him and had been shouting encouragement to his mother and sisters to remain steadfast in their Judaism.

The dignitaries marched after the prisoners. First came the senior inquisitor, with the viceroy on his right and the junior inquisitor on his left. Then came the inquisitorial prosecutor, with the crimson standard of the Holy Office. The banner was tasseled with silk and golden cords and fastened to a silver pole capped with an aureate cross. Behind the prosecutor marched numerous other churchmen and lay officials, as well as private citizens of note.

The multitude of marchers snaked toward the Great Square, jammed with people from all walks of life who had been thronging there for hours. The criminals were led to a tiered, semicircular pyramid at one side of the staging and made to sit in places corresponding to the severity of their guilt. Those with lesser offenses were put on the bottom rungs and those with more serious crimes near the top. Luis de Carvajal's seat overlooked the entire assembly.[6] Before he sat down, he caught a glimpse of the effigy of a Judaizer destined for relaxation and heaved a plaintive sigh. The statue may well have been the one representing his brother Miguel.[7]

The dignitaries, too, had their appointed seats. Walnut chairs had been provided for the inquisitors and the viceroy. The viceroy's was adorned with several cushions, including one for his feet. In a building adjacent to the scaffolding the viceroy even had a three-room, handsomely appointed apartment waiting for him.

The ceremony began with the usual verbose sermon. The preacher for the occasion was no less a personage than the archbishop of the Philippines.

The Inquisition's secretary then administered the oath of faith. The people roared their promise to defend the Holy Office and its agents and to denounce all heretics, "revealing them and not concealing them." They also invoked an entire panoply of curses on themselves should they ever break this commitment.

The secretary then turned to the monotonous and time-devouring reading of the sentences, beginning with the blasphemers. These included some Negro slaves who, when starved and inhumanely lashed, had expressed the wish that they were not alive and said it was better to be a monkey than a Christian. They were sentenced to be corrected by more lashes and mistreatment. They were followed by the fornicators, the witches, and the bigamists. Finally came the Judaizers: forty-five in person, and eight in effigy, including the wife and nephew of Dr. Morales and Luis's own brother Miguel. In addition to the Carvajals, four other Judaizers were to be relaxed in person. These were Manuel Díaz, Beatriz Enríquez de Payba, Diego Enríquez, and Manuel de Lucena. Among the Judaizers reconciled to the church were Lucena's wife, Catalina Enríquez, Díaz's wife, also named Catalina Enríquez, Diego Díez Nieto, Manuel Gómez Navarro, Clara Enríquez and her daughter, Justa Méndez, and Lucena's brother-in-law, Pedro Enríquez. Manuel Gómez Navarro was sent to the galleys for six years and Pedro Enríquez for five.[8]

During the sentencing various members of the clergy kept importuning Luis to convert, but Luis paid them no heed. When Justa Méndez was about to be sentenced Luis managed to throw off his gag and cry out, "Let me hear the sentence of that fortunate and blessed girl."[9]

After the sentences Luis, his mother, and sisters had their hands tied and were placed on beasts of burden. Under guard they were led in a procession to San Francisco Street and the Merchants' Gate (*Portal de los Mercaderes*). As they moved, a crier kept proclaiming the heinousness of their misdeeds. At their destination stood a carpeted stage. Here, in the presence of a scribe and familiar of the Holy Office, the mayor, Licentiate Bibero, pronounced their sentences of death and sent them on their way to the burning grounds or *quemadero*. The *quemadero* was located in the marketplace of Saint Hippolytus (*tiangues de San Hipólito*) at the east end of the Alameda, the city's central park. It had been constructed for this occasion at a cost of four hundred pesos.[10]

Shortly before they were put to death, Doña Francisca and her daughters agreed to embrace the church. They were accordingly garroted before the pyre was kindled.[11]

Immediately upon Luis's death, Alonso de Bernal, the notary in attendance, made a formal report, attesting to Carvajal's trek to the *quemadero* and the burning of his body to ashes, in the presence of the chief constable, Baltasar Mexía Salmerón, and his lieutenants, Pedro Rodríguez and Juan de Budía, "and many other people." But, said Bernal, as Luis was being led to execution, "he showed signs of having converted: he took a crucifix in his hands and said some words by which it was understood that he had converted and repented. Whereupon, on arriving at the site of the execution, he was garroted until he died . . . and his body was consigned to the flames."[12]

A Dominican friar named Alonso de Contreras wrote a lengthy statement, dated December 9, 1596, confirming Bernal's claim.

He had come to the auto-da-fé on Dr. Bohorques's invitation, said Contreras, and there he was attracted to Luis de Carvajal. Aware of the prisoner's staunch commitment to Judaism, he had no doubt "that if he had lived before the incarnation of our redeemer, he would have been a Hebrew worthy and would have had renown in the Bible today." Indeed, said Contreras, "even in New Spain, if God, for His own sake, had not stopped him, he would have uprooted large and venerable stocks from the vineyard of the church."

After the sentencing, as Luis was being led away, Contreras claimed that he approached him. He heard several monks and priests who were desperately trying to convert Luis but were succeeding only in kindling his fury. Deciding to try his hand, Contreras asked politely in Spanish, "Do you know, Luis, what the Inquisition and Holy Office really is?"

To this Luis shouted in Latin, "The council of the wicked and the seat of pestilence." Then he added pathetically, "Is there a worse torture in the world than for a man to have his hands tied and be surrounded by rabid dogs?"

Contreras said that he then exhorted Luis to forbearance and engaged him in a lengthy but fruitless theological discussion that continued until they reached the mayor's stand. After the sentencing to the *quemadero*, everyone but Luis's confessor was ordered to stay away from him, and Contreras began to leave. At that moment he saw the chief magistrate winking at him and indicating that he should remain at Luis's side.

He therefore resumed his efforts to convert Luis, said Contreras. Finally Luis promised that he would convert if Contreras proved that a biblical verse he was citing came, as he claimed, from the prophet Jeremiah. After fumbling helplessly through the pages of a Bible, much to Luis's amusement, Contreras managed to borrow a concordance and found the verse in the Book of Lamentations, which is traditionally attributed to Jeremiah.

Thereupon, said Contreras, Luis kept his word. He received a cross with tender emotion, affirming his belief in the divinity of Jesus and the grace-giving potential of the church's sacraments. Contreras said that he then had himself appointed Luis's confessor in Father Medrano's place.[13]

As Luis approached his stake, he took his final confession. In these last words Luis revoked the damning testimony he had given against eight Judaizers. One of these was his brother-in-law Díaz de Cáceras. Another was Tomás de Fonseca of Tlalpujahua, the uncle and erstwhile manager of the estate of his other brother-in-law, Jorge de Almeida.[14]

Contreras reported that he was with Luis de Carvajal when he was garroted and that he died clutching his crucifix.[15]

To judge from the concluding section of Contreras's report, its motivation was clearly apologetic. The conclusion goes to great lengths to refute the charges made by others, clerics among them, that Luis de Carvajal had not converted sincerely but only to escape the ordeal of burning alive. There were even those who said that before his death Luis had uttered words and made gestures that were used by the secret Jews.

Despite certain challenges to Contreras's theological asides made by an official of the Holy Office in the margins, his document was accepted by the Inquisition and was eventually appended to the minutes of Luis de Carvajal's trial. It was certainly in the Inquisition's interest to claim that the spirit of so notorious a Judaizer had been conquered.

Nor were Luis de Carvajal's contemporaries any surer about it. A certain lady named Doña Damiana had been watching the procession of prisoners, particularly Luis de Carvajal, being led to the auto-da-fé. Looking at Luis, she inwardly prayed to God to reveal to her whether or not he would convert and receive salvation. According to a friend, Doña Ana de Guillamas, God answered Doña Damiana's prayer and revealed that Luis would convert, "as he did convert after he had passed by the place where they had been standing for a long time."[16]

However, Manuel Tavares, a Portuguese Judaizer arrested by the Inquisition, insisted that Carvajal did not convert. "You never get a good Christian from a good Jew," he later told his cellmate in the

Inquisition's jail. His cellmate, a priest named Juan Plata, reminded Tavares of the incident involving Father Contreras and the biblical verse, as a result of which Luis was said to have converted. Plata even suggested that Luis converted because he was afraid of eternal damnation. Tavares was unmoved by such arguments. He responded by saying that "Carvajal knew well whether he was being damned or not." He praised Carvajal's religious knowledge and reminded Plata that the inquisitorial tribunal had failed in numerous previous attempts to convince Carvajal.[17]

Did Luis de Carvajal really convert? Was he garroted against his will in order to give the impression that he had embraced the church? Or did Luis de Carvajal only feign conversion? We do not know.

Jewish history records numerous cases of Jews under the threat of death who converted to save their lives and property. Luis de Carvajal may well be an example of a secret Jew who, in the face of inescapable death, converted at least in part in an attempt to save the lives and property of people dear to him.

On March 25, 1601, four and a half years after the holocaust that consumed her mother, brother, and three sisters, Doña Mariana Núñez de Carvajal followed them to the stake. She too was converted and garroted before her body was set afire, but in her case the conversion had been unimpeachably sincere. The last several years of her life, fragmented into alternating periods of lucidity and madness, were tragic beyond description. And the days of her sanity were palled by the fate of her loved ones and the certain future that lay in store for her.[18]

The Inquisition had assigned her to the care of one of its familiars, Bernardino Vázquez de Tapia, around Easter of 1596.[19] When she first came to his home, Mariana suffered from extreme melancholia and fits of rage. She broke open a locked chest with her head, tore her clothing to pieces, and refused food and drink; when she was not babbling unintelligibly she often used the foulest of language. This situation lasted for about two months, according to Vázquez de Tapia's wife, Doña Luisa de Castilla. It was probably prolonged by the beatings and whippings administered as a cure. Mariana, however, remained melancholy after this violent phase, and for long periods of time refused to leave her room.[20]

But by November 1597 she showed signs of recovery. To restore her health fully, Bernardino Vázquez de Tapia decided to transfer her to the home of his mother, Doña María de Peralta.[21] Doña Luisa de

The Martyrdom of Mariana de Carvajal (from El Libro Rojo)

Castilla accompanied Mariana there. When she was called by the Inquisition to testify about Mariana's sanity on July 23, 1598, Doña Luisa was able to say that since her transfer "she had not done anything imprudent except sing and talk too much sometimes." But, Doña Luisa added, "when told to be quiet, she quiets down and is calm."[22]

When her judgment was restored, Mariana later claimed, she returned wholeheartedly to the church. She regularly recited the Lord's Prayer, the Hail Mary, the credo, and the Hail Holy Queen and dutifully fulfilled all her obligations as a Catholic. She taught the children in Doña María de Peralta's house and chided people for not praying with sufficient devotion. She became a model of Catholic piety. María de Peralta came to regard her as "a little saint." Whenever anyone mentioned her parents, Mariana asked them not to because they had offended God.[23] She liked to think that she had been a good Catholic since December 8, 1596, when she realized "that the keeping of the Law of Moses was a deceit and that the Christians who kept the holy Catholic faith would not be damned."[24]

Mariana fully revealed her prior Judaizing to Fray Juan de Santiago, a Franciscan then serving as her confessor. She even expressed a desire to rush to the Inquisition with this information, but Fray Juan dissuaded her, saying that the acceleration of one's own death was not a prerequisite for salvation.[25]

By May 1600, after numerous inquiries and depositions had pointed to her recovery, the inquisitors proceeded to try Mariana on the charge of having relapsed into Judaism after her reconciliation to the church. In her trial Mariana testified fully and candidly, displaying a sincere love for the church. Her testimony accorded fully with the information the Inquisition had already accumulated from her family and friends and provided conclusive proof of her guilt.

Unmoved by Mariana's mental ordeals and unmindful of her sincere conversion and exemplary Catholic life since she regained control of her faculties, the Inquisition proceeded to sentence her to relaxation. According to one account, Mariana died "with much contrition, asking God's mercy for her sins and confessing the holy Catholic faith with such emotion and tears that she stirred her listeners. She spoke tenderly to the cross she carried, kissing and embracing it with such sweet words that the monks and priests accompanying her were moved to silence, and all gave infinite thanks to God our Lord."[26]

Tomás de Fonseca of Taxco was also burned at the stake on that day, and some sixteen other Judaizers were relaxed in absentia or posthumously. Among those who had succeeded in escaping the

Inquisition by prior death were Cristóbal Gómez, Jorge Díaz, and Blanca de Morales. Foremost among the deceased whose bodies were carried to the *quemadero* was Antonio Machado.[27]

In addition, a large number of Judaizers were officially reconciled to the church. Among them were Isabel Machado, Hector de Fonseca, Gonzalo Pérez Ferro, Antonio Díaz Márquez, and Tomás de Fonseca of Tlalpujahua. Among them also were three members of Luis de Carvajal's family: his sister Anica, his niece, Leonor, and her father, Antonio Díaz de Cáceres.[28]

Luis's death-hour retractions were to prove of inestimable help to Antonio Díaz de Cáceres. Shrewd and politically well-connected, Luis's brother-in-law had managed to keep out of the Inquisition's clutches until 1596, despite the fact that for some time it had had ample evidence to arrest him. From his very first audience, on December 19 of that year, Díaz de Cáceres vigorously insisted on his innocence. He rested his defense on the contention that his in-laws, including Jorge de Almeida, had testified against him out of ineradicable malevolence.[29]

He explained that they were his mortal enemies for three reasons: he had slapped Leonor; he had once attacked some of the members of the family with a knife; and he had shut the door in their faces when they came to visit his ailing wife. At the same time he repeatedly discredited the women in the family. He said that Leonor, who blamed him for Mariana's imprisonment, had no sense, and that his mother-in-law "was simple and without natural understanding."[30]

Díaz de Cáceres named a number of people who he believed would substantiate the family's antipathy toward him. They included Jorge de León, Catalina de León, wife of Gonzalo Pérez Ferro, and even Hector de Fonseca, Diego Díez Nieto, and some servants. The Inquisition proceeded to interview ten such witnesses on Thursday March 27, 1597, and found their testimony conflicting. Some, like Almeida's brother and Jorge de León, supported Díaz de Cáceres's contention, while others denied any knowledge of the alleged animosity.[31] In the meantime Díaz de Cáceres had a change of heart about Hector de Fonseca. Apparently not certain how he would testify, he decided to petition the inquisitors to reject him as untrustworthy. In his petition, finally presented in mid-April, Díaz de Cáceres lamely explained that he had originally named him because he believed there was a dearth of witnesses on his behalf. Díaz de Cáceres did not know, of course, that Hector de Fonseca had testified in his favor.[32]

After the reading of the second admonition to Díaz de Cáceres on April 29, 1597, he was not recalled to audience until December 2, 1600. In the intervening years the Inquisition was patiently collecting additional incriminating evidence against him. Mariana, Gonzalo Pérez Ferro, Diego Díez Nieto, and Díaz de Cáceres's own daughter, Leonor, gave devastating evidence of his Judaizing activities and the practices carried on with his knowledge in his home.[33] Others spoke of his attempts to communicate with fellow prisoners like Gonzalo Pérez Ferro by boring holes in the walls of his cell and sending messages to other parts of the secret compound. One of these messages was intended for his sister-in-law Ana, arrested shortly after the auto-da-fé of 1596. The message accused Ana of giving testimony that led to his arrest, but went on to tell her that "he did not hate her but that rather, on leaving jail, he intended to give her five hundred pesos so that she could get married and that he would do everything possible to protect and favor her, for after all, she was his wife's sister, and he would fulfill his promises to her as to his own daughter." He asked Jorge Rodríguez, a fellow prisoner, to deliver this message. Through him, Ana expressed her gratitude to her brother-in-law and prayed "that God grant him health and freedom that he might always do good."[34]

Despite the presentation of this evidence against him, Díaz de Cáceres insisted on his innocence throughout his audiences in December 1600 and the first two months of the following year. He denied knowing that Diego Díez Nieto or his father were secret Jews. He denied that it was his wife's Judaizing that had impelled him to take his daughter away from home. He denied awareness that the food served him adhered to the Judaizers' dietary laws. After all, he said, "I am not a cook. I ate what I was given."[35]

Díaz de Cáceres's stance inevitably led him to the torture chamber. After voting torture *in caput proprium* on March 2, 1601, the inquisitors subjected Díaz de Cáceres to a terrible ordeal. As usual they recorded every step of the proceedings for posterity with dispassionate detail.

They first submitted him to the rope treatment, giving him twelve hoists and an opportunity after each application to confess the information they knew he was concealing. When he said he had already revealed everything, they stretched him on the rack and began to apply exquisite torture to his calves, thighs, and shins. After this infliction, they started another round with several minor variations. During the experience Díaz de Cáceres recited the Lord's Prayer, the Hail Mary, and Psalm 130, which begins: "Out of the depths have I called Thee, O Lord./Lord, hearken unto my voice;/Let Thine ears be attentive/To the voice of my supplications." But he revealed no new information.

When the inquisitors demanded that he tell the truth, all he would say was, "Kill me. . . . I have already told it."

The inquisitors unbound him, again admonished him to tell the truth, and when he refused to speak further, they stretched him on the rack again. But this time they did not torture him. They decided that he had had enough.[36]

The iron-willed Díaz de Cáceres had thus overcome his torture. Normally with such a victory came a presumption of the defendant's innocence, especially when the evidence against him was inconclusive. But since there was an accumulation of damning testimony against Díaz de Cáceres, the natural step for the inquisitors to take was to have him declared an impenitent and condemn him to relaxation to the secular arm.

Yet they did not. Instead they decided to reconcile Díaz de Cáceres and give him an unusually light sentence. They decreed that he appear as a penitent at the auto-da-fé on March 25, 1601, abjure *de vehementi,* and pay a thousand Castilian ducats for the "extraordinary expenses of this office" incurred in his case. He was spared from lashes "because he was a man of esteem and had served the king on several occasions."[37] It is easy to imagine that this light sentence was the result of confidential efforts by Díaz de Cáceres's friends and political connections.

After his reconciliation Díaz de Cáceres disappears from the records, but his name continues to be recorded again and again in the trials of his progeny before the Inquisition.

Jorge de Almeida, too, disappeared from sight after obtaining the liberty of his in-laws. He did not return to New Spain, and after his letter to Luis, he is heard from no more. For some reason, perhaps because it expected Almeida to return, the Inquisition did not rush to try him in absentia after its abortive attempt to reach him in 1590. In 1594 it sued Almeida's estate for the value of his wife's dowry, though it had already confiscated what was left of Leonor's possessions. Almeida's funds were in the hands of his administrator, Felipe de Palacios, and he did not display any eagerness to release them.[38]

Since the suit did not involve the question of Judaism, witnesses for the defense felt freer to appear. Relatives like Gonzalo Pérez Ferro and Diego Márquez de Andrada and friends like Cristóbal Gómez, Fernando de Vega, and Gaspar Delgado all argued that Doña Leonor never really had a dowry from her family, that the money constituting the so-called dowry was really part of Almeida's possessions and hence beyond the Inquisition's claim. One witness, María Ortiz, even said that some of the property did not belong to Almeida, that the writ of dower had been drawn up to postpone the payment of debts Almeida owed. At the same time, creditors came forward to present claims against the estate. Among them was Antonio Díaz de Cáceres.[39]

From the beginning Felipe de Palacios systematically blocked the Inquisition's efforts with one delay after another. The Inquisition finally put him in jail for thirty days and sentenced him to a second term, though this time he did not serve. In the long run, neither relatives nor friends could delay the inevitable outcome of the proceedings. Felipe de Palacios was forced to hand over the money corresponding to Leonor's dowry. The final installment, in the amount of 2,005 pesos, was received on February 16, 1599.[40]

Within a decade the balance of Almeida's estate was confiscated. In 1607 the Inquisition decided to try him again in absentia, resting its case on evidence it had obtained from the trials of Manuel de Lucena, Diego Díez Nieto, Almeida's sister-in-law Mariana, and his brother-in-law Luis. After publishing three summonses, each allowing him a period of twenty days in which to appear to answer charges, the inquisitors proceeded against Almeida. Finding him guilty, they confiscated his estate and condemned him to be relaxed in effigy at the auto-da-fé of March 22, 1609.[41]

Luis de Carvajal's brothers also survived the holocaust of 1596. Fray Gaspar remained on in New Spain and was sufficiently well regarded by the Inquisition to be consulted on the future of his niece, Leonor.[42] Baltasar and Miguel, alias David and Jacob Lumbroso respectively, were safely in Europe. Sometime before Luis was arrested as a relapsed heretic, he had received a letter from Baltasar informing him that Miguel "had gone to Salonika, near Constantinople, the city of the Turk, to study, and that he had become a great scholar in the Law of Moses and that he was a saint."[43]

We do not know by what standard, that of the Jews of Europe or the secret Jews of New Spain, Baltasar judged the scholarship of his brother. But we do know that tempting as it is, it is wrong to identify our Jacob Lumbroso with the famous rabbi and physician of the same name living in Venice at the beginning of the seventeenth century.

In 1638/39 Rabbi Jacob Lombroso (Lumbroso in Spanish) published his *Melo Kaf Naḥath* (A Handful of Pleasure), an edition of the Hebrew Bible with an introduction, and a commentary that included Spanish words and phrases. Several decades earlier he had produced a work called *Ḥesheḳ Shlomo* (Solomon's Desire), a glossary in Spanish of difficult words in the Bible.[44]

One simple fact makes it certain that there were two Jacob Lumbrosos. The first edition of the *Ḥesheḳ Shlomo* appeared in 1588.[45] At the time Miguel was twelve or thirteen years old, had had no Hebrew instruction, and was still living with his family in the capital of New Spain.

Justa Méndez also survived the auto-da-fé of 1596. Sometime later she married a rich widower with children. He was the merchant Francisco Núñez, also known as Francisco Rodríguez. Of Portuguese descent and a Judaizer, he had also been reconciled in the auto-da-fé of 1596.[46]

For her part, Justa Méndez Núñez could not accept the sumptuary regulations imposed upon her as a reconciled penitent. Not long after the removal of her penitential garb, on December 11, 1599, she was flouting the Inquisition's rules.[47]

On July 6, 1604, Ángel Guillaza, a Genoese merchant living in Mexico City, appeared before the Inquisition to testify that he saw Justa Méndez Núñez "traveling on a chair covered with white oilcloth . . . on the shoulders of a Negro or one Negro and one Indian." And, said Guillaza, "he heard the said Justa Méndez tell them to open the curtains so that she could be seen by all." He then observed that Justa Méndez was richly attired in an oriental black taffeta dress and a Mexican mantle made of silk and wool. He then saw her stop at the home of Sebastián and Constanza Rodríguez, both reconciled by the Inquisition for Judaizing.

On other occasions Guillaza saw Justa Méndez using silver tableware, including jugs, goblets, and saltcellars.[48]

Twenty months later, on February 25, 1606, Diego de Espinosa, the warden of the perpetual jail that the Inquisition had finally managed to establish, and Andrés de Mondragón, the "barber and surgeon" of the Holy Office, were passing by a shop owned by Justa Méndez on Santo Domingo Street, where most of the reconciled Judaizers had their places of business. They happened to look in and saw Justa bedecked in her finery. She was wearing gold rings on her fingers and a dress of dyed Castilian cloth with silk edging. Manuel de Lucena's daughter, Clara Enríquez, was there too. She had been reconciled in 1603, but she did not have on the *sambenito* she was still required to wear.

Andrés de Mondragón, astounded, asked Justa Méndez, "Why are you dressed this way, knowing you are not permitted to be?"

Justa Méndez replied, "Why shouldn't I be? Any black slave wears more than that."[49]

Such testimony, reinforced by other witnesses, led the Inquisition to reopen proceedings against Justa Méndez for failing to adhere to the sumptuary restrictions placed upon her. These proceedings ended startlingly with a decree from Madrid dated June 4, 1608, permitting her, "despite her condemnation and without danger of incurring further penalty" to "don and wear silk, fine cloth, gold, silver, precious stones, and to use and enjoy all the other things arbitrarily prohibited to those reconciled by the Holy Office that are not forbidden by common law."[50]

How Justa Méndez managed to obtain this exemption remains a mystery. If it points to nothing else, it at least testifies that she and her husband were people to conjure with in the community of New Spain.

Two decades later, in 1629, Justa Méndez is mentioned again in the records of the Holy Office. At that time an officer of the Inquisition in the town of Texcoco quoted Manuel de Lucena's son, Simón de Paredes, as saying that he suspected Justa Méndez of killing his sister Clara because she refused to Judaize.[51]

In 1633 Justa and her husband filed a complaint against a man named Gaspar Gerónimo because he had referred derogatorily to their Jewish ancestry.[52]

Justa Méndez Núñez died around 1635, but her memory continued to play an important role in the proceedings of the Inquisition. In 1642 Blanca de Rivera, arrested as a Judaizer, testified that Justa had indoctrinated her and her children into Judaism.[53] As a result of such testimony, Justa Méndez Núñez was posthumously charged with a relapse into heresy and was condignly sentenced to be relaxed in effigy. The sentence was executed on April 11, 1649, at the end of the so-called Great Auto-da-fé, where over a hundred prisoners were involved and fifty-seven were sentenced to relaxation in effigy. The most renowned victim of this auto-da-fé, the fervent Judaizer Tomás Treviño de Sobremonte, was burned alive at the stake.[54]

Luis's sister Ana, now a dowager of close to seventy, was also among the victims of this auto-da-fé.

After her reconciliation in 1601 she had married a merchant named Cristóbal Miguel. The couple had six children: Gaspar de Sosa, Tomás, Catalina, Mariana or María, Juana, and Ana. Tomás was married in Mexico City, but his wife's name is unknown. Catalina married a man

named Nieto, also of Mexico City, while María wed Diego Núñez
Pacheco, who was arrested by the Inquisition on the charge of Judaizing in October 1642 and died in prison the following May.[55]

Earlier in 1643 Ana had been arrested as a relapsed Judaizer. She
languished in her cell for six years, adhering to her secret faith through
prayer and fasting, unaware that spies were carefully observing her
every move. She might have looked forward to her death at the auto-
da-fé, for at the time she was suffering grievously from an advanced
case of cancer.[56]

Ana's niece, Leonor de Cáceres, was only fourteen years old when
she was reconciled to the church in the auto-da-fé of March 25, 1601.
After the auto-da-fé of 1596, the Inquisition took her from Agustín
de Espindola and placed her in the home of Doña María de Peralta,
where less than a year later she was to be reunited with her Aunt
Mariana.[57] Testimony by both Ana and Mariana led to Leonor's arrest
by the Inquisition in 1600. In her audiences she revealed that her
mother, her aunts, and her Uncle Luis had been teaching her Judaism
since she was five years old. Though she had been away from the
family since 1595, she could still recite numerous prayers by heart.[58]

Sometime after Leonor's reconciliation the inquisitors decided that
she should be placed with someone who could be relied upon to look
after her spiritual welfare. They turned for advice to Fray Gaspar de
Carvajal, and he suggested that Leonor be turned over to the custody
of his sister Ana. The inquisitors agreed, but Leonor balked at the
arrangement. She managed to persuade the inquisitors to permit her to
go instead to the home of her half sister, the mulatto Agustina de
Quiñones, now the wife of a barber named Gaspar de Pastraña.[59]

In 1608 Gaspar managed to take Leonor to Ana's house. And
though she later claimed that she hated her family more than the devil,
Leonor did permit herself a visit and a stay with her Aunt Ana in
1632.[60]

Around 1612 Leonor was married to a muleteer named Lope
Núñez. Some three years later the couple established their home in
Núñez's native town of Tulancingo, about seventy miles north of
Puebla. Four children were born of their marriage: Nicolás, around
1614; Ana, around 1618; Juan, around 1621; and Antonio, around 1624.
Leonor also raised a waif named María de Jesús who eventually be-
came Antonio's wife.[61]

Leonor apparently led a tranquil and Christian life in Tulancingo.
Toward the middle of the century she served as a volunteer nurse for

the indigent in the region. But on April 4, 1650, forty-nine years after her reconciliation, the Inquisition again became interested in Leonor when she made a sweeping revocation of the confessions she had given as a child. She now contended that she had not only never Judaized but that she had never learned anything about Judaism either at home or outside. She insisted that as a child she had never heard a word spoken against the Catholic faith. She falsely claimed that at the time of the auto-da-fé of 1601 she was only seven years old and explained that if she had confessed to the practice of Judaism, it was only because she frantically feared that she would be tortured if she did not.[62]

What motivated Leonor to make this unusual declaration is nowhere stated, but perhaps it does not have to be. For at least the last fifty of her sixty-three years she appears to have been a devout Catholic and raised her children as loyal sons and daughters of the church. In view of the serious disadvantages incurred by the descendants of every Judaizer, it was only natural that she should want to disencumber them by clearing her own name. Perhaps as time and desire transmuted her memory of the past she may even have unwittingly re-created the events of a half century before and could no longer imagine her childhood confessions to be true.

But the Inquisition's memory had not dimmed. Armed with their records, the inquisitors not only rejected Leonor's request but ordered her arrest and the sequestration of her possessions on January 12, 1652.

The Great Auto-da-fé of 1649

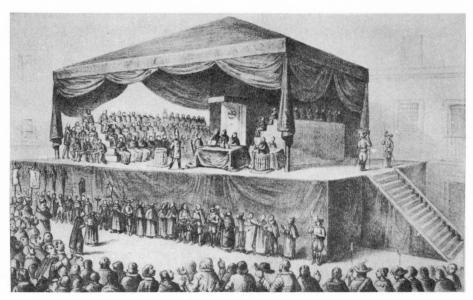

Charging her with having falsely revoked her testimony, the prosecuting attorney demanded a "severe and exemplary punishment."[63]

The trial that followed was bizarre. The Inquisition recited in detail the unimpeachable evidence of Leonor's youthful participation in the Judaizers' rites, and Leonor soon recognized that her case was lost. At first she softened her position, admitting that she had indeed Judaized as a child, but claiming that she no longer remembered what she had done because she stopped her Judaizing the moment she was taken to the home of Agustín de Espindola. But finally she had no choice but to reaffirm her original testimony, concede that she remembered her youthful crimes, and demonstrate repentance for the serious offense of having tried to erase the record.

The inquisitors, Francisco de Estrada y Escobedo and Pedro Saenz de Mañozca, then displayed an amazing charity toward Leonor. They set her free and restored her possessions. They limited her punishment to a reprimand for her recent actions and a warning "to calm down and forget about this matter."[64]

But that is not the last we hear about Doña Leonor. In August 1688, thirty-five years after her surprising release by the inquisitors and long after her death, a grandson of hers named José Núñez sought to clear her name in an effort to attain ordination as a priest. He had received minor orders, but recognized that he could not advance "because he had heard it said that he derived from the evil race of Jews and that his grandparents had been penanced by the holy tribunal of the Inquisition, for this was common knowledge in the town of Pachuca and this town of Tulancingo."[65] A friend of his, a priest named Tristán de Lara, who came from Pachuca, took up the cudgels on his behalf. He went back home to discuss the matter with his father, Agustín de Lara, and not long thereafter brought back the report concerning José Núñez "that everything with which he was being charged was false and a pack of lies." Don Agustín, his son said, had spoken to his own father about Doña Leonor and was persuaded not only that "this woman was very virtuous and proper," but that her "lineage was free of every evil race."

Armed with this information, the young priest visited the headquarters of the Inquisition in Mexico City and asked for a document attesting to José Núñez's Old Christian status, affirming that if he were not an Old Christian "he would not have him for a friend and would not keep his company." The inquisitor, persuaded that Tristán de Lara was not a relative of José Núñez's and was moved only by a desire for truth, told him to return in a week. When he did, the inquisitor informed him that he had good news. He had ordered the Inquisition's records searched but had found nothing to impugn the blood purity of José Núñez! Indeed, he had already passed this information on to the archbishop, who instructed that José Núñez be informed so that he could proceed with his plans for ordination.

Thus shown to be an Old Christian, José Núñez was ordained "within a few days." Sometime later his two nephews, Francisco Carlos de Espinosa and Ignacio de Espinosa, sons of his sister, Jerónima, also received ordination. Why the inquisitor was unable to find the record of José Núñez's true identity is nowhere told.[66]

In view of José Núñez's good fortune it is not surprising that seventeen years later another descendant of Leonor de Cáceres's tried to achieve a similar acknowledgment of untainted ancestry. This descendant was José de la Rosa, also of Tulancingo, Leonor de Caceres's great-grandson and her daughter Ana's grandson.

On February 4, 1706, José de la Rosa presented an unusual petition to the inquisitors. It alleged that virulent rumors, fanned by a fellow townsman, Miguel López, were identifying him as a descendant of the Leonor de Cáceres who had been reconciled years before by the Inquisition, and whose name appeared on a list of infamy hung in the cathedral of the city. The petition went on to claim that the identification was being made for no other reason than "because my maternal great-grandmother had the same first and last names." Since these rumors implied that he was of unclean blood, José de la Rosa asked the inquisitors to certify "that I am an Old Christian, free of any evil trace of Jew, Moor, heretic, or anyone penanced by this Holy Office, and that the said Leonor de Cáceres, my maternal great-grandmother, was not the one mentioned on the aforesaid document of infamy, but someone else."[67]

To support his claim, José de la Rosa presented an impressive array of witnesses, including Tristán de Lara.

But finally, on May 7, 1706, after a thorough examination of all the evidence, including a report of an investigation of the Inquisition's records, the inquisitor, Dr. Francisco de Deza y Ulloa, concluded that the Leonor de Cáceres who had been reconciled was indeed José de la Rosa's great-grandmother. He therefore rejected the petition, and the case was closed.[68]

By this time the Inquisition in the viceroyalty of New Spain had long passed its heyday. After 1649 the Judaizers haled before the Inquisition in New Spain were comparatively few in number, and the charges against them were often minor. There were no Judaizers among the twelve prisoners at the auto-da-fé of 1652 or the thirty-one sentenced in 1656, and only four out of the thirty-two paraded in 1659. Two of these, Diego Díaz and Francisco Botelho, paid the supreme penalty. From then on the Judaizers were noteworthy by the extreme infrequency of their appearance. Until well into the following century the inquisitors spent most of their time chasing bigamists and blasphemers, sorcerers and peccant priests.

The death at the stake of Fernando de Medina on June 14, 1699, closed the last important case of Judaizing in New Spain. A number of people, one of them a priest, are known to have been arrested on charges of Judaizing during the course of the eighteenth century, and even the beginning of the nineteenth. Many of the charges were flimsy, even spurious—as, for example, in the case of the great Mexican patriot in the war for independence, Miguel Hidalgo y Costilla. There is no evidence for the belief, occasionally articulated by scholars, that there were massive arrests of Judaizers during this period. The unmistakable impression left by the trial records is that the manifestations of secret Judaism in the last century of colonial New Spain were the distorted death gasps of a movement whose fate had been sealed long before.

The coming of the Bourbons to the Spanish throne in 1700 generated new attempts to restrain the reach of the Inquisition, and when Charles III expelled the Jesuits in June 1767, it was widely believed that the Inquisition would be suppressed within a matter of months.

The Inquisition was not suppressed, however, and it actually accelerated its activity, as if to announce that it was still very much alive. But the lethal blow was only a few decades in coming.

The cortes in Cádiz dissolved the Inquisition in Spain and in the colonies by its decree of February 22, 1813. The decree was published in Mexico on June 8 of that year. Though the restoration of Ferdinand VII returned the Inquisition, the revolution of 1820 effectively brought it to an end.

In the two and a half centuries of its existence the Inquisition in New Spain had done its work well against the children of Abraham. It had sent over a hundred alleged Judaizers to their death, put scores of others to flight, many of them among the most prominent citizens of New Spain, and had frightened countless others into unswerving conformity to the church.[69]

This does not mean that New Spain was swarming with secret Jews. In the three centuries of the colony's existence the number of known indictments handed down by the Inquisition against Judaizers does not by any count exceed fifteen hundred, and actually appears to have been considerably less. Some allowance also has to be made for those who were mistakenly or unjustly accused and the small number whose cases were dismissed. How many other secret Jews there were is impossible to tell, since only those whose secrecy failed have come to our attention. We do know that of those who were tried by the Inquisition, the vast majority were reconciled to the church and never heard from again, thus leaving open the possibility that they faithfully reembraced Catholicism. Charges by enemies of the New Christians that they were all secret Jews at heart lose their force in view of the few indictments made by the Inquisition from the sixteenth through the eighteenth centuries, despite its concern to uproot the Judaizers. From the records available, one must conclude that the Judaizers, if numbering some of the most important people in society, constituted only a small percentage of the New Christians in New Spain.

With Governor Carvajal's removal from the New Kingdom of León, the territories that had been under his control began to experience a precipitate decline. The inhabitants of the New Kingdom of León, especially those in the outlying regions, began to abandon their homes. Many sought refuge in Saltillo. Carvajal's lieutenant governor and successor, Castaño de Sosa, also suffered a tragic end. During an expedition to the north country, arranged in an effort to gain more land and resources, he was arrested on the treachery of Captain Juan Morlete and charged with rebelling against the crown. Castaño's arrest accelerated the deterioration of Carvajal's old region. The New Kingdom of León again saw men brutally killed, Indians enslaved, and people forced to leave their homes. As usual, many fled to Saltillo. It was not long before Saltillo found itself once more on the Indian frontier.[70]

In the spring of 1894, more than three hundred years after Governor Carvajal's death, an American named Charles A. Landis claimed that he had heard a number of legends about the governor on a visit to the state of Nuevo León. Later that year he published these accounts in a booklet entitled *Carabajal, the Jew: A Legend of Monterey* (sic).

According to Landis's account, the following are the highlights of the legends:

King Philip II, pained by the massacres inflicted on settlers by the savage Indians in the viceroyalty of New Spain, realized that there was only one man, Don Louis de Carabajal Y Cueva (sic) who could cope with the situation. He therefore decided to give him this responsibility, offering him in return the governorship of the Kingdom of New Leon (sic). At the same time, he apparently asked Carvajal for a loan of two million ducats.

Carvajal was a Jew and a humanitarian. In Spain he had already established hospitals, foundling homes, and other charitable institutions. He was also a lover of art and music, "so often characteristic of this people," and had enriched the art galleries and universities of Spain. And, "without possessing shrewdness or cunning," he "had all the business sagacity of his race," converting to gold whatever he touched. He had already purchased a large hacienda in New Spain years before.

Carvajal now accepted King Philip's offer and came to the New World, willingly bringing along holy friars and members of the poor and Old Christian nobility of Spain. In the New World he established many settlements and cities, including one "on the stream of Santa Lucia in Monterey." He planned the cities with an eye to their beauty and salubrity. "He adopted Jewish sanitary regulations and a special board for carrying them out."

He routed the Yako and Apache Indians and instituted a period of peace. Unlike other conquistadors, he allowed no slavery but created cooperative settlements for mining, agriculture, and manufacturing.

Carvajal's downfall appeared to have resulted from the viceroy's jealousy at his achievements and the animosity on the part of some priests who were angered by Carvajal's secularization of education. With the help of several noblemen, the priests plotted against him. Realizing they could not take any public measures against him, they had him secretly arrested by the Inquisition. They then charged him with being a Jew, sacrificing Christian children, enslaving and destroying the Indians, and taking education out of the hands of the church. They succeeded in having not only Carvajal but his entire family sentenced to death.

The death of the illustrious governor was followed by a period of reaction. Repressive laws were imposed upon the lands formerly under his control.

Soon, however, the Jews in the area left and the Indians disappeared from the mines. The Indians attacked and severely mauled the Spaniards. The priests in the region could not refrain from wishing that they might again have "a day of Carabajal." The people were furious with the inquisitors. The members of the inquisitorial court that had convicted Carvajal took refuge in the torture chamber, but they were dragged out and ignominiously put to death.[71]

If these legends were really widely preserved in and around Monterrey, they fittingly bespeak the high regard in which the memory of Carvajal, and ironically his Jewish ancestry, were held by segments of the populace. For all their confusion of detail, the legends manifest a recognition of the contribution made to the land of New Spain by Governor Carvajal and his people, and the damaging blow dealt not only to him but to the entire society by the forces of obscurantism.

Mr. Landis at no time cites the sources for his web of legends, and one might suspect that he invented some or most of them. However, the well-known Mexican scholar Vito Alessio Robles said in 1904 that he too collected the legends regarding Carvajal. His version appears to be identical with Landis's.[72]

Whether the legends are accurately reported or not, they reflect the idealism and contribution of the secret Jews as a group. They reflect as well the idealism of the modern nation of Mexico, where men of different faiths and different backgrounds, each respecting the other, strive to work together for the common good.

Appendix

THE INQUISITORIAL SOURCES

Every trial record includes the testimony of witnesses other than the defendant. In the Notes the manuscript sources in the trial records are identified by the name of the witness, the date of his testimony, and name of the defendant in the trial record, in italics. In cases where the defendant himself gave testimony or where official documents, such as an indictment or sentence, were presented against him, the defendant's name appears in italics before the date.

Not all the testimony offered by a defendant before the inquisitors necessarily appears in his trial record. Where such testimony dealt primarily with other prisoners and had no direct bearing on a defendant's case, it was not usually included in his own trial record.

The names of the witnesses appearing most frequently have been abbreviated as follows:

LCG: Luis de Carvajal, governor of the New Kingdom of León
LCM: Luis de Carvajal the Younger
ADC: Antonio Díaz de Cáceres, LCM's brother-in-law
ADM: Antonio Díaz Márquez, cousin of Francisca Núñez de Carvajal
ALC: Ana (Anica) de León Carvajal, LCM's youngest sister
BRC: Baltasar Rodríguez (de Andrada) (de Carvajal), LCM's brother
CC: Catalina de la Cueva (de León) (de Cáceres), LCM's sister
DDN: Diego Díez Nieto
FNC: Francisca (Núñez) de Carvajal, LCM's mother
GRC: Gaspar (Rodríguez) de Carvajal, LCM's brother
IRA: Isabel (Rodríguez) de Andrada (de Carvajal), LCM's sister
JA: Jorge de Almeida, LCM's brother-in-law
JM: Justa Méndez
LAC: Leonor (de Andrada) (de León) (de la Cueva) de Carvajal (de Almeida), LCM's sister
LC: Leonor de Cáceres, LCM's niece
LD: Luis Díaz

ML: Manuel de Lucena
MNC: Mariana (Núñez) de Carvajal, LCM's sister

Many invaluable records pertaining to the family are no longer available. Luis's memoirs and most of his letters disappeared mysteriously around July 1932, as Alfonso Toro records in the introduction to *La familia Carvajal*. Most of the letters were thereafter returned. Fortunately Toro had made a copy of the autobiography and published it along with the letters. His transcript of these writings by Carvajal were used for this study.

In addition, records as important as those of the two trials of Luis's sister Catalina de León and those of the second trials of Isabel, Leonor, and Doña Francisca have also been lost or destroyed. Some of the testimony of these defendants has been preserved in other trial records. Since this testimony is often found in more than one trial record, those that were actually used are cited.

Where we have records of two or more cases against the same individual we distinguish them by Roman numerals.

The major trial records utilized in this study and their locations are as follows:

I: *LCG:* Year 1589 *Inquisition Documents (Ramo de la Inquisición,* henceforth identified as *ID*), Vol. 1487 (*Colección Riva Palacio,* Vol. 11), Dossier 3 (located in the Archivo General de la Nación, Mexico City, henceforth abbreviated AGN). Published by Alfonso Toro in *Los judíos en la Nueva España, Publicaciones del Archivo General de la Nación* (Mexico, 1932), 20: 205–372.

LCM I: Year 1589. *ID*, Vol. 1487 (*Colección Riva Palacio,* Vol. 11), Dossier 2 (AGN). Published almost in its entirety by Luis González Obregón and Rodolfo Gómez in *Procesos de Luis de Cavajal (El Mozo), Publicaciones del Archivo General de la Nación* (Mexico, 1935), 28: 1–113.

LCM II: Year 1595. *ID*, Vol. 1489 (*Colección Riva Palacio,* Vol. 14), entire volume (AGN). Published by Luis González Obregón and Rodolfo Gómez in *Procesos de Luis de Cavajal (El Mozo)*, pp. 115–459.

LCM-A: The *Autobiography* or *Memoirs*, original missing from AGN. Published by Luis González Obregón and Rodolfo Gómez in *Procesos de Luis de Carvajal (El Mozo)*, pp. 461–96.

LCM-Letters: Originals now missing again from AGN. Published by Luis González Obregón and Rodolfo Gómez in *Procesos de Luis de Carvajal (El Mozo)*, pp. 497–534.

Page references to the printed editions are given in parentheses or brackets in the notes. Occasionally references to the folio of the original manuscripts of *LCG, LCM I,* and *LCM II* may be cited, where the original manuscript is of particular interest. This is the case, for example, where the printed text omits certain items of testimony. The printed text of *LCM I* omits some significant material.

II: *ADC:* Year 1596. *ID*, Vol. 159, Dossier 1 (AGN).

ADM: Year 1596. *ID*, Vol. 158, Dossier 4 (AGN).

ALC: Year 1590. (American Jewish Historical Society, Waltham, Massachusetts).

BRC: Year 1589. *ID*, Vol. 1488 (*Colección Riva Palacio*, Vol. 12), Dossier 3 (AGN).

DDN: Year 1596. *ID*, Vol. 159, Dossier 2 (AGN).

FNC: Year 1589. *ID*, Vol. 1488 (*Colección Riva Palacio*, Vol. 12), Dossier 1 (AGN).

GRC: Year 1589. *ID*, Vol. 126, Dossier 12 (AGN).

IRA: Year 1589. *ID*, Vol. 558, entire volume (AGN).

JA I: Year 1590. *ID*, Vol. 150, Dossier 1 (AGN).

JA II: Year 1594. *ID*, Vol. 251a, Dossier 5, to which add Year 1607, *ID*, Vol. 254a, folios 506–12 (AGN).

JA III: Year 1607. (American Jewish Historical Society, Waltham, Massachusetts).

JM I: Year 1595. *ID*, Vol. 154, Dossier 1 (AGN).

JM II: Year 1604. *ID*, Vol. 1495 (*Colección Riva Palacio*, Vol. 20), Dossier 2 (AGN).

LAC: Year 1589. *ID*, Vol. 1488 (*Colección Riva Palacio*, Vol. 12), Dossier 2 (AGN).

LC I: Year 1601. (Henry E. Huntington Library, San Marino, California).

LC II: Year 1652. *ID*, Vol. 560, Dossier 1 (AGN).

LD: Case missing. LD is quoted in *LCM II*.

ML: Case missing. ML is quoted in other cases.

MNC I: Year 1589. *ID*, Vol. 126, Dossier 13 (AGN).

MNC II: Year 1596. *ID*, Vol. 1490 (*Colección Riva Palacio*, Vol. 15), Dossier 3 (AGN).

III: *Luis Díaz* (Díez), silversmith (not to be confused with LD, the priest). Year 1597. *ID*, Vol. 161, Dossier 2 (AGN).

Diego Díez Nieto: Year 1596. *ID*, Vol 159 Dossier 2 (AGN).

Catalina Enríquez, wife of Manuel de Lucena: Year 1595. *ID*, Vol. 152, Dossier 4 (AGN).

Clara Enríquez, mother of Justa Méndez: Year 1595. *ID*, Vol. 153, Dossier 7 (AGN).

Hector de Fonseca, brother of Jorge de Almeida: Year 1596. *ID*, Vol. 158, Dossier 1 (AGN).

Tomás de Fonseca Castellanos, of Taxco: Year 1595. *ID*, Vol. 156, Dossier 4 (AGN).

Tomás de Fonseca, of Tlalpujahua: Year 1596. *ID*, Vol. 158, Dossier 3 (AGN).

Manuel Gómez Navarro: Year 1594. *ID*, Vol. 151, Dossier 5 (AGN).

Manuel Gil de La Guarda (Guardia): Year 1597. *ID*, Vol. 160, Dossier 1 (AGN).

Ana de Guillamas, alias de Peralta. Year 1598. *ID*, Vol. 176, Dossier 9 (AGN).

Isabel Clara (Hernández), wife of Franco (Francisco) Hernández, brother of Dr. Morales: Year 1595, *ID*, Vol. 153, Dossier 3 (AGN).

Miguel Hernández, brother of Jorge de Almeida: Year 1596. *ID*, Vol. 158, Dossier 2 (AGN).

Antonia Machado, granddaughter of Antonio Machado: Year 1604. *ID*, Vol. 273, Dossier 16 (AGN).

Francisco Machado, grandson of Antonio Machado: Year 1604, *ID*, Vol. 274, Dossier 11 (AGN).

Gonzalo de Molina, grandson of Antonio Machado: Year 1615, *ID*, Vol. 308, Dossier 1 (AGN).

Antonio de Morales, nephew of Dr. Morales: Year 1599. *ID*, Vol. 168, Dossier 1 (AGN).

Blanca de Morales, sister of Dr. Morales: Year 1595. *ID*, Vol. 153, Dossier 8 (AGN).

Manuel de Morales, the physician: Year 1589, *ID*, Vol. 127, Dossier 3 (AGN).

Sebastián de la Peña: Year 1598. *ID*, Vol. 167, Dossier 3 (AGN).

Juan Plata. Year 1596. *ID*, Vol. 180, Dossier 1 (AGN).

Gonzalo Pérez Ferro, Jr., son of Gonzalo Pérez Ferro: Year 1589. *ID*, Vol. 126, Dossier 11 (AGN).

Francisco Ríos (Rodríguez), husband of Justa Méndez: Year 1595, *ID*, Vol. 156, Dossier 3 (AGN).

Juan Rodríguez: Year 1596. *ID*, Vol. 157, Dossier 2 (AGN).

IV: In addition, the following inquisitorial documents and dossiers were consulted:

A. Vol. 169, no. 2 (AGN), *Visita de las naos que forman la flota en que vino por general Don Francisco de Luxán, que llegó a San Juan de Ulúa a 25 de agosto de 1580 conduciendo al Virrey conde de la Coruña.*

Vol. 213, no. 12 (AGN), listing the daily and special rations received by the prisoners in the secret cells of the Holy Office.

Vol. 213, no. 16 (AGN), dealing with the cases involved in the auto-da-fé of 1590.

Vol. 216, no. 20 (AGN), describing the auto-da-fé of 1596.

Vol. 223, no. 31 (?) (folio 223a) (AGN), correspondence sent to the inquisitor-general and others regarding the fate of Francisco Rodríguez de Matos, Francisca Núñez Carvajal, Catalina de Cáceres, and others, along with transcripts of their trial records.

Vol. 251, no. 3 (f. 253a) (AGN), containing a facsimile of the *sambenito.*

B. Vol. 277, no. 6 (ff. 210–11) (AGN), denunciation of Justa Méndez for failure to wear her penitential garb.

Vol. 366, no. 27, Letter no. 4 (f. 339a) (AGN), testimony against Justa Méndez by Simón de Paredes.

Vol. 373, no. 28 (AGN), complaint by Justa Méndez and her husband against Gaspar Gerónimo.

Vol. 393, no. 6 (7 folios) (AGN), testimony against Justa Méndez by Blanca de Rivera.

Vol. 415, no. 2 (AGN), testimony against Justa Méndez by Isabel Núñez.

Vol. 417, no. 16 (AGN), testimony against Justa Méndez by Felipa de la Cruz.

Vol. 560, no. 3 (AGN), petition of José de la Rosa.

Vol. 1495 (=Riva Palacio 20), no. 2 (AGN), testimony against Justa Méndez by Ángel Guillaza, Diego de Espinosa, Francisca Núñez and Andrés de Mondragón.

C. Vol. 273, no. 16; Vol. 274, no. 11; Vol. 279, no. 9; and Vol. 308, no. 1 (all AGN), all dealing with various members of the Machado family.

D. Vol. 223, nos. 33, 34, 34; Vol. 271, no. 1; Vol. 276, no. 14 (folios 412 ff.); and Vol. 279, no. 9 (all AGN), all related to various other Judaizers whose cases are mentioned above.

Notes

Full references will be found in Bibliography

*Abbreviations of Journals and Encyclopedias used in the following notes**

AHR	*American Historical Review*
AJA	*American Jewish Archives*
AJHQ	*American Jewish Historical Quarterly*
BAGN	*Boletín del Archivo General de la Nación*
HAHR	*Hispanic American Historical Review*
EJ	*Encyclopaedia Judaica*
HM	*Historia Mexicana*
HR	*Hispanic Review*
HUCA	*Hebrew Union College Annual*
JE	*The Jewish Encyclopedia*
JAOS	*Journal of the American Oriental Society*
JQR (N.S.)	*The Jewish Quarterly Review (New Series)*
MAMH	*Memorias de la Academia Mexicana de la Historia*
PAJHS	*Publications of the American Jewish Historical Society*
REJ	*Revue des Études Juives*

CHAPTER I

1. The descriptions are a composite of *LCM I,* May 13, 1589 (p. 22); *BRC, Instrucción para la prisión,* Apr. 20, 1589; Diego Márquez de Andrada, June 8, 1589 (in *BRC*). Márquez's description of Luis and Baltasar differs in some detail from the others and leads to the conjecture that he was trying to confuse the Inquisition.

On the Spanish population, see J. López de Velasco, *Geografía y descripcíon universal de las Indias,* p. 187; H.I. Priestly, *The Coming of the White Man,* p. 22; E. R. Wolf, *Sons of the Shaking Earth,* p. 31; G. Kubler, "Population Movements in Mexico," *HAHR* 22: 606–43; S.F. Cook and L.B. Simpson, *The Population of Central Mexico in the*

---

* For key to other abbreviations see Appendix.

Sixteenth Century; C.C. Cumberland, *Mexico: The Struggle for Modernity*, p. 48. For a valuable survey, see E.G. Bourne, *Spain in America, 1450–1580*, pp. 243 ff.

2. B. de Balbuena, *Grandeza Mexicana*, p. 80; see also pp. 14–15, 35, 44–45. Cf. also J. Van Horne, *La "Grandeza Mexicana" de Bernardo de Balbuena*. Las Ventas, also called Las Ventas de Perote or La Venta de Perote, and today called Perote, is located between Jalapa and Puebla in the state of Veracruz. For a contemporary description of the areas traversed by Luis, see "The Voyage of Robert Tomson, Merchant, into Nova Hispania in the Yere 1555," in R. Hakluyt, *The Principal Navigations, Voyages, Traffiques and Discoveries of the English Nation,* 9: 338–58.

3. See, for example, W.H. Prescott, *The Conquest of Mexico*, pp. 10 ff., 210 ff.; H.H. Bancroft, *History of Mexico*, Vol. 2; A. Toro, *La familia Carvajal*, 1:87; L.B. Simpson, *Many Mexicos;* and the general histories and descriptions of Mexico, including short surveys like N. Cheetham, *Mexico: A Short History*, though it is not quite accurate on a number of points regarding the Carvajals (pp. 102 ff.). See also T. Gage, *A New Survey of the West Indies;* J. F. de Cuevas Aguirre y Espinosa, *Extracto de los autos de diligencias y reconocimientos de los ríos, lagunas, vertientes y desagües de la capital México y su valle*; A. de Valle-Arizpe, *Historia de la ciudad de México según los relatos de sus cronistas*; and broader surveys like S. de Madariaga's *The Rise of the Spanish American Empire,* especially chapters 8 ("Economic Life," pp. 127–41), 9 ("The Church: The Inquisition," pp. 142–68), and 10 ("Intellectual Life," pp. 169–86); P. Henríquez Ureña, *A Concise History of Latin American Culture* (trans. with a supplementary chapter by Gilbert Chase), especially pp. 7 ff. and 29 ff.

4. See sources in note 3 above and H. Cortés, *Cartas y Documentos,* ed. Hernández Sánchez-Barba, p. 71.

5. F. Cervantes de Salazar, *México en 1554,* pp. 89–90.

6. I.A. Leonard, *Books of the Brave,* p. 26.

7. L. González Obregón, *Las calles de México,* 2: 17.

8. On the Aztecs, in addition to the histories cited above, see V.W. Von Hagen, *The Aztec: Man and Tribe*; F.A. Peterson, *Ancient Mexico: An Introduction to the Pre-Hispanic Cultures*; G.C. Vaillant and S.B. Vaillant, *The Aztecs of Mexico*, books all still valuable, even if outdated in some places. See also the popular accounts by J. Soustelle, *Daily Life of the Aztecs on the Eve of the Spanish Conquest,* trans. from the French by Patrick O'Brian, especially pp. 120 ff.; I. Bernal, *Mexico before Cortes*; and the more comprehensive work by C. Gibson, *The Aztecs under Spanish Rule*, pp. 9 ff. See also Gibson's *Spain in America* and the classical accounts from the early colonial period, including Diego Durán's *Historia de las Indias de Nueva España e islas de la tierra firme,* ed. Ángel María Garibay, 2 vols. (see introduction, 1: xiv ff.); English translation entitled *The Aztecs: The History of the Indies of New Spain,* with notes by Doris Heyden and Fernando Horcasitas, and introduction by Ignacio Bernal; Motolinía's *History of*

the Indians of New Spain, trans. Elizabeth Andros Foster, and a second excellent translation entitled *Motolinía's History of the Indians of New Spain,* with notes and a biographical-bibliographical study of Motolinía by Francis Borgia Steck; Manuel Orozco y Berra's *Historia antigua de la conquista de México,* ed. Miguel León Portilla, 4 vols.; Bernardino de Sahagún's *Historia general de las cosas de Nueva España,* ed. Ángel María Garibay, 4 vols. (see especially book 12, comprising Vol. 4); Agustín de Vetancourt's *Teatro Mexicano,* 4 vols., ed. Madrid; Alonso de Zurita's *Life and Labor in Ancient Mexico: The Brief and Summary Relation of the Lords of New Spain,* trans. Benjamin Keen (see especially pp. 127 ff., "The Valley of Mexico in Zurita's Time").

9. Sahagún, *Historia general,* pp. 169–70.

10. On the rebuilding of the city see Prescott, *Conquest,* pp. 624 ff. Cf. A. Vázquez de Espinosa, *Compendium and Description of the West Indies* (c. 1612), pp. 155 ff. On the building of the church and the cathedral, see A. de Montúfar, *Descripción del arzobispado de México hecha en 1570,* ed. L. García Pimentel, p. 19; S. Baxter, *Spanish-Colonial Architecture in Mexico,* 1:25–26, 876; A.C. Bossom, *An Architectural Pilgrimage in Old Mexico,* passim: G. Kubler, *Mexican Architecture of the Sixteenth Century,* 1:68 ff.; 2: passim. See also W.H. Kilham, *Mexican Architecture of the Vice-Regal Period,* passim.

11. See sources in note 3 above. In 1576 the number of Negroes in New Spain exceeded that of the Spaniards. See G. Aguirre Beltrán, "The Slave Trade in Mexico," *HAHR* 24: 412 ff.; idem, "Tribal Origins of Slaves in Mexco," *Journal of Negro History* 31: 269–352; idem, *La población negra de México.* For Mexican demography, see, M. O. de Mendizábal, "La demografía mexicana. Época colonial. 1519–1810," *Boletín de la Sociedad Mexicana de Geografía y Estadística* 48 (1939): 301 ff.

12. F. Hernández, *Antigüedades de la Nueva España,* pp. 69–70; J. Miranda, *España y Nueva España en la época de Felipe II,* pp. 61 ff.; Prescott, *Conquest,* pp. 632 ff.; Vaillant and Vaillant, *The Aztecs,* pp. 75 ff., 223, passim; and the other histories cited above.

13. *LCM I,* May 12, July 27, Aug. 11, 1589 (pp. 13, 31, 35, 57, 64). In view of the total evidence in the case, the year when Francisco Rodríguez de Matos became ill and began to teach his son is 1584 rather than 1585. This is inferable from *LCM I,* Aug. 11, 1589 (p. 68). It should be noted that in that passage Luis says "que serán cinco años *poco más o menos"* (italics mine) since his father had begun to teach him.

14. *GRC,* April 18, 1589.

15. *LCM I,* May 12, 1589 (p. 14 and passim); trial records of rest of family, passim. On Peter of Ghent (1480–1572), see "Pedro de Gante," in *Diccionario Porrúa,* p. 582. Peter of Ghent was reputed to be a blood relative of Emperor Charles V. For this and for his efforts in the field of education in New Spain, see J. García Icazbalceta, "Education in the City of Mexico during the Sixteenth Century," trans. Walter J. O'Donnell, in *Texas Catholic Historical Society, Preliminary Studies* 1, no. 7: 9 ff. See also A.M. Carreño, "Una desconocida carta de Fray

Pedro de Gante," *MAMH* 20 (1961): 14–20, a study based on a manuscript letter found in the Biblioteca Nacional in Madrid.

16. *IRA*, beginning; *FNC*, Sept. 28, 1589. Cf. *LCM I*, Aug. 7, 1589 (p. 44); *LCM-A* (p. 473). For the name Flat House, see "Luis de Carvajal (el Mozo)," *Enciclopedia judaica castellana*, 2: 574 and Toro, *La familia Carvajal*, 1: 228.

17. *LCG, Auto de prisión*, Apr. 14, 1589 (p. 211).

18. *LCM I*, beginning (pp. 5 ff.).

19. *BRC*, beginning.

20. Rodrigo de Ávila, Apr. 22, 1589, in *LCM I*, beginning (p. 7).

21. Rodrigo de Ávila, May 6, 1589, in *BRC*.

22. H.C. Lea, *A History of the Inquisition of Spain*, 2: 457 ff.; 3: 121 ff; C. Roth, *A History of the Marranos*, pp. 118 ff. Cf. also A.M. Carreño, "Luis de Carvajal (El Mozo)," *MAMH* 15: 93–94.

   For background material on the church's legal basis for the prosecution of heretics, see E. Vacandard, *The Inquisition: A Critical and Historical Study of the Coercive Power of the Church*, trans. Bertrand L. Conway; H. Maillet, *L'Église et la répression sanglante de l'hérésie*, ed. Karl Hanquet. On torture and the death penalty, see G.G. Coulton, *The Death Penalty for Heresy from 1184 to 1917 A.D. Medieval Studies*, Second Series, no. 18. For examples of the rare restoration of confiscated property, see H. Beinart, "Two Documents concerning Confiscated Converso Property," *Sefarad* 17: 280 ff.

   A facsimile of the *sambenito* is to be found in the AGN,, *ID*, Vol. 251a, Dossier no. 3. The word is sometimes spelled *sanbenito*.

23. L. González Obregón, *México Viejo*, pp. 675 ff.; A. Toro, ed., *Los judíos en la Nueva España*, Document 3, pp. 17 ff.; H.C. Lea, *The Inquisition in the Spanish Dependencies*, p. 196, incorrectly states that "it would seem that the *sanbenitos* were not hung in the cathedral until 1667."

24. On Hernando Alonso, see B. Lewin, *Mártires y conquistadores judíos en la América Hispana*, pp. 11–19. Cf. also G.R.G. Conway, "Hernando Alonso, a Jewish Conquistador with Cortes in Mexico," *PAJHS* 31: 9–31. In both cases the term "Jewish" is misleading. Though Hernando Alonso may have considered himself a Jew, he was born and raised a Catholic and had at best a negligible knowledge of Judaism.

25. Lea, *The Inquisition in the Spanish Dependencies*, pp. 209 ff., 332. Cf. H.B. Parkes, *A History of Mexico*, p. 89. It is important to distinguish between the Inquisition proper, that is, the Holy Office of the Inquisition instituted in Mexico in 1571, and the preceding inquisitions existing there. The list of cases handled by inquisitions in Mexico prior to the establishment of the Dominican Inquisition is available in Toro, *Los judíos en la Nueva España*, pp. 91–161, and includes a number of Indians. See also Y. Mariel de Ibáñez, *La Inquisición en México durante el siglo XVI*, passim, and below, chapter 3, note 48.

26. That is, Mexico City.

27. F. Hernández, *Antigüedades*, pp. 71–72.

28. Prescott, *Conquest*, pp. 148 ff. Parkes, *History*, pp. 106 ff. See also C.S. Braden, *Religious Aspects of the Conquest of Mexico*, especially chap-

ters 3 ("The Religion of the Mexican Indians at the Time of the Conquest," pp. 20–75, with a section on "Similarities between the Mexican Religion and Christianity," pp. 61 ff.); 6 ("Conditions Favoring and Hindering Conversion," pp. 180–221); and 7 ("Results of the Efforts at Conversion," pp. 222–59).

29. F. Hernández, *Antigüedades*, pp. 38 ff.
30. Lea, *A History of the Inquisition of Spain*, 2: 457 ff. Cf. J.T. Medina, *Historia del Tribunal . . . de la Inquisición en México*, pp. 15 ff.
31. *LCM I*, May 12, 1589 (pp. 12–13, 17), ML, May 12, 1589 (in *BRC*).
32. *LCM I*, May 13, 1589 (pp. 20 ff.) and passim; ML, Nov. 3, 1589, in *Blanca de Morales; LCM-A* (pp. 474 ff.). For the Italian cities, see C. Roth, *The History of the Jews of Italy*, passim; A. Milano, *Storia degli ebrei in Italia*, pp. 212 ff.; C. Roth, *Venice (History of the Jews in Venice)*, pp. 63 ff. In the 1580s, after a reaction against the Jews of Ferrara, Venice eclipsed Ferrara as a haven for the Judaizers. See also S. Della-Pergola, "Pisa," in *EJ* 13, cols. 561–63; A. Milano, "Ferrara," ibid. 6, cols. 1231–33.
33. *LCM II*, Sept. 28, 1596 (p. 420), and by inference from *LCM-A* (p. 475), and *LCM I* and *LCM II*, passim, where Miguel is mentioned only in connection with Baltasar and eventually escapes with him.
34. Francisco Díaz, Feb. 19, 1592, in *JA I*.
35. *LCM II*, Sept. 28, 1596 (pp. 420 ff.).
36. Ibid.
37. Ibid.; ML, Nov. 3, 1594 (in *JA III*).
38. Ibid. Cf. *LCM I*, Aug. 7, 1589 (p. 41).
39. *LCM I*, Aug. 11, 1589 (pp. 61–62); *MNC II*, May 31, 1600.
40. *LCM I*, Aug. 7, 1589 (p. 44).
41. Ibid. (p. 44). On the departure and vicissitudes of the fleet, see H. Chaunu and P. Chaunu, *Séville et l'Atlantique*, 3: 442.
42. LCM, May 30, 1589 (in *Diego Márquez de Andrada*). This testimony does not appear in *LCM I*, either in the manuscript or in the printed version.

   On Veracruz as a port and center of communications in the sixteenth century, see P. Chaunu, "Veracruz en la segunda mitad del siglo XVI y primera del XVII," *HM* 9: 521–57, especially p. 526. For its continuing significance, see J. I. Rubio Mañe, *Movimiento marítimo entre Veracruz y Campeche, 1801–1810*, pp. 3 ff. Campeche, as we have seen above, was already important in the sixteenth century and retained that importance throughout the colonial period.
43. *LCM-A* (p. 474).
44. Ibid.
45. See note 42 above.
46. Cristóbal Gómez, May 12, 1589 (in *LCM I*, pp. 18–19).
47. The phases of the moon were determined by consulting B. Zuckerman, *Anleitung und Tabellen zur Vergleichung jüdischer und christlicher Zeitangaben*.
48. On Mexico City in the sixteenth century and its streets at night, see M. Carrera Stampa, "Planos de la ciudad México," p. 285; González Obregón, *México Viejo*, pp. 21–22; idem, *Las calles de México*, 2: 72.

For interesting sidelights on the problem of urban cleanliness, see J.I. Rubio Mañé, "Ordenanzas para la limpieza de la ciudad de México," *BAGN* 27: 19–24. On the names of the streets, see the essay by J.L. Cossío, "La nomenclatura y la historia de la ciudad," in his *Del México Viejo*, pp. 153–77. For other maps and discussions of the plan of the city, see M. Orozco y Berra, *Memoria para el plano de la ciudad de México; Atlas general del Distrito Federal*, Vol. 2, especially plate 3, "La ciudad de México a mediados del siglo XVI"; Ola Apenes, *Mapas antiguos del valle de México*; F. Chueca Goitia and L. Torres Balbás, *Planos de ciudades íberoamericanas y filipinas existentes en el Archivo de Indias*, especially no. 227 and no. 229.

49. Composite of *LCM II*, Feb. 9, 1596 (p. 327), and FNC, Sept. 25, 1595 (in *MNC II*).
50. *FNC, Auto de prisión*, beginning.
51. *LCM-A* (p. 474).
52. Ibid.
53. Ibid.
54. *Expediente de las raciones diarias que recibían los presos de las cárceles secretas del Santo Oficio* (beginning Feb. 1589), Inquisition. Vol. 213, Document 12.

CHAPTER 2

1. "Medina del Campo," in *Enciclopedia universal ilustrada,* 34: 119; J. Lynch, *Spain under the Habsburgs,* 1: 101 ff., 139; and for the population, Miranda, *España y Nueva España,* p. 36; J. Ruiz Almansa, "La población de España en el siglo XVI: Estudio sobre los recuentos de vecindario de 1594, llamados comúnmente 'Censo de Tomás González,' " *Revista internacional de sociología* 3: 114–36, with an interesting comparison between the population of Portugal (16.7 inhabitants per square mile) and Castile (22.0 inhabitants per square mile) at the end of the sixteenth century (p. 120). On the fairs, see C. Espejo and J. Paz, *Las antiguas ferias de Medina del Campo,* esp. p. 298. On the economic life of the period, see, inter alia, R. Carande Thovar, *Carlos V y sus banqueros,* Vols. 1 and 2; J. Vicens Vives, ed., *Historia social y económica de España y América,* especially Vol. 3; F. Braudel, *La Méditerranée et le monde méditerranéen à l'époque de Philippe II,* 2 vols. On the entire period, see also R.B. Merriman, *The Rise of the Spanish Empire in the Old World and in the New,* Vols. 3 and 4.
2. See Felipe Núñez, Mar. 7, 1589 (in *LCM I* [p. 9]), where the text reads "*rua de Medina.*" Felipe Núñez himself corrects this in his testimony of Sept. 22, 1589 (in *IRA*). See also LAC, Jan. 8, 1590 (in *MNC I*). Mariana, however, said that the family lived on Salamanca Street (*MNC I*, Jan. 8, 1590).
3. See, for example, Leonard, *Books of the Brave,* p. 37.
4. On this period, see, inter alia, M. Lafuente y Zamalloa, *Historia general*

de España, Vol. 3; R. Altamira y Crevea, *Historia de España,* Vol. 2; the survey by R. Trevor Davies, *The Golden Century of Spain: 1501–1621;* Merriman, *The Rise of the Spanish American Empire,* Vol. 3; Lynch, *Spain under the Habsburgs.* For the intellectual and social milieu of Spain and the Hispanic world, see O.H. Green, *Spain and the Western Tradition: The Castilian Mind in Literature from El Cid to Calderón,* 4 vols. (for Mexico, see Vol. 3, pp. 60 ff.); Roth, *A History of the Marranos,* pp. 52 ff.; M.A. Cohen, in Samuel Usque, *Consolation for the Tribulations of Israel,* pp. 3 ff.

5. *LCM I,* July (read August) 2, 1589 (p. 39).
6. *LCM I,* May 12, 1589. See also *ALC,* Jan. 19, 1590, and *LAC,* Dec. 23, 1589 (in *FNC*).
7. *LCM I,* May 12, 1589 (p. 15) and by inference from the introduction to *LCM-A* (p. 463). For the Jesuit curriculum, see René Fülöp-Miller, *The Jesuits: A History of the Society of Jesus,* p. 408; T. Maynard, *Saint Ignatius and the Jesuits,* pp. 181 ff. See also A. Astraín, *Historia de la compañía de Jesús,* Vol. 1.
8. On the question of blood purity (*limpieza de sangre*), see A.A. Sicroff, *Les controverses des statuts de "pureté de sang" en Espagne du XVᵉ au XVIIᵉ siècle,* pp. 32 ff.; idem, "Limpieza de sangre," *EJ* 11, cols. 255–56; C. Roth, "Jews, Conversos and the Blood-Accusation in Fifteenth-Century Spain," *The Dublin Review,* no. 383, pp. 219–31, a trenchant critique of W. Walsh's book, *Isabella of Spain,* and Walsh's reply in the same journal, pp. 232–52; A. Castro, *The Structure of Spanish History,* pp. 521 ff. See also Green, *Spain and the Western Tradition,* 4: 166 and the earlier studies by Lea in *A History of the Inquisition of Spain,* 2: 285–314 ("Limpieza"); A. Domínguez Ortiz, "Los cristianos nuevos: Notas para el estudio de una clase social," *Boletín de la Universidad de Granada* 21 (1949): 249–97, and the development of its thesis in his subsequent work, *La clase social de los conversos en Castilla en la Edad Moderna;* and E. Asensio, "El erasmismo y las corrientes espirituales afines," *Revista de filología española* 36 (1952): 31–99, especially 57 ff. See now also the study of I.S. Révah, "La controverse sur les statuts de pureté de sang: Un document inédit: 'Relación y consulta del Cardenal Guevara sobre el negocio de Fray Agustín Saluzio' (Madrid, 13 août 1600)" *Bulletin Hispanique* 73 (1971): 263–306. The article and the accompanying document reveal the political use to which the concept of *limpieza de sangre* might be put, regardless of the accuracy of its application to an individual. See for example, in the study, pp. 267–68 and in the document, p. 306.
9. For defenses of this position and the right of New Christians to fair and equal treatment with all other Christians, see the tract by the Dominican padre Juan de Torquemada (1388–1468), *Tractatus contra madianitas et ismaelitas,* written in the aftermath of the Toledo riots of 1449, and edited, with the subtitle *Defensa de los judíos conversos,* by Nicolás López Martínez and Vicente Proaño Gil, especially chapter 13 (pp. 99 ff.), where the author objects to the assumption that New Christians are to be considered suspect in their faith through three

generations; and chapters 14 and 15 (pp. 109 ff.), where he stresses the unity of all Christians and deplores the discriminatory separation of New Christians from this unity ("ponere talem differentiam inter fideles dampnabile est, ex eo quod contradicit divine Scripture in multis locis," p. 117). Torquemada's work is amply spiced with quotations from the Bible and postbiblical authorities of the church.

Fray Alonso de Oropesa wrote his *Lumen ad revelationem gentium et gloriam plebis tuae Israel*, "to remove from the converts the reproach and opprobrium with which wicked Christians were seeking to crush and destroy them." Cf. Padre José de Sigüenza, *Historia de la orden de San Jerónimo*, part 2, book 3, chapter 18, in *Nueva biblioteca de autores españoles*, 8: 370.

It is significant that no invidious discrimination between Old Christians and New Christians, such as is present in the concept of *limpieza de sangre*, is to be found in Gratian's *Decretum*. Baptism into the faith was regarded to bring a "regeneration of man and rebirth." See Thomas Aquinas, *Summa Theologica*, translated by the Fathers of the English Dominican Province, part 3, question 65, pp. 2375 ff., especially A 2 (p. 2376), and passim. See also C. Williams, s.v. "Conversion, Theology of," *New Catholic Encyclopedia*, 4: 288.

10. There is an extensive bibliography on the New Christians. By far the most comprehensive account (though in need of revision) is that of Roth, *A History of the Marranos*. See also the standard histories of the Jews in Spain like J. Amador de los Ríos, *Estudios históricos, políticos y literarios sobre los judíos de España;* idem, *Historia social, política y religiosa de los judíos de España y Portugal*, Vols. 2 and 3; I. Baer *Toledot ha-Yehudim bi-Sefarad ha-Noṣrit;* B. Netanyahu, *The Marranos of Spain;* M.A. Cohen, "New Christians," *EJ* 12, col. 1022. For a general survey of conversion of Jews to Christianity in Spain, beginning with the Middle Ages, see H. Guttmann, "Marranen and Apostaten unter den spanischen Juden," in *Jewish Studies in Memory of Michael Guttmann*, ed. Samuel Löwinger, pp. 129–74.

11. For the history of the Jews in Christian Spain, see Baer, *Toledot ha-Yehudim bi-Sefarad ha-Noṣrit* (English translation by Louis Schoffman with the title *A History of the Jews in Christian Spain*, 2 vols.); Amador de los Ríos, *Historia social, política y religiosa de los judíos;* (a new edition of this work is now being prepared by Francisco Cantera Burgos, with up-to-date bibliographical revisions, it is scheduled for publication by the Alianza publishing house of Madrid); idem, *Estudios históricos, políticos y literarios;* A. de Castro y Rossi, *Historia de los judíos de España;* the still useful *An Inquiry into the Sources of the History of the Jews in Spain* by Joseph Jacobs. See also the excellent survey by Federico Pérez Castro, "España y los judíos españoles: Interpretación de algunos aspectos de su cultura," in *The Sephardi Heritage*, ed. R.D. Barnett, pp. 275–322. For the period of turbulence in fourteenth-century Spain, see J. Valdeón Baruque, *Enrique II de Castilla, la guerra civil y la consolidación del régimen, 1366–1371*.

12. See Andrés Bernáldez, *Historia de los Reyes Católicos,* 1: 129 ff. See also H.C. Lea, *Ferrand Martinez and the Massacres of 1391;* I. Loeb, *Le sac des juiveries de Valence et de Madrid en 1391.*

13. One of the classic expressions of this position is found in Andrés Bernáldez, *Historia de los Reyes Católicos,* 1: 126: "Y puesto caso que algunos fueron baptizados, mortificado el carácter del baptismo en ellos por la credulidad, e por judaizar, hedían como judios." On the conversos as a caste (with especially interesting remarks on the marriages of poor Old Christians to wealthy New Christians) see S. Gilman, *The Spain of Fernando de Rojas: The Intellectual and Social Landscape of LA CELESTINA,* pp. 113–22.

14. For interesting insights into the libels and anti-Semitic references aimed at Jews and their descendants, see E. Glaser, "Referencias antisemitas en la literatura peninsular de la Edad de Oro," *Nueva Revista de Filología Hispánica* 8: 39–62.

15. On the Marranos, see A. Farinelli, *Marrano: Storia di un vituperio;* H. Kahane and R. Kahane, "Christian and Un-Christian Etymologies," *Harvard Theological Review* 57: 23–38, especially 28–33; Y. Malkiel, "Hispano-Arabic Marrano and Its Hispano-Latin Homophone," *JAOS* 68: 175–84; D.G. Maeso, "Sobre la etimología de la voz *marrano* (criptojudío)," *Sefarad* 15: 373–85; J. Corominas, *Diccionario crítico etimológico de la lengua castellana,* 3: 272–75. See also M.A. Cohen "Marrano," *EJ* 11, col. 1018.

16. On the medieval Inquisition, see H.C. Lea, *A History of the Inquisition in the Middle Ages,* 3 vols.; C. Douais, *L'Inquisition: Ses origines, sa procédure,* with important documents, pp. 275–351; J. Guiraud, *Histoire de l'Inquisition au moyen âge,* 2 vols., with excellent bibliography, 1: xi–xlviii; H. Maisonneuve, *Études sur les origines de l'Inquisition,* especially chapter 5, "Les Débuts de l'Inquisition," pp. 242–86; G.G. Coulton, *Inquisition and Liberty,* especially pp. 119 ff., for inquisitorial procedure.

17. On the Inquisition in Spain, see Lea, *A History of the Inquisition of Spain;* C. Roth, *The Spanish Inquisition;* and H. Kamen, *The Spanish Inquisition.* See also the older work by A. de Castro y Rossi, *A History of Religious Intolerance in Spain,* and, for a pro-Inquisition viewpoint, W.T. Walsh, *Characters of the Inquisition* (see, for example, his chapter 8, "Llorente," pp. 266–301). See also Haim Beinart, "The Records of the Inquisition as a Source of Jewish and Converso History," *Proceedings of the Israel Academy of Sciences and Humanities* 2: 212 ff. For a summary of the relationship of the Inquisition to heterodoxy, see Domínguez Ortiz, *The Golden Age of Spain 1516–1659,* trans. James Casey, pp. 214–28.

Much work remains to be done on the question of the extent of the reliability of the Inquisition documents for unbiased information about the Judaizers or Judaizing practices. Ellis Rivkin's "The Utilization of Non-Jewish Sources for the Reconstruction of Jewish History," *JQR (N.S.)* 48: 183–203, esp. pp. 193 ff., is a pioneering attempt to cope with this problem. António José Saraiva, writing about Portugal, expresses the opinion that the reaction against New Christians there was based almost exclusively on economic grounds. See his *História da cultura em Portugal,* 3: 29 ff., 107–8; idem, *Inquisição e Cristãos-Novos,* pp. 199 ff. His writings naturally suggest the question of a possible parallel in Spain. Saraiva has recently been engaged in a controversy with I.S. Révah over his views (see *Diário de Lisboa,* May 6, 13, 27; June 3, 17; July 15, 22, 29; August 5, 12, 19, 26; and September 2, 1971). See also the earlier attack on Saraiva by J. Alcambar, *O Estatismo e a Inquisição,* a slender volume with a number of sharp observations. Saraiva's position may be somewhat strongly stated, but the fact remains that, regardless of the existence of numbers of committed Judaizers, economic, political, and social elements did play a significant role in the creation of a Marrano myth.

On this controversy, see H.P. Salomon, "The Portuguese Inquisition and Its Victims in the Light of Recent Polemics," *The Journal of the American Portuguese Cultural Society* 5 (1971): 19–28, 50–55.

The controversy has recently flared in connection with the Mallorcan Inquisition. Miquel Forteza y Pinya, in his *Els descendents dels jueus conversos de Mallorca. Quatre mots de la veritat,* claims that the massive arrests in Mallorca's *call menor* in 1675 by the suddenly energized Inquisition was not so much a roundup of Chuetas by descent as of the people who happened to reside in the *call menor.* He claims (p. 218, for example) that the desire to despoil its victims was a paramount motive of the inquisitors. See also the review of this book by Thomas F. Glick in *Jewish Social Studies* 33 (1971): pp. 230–32. Now challenging this view is Ángela Selke's *Los chuetas y la Inquisición,* pp. 18 ff. See, in connection with Mallorca, B. Braunstein's indispensable *The Chuetas of Majorca: Conversos and the Inquisition of Majorca,* first published in 1936 and reprinted in 1972 with a new introduction by the author.

Considerable study remains to be done on this entire problem. On the lack of sufficient information on the economic aspect of the Inquisition itself, see the remarks of H. Kamen, "Confiscations in the Economy of the Spanish Inquisition," *The Economic History Review, Second Series* 18: 511 ff.

18. It is important to stress the distinction between the terms "Jew" and "Judaizer." The Judaizer, though he regarded himself as a Jew, was officially and, according to canon law, legally a Christian. To add to the confusion, the Inquisition, in prosecuting Judaizers (*judaizantes*) called them Jews (*judíos*). It prosecuted them, however, not because they were Jews, but as Mariel de Ibáñez says, "because they were traitors to the Catholic faith" (*La Inquisición en México,* pp. 151–52). The distinction between *judios* and *judaizantes* is thus much more than academic, for, as will be seen below (chapter 5 and especially chapter 6) the outlook and beliefs of the *judaizantes* diverged sharply from those of the *judíos.*

It should be noted that the Inquisition had the right to arrest unconverted Jews for a variety of offenses. These included sorcery, blasphemy, disrespect for Christian ceremonies or objects of veneration, and efforts to bring Jewish converts to Christianity back to Judaism. This right had especial meaning in Spain before 1492, when Jews could still officially live there. However, the Inquisition did not have the authority to arrest unconverted Jews for the practice of their faith. In every case people of Jewish descent who were arrested on this charge were presumed on the basis of evidence to be duly baptized New Christians. On this subject see the review by H.P. Salomon of Seymour Liebman's *The Jews in New Spain, AJHQ* 61 (1972): 190–201.

19. On the Judaizers of the fifteenth and sixteenth centuries, add to the aforementioned sources B. Llorca, "La Inquisición española y los conversos judíos o 'marranos,'" *Sefarad* 2: 113–51; N. López Martínez, *Los judaizantes castellanos y la Inquisición en tiempo de Isabel la Católica;* A. Domínguez Ortiz, "Los conversos de origen judío después de la expulsión," in *Estudios de historia social de España,* pp. 223–345; H. Beinart, "The *Converso* Community in 15th Century Spain," in *The Sephardi Heritage,* ed. R.D. Barnett, pp. 425–56; idem, "The *Converso* Community in 16th and 17th Century Spain," ibid., pp. 457–78. For relevant monographs on Judaizers at this time, see H. Beinart, "The Judaizing Movement in the Order of San Jerónimo in Castile," *Scripta Hierosolymitana* 7: 167–92, covering two trials, 1487–1490; A.A. Sicroff, "Clandestine Judaism in the Hieronymite Monastery of Nuestra Señora de Guadalupe," in *Studies in Honor of M.J. Benardete,* pp. 89–125; H. Beinart, *Ha-Mishpatim mi-Ta'am ha-Inqvizisia be-Toledo . . .* (Hebrew) (Trials of Judaizers by the Toledan Inquisition: From Its Establishment till the Beginning of the Sixteenth Century), pp. 20 ff.; idem. "Ha-Nidonim be-Vet-Din ha-Inqvizisia she-be-Toledo" (Hebrew) (The Defendants before the Inquisitorial Court in Toledo), *Tarbiz* 26: 71–86; idem, *Anusim be-Din ha-Inqvizisia* (Hebrew) (Conversos on Trial by the Inquisition). See also F. Cantera Burgos, *El poeta Cota y su familia de judíos conversos;* M. de la Pinta Llorente, *Proceso criminal contra el hebraista salmantino Martín Martínez de Cantalapiedra;* A. Domínguez Ortiz, "Historical Research on Spanish Conversos in the Last 15 Years," in *Collected Studuies in Honour of Americo Castro's Eightieth Year,* ed. Michael Paul Hornik, pp. 63–82.

For some excellent insights on this period, see also B. Netanyahu, *Don Isaac Abravanel: Stateman and Philosopher*; Cantera Burgos, *El poeta Cota y su familia de judíos conversos,* especially pp. 44 ff., 74 ff., 82; Gilman, *The Spain of Fernando de Rojas: The Intellectual and Social Landscape of LA CELESTINA,* especially pp. 113 ff.

20. For the history of Portugal, see J. Ameal, *História de Portugal;* J.P. Oliveira Martins, *História de Portugal;* H.M. Stephens, *Portugal;* H.V. Livermore, *A History of Portugal.* See also H. de Gama Barros, "Judeus e Mouros em Portugal em tempos passados," *Revista Lusitana* 34: 165–265; 35: 161–238; H. Beinart, "La formación del mundo

sefardí," in *Actas del primer simposio de estudios sefardíes,* ed. I.M. Hassan, with the collaboration of María Teresa Rubiato and Elena Romero, pp. 43–48, and discussion on pp. 371–76. On the economic development of Portugal, its place in international trade, and particularly the role within that trade of the traffic in precious metals, see M.N. Dias, *O capitalismo monárquico português (1415–1549): Contribuição para o estudo do capitalismo moderno,* 2 vols. For primary source material on the relations between Spain and Portugal during this period, including material on Jews, see A. de la Torre and L. Suárez Fernández, *Documentos referentes a las relaciones con Portugal durante el reinado de los Reyes Católicos,* 3 vols., especially 1: 158, 161; 2: 295, 330, 333, 352, 398, 406; 3: 1–14.

See also A. Paulo, "Os Marranos nas Beiras," *Beira Alta,* 19 and 20; idem, *Os Judeus em Trás-os-Montes;* I.S. Révah, "Les Marranes portugais et l'Inquisition au XVIe siècle," in *The Sephardi Heritage,* pp. 479–526.

On the Inquisition in Portugal, the standard work remains A. Herculano (de Carvalho e Araujo), *História da origem e estabelecimento da Inquisição em Portugal,* 3 vols. For our period, see 1: 87 ff. Herculano's work has been translated by John C. Branner (1926), and this translation has since been republished twice, in 1968 and again, with an introduction by Y. H. Yerushalmi, in 1972.

For the later presence of Portuguese New Christians in Spain, see J. Caro Baroja, *La sociedad criptojudía en la corte de Felipe IV.*

On the Portuguese Jews and New Christians, see also M. Kayserling, *Geschichte der Juden in Portugal* (see the translation of this work under the title *História dos judeus em Portugal,* by Gabriele Borchardt Correa da Silva and Anita Novinsky, with introduction, revised bibliography and notes by Anita Novinsky); J. Mendes dos Remédios, *Os Judeos em Portugal,* Vols. 1 and 2; J.L. d'Azevedo, *História dos Christãos-Novos portugueses.* Occasionally scholars do not understand that all the Jews of Portugal were converted or considered to be converted as of 1497. So, for example, R. de Lafuente Machaín, *Los portugueses en Buenos Aires (siglo XVII),* p. 41. For an excellent summary of the Jews in medieval Portugal and the origins of the New Christians there, see A. Novinsky, *Cristãos Novos na Bahia,* pp. 23 ff. See also the references to the Jews and New Christians of Portugal in A. H. de Oliveira Marques, *History of Portugal,* 1: 167–68, 210 ff., and passim. For a readable account of the important reign of Manuel I, see E. Sanceau, *The Reign of the Fortunate King,* 1495–1521, especially pp. 18, 21, 40, and 128–29.

21. On the Portuguese New Christians, see I.S. Revah, "Les Marranes," *REJ* 108: 29–77; H. Kellenbenz, *Sephardim an der Unteren Elbe: Ihre Wirtschaftliche und Politische Bedeutung vom Ende des 16. bis zum Beginn des 18. Jahrhunderts,* with an excellent summary of the origins of the Marranos, pp. 13–22; Domínguez Ortiz, "Los conversos de origen judío"; M.A. Cohen, "Marrano Diaspora," *EJ* 11, cols. 1019–25. On various halakhic problems engendered by the Marranos, see H.J.

Zimmels, *Die Marranen in der Rabbinischen Literatur,* pp. 12 ff. See also Zimmels's *Ashkenazim and Sephardim* and S. Assaf, "Spanish and Portuguese Marranos in the Responsa Literature" (Hebrew), in his *Be-Oholei Yaakov,* pp. 177 ff.

On the equation of "Jews" and "Portuguese," see Glaser, "Referencias antisemitas," p. 41, where he quotes Antonio Vieira's famous statement "Portuguezes e judeus ja são synónimos."

22. On the population of Mogadouro, see A. Braamcamp Freire, "Povoação de Trás os Montes no XVI. século," *Archivo histórico portuguez* 7: 262. On the Jews of Trás-os-Montes, see especially F.M. Alves, *Memorias arqueológico-históricas do Distrito de Bragança, Os Judeus no Distrito de Bragança,* 1925. On Trás-os-Montes as one of the two major concentrations of Judaizers in Portugal (the other being Beira Baixa), see R. Ricard, "Pour une étude du judaisme portugais au Mexique pendant la période coloniale," *Revue d'histoire moderne* 14: 523–24, reprinted in his *Études sur l'histoire morale et religieuse du Portugal,* pp. 203–4. For a note on contemporary Mogadouro and its "Marranos," see A. Paulo, *Os Marranos em Portugal: Reminiscências judio-portuguesas,* p. 6.

23. *GRC,* Apr. 17, 1589; *LCG,* Apr. 17, 1589 (pp. 278 ff.); *LCM I,* May 12, 1589 (p. 12 ff.); *FNC,* May 12, 1589, and Jan. 17, 1590; *IRA,* Nov. 27, 1589. The name Andrada is occasionally spelled Andrade in the sources.

24. See below, chapter 3. One cannot help but wonder what relationship, if any, existed between Luis de Carvajal, his uncle, and their namesake, Fray Luis de Carvajal, the famous Franciscan monk who flourished in the early sixteenth century. A scion of one of Spain's finest families, Fray Luis had studied at the Sorbonne and became a friend to Juan Luis Vives and an admirer of Erasmus. Yet it was in opposition to Erasmus that he wrote his most famous work, his apology for religious orders (*Apologia monasticae religionis diluens nugas Erasmi,* Salamanca, 1528). At present, however, there is no evidence to link Fray Luis with our Carvajals. The same may be said of many other Carvajals found on the Hispanic peninsula and in New Spain around this time. See M. Bataillon, *Erasmo y España,* pp. 318–27. See also 264–65, 506–7, and passim; on the Captain Carabajal who accompanied Pizarro, see G.A. Kohut, "The Martyrdom of the Carabajal Family in Mexico, 1590–1601," *The Jewish Tribune* (Portland, Oregon), March 25, 1904, p. 3.

25. See the standard histories of the period. On the inflation, see, for example, E. Hamilton, *American Treasure and the Price Revolution in Spain, 1501–1650,* p. 261; Lynch, *Spain under the Habsburgs,* 1: 124 ff., 272 ff., 303 ff. See also J.H. Parry, *The Spanish Seaborne Empire,* passim.

26. *LCM II,* Feb. 11, 1595 (pp. 221 ff.); *LCM-A,* beginning (p. 463).

27. CC, Dec. 20, 1589 (in *FNC* and *MNC I*).

28. *IRA,* Nov. 27, 1589; *FNC,* Jan. 10, 1590; *MNC I,* Jan. 18, 1590.

29. On this subject, see C. Roth, "The Religion of the Marranos," *JQR*

(*N.S.*) 22: 1–33, reprinted in C. Roth, *Gleanings: Essays in Jewish History, Letters and Art*, pp. 119–51; M.A. Cohen, "The Religion of Luis Rodríguez Carvajal," *AJA* 20: 33–62.

30. *LCM-A* (p. 463). Although the calendar of the Judaizers in New Spain was different from that of traditional Judaism (see below, chapter 5), the Day of Pardon in 1579 happened to coincide with the traditional date of Yom Kippur.

31. See note 29 above; see also chapter 6, below.

32. See Roth, *A History of the Marranos,* p. 175. Occasionally assertions are made, without evidence, that "the Law of Moses" was a term of inquisitorial invention and that it was used by the Judaizers only rarely and only in contrast with the phrase "the Law of Jesus." This viewpoint is contradicted by the evidence of the primary sources, manuscript as well as printed. "The Law of Moses" was the Judaizers' normal appellation for their faith, even when they were not contrasting it with Christianity.

It is a direct translation of the Hebrew *Torat Moshe,* a phrase used regularly by Jewish writers in Christian Spain, for example, Joseph Albo, in his *'Ikkarim.* Albo lived at a time when there were already numerous New Christians.

An interesting example of the use of the term is found in the *Rópica Pnefma* (1531) by the well-known anti-Jewish controversialist João de Barros. There "Vontade," speaking from a Jewish perspective, says: "Sabes donde veo entenderes a minha inclinação à Lei de Moses?"

Indeed, the term "Law of Moses" is a much more natural description of Judaism than the corresponding "Law of Christ," regularly found in the primary sources, is of Christianity. A strong case may be made for the derivation of the latter term from a Jewish model.

There is no evidence whatsoever that the term was invented by the Inquisition.

33. *GRC,* Apr. 17, 1589. Cf. *IRA,* Apr. 11, 1589. It should be noted that by the closing decades of the sixteenth century a number of religious orders, following the lead of the Jeronymites, had been closing their doors to descendants of Jews. See Domínguez Ortiz, "Los conversos de origen judío," p. 80.

34. *IRA,* Apr. 11, Nov. 29, 1589; *LCG,* Sept. 22, 1589 (p. 318).

35. Cf. note 13 above. Luis's brother is not to be confused with the more famous Fray Gaspar de Carvajal who accompanied Francisco de Orellana, the explorer of the Amazon, half a century earlier and became archbishop of Lima. On this Fray Gaspar, see P. Hermann, *The Great Age of Discovery,* trans. Arnold J. Pomerans, pp. 210 ff. The *Diccionario Porrúa* includes an article on Luis's brother (p. 278), but misnames him Fray Gabriel de Carvajal. The name appears nowhere in *GRC* or the trial records of the other members of the family. The author of the article errs again in stating that our Fray Gaspar died at the end of the century. He was still very much alive in the following century. See chapter 10 below. Antonio Domínguez Ortiz, *Los judeoconversos en España y América,* p. 33, likewise calls Gaspar Gabriel.

36. The possibility remains after examining Gaspar's early depositions, *GRC*, April 17–22, 1589.
37. *IRA*, Nov. 29, 1589; CC, Dec. 20, 1589 (in *FNC*); *FNC*, Jan. 11, 1590.
38. *LCG*, Apr. 19, 1589 (p. 287); *FNC*, Jan. 11, 1590; *MNC II*, Mar. 14, 1601. In *LCM II*, Feb. 14, 1596 (pp. 361–62), LCM mentions that his father later told him that another brother of his, Hernán Rodríguez, and his son Diego were secret Jews.
39. *MNC II*, Mar. 14, 1601. Cf. *LCM I*, Aug. 11, 1589 (p. 56), and *GRC*, Apr. 17, 1589. Even Gaspar admitted this, saying that though he had reports "de que la dicha su madre es hija de algo también la tiene de la misma casta de cristianos nuevos de judíos por haberlo entendido y oído así en España y él lo entiende así." The statement by S.B. Liebman, *The Enlightened*, p. 26, that "Luis' mother was of Jewish descent only on her maternal side," is not supported by the evidence. S. Roel, *Nuevo León: Apuntes históricos*, p. 7, agrees regarding Luis de Carvajal the governor that "sus padres habían sido judíos antes de hacerse cristianos."
40. *FNC*, Jan. 11, Jan. 17, 1590.
41. *LC MII, Feb.* 12 (p. 349), Feb. 14, 1596 (pp 364–65); *MNC II*, Mar. 14, 1601; CC, Dec. 11, 1589 (in *MNC I*). The original quotation found in Mariana's trial record, reads "Mayor es tu misericordia para nos salvar que nuestros pecados para nos condenar."
42. See the case against Morales, *ID*, Vol. 127, Year 1589; CC, Dec. 16, 1589 (in *MNC I*).
43. See below, chapter 3.

CHAPTER 3

1. *LCG*, Defense, Oct. 6, 1589 (p. 322).
2. See S. Guerra, *Terras da Guiné e Cabo Verde*, pp. 7–11. See also S. Zavala, *La filosofía política en la conquista de América*, pp. 105 ff.
3. G. Scelle, *La traite négrière aux Indes de Castille*, passim. See also Bourne, *Spain in America*, pp. 273 ff.; P.A. Means, *The Spanish Main, Focus of Envy*, pp. 60 ff.; Chaunu and Chaunu, *Séville et l'Atlantique*, 6: 41, 396 ff.; and especially Aguirre Beltrán, "The Slave Trade in Mexico," pp. 412–31. See also J.A. Saco, *Historia de la esclavitud de la raza africana en el Nuevo Mundo*, 1: 48 ff., 57 ff.; 2: 77 ff.
4. *LCG*, Apr. 14, 1589 (pp. 280–81).
5. On the slave trade, see D.B. Davis, *The Problem of Slavery in Western Culture*, pp. 223 ff. On the death of Miguel Núñez, see note 38 below.
6. Report by Juan de Ubilla dealing with Hawkins's attack on the fleet arriving in New Spain in 1568, published in F. del Paso y Troncoso, *Epistolario de Nueva España*, 10: 286.
7. *LCG*, Apr. 17, 1589 (p. 280). The date of the marriage is inferred from the various data of Carvajal's life.
8. *IRA*, Mar. 16, Apr. 11, Apr. 12, 1589 (also in *LCG*, pp. 212 ff.)
9. J.T. Medina, *Historia . . . de la Inquisición en México*, p. 74. (Page numbers will always refer to the second edition.)

10. *LCG,* Apr. 17, 1589 (p. 281).
11. For general background, see H.M. Bailey and A.P. Nasatir, *Latin America: The Development of Its Civilization,* pp. 89 ff.; S.A. Zavala, *La encomienda indiana,* pp. 40 ff.; idem, *New Viewpoints on the Spanish Colonization of America,* passim; idem, *Los esclavos indios en Nueva España,* passim; J.H. Parry, *The Spanish Theory of Empire in the Sixteenth Century,* pp. 27 ff.; L.B. Simpson, *The Encomienda in New Spain,* pp. 3 ff., 183, 196–97, and passim; idem, *The Repartimiento System of Native Labor in New Spain and Guatemala,* which forms part 3 of the *Studies in the Administration of the Indians in New Spain,* pp. 44 ff.; J.M. de Ots Capdequí, *Instituciones sociales de la América española en el período colonial,* p. 35; idem, *El estado español en las Indias,* with an excellent overview of the legal, social, and institutional aspects of the Spanish conquest; idem, *España en América: El régimen de tierras en la época colonial,* pp. 82 ff.; M.B. Trens, "La legislación española de Indias en la Nueva España," *BAGN* 23: 415–51. See also J. Miranda, *El tributo indígena en la Nueva España durante el siglo XVI,* pp. 9 ff., 45 ff.; idem, *La ideas y las instituciones políticas mexicanas. Primera Parte, 1521–1580,* passim; the still valuable work by Arthur Helps, *The Spanish Conquest in America,* Vols. 1, 2, and 3 to p. 288; S. Uribe de Fernández de Córdoba, "Bibliografía histórica mexicana," *HM* 15: 132–54.
12. See Priestley, *The Coming of the White Man,* pp. 119 ff.; L. Hanke, *The Spanish Struggle for Justice in the Conquest of America,* pp. 39 ff.; Simpson, *Many Mexicos,* pp. 112 ff. For an excellent picture of the conditions of Indian life in the colonial era a few decades after the period of this study, see Gage, *A New Survey of the West Indies,* chapter 19.
13. Bernal Díaz, *The True History and Conquest of Mexico,* trans. M. Keatinge, 2: 550.
14. *LCG,* Defense, Oct. 6, 1589 (p. 338).
15. Chaunu and Chaunu, *Séville et l'Atlantique,* 3: 116–17.
16. On the role of mercury, see C.B. Dahlgren, *Historic Mines of Mexico,* p. 18.
17. On the viceroys see J.I. Rubio Mañé, *Introducción al estudio de los virreyes de Nueva España.* Cf. also "Virrey," in *Diccionario Porrúa,* p. 1571. See also M. Rivera Cambas, *Los gobernantes de México,* and A. Villaseñor y Villaseñor, *Gobernantes de México y formas de gobierno.*
18. *LCG,* Defense, Oct. 6, 1589 (p. 338). Carvajal's title was *alcalde ordinario.* For the functions of this office and its points of similarity with the *alcalde mayor,* the equivalent of mayor, in New Spain, see J. Escriche, *Diccionario razonado de legislación y jurisprudencia,* 1: 424.
19. *LCG,* Defense, Oct. 6, 1589 (pp. 338–39).
20. The letter sent by Martín Enríquez to John Hawkins can be found in translation in I.A. Wright, *Spanish Documents concerning English Voyages to the Caribbean,* Document 25, p. 128. Cf. also ibid., Document 27, pp. 131–52, including depositions taken on September 27–30, 1568, by Francisco Maldonado, Antonio Delgadillo, Juan de Ubilla, and Francisco Bustamante.

21. For these events, see Means, *The Spanish Main*, pp. 67 ff.; J.A. Williamson, *Hawkins of Plymouth*, pp. 48 ff., 132 ff.; C.R. Markham, ed., *The Hawkins' Voyages*, pp. 70–81.

22. A. Rumeu de Armas, *Los viajes de John Hawkins a América*, pp. 311 ff., with a good summary of the "Diligencias hechas por el muy magnifico señor Luis de Carvajal, alcalde ordinario en esta villa por Su Magestad sobre los Ingleses," found in the Archivo de Indias: Patronato Real, in Seville. Cf. the report by the sailor William Collins (Guillermo Calens), a member of Hawkins's crew, in V. Riva Palacio, *México a través de los siglos*, 2: 507 ff. Cf. also C. Sanz Arizmendi, "Cuatro expediciones de Juan Haquinés," *Boletín del Instituto de Estudios Americanistas de Sevilla* 1: 59–69, the report by Francisco de Luján to the king on Oct. 20, 1568, found in Paso y Troncoso, *Epistolario*, pp. 260–61; A. Caso, *Los tres siglos de México*, 1: 188.

On Hawkins's sailors, see F. Aydelotte, "Elizabethan Seamen in Mexico and Ports of the Spanish Main," *AHR* 48: 1–19 (he does not, however, give credit to Carvajal); P. Martínez del Río, "La aventura mexicana de Sir John Hawkins," *MAHM* 2: 241–95; J. Jiménez Rueda, *Corsarios franceses e ingleses en la Inquisición de la Nueva España*. On individual sailors, see, for Robert Thompson, Conway, *An Englishman and the Mexican Inquisition*, and for Miles Philips, Philips's own account entitled "A Discourse Written by One Miles Philips, Englishman, One of the Company Put on Shore Northward of Panuco, in the West Indies, by M. John Hawkins, 1568," in Hakluyt, *The Principal Navigations, Voyages, Traffiques and Discoveries*, 9: 398–445; J. García Icazbalceta, "Relación escrita por Miles Philips, inglés," in his *Obras*, 7: 151–296 (see also *BAGN* 20: 467 ff., 615 ff.). For a list of the trial records involving Hawkins's crew, see S. Williams, "The G.R.G. Conway Collection in the Library of Congress: A Checklist," *HAHR* 35: 386–97, especially pp. 387–94.

23. For a summary of this period, see Parkes, *A History of Mexico*, pp. 95–96; Simpson, *Many Mexicos*, pp. 129 ff. Cf. M. Orozco y Berra, *Historia de la dominación española en México*, 238 ff.

24. P.W. Powell, *Soldiers, Indians and Silver*, pp. 28 ff. See also idem, "Spanish Warfare against the Chichimecas in the 1570s," *HAHR* 24: 580–604. Cf. G. de las Casas, *La guerra de los chichimecas*, ed. J.F. Ramírez, pp. 21 ff. The quotation is from Miles Philips's "Discourse," loc. cit., pp. 410–12.

25. Paso y Troncoso, *Epistolario*, 11: 179.

26. Powell, *Soldiers, Indians and Silver*, chapter 7. Cf. "Relación de la conquista de los teules chichimecas que dió Juan de Sámano," in J. García Icazbalceta, *Colección de documentos inéditos para la historia de México*, 2: 262–87.

27. *LCG*, Defense, Oct. 6, 1589 (p. 339). Cf. Powell, *Soldiers, Indians and Silver*, pp. 145–46.

28. *LCG*, Apr. 17, 1589 (p. 281) and Defense, Oct. 6, 1589 (p. 339).

29. See below, note 57, and accompanying text.

30. *Catálogo de los fondos americanos del archivo de protocolos de Sevilla*, Vol. 1, Document 1828, p. 435.

31. V. Alessio Robles, *Monterrey en la historia y en la leyenda,* p. 91.

32. A. de Lenón, *Historia de Nuevo León,* ed. G. García, pp. 73 ff., 89–90.

33. W.W. Borah, *New Spain's Century of Depression,* pp. 18–19; Chaunu and Chaunu, *Séville et l'Atlantique,* 8: 518–19, 560 ff. Cf. Lynch, *Spain under the Habsburgs,* 1: 163–64.

34. Cf. Powell, *Soldiers, Indians and Silver,* pp. 172–73.

35. The document is to be found in the *Instrucciones que los vireyes* [sic] *de Nueva España dejaron a sus sucesores.* The report is entitled "Instrucción y advertimientos que el Virey [sic] D. Martín Enríquez dejó al Conde de la Coruña (D. Lorenzo Suárez de Mendoza), su sucesor en los cargos de Nueva España." Cf. Medina, *La Inquisición en México,* pp. 99 ff., and V. Alessio Robles, *Coahuila y Texas en la época colonial,* p. 115.

36. León, *Historia de Nuevo León,* pp. 73 ff.; C.C. Colby, *Source Book for the Economic Geography of North America,* pp. 346 ff.; J.L. Tamayo, *Geografía general de México,* 2 vols.; J.A. Vivó, *Geografía de México.* Cf. Roel, *Nuevo León,* pp. 12 ff.; and A. de la Mota y Escobar, *Descripción geográfica de los reinos de Nueva Galicia, Nueva Vizcaya y Nuevo León,* ed. J. Ramírez Cabañas.

37. León, *Historia de Nuevo León,* pp. 79 ff. Cf. Roel, *Nuevo León,* pp. 12 ff. For a description essentially corroborating León's, see Henry Hawks, "A Relation of the Commodities of Nova Hispania, and the Manners of the Inhabitants (1572)," in Hakluyt, *The Principal Navigations, Voyages, Traffiques and Discoveries,* 9: 382.

38. Núñez's death is derived from the *Catálogo de los fondos americanos,* Vol. 2, Document 1049, pp. 240–41.

39. *LCG,* Defense, Oct. 6, 1589 (p. 339).

40. "Inundaciones de la ciudad de México," in *Diccionario Porrúa,* p. 809. See also Rubio Mañé, *Movimiento marítimo,* 4: 15 ff.

41. Chaunu and Chaunu, *Séville et l'Atlantique,* 3: 258 ff.; Leonard, *Books of the Brave,* pp. 124 ff.

42. Felipe Núñez, Sept. 22, 1589, in *IRA.* The date of late 1578, rather than early 1579, is derived from this testimony.

43. The document is reproduced by V. Alessio Robles in *Actividad* (Monterrey, Mexico, March 1, 1938) and Roel, *Nuevo León,* pp. 155–58. The original is found in the AGN, *Ramo Civil,* Vol. 672, folio 254 ff. See also V. Alessio Robles, *Saltillo en la historia y en la leyenda,* pp. 64 ff.; idem, *Monterrey en la historia y en la leyenda,* pp. 97 ff.; idem, *Coahuila y Texas en la época colonial,* pp. 90 ff.

    In one document Carvajal is listed as "Governor and Captain General of the New Territory of the New Kingdom of León and the Mines of Mazapil in the Indies," *Catálogo de los fondos americanos,* Vol. 2, Document 1368, p. 320. The statement by A. Toro, *La familia Carvajal,* 1: 41, that Carvajal was permitted to take more than a hundred people to the New World is based on a confusion of the number allotted to him and the number he actually took. See below, p. 62.

44. Most writers, unaware of the existence of two documents, generally speak of only one, that of June 14, 1579—for example, E. Schäfer,

El Consejo real y supremo de las Indias, 1: 546. Works like those of M. Cuevas, *Historia de la iglesia de México,* 2: 43–44, 282, which blame Jews (by which, one supposes, New Christian Judaizers are meant) for all kinds of troubles in Mexico (including those of the twentieth century) are at a total loss to explain why the Judaizers were permitted to emigrate to the New World "with a dispensation positively granted by the crown" (pp. 43–44). The idea that Philip II, a pillar of Catholic religiosity, might have permitted the Judaizers to emigrate because he recognized their potential beneficent contribution to the development of the New World, a potentiality that they soon actualized, escapes their recognition. See also M. Cuevas, *Historia de la nación mexicana,* p. 267.

45. Lea, *The Inquisition in the Spanish Dependencies,* pp. 193 ff.; Bourne, *Spain in America,* pp. 207, 243 ff., 269; J.T. Medina, *La primitiva inquisición americana,* 1: 17 ff. Cf. A. de Herrera y Tordesillas, *Historia general de los hechos de los castellanos en las islas y tierra firme del mar Océano,* 2: 389; B. Lewin, *El Santo Oficio en América,* pp. 35 ff., with good bibliography; idem, *La Inquisición en Hispanoamérica (Judíos, protestantes, patriotas),* pp. 139 ff.; Roth, *A History of the Marranos,* pp. 272 ff.; and Ots Capdequí, *El estado español en las Indias,* p. 47. On the emigrants from Spain, see also V.A. Neasham, "Spain's Emigrants to the New World," *HAHR* 19: 147–60; and the passenger lists, though relating to the early part of the sixteenth century, in L. Rubio y Moreno, *Pasajeros a Indias,* 2 vols., and C. Bermúdez Plata, *Catálogo de pasajeros a Indias durante los siglos XVI, XVII y XVIII,* 3 vols. (covering only to 1559); and the following related studies: J. Friede, "The *Catálogo de Pasajeros* and Spanish Emigration to America to 1550," *HAHR* 31: 333–48; idem, "Algunas observaciones sobre la realidad de la emigración española a América en la primera mitad del siglo XVI," *Revista de Indias* 12: 467–96; P. Boyd-Bowman, "La emigración peninsular a América: 1520 a 1539," *HM* 13: 165–92; R. Konetzke, "Grundzüge der spanischen Gesetzgebung über die Auswanderung nach dem amerikanischen Kolonialreich," *Festschrift Percy Ernst Schramm,* 2: 105–13, especially pp. 108–9. In his supplementary material to his edition of Medina's *Historia . . . de la Inquisición en México,* p. 98, Jiménez Rueda points out that following the union of Spain and Portugal in 1580 there was an exodus of New Christians from Portugal to New Spain and Peru. Cf. L. García de Proodián, *Los judíos en América,* p. 21.

46. Medina, *La Inquisición en México,* pp. 24 ff. See also G García and C. Pereyra, *La Inquisición de México* (in *Documentos inéditos o muy raros . . .* vol. 5), pp. 225 ff. See also G. García, *El clero de México durante la dominación española,* p. 181, for royal instructions regarding the honoring of the inquisitors in the church, and, on important data concerning the personnel of the Inquisition on the basis of a document of 1646, "Nómina del tribunal de la Inquisición de Nueva España, 1571–1646," *BAGN* 26: 53–90; 293–313; 487–518; 687–707; 27: 315–61; 495–559; 703–48.

47. Medina, *La Inquisición en México,* pp. 33 ff. All told there were only

some fifteen alleged Judaizers tried before the inquisitions in Mexico City prior to 1574. See Mariel de Ibáñez, *La Inquisición en México,* p. 10.

On the Protestants tried in Mexico, see G. Baez Camargo, *Protestantes enjuiciados por la Inquisición en Iberoamérica,* pp. 23 ff.; P. Gringoire, "Protestantes enjuiciados por la Inquisición," *HM* 11: 161–79. For the broader picture of the attitudes in the Peninsula toward the Protestants and humanists, see M. Bataillon's classic *Érasme et l'Espagne,* now available in revised and up-to-date form in a Spanish translation (*Erasmo y España*) by Antonio Alatorre; H.C. Lea, *Chapters from the Religious History of Spain,* pp. 36 ff.; E. Schäfer, *Beiträge zur Geschichte des spanishen Protestantismus und der Inquisition im sechzehnten Jahrhundert,* 3 vols.; M. de la Pinta Llorente, *La Inquisición española y los problemas de la cultura y de la intolerancia,* 2 vols. (see especially 1: 23, on the concern for "Protestant" Bibles entering Spain, and 2: 59 ff., for a discussion of the Reformation); E. Boehmer, *Bibliotheca Wiffeniana: Spanish Reformers of Two Centuries, from 1520,* 3 vols.; E. Asensio, "El erasmismo y las corrientes espirituales afines," *Revista de filología española* 36: 31–99; and, for individuals, the following: Miguel de la Pinta Llorente, ed., *Procesos inquisitoriales contra Francisco Sánchez de las Brozas,* especially pp. 6 ff.; J.E. Longhurst, *Erasmus and the Spanish Inquisition: The Case of Juan de Valdes;* idem, *Luther and the Spanish Inquisition: The Case of Diego de Uceda, 1528–1529.* See also B. Llorca, *Die Spanische Inquisition und die "Alumbrados" (1509–1667),* especially pp. 46 ff. For a fine overview of Erasmism in Spain, see H. Piñera, *El pensamiento español de los siglos XVI y XVII,* pp. 62–92. For the trial of a follower of Erasmus in Mexico, see J. Jiménez Rueda, "Proceso contra Francisco de Sayavedra, por erasmista, 1539," *BAGN* 18: 1–15.

48. The inventory is published by Toro in *Los judíos en la Nueva España,* pp. 91 ff. See also Mariel de Ibáñez, *La Inquisición en México,* p. 10. On Zumárraga, see R.E. Greenleaf, *Zumarraga and the Mexican Inquisition,* pp. 93 ff., though Greenleaf does not clearly distinguish between "Jews" and "Judaizers"; J. García Icazbalceta, *Don Fray Juan de Zumárraga, primer obispo y arzobispo de México,* new ed. rev. by Rafael Aguayo Spencer and Antonio Castro Leal.

49. Medina, *La Inquisición en México,* pp. 47 ff.

50. Ibid. Cf. Simpson, *Many Mexicos,* p. 188.

51. Medina, *La Inquisición en México,* pp. 76 ff. Lea, *The Inquisition in the Spanish Dependencies,* p. 207, claims that two Judaizers were burned at the stake in 1578, but does not give their names.

52. *LCG,* Apr. 19, 1589 (p. 288). On New Christians in France, see I. Bédarride, *Les Juifs en France, en Italie et en Espagne,* still useful even if somewhat outdated, pp. 323 ff.; R. Anchel, *Les Juifs de France,* pp. 132 ff.; T. Malvézin, *Histoire des Juifs à Bordeaux,* pp. 87 ff.; H. Léon, *Histoire des Juifs de Bayonne,* pp. 13 ff.; G. Cirot, *Rechesches sur les Juifs espagnols et portugais à Bordeaux,* especially chapter 2, "Quelques sources à consulter sur les Juifs 'portugais' de Bordeaux aux XVIIe

et XVIIIe siècles." See also L. de Matos, *Les Portugais en France au XVIe siècle: Études et documents*; idem, *Les Portugais à l'Université de Paris entre 1500 et 1550*. For the maritime contacts between France, Spain, and Portugal at the time, see Z. Szajkowski, "Trade Relations of Marranos in France with the Iberian Peninsula in the Sixteenth and Seventeenth Centuries," *JQR (N.S.)* 50: 69–78, and in connection with this, M. Grünwald, "Note sur les Marranes à Rouen et ailleurs," *REJ* 89: 381–84. Reciprocally, there was a French colony in Andalusia. On the presence of the French in Spain and their growing role in the sixteenth century, see A. Girard, *Le commerce français à Séville et Cadix au temps des Hapsbourg.*

53. *FNC*, Aug. 31, 1589; *LCG*, Defense, Oct. 6, 1589 (pp. 334–35).

54. Felipe Núñez, Sept. 22, 1589 (in *IRA*). Felipe Núñez at first believed that Gabriel and Isabel were planning to accompany the governor to the New World, but Isabel's reaction after Gabriel's death tells another story.

55. On the passenger list, see *LCG*, Apr. 27, 1589 (p. 292); and *Cátalogo de los fondos americanos*, Vol. 2, Documents 955 (p. 216), 969 (p. 220), 1023 (p. 234), and 1031 (pp. 235–36). On Águila's full name and occupation, see *IRA*, Mar. 16, 1589 (also in *FNC* and *LCG* [p. 213]). On Dr. Morales, see also *LCM I*, Aug. 11, 1589 (p. 53).

56. See, for example, *IRA*, July 20, 1589, and chapter 4, below, for mention of correspondence regarding Guiomar's death. In his defense (*LCG*, Oct. 6, 1589) Governor Carvajal understandably denied that his wife Judaized, but all the facts in the case, including Isabel's testimony under torture (*IRA*, Nov. 29, 1589) militate against this position.

57. *Catálogo de los fondos americanos*, volume 2: Doña Blanca, executrix: Document 1049, p. 240; payment for slaves: Document 1051, p. 241; payment to Morales: Document 889, pp. 199–200; sale of cochineal: Document 1075, p. 247; Alonso Rodríguez: Document 1061, pp. 243–44; Diego Ruiz de Ribera: Document 1078, p. 248; power of attorney to Cristóbal Ortiz: Document 1105, pp. 254–55; acquisition of ship: Document 804, p. 179; purchase of hardtack: Document 1368, p. 320. All the documents pertaining to Carvajal in the *Catálogo,* save two (Vol. 1, no. 1828, pp. 435–36 [cf. above, note 30], and Vol. 2, no. 1105, pp. 254–55) are listed in J.B. Goldmann's "The Tragic Square of Don Luis de Carbajal y de la Cueva," *The Historian*, Autumn 1946, pp. 74–75, with one or two slight errors, such as the name of Carvajal's father-in-law.

58. *LCM I*, Sept. 13, 1589 (p. 80); *LCG*, Defense, Oct. 6, 1589 (p. 325).

59. CC, Dec. 20, 1589 (in *LCG* [p. 274] and *MNC I*).

60. *IRA*, Mar. 16, 1589; *FNC*, Sept. 13, 1589; *LCG*, Defense, Oct. 6, 1589 (p. 325).

61. *LCG*, Defense, Oct. 6, 1589 (p. 325); *IRA*, Sept. 13, 1589.

62. See, for example, Leonard, *Books of the Brave*, pp. 135–36.

63. *LCG*, Defense, Oct. 6, 1589 (p. 340). Cf. Bourne, *Spain in America,* p. 252, who says that the peso in 1581 "was equivalent to about three dollars" at the beginning of the twentieth century.

64. *FNC,* Jan. 11, 1590.
65. *IRA,* Mar. 16, 1589.
66. *FNC,* Jan. 11, 1590.
67. *IRA,* Mar. 16, Apr. 11, 14, and July 20, 1589. Cf. the publication of IRA's testimony in *LCG* (p. 308).
68. J. de Veitia Linaje, *The Spanish Rule of Trade to the West Indies,* trans. J. Stevens, pp. 136, 232, 259. Cf. Williamson, *Hawkins of Plymouth,* p. 47; C.H. Haring, *Trade and Navigation between Spain and the Indies in the Time of the Hapsburgs,* chapters 5, 6, and 9; G. de Artíñano y Galdácano, *Historia del comercio con las Indias durante el dominio de los Austrias,* pp. 51, 78, 105; Means, *The Spanish Main,* pp. 58 ff.; Leonard, *Books of the Brave,* pp. 142–43.
69. See preceding note and cf. Chaunu and Chaunu, *Séville et l'Atlantique,* 6: 928 ff.
70. *LCM I,* Sept. 13, 1589 (pp. 80–81). On Seville, see R. Pike, "Seville in the Sixteenth Century," *HAHR* 41: 1–30.
71. Chaunu and Chaunu, *Séville et l'Atlantique,* 3: 276 ff.
72. López de Velasco, *Geografía y descripción universal de las Indias,* p. 87; Leonard, *Books of the Brave,* pp. 140 ff.

CHAPTER 4

1. The quotation is from Escalante de Mendoza, *Itinerario de navegación de los mares y tierras occidentales* (circa 1571), and is found in G. de Artíñano y Galdácano, *La arquitectura naval española,* p. 113.
2. Artíñano y Galdácano, *La arquitectura naval española,* pp. 66 ff.
3. Leonard, *Books of the Brave,* pp. 143 ff.
4. *Visita de las naos que forman la flota en que vino por general Don Francisco de Luxán, que llegó a San Juan de Ulúa a 25 de agosto de 1580 conduciendo al Virrey conde de la Coruña,* AGN, *ID,* Vol. 169, Document 2. The document has been reproduced in F. Fernaídez del Castillo, *Libros y libreros en el siglo XVI,* pp. 385–87. Cf. Toro, *La familia Carvajal,* 1: 58. Toro, however, makes the mistake of assuming that the books of Fray Luis de Granada included the *Introducción al símbolo de la fe* (first published in Salamanca in 1582). Cf. also Leonard, *Books of the Brave,* pp. 42, 78, 106, 120; idem, "On the Mexican Book Trade, 1576," *HR* 17: 18–34. On the literature, see also the appropriate discussions in a history like that of J. Hurtado and A. González-Palencia, *Historia de la literatura española,* pp. 316–17, 390–91. Cf. also García de Proodián, *Los judíos en América,* pp. 211–12.
5. Chaunu and Chaunu, *Séville et l'Atlantique,* 3: 276 ff. Cf. Artíñano y Galdácano, *La arquitectura naval española,* pp. 79–80. Cf. J. de Veitia Linaje, *Norte de la contratación de las Indias occidentales,* p. 260. Ocoa was located on the eastern shore of the Bay of Ocoa on the island of Española (Hispaniola), now Santo Domingo. Chaunu and Chaunu, *Séville et l'Atlantique,* 1: maps.
6. León, *Historia de Nuevo León,* pp. 80–81. See, however, Alessio Robles,

Monterrey en la historia y en la leyenda, pp. 97 ff. and idem, *Coahuila y Texas en la época colonial,* pp. 89–90. Believing incorrectly that Carvajal's territory was a square two hundred leagues in each direction, Alessio Robles calls the region "Carvajal's tragic square." This term is repeated by Goldmann, "The Tragic Square of Don Luis de Carbajal y de la Cueva," pp. 69 ff., Lewin, *El Santo Oficio en América,* pp. 51–52, and numerous others. Since the territory could not go beyond the borders of New Biscay and New Galicia, it was certainly not a square. On the territorial divisions, see E. O'Gorman, *Historia de las divisiones territoriales de México,* pp. 3 ff.

7. Roel, *Nuevo León,* pp. 155, 158.
8. Priestley, *The Coming of the White Man,* p. 12; F. Chevalier, *Land and Society in Colonial Mexico,* p. 47; Miranda, *España y Nueva España,* pp. 66–67. See also Domingo Lázaro de Arregui, *Descripción de la Nueva Galicia,* ed. François Chevalier, and the editor's introductory study, "La vida económica y social en la obra de Arregui," pp. lv–lxx; G. Gómez de Cervantes, *La vida económica y social de Nueva España al finalizar el siglo XVI,* ed. Alberto María Carreño. On the history of the entire northeast region to and beyond the time of Carvajal, see M.B. Trens, "Apuntes históricos sobre el nordeste de México," *BAGN* 28: 325 ff. See also W. Jiménez Moreno, "El noreste de México y su cultura," *MAMH* 19: 176–87. Jiménez Moreno agrees (p. 180) with those who hold that Monterrey was founded first in 1577, then for a second time by Carvajal, and finally for a third time by Diego de Montemayor in 1596.
9. Carvajal's charter, in Roel, *Nuevo León,* pp. 155 ff.
10. *IRA,* Mar. 18, 1589; *FNC,* Jan. 10, 11, 1590, CC, Dec. 16, 1589 (in *FNC*).
11. *FNC,* Sept. 25, 1589.
12. *LCM I,* Aug. 11, 1589 (p. 53); *LCM II,* Aug. 14, 1596 (p. 400), Oct. 14, 1596 (pp. 424 ff.). See also the trial record of Luis Díaz (Díez), silversmith, AGN, *ID,* Vol. 161, Dossier 2, passim. Luis Díaz was tried in absentia.
13. *LCM I,* Aug. 11, 1589 (p. 53); Juan de Micina, Apr. 15, 1589, in *IRA*; *FNC,* Sept. 25, 1589, and, for the date of Dr. Morales's departure, Chaunu and Chaunu, *Séville et l'Atlantique,* 3: 352. See also trial records of Manuel de Morales, Isabel Clara, Antonio de Morales, and Blanca de Morales. For locations of the records, see Appendix.
14. *LCM-A* (p. 464).
15. *LCM-A* (p. 464); Simpson, *Many Mexicos,* p. 8; Parkes, *A History of Mexico,* p. 33. Tampico was located in the province of Pánuco, not "Parmco," as is stated in C. Adler, "Trial of Jorge de Almeida by the Inquisition in Mexico," *PAJHS* 4:49, and frequently repeated. When the trial records speak of the family's living in Pánuco, they refer to the region, not the town of Pánuco. All available evidence points to the fact that the family continued to live in the town of Tampico until it moved to the capital, after which it never reestablished residence in the coastal regions. There is no evidence that the family ever moved

from Tampico, in the region of Pánuco, to the town of Pánuco. See, for example, *LCM I*, Sept. 7, 1589 (p. 75). See also chapter 5, below and Toro, *La familia Carvajal*, 1: 63 ff. and 112 ff.

16. *LCM-A* (p. 464); *FNC*, Jan. 10, 1590.
17. *LCG*, Defense, Oct. 6, 1589 (p. 340). Cf. P.W. Powell, "Presidios and Towns on the Silver Frontier of New Spain 1550–1590," *HAHR* 24: 195 ff. The names of at least two adventurers are known to us. They are Domingo Martínez Learreta and his son, Pedro de Learreta Buitrón. In a document dated May 24, 1590, asking for consideration for his services, Domingo Martínez Learreta, petitioning for himself and his son, indicated that nine years earlier he had entered into the service of Governor Carvajal, and that he and his son had furnished their own arms and horses and received no salary or other recompense. In another document, Governor Carvajal himself revealed that Robert Plimpton (Plinton), of Plymouth, England, one of the members of John Hawkins's crew who had been tried for heresy by the Inquisition and reconciled in 1574, subsequently went along with him, apparently against his will, in the expedition of discovery in the mining area of Mazapil. In his declaration, Carvajal denied that Plimpton was ever officially in his service, as the Englishman had apparently alleged, or that he ever took a dappled horse from Plimpton. Plimpton had left the horse with him after it had had its leg cut off, the governor insisted. The only other item he had of Plimpton's, he said, were several yards of sackcloth, which he took from him in exchange for a nearly jet-black horse. To the question of whether his slave Agustín had ever taken a jet-black horse from Plimpton, Carvajal responded with a categorical denial. Carvajal's testimony was included in the trial against Plimpton held in 1573 and now found in the AGN, *Ramo Criminal*, Vol. 685. See R. Gómez, "Dos documentos relativos a Luis de Carvajal, el Viejo," *BAGN* 22: 551–58. Gómez incorrectly gives 1593 as the date of the trial. The petition of Domingo Martínez Learreta forms document no. 501 in the "Catálogo de pobladores de Nueva España," *BAGN* 13: 155.
18. *LCG*, Defense, Oct. 6, 1589 (p. 340). For general background, see also H.E. Bolton, "The Mission as a Frontier Institution in the Spanish-American Colonies," *AHR* 23: 42–61.
19. León, *Historia de Nuevo León*, p. 91.
20. Powell, *Soldiers, Indians and Silver*, p. 146.
21. *LCG*, Defense, Oct. 6, 1589 (p. 340).
22. León, *Historia de Nuevo León*, p. 90.
23. *LCG*, Defense, Oct. 6, 1589 (p. 333).
24. *LCM I*, Aug. 9, 1589 (pp. 45–46); *LCG*, Apr. 19, 1589 (p. 285); Defense, Oct. 6, 1589 (p. 333), and the governor's conversations with Baltasar, Gaspar, and Luis, below.
25. *LCM-A* (p. 464).
26. *FNC*, Jan. 11, 1590. Cf. *MNC I*, Jan. 17, 1590.
27. *IRA*, Apr. 14, 1589. CC, Dec. 20, 1589 (in *FNC*); *FNC*, Nov. 10, 1589, Jan. 17, 1590; *MNC I*, Jan. 17, 1590.

28. *LCM II,* Oct. 15, 1596 (pp. 427ff.). The original reads as follows:

> Osen otros responder,
> no es tiempo de bien obrar;
> pues sin algo merecer
> ¿cómo se puede creer
> que el tal tiempo ha de llegar?
>
> Yo tengo por herejía
> posar el entendimiento
> en tan torpe atrevimiento,
> y aquel que en tal confía
> espera su perdimiento.
>
> Que querer cojer aceite
> Sin plantar el olivar
> venirle ha por eso mal,
> y sin ganado deleite
> de leche es mala señal.
>
> Y el que no siembre la viña
> y la osa vendimiar,
> no piense bien esperar,
> que el que vive de rapiña
> a la horca va a parar.
>
> Y el que no siembra la tierra
> sin plantarla con sudor,
> quiere gustar su sabor,
> morirá en la justa guerra
> a manos del Plantador.
>
> Así que es cosa errada
> contra Dios Omnipotente
> pedirle el hombre posada
> dentro en su santa morada,
> si no le fuere obediente, etc. . . .

29. The original reads:

> Recibe mi ayuno en penitencia,
> Señor, de todo mal que he cometido;
> no permitas me falte tu clemencia
> pues ves con cuanta angustia te la pido;
> ensalzaré tu suma omnipotencia,
> será de mí tu nombre engrandecido
> y no me des, Señor, lo que merezco,
> pues ves que aún en pensarlo estremezco.
>
> Si te he ofendido gravemente,
> era por falta de entendimiento . . .

CC, Dec. 23, 1589, Feb. 16, 1590 (in *FNC* and *MNC I*); *LCM I,* Jan. 15, 1590 (pp. 86–91). Many who have written on the Carvajals have failed to realize that the appearance of the poem in the trial records of Luis de Carvajal the Younger does not automatically mean that he is the author. Nowhere in any of the trial records is authorship attributed to him, while Catalina's evidence points to authorship by Dr. Morales.

Failing to realize this fact, several writers have proceeded to attribute the composition to Luis. Thus, for example, Toro, *La familia Carvajal*, 1: 328; Liebman, *The Enlightened,* p. 49; "Carvajal, Luis de (El Mozo)," in *Enciclopedia de México,* 2: 384 (author unidentified). On the basis of this incorrect attribution, the writer of this article, following other writers, calls Luis a mystic. Luis did possess a mystical strain, perhaps influenced by Gregorio López (see chapter 6, below). While strong, this was not the predominant element in his complex personality. See also *Enciclopedia Judaica Castellana,* 2: 571, the probable source of the article.

Like other Judaizers, Dr. Morales's knowledge of Judaism was extremely limited. There is no evidence whatever that he knew any Hebrew, or had any acquaintance with rabbinic literature, or had a knowledge of the tradition of Judaism beyond a few practices, an even smaller number of prayers, and some explanations, all acquired second hand and all distorted. The Inquisition called him "rabbi and dogmatizer," and occasionally this fools an unsuspecting scholar into a posthumous and unmerited ordination of Dr. Morales.

30. *IRA*, Nov. 29, 1589; *LCM-A* (p. 470); *LCM II*, Feb. 25, 1595 (p. 241).
31. By inference from *FNC*, Jan. 16, 1590.
32. *GRC*, Apr. 20, 1589, and CC, Dec. 20, 1589 (in *FNC*). The verse is from Psalms 130:7–8. Gaspar's words are translated literally.
33. Reconstructed from information about inquisitorial procedure and trial records, especially *GRC*, and within *GRC*, especially Apr. 17, 1589.
34. *IRA*, July 3, July 10, 1589; *Gonzalo Pérez Ferro (Jr.),* Year 1589, AGN, *ID*, Vol. 126, Dossier 11, audiences beginning with arrest on Dec. 2, 1589.
35. *LCG*, Defense, Oct. 6, 1589 (pp. 331–32).
36. Reconstructed from *IRA*, Mar. 16, Apr. 11, 1589; *FNC*, May 13, 1589; *LCM I*, Aug. 9, Sept. 7, 1589 (pp. 46, 77); *LCG*, Apr. 17 (p. 282), Apr. 19 (pp. 289–90), Aug. 23 (pp. 302–3), Sept. 12 (p. 307), Oct. 6 (pp. 322–23, 335–36), Oct. 9 (p. 347), Oct. 25 (p. 349), Nov. 17 (p. 352), Nov. 21 (p. 355), 1589, Jan. 5, 1590 (pp. 356 ff.).
37. *MNC I*, Dec. 4, 1589, Jan. 17, 1590; CC, Dec. 20, 1589 (in *LCG*, pp. 273–74); *LCM I*, Sept. 7, 1589 (p. 77). Cf. *LCG*, Feb. 8, 1590 (pp. 358–59), Feb. 13, 1590 (p. 362).
38. *FNC*, May. 13, Nov. 13, 1589; *LCM I*, Sept. 7, 1589 (p. 77).
39. *LCG*, Feb. 13, 1590 (p. 362).
40. *LCG*, Apr. 17, 1589 (p. 282).
41. *FNC*, May 13, Nov. 13, 1589.
42. *LCG*, Apr. 17 (p. 282), Apr. 19, 1589 (pp. 289–90) and Defense, Oct. 6, 1589 (p. 332).
43. *LCG*, Defense, Oct. 6, 1589 (pp. 332–33).

44. *GRC,* Apr. 17, Aug. 23, 1589.
45. *GRC,* Oct. 16, 1589.
46. *GRC,* Apr. 18, Apr. 22, 1589.
47. *GRC,* Apr. 18, June 25, 1589.
48. *GRC,* Apr. 17, Apr. 18, 1589, Feb. 6, 1590.
49. *IRA,* Apr. 12, 1589.
50. *LCG,* Apr. 19, 1589 (p. 285).
51. Ibid. (pp. 289–90); *LCM I,* Oct. 20, 1589 (not in printed *LCM I,* but in manuscript and in *LCG,* p. 265).
52. *LCM I,* Aug. 9, Sept. 7, 1589 (pp. 49, 77); *LCG,* Oct. 9, 1589 (p. 347). It is unlikely, as Luis claimed (Sept. 7, 1589) that Baltasar tried to convert the governor to secret Judaism immediately after the incident with Isabel. All the testimony in the cases seems to indicate that some time elapsed.
53. *LCG,* Defense, Oct. 6, 1589 (pp. 334–35).
54. *LCG,* Apr. 19, 1589 (pp. 389–90); *LCM I,* Aug. 9, Aug. 12, 1589 (pp. 45, 67).

CHAPTER 5

1. *LCM I,* July 27, 1589 (p. 35).
2. *LCM I,* Aug. 9, 1589 (pp. 45 ff., 48 ff.), Aug. 11, 1589 (pp. 52 ff.), Aug. 12, 1589 (pp. 64 ff.); *MNC II,* May 30, 1600. On the gold coin, see especially CC, Dec. 20, 1589 (in *MNC I* and *FNC*); and *FNC,* Jan. 16, 1590. On the calendar, see especially *LCM I,* Aug. 9, 1589 (pp. 47–48), and the sentence against LCM, *LCM I* (p. 97).

The information on the conversations between Don Francisco and his son, derived entirely from LCM's first trial, appears to be basically trustworthy, despite one serious untruth told by LCM: Luis claimed that in these conversations his father indoctrinated him for the first time into Judaism. This fact is manifestly incorrect, as is shown from evidence in Luis's second trial and autobiography, and corroborated in the trial records of other members of his family.

It is known that Judaizers often pleaded that their activities were of recent origin and sought to implicate only the deceased, especially if they left no appreciable estate for the Inquisition to sequester. One might wonder under these circumstances whether Luis's entire testimony about his conversations with his father should therefore be dismissed as spurious.

Yet from this testimony it is patent that Luis had no intention of using the story of his indoctrination to shield his family. He implicated his mother and sister Isabel, both already under arrest, his brother Baltasar, a fugitive from the Inquisition, and his sisters Catalina and Leonor, both still free though on the brink of arrest. All of these, he claimed, were actively Judaizing before his indoctrination.

In view of the fact that Luis continued to work zealously with his uncle, maintained his position as heir apparent to the governorship, and returned to his uncle's side less than a month after his father's death, it is likely that Luis was not an unconditionally committed secret Jew, and that his father's deathbed conversations were intended to prepare him for the spiritual leadership of the family. It is a fact that it was eventually Luis and not Baltasar who assumed this leadership. Besides, nowhere in the trial records of any member of the family is there a suggestion that Don Francisco regarded any other member of the family, with the exception of Gaspar (see above, chapter 4) for this role.

Thus, while one cannot be certain about the details, I regard the above reconstruction as the most plausible.

3. See Cohen, "The Religion of Luis Rodríguez Carvajal," pp. 33 ff.; Roth, "The Religion of the Marranos," pp. 1 ff.; note 2 above. To this add *LCM I*, Aug. 7, 1589 (p. 40). Luis's claim that his father knew no Latin, found in *LCM I*, Aug. 11, 1589 (p. 56), is contradicted by the rest of his testimony. Cf. also *IRA*, Nov. 27, 1589, where Isabel, who knew Latin, said she overheard her father praying in that language. On the use of the title saint, see *LCM II*, Mar. 2, 1595 (p. 250); June 10, 1595 (p. 279); Feb. 14, 1596 (p. 356); Aug. 20, 1596 (p. 402); *LCM II, Last Will* (p. 414); *LCM-A* (p. 476). In the last four cases the word *santo* may be merely an adjective meaning holy, capitalized by the inquisitorial scribe. The belief in saints among the Judaizers, however, is well documented from other sources.

Writers unaware of Jewish practice occasionally attempt to equate the Judaizers' liturgy with the various forms that could be called normative for the Judaism of the time. Some even draw a parallel between the novelty in the Judaizers' liturgy and the innovations found in Conservative or Reform Judaism. But such analogies are misleading. Conservative and Reform Judaism, however original their forms may occasionally be, are direct descendants of the tradition of Judaism, with its Hebraic and rabbinic context. They are the products of lands where Judaism could be practiced openly and freely and where the traditions of Judaism were available for study. By contrast, the New Christians in Spain, Portugal, and their territories lived, after 1497, in lands where Judaism and Jewish studies were strictly forbidden. By the middle of the sixteenth century the chief source of Jewish knowledge available to them was the Vulgate. In addition, the Judaizers in New Spain had vague reminiscences of rabbinic customs and prayers handed down through the decades and amazingly limited in quantity and scope by the end of the sixteenth century. In the following century a small number of New Christians who had lived in lands like Italy, where Judaism was practiced openly, came to New Spain and brought with them a knowledge of more authentic traditions. But these cases were rare and they exerted but little influence on the practices of the Judaizers as a whole. See M.A. Cohen, "Some Misconceptions about the Crypto-Jews in Colonial Mexico," *AJHQ* 61 (1972): 288 ff.

4. *LCM II*, Aug. 14, 1596 (pp. 397–98); Aug. 30, 1596 (p. 406).

5. *LCM I*, Aug. 11, 1589 (p. 57).
6. *GRC*, Apr. 17, 1589.
7. *LCM I*, July 27, 1589 (p. 35), Aug. 11, 1589 (p. 57), and see below, note 8.
8. CC, Dec. 20, 1589 (in *MNC I*, and *FNC*); *MNC II*, May 30, 1600. Cf. *FNC*, Jan. 16, 1590. On the custom of placing a gold coin on the body of the deceased, practiced by the Jews of Portugal, see Alves, *Memorias arqueológico-históricas do Distrito de Bragança*, p. xc; and M. J. Pimenta Ferro, *Os Judeus em Portugal no século XIV*, p. 42, note 141.
9. *LCM I*, Aug. 7, 1589 (pp. 40–41); CC, Dec. 22, 1589 (in *MNC I*).
10. *LCM I*, Aug. 11, 1589 (p. 58).
11. *LCM I*, Aug. 7, 1589 (p. 41).
12. *LCM I*, Aug 9, 1589 (p. 47); *LCM-A* (p. 464); *LCM II*, Feb. 11, 1595 (pp. 222–23). Cf. *FNC*, Jan. 11, 1590.
13. *LCM I*, Aug. 9, 1589 (pp. 47–48).
14. Ibid. (p 50).
15. *LCM-A* (pp. 464–65); *LCM II*, Feb. 11, 1595 (p. 222); Feb. 15, 1595 (p. 231).
16. *LCM I*, Aug. 7, 1589 (p. 41).
17. *LCG*, Defense, Oct. 6, 1589 (pp. 341 ff.). Cf. Roel, *Nuevo León*, p. 8.
18. *LCG*, Defense, Oct. 6, 1589 (p. 341). Cf. Priestley, *The Coming of the White Man*, pp. 20–21.
19. Alessio Robles, *Monterrey en la historia y en la leyenda*, p. 88; idem, *Coahuila y Texas en la época colonial*, pp. 89, 114. See also M. Alessio Robles, *La ciudad del Saltillo* and *Perfiles del Saltillo*, modern portraits with sensitive insights into the city's heritage.
20. Alessio Robles, *Coahuila y Texas en la época colonial*, p. 113.
21. D.A. Cossío, *Historia de Nuevo León*, 1: 19; Alessio Robles, *Monterrey en la historia y en la leyenda*, pp. 40, 87, 103–4. On the legends regarding the founding of Monterrey, such as the one about the mythical Friar Cebrián de la Nada, see ibid., pp. 53 ff. Alessio Robles's contention that the Monterrey area was swarming with Jews or Judaizers has no basis in fact (see ibid., pp. 105 ff.). Cf. also J. Eleuterio González, *Colección de noticias y documentos para la historia del Estado de Nuevo León*, pp. xvi ff., 5–6.
22. *LCG*, Defense, Oct. 6, 1589 (p. 341); *LCM II*, Feb. 14, 1596 (p. 361). Cf. León, *Historia de Nuevo León*, p. 95.
23. Alessio Robles, *Coahuila y Texas en la época colonial*, p. 92, note 7; idem, *Monterrey en la historia y en la leyenda*, pp. 107–8.
24. Powell, *Soldiers, Indians and Silver*, p. 110.
25. León, *Historia de Nuevo León*, pp. 76–77, 86 ff.; Roel, *Nuevo León*, p. 22.
26. *LCG*, Defense, Oct. 6, 1589 (p. 341). This may well have been the journey begun by Espejo on November 10, 1582, with fourteen soldiers and a friar or priest. The primary object of this mission appears to have been the rescue of two Franciscan friars, Agustín Rodríguez and Francisco López, who had penetrated to the region of the upper Rio

Grande and had failed to return. See J.L. Mecham, "Antonio de Espejo and His Journey to New Mexico," *Southwestern Historical Quarterly* 30: 114 ff. Espejo's own account of the expedition surprisingly does not mention Carvajal. See G.P. Hammond and A. Rey, eds., *Expedition into New Mexico Made by Antonio de Espejo . . . , as Revealed in the Journal of Diego Pérez de Luxán . . . ,* pp. 45 ff. The royal decree for the conquest of New Mexico was dated April 19, 1583, and only in 1595 was Juan de Oñate awarded the conquest of New Mexico. See G.P. Hammond, *Don Juan de Oñate and the Founding of New Mexico,* pp. 10, 13. See also the instructions given to Juan de Oñate on October 21, 1595, and the acceptance of the contract on his behalf by Luis Núñez Pérez and Cristóbal de Oñate on December 15, 1595, in G.P. Hammond and A. Rey, *Don Juan de Oñate, Colonizer of New Mexico, 1595–1628,* 1: 65–69. The original documents are to be found in the Archivo General de Indias, Audiencia de México, *legajos* 26 and 24 respectively.

27. León, *Historia de Nuevo León,* p. 77.
28. Roel, *Nuevo León,* p. 22.
29. *LCG,* Defense, Oct. 6, 1589 (p. 343).
30. León, *Historia de Nuevo León,* p. 77.
31. *LCM I,* Aug. 7, 1589 (p. 41), where Luis says that his uncle "a esta sazón andaba por la Huaxteca"; *LCM I* and *LCG,* passim.
32. *LCM-A* (p. 468).
33. León, *Historia de Nuevo León,* p. 91.
34. For a description and pictures of contemporary armor, see J. Hefter et al., *Crónica del traje militar en México del siglo XVI al XX,* pp. 20 ff. See also Powell, "Spanish Warfare against the Chichimecas in the 1570s," pp. 593–94.
35. *LCM-A* (pp. 466 ff.).
36. *LCM-A* (pp. 465–66), and by inference from *LCM I,* Aug. 9, 1589 (p. 50), and passim.
37. Alessio Robles, *Monterrey en la historia y en la leyenda,* pp. 105 ff.; idem, *Coahuila y Texas en la época colonial,* p. 99; Parkes, *A History of Mexico,* p. 34; and Simpson, *Many Mexicos,* pp. 50 ff., 61 ff.
38. Simpson, *Many Mexicos,* p. 61; idem, *The Encomienda in New Spain,* pp. vii ff.
39. León, *Historia de Nuevo León,* p. 90.
40. Ibid. Cf. *LCG,* Defense, Oct. 6, 1589 (p. 326); *IRA,* April 11, 1589. Also intervening in Carvajal's apprehension was the inquisitorial scribe Juan Morlete. See Alessio Robles, *Coahuila y Texas en la época colonial,* p. 106; León, *Historia de Nuevo León,* pp. 93 ff. Cf. Lewin, *Mártires y conquistadores judíos en la América Hispana,* p. 26. The Huaxteca, named after the local Huaxtec Indians, refers to the region comprising the northern part of the present state of Veracruz, in the area of Tampico and westward, and the eastern part of the present state of San Luis Potosí. The official document (a royal rescript) of August 8, 1587, is to be found in R. Konetzke, *Colección de documentos para la historia de la formación social de Hispanoamérica, 1493–1810,* 1: 583–84.

41. *LCM-A* (p. 468).
42. Manuel de Lucena, Nov. 3, 1594 (in *JA III*); DDN, Jan. 3, 16, 17, 26, 1601 (also in *JA III*); *IRA,* Nov. 29, 1589; sentence of JA, *JA III* and, for Mariana's statement, *MNC II,* May 30, 1600. For an evocation of many of the past beauties of Taxco, as well as those of the present, see the descriptions in poetic prose in F. Monterde's *Perfiles de Taxco.*
43. *ADC,* Dec. 19, 1596.
44. *MNC II,* May 29, May 30, 1600.
45. *GRC,* Apr. 17, 1589. Cf. *IRA,* Apr. 12, Apr. 20, Sept. 12, Oct. 16, 1589, and dates of Gaspar's second visit.
46. *GRC,* Apr. 17, 1589.
47. *GRC,* Apr. 17, 1589; *IRA,* Apr. 20, Sept. 12, 1589.
48. *IRA,* July 5, 1589.
49. *GRC,* Apr. 18, 1589.
50. *LCM-A* (p. 468).
51. *FNC,* Jan. 16, 1590; *MNC II,* May 30, June 13, 1600.
52. *IRA,* Apr. 12, 1589.
53. *IRA,* Apr. 12, 1589; *MNC I,* Feb. 7, 1590.
54. *LCM-A* (p. 469).

CHAPTER 6

1. *LCM I,* May 12 (p. 15), Aug. 7, 1589 (p. 41). Michoacán, a state of extensive agricultural and mineral resources in modern Mexico, to the west of the State of Mexico, was a vast, sparsely inhabited region in Luis de Carvajal's day. Its present capital, Morelia, has many buildings dating from the viceregal period.
2. M. Othón de Mendizábal, "Carácter de la conquista y colonización de Zacatecas," *Obras Completas,* 5: 73 ff.; idem, "Compendio histórico de Zacatecas," ibid., pp. 83 ff., esp. pp. 113, 115, 151. See also "Guadalajara," *Enciclopedia Universal Ilustrada,* 26: 1494–95; M. Toussaint, *Tasco,* pp. 26–27.
3. See P.J. Bakewell, *Silver Mining and Society in Colonial Mexico, Zacatecas, 1546–1700,* pp. 12 ff. See also W. Jiménez Moreno, *Estudios de historia colonial,* pp. 99–100; S. Zavala, "La amalgama en la minería de Nueva España," *HM* 11: 416 ff. On the role that mercury played in the mining process after its introduction into the mines of Pachuca, see M.F. Lang, "La búsqueda de azogue en el México colonial," *HM* 18: 473 ff.
4. *LCM-A* (p. 469). For dress in sixteenth century New Spain see A. Carrillo y Gariel, *El traje en la Nueva España,* pp. 51 ff.
5. *JA II, Presentación,* April 14, 1590.
6. *LCM I,* Aug. 7, 1589 (p. 42); *MNC I,* Jan. 8, 1590, and subsequent hearings, passim; and Toro, *La familia Carvajal,* 1: 139.
7. *MNC II,* June 2, 1600.
8. Inferred from the circumstances; see *MNC II,* June 2, 1600, and following.

9. *MNC II*, June 13, 1600.
10. On ADC's slapping of Leonor, see *ADC*, Mar. 22, 1597; on his stabbing of Almeida, see *Hector de Fonseca*, AGN, *ID*, Vol. 158, Dossier 1, Feb. 25, 1597. Cf. also CC, Dec. 16 1589 (in *MNC I*). On the dating of these events beginning shortly after the marriages of Catalina and Leonor and the family's transfer to Mexico City, see *GRC*, Apr. 17, 1589.
11. *MNC II*, June 13, 1600.
12. *Hector de Fonseca*, May 4, 1598.
13. *MNC II*, June 13, 1600.
14. *MNC I*, Jan. 8, 1590. Cf. *MNC II*, May 30, June 2, June 5, 1600.
15. *MNC II*, May 30, 1600. This Jorge de León (de Andrada) is not to be confused with the Jorge de León appearing toward the middle of the seventeenth century, as, for example, in *ID*, Vol. 426 (AGN), f. 530.
16. *GRC*, Apr. 17, 1589.
17. Felipe Núñez, Sept. 22, 1589 (in *IRA*).
18. *LCM-A* (p. 469).
19. *LCM I*, Aug. 7, 1589 (p. 42); *FNC*, Aug. 23, 1589; *MNC I*, Jan. 17, Jan. 18, 1590. On the nature of mining operations in New Spain, see M. Othón de Mendizábal, "La minería y la metalurgia mexicanas, 1520–1943," *Obras Completas*, 5: 25 ff., and the comment by Henrie Hawk to the effect that the miners "were princes in the keeping of their houses and bountiful in all manner of things." Quoted from Hakluyt, *The Principal Navigations, Voyages, Traffiques and Discoveries*, 6 (London, 1926): 289, by Wolf, *Sons of the Shaking Earth*, p. 178.
20. *LCM I*, Aug. 7, 1589 (p. 42), and by inference from *LAC*, Dec. 23, 1589.
21. *LCM I*, Aug. 7, 1589 (p. 42).
22. *LCM-A* (p. 472).
23. *LCM II*, Feb. 25, 1595 (p. 248). Thus, for example, Gregorio López was called a "*siervo de Dios*." See M.A. Cohen, "Don Gregorio López: Friend of the Secret Jew," *HUCA* 38: 259 ff., especially p. 259, note 1. When Isabel wanted to explain that her uncle was an exemplary Christian, she called him a "*siervo de Dios*." See also above, chapter 5, p. 116 and note 53. *IRA*, July 24, 1589.
24. *LCM II*, Feb. 14, 1596 (p. 358).
25. *LCM II*, Feb. 8, 1596 (pp. 314, 316); *MNC II*, June 15, 1600. See also the trial record of Hector de Fonseca, AGN, *ID*, Vol. 158, Document 1, Feb. 25, 1597.
26. *LCM II*, Feb. 8, 1596 (p. 313).
27. *LCM II*, Feb. 10, 1596 (pp. 337–38).
28. *LCM II*, Feb. 12, 1596 (p. 354). For other Judaizers, see *LCM II*, Aug. 14, 1596 (p. 400) (Luis Díaz [Díez]); *LCM II*, Feb. 14, 1596 (p. 356) (Juan Méndez); and in this connection the statement by Luis on mutual confessions of Judaizing such as he and Juan Méndez made, in *LCM II*, Feb. 9, 1596 (p. 325); and, for Hernando Rodríguez de Herrera, the statements made by that Judaizer on September

25 and October 5, 1589, and found in *LCM I,* in the manuscript, but not included in the printed text of the trial.

29. *LCM II,* Feb. 10, 1596 (pp. 330 ff.); Cf. ML, Nov. 3, 1594 (in *JA III*). See chapter 1, note 37 and also the cases against Catalina Enríquez and Beatriz Enríquez. On Pachuca as a principal mining town, see Bakewell, *Silver Mining and Society,* p. 139.

30. *LCM II,* Feb. 9, Feb. 10, 1596 (pp. 328–29, 332); Aug. 14, 1596 (pp. 398–99).

31. *LCM II,* Feb. 15, 1595 (p. 151), Feb. 8 (pp. 311–12, 322), Feb. 17, 1596 (p. 371); Cohen, "Don Gregorio López: Friend of the Secret Jew," pp. 259 ff. Gregorio López is mentioned by numerous writers as a mystic. See, for example, J. Jiménez Rueda, "La secta de los alumbrados en la Nueva España," *BAGN* 16: 29–30. For additional remarks and reminiscences on Gregorio López, see Catalina de la Dueña, Dec. 29, 1597; Juan Salguero, Dec. 31, 1597; Mariana de Jesús, Jan. 11, 1598; and Juana de San José (Sanct Joseph), Jan. 11, 1598, all in *Juan Plata.*

32. *LCM-A* (pp. 469–70). See also *Antonio Machado, Isabel Machado, Isabel Clara, Blanca de Morales,* and *Antonio de Morales.*

33. *LCM II,* Sept. 30, 1596 (p. 423); *LCM-A* (pp. 469–70).

34. *LCM-A* (p. 470).

35. *LCM-A* (pp. 470–71).

36. *IRA,* Dec. 12, 1589. Contrary to statements occasionally found in the literature, there were no synagogue buildings in New Spain. Inquisition texts often use the word "synagogues" for the rooms where the Judaizers prayed, but these rooms lacked ark, Torah, prayer books, and the other traditional appurtenances of Jewish houses of worship. Just as often the term synagogue in these documents may refer to the group or quorum of Judaizers praying together. It is instructive to compare Luis de Carvajal's religion with that of Uriel da Costa in Amsterdam half a century later. See I. S. Révah, "La religion d'Uriel da Costa, Marrane de Porto," *Revue de l'histoire des religions* 161: 45–76, especially pp. 60 ff. See also Cohen, "The Religion of Luis Rodríguez Carvajal," pp. 33–62, and, for the broader picture of Judaizing practice, Roth, "The Religion of the Marranos," pp. 1–33.

37. *IRA,* Apr. 20, 1589; *LCM I,* Aug. 11, 1589 (p. 63); CC, Dec. 16, 1589 (in *FNC*); *MNC I,* Jan. 8, 1590; *FNC,* Jan. 10, 15, 16, 1590; *ALC,* Jan. 19, July 10, Aug. 17, 1590; *MNC II,* June 2, 1600.

38. *IRA,* Nov. 29, 1589; CC, Dec. 16, 1589 (in *IRA* and *FNC*); *LAC,* Dec. 19, 1589; *FNC,* Jan. 11, Jan. 15, 1590. The quotations are from *LAC,* Dec. 19, 1589.

39. CC, Dec. 16, 1589 (in *FNC* and *MNC I*).

40. *FNC,* Jan. 15, 1590.

41. *LCM I,* Aug. 11, Aug. 12, 1589 (pp. 63, 66–67) and Francisco Díaz, Feb. 19, 1592 (morning session), in *JA I.* Cf. Lea, *A History of the Inquisition of Spain,* 3: 300.

42. Don Francisco, his wife, and several of his children, but apparently not Luis, had celebrated the Great Day regularly in Pánuco. The family

continued the practice both in Mexico City and in Taxco. CC, Dec. 16, Dec. 23, 1589 (in *FNC* and *MNC I*); *LAC*, Dec. 19, 1589; *IRA*, Jan. 3, 1590; *FNC*, Nov. 13, 1589; *MNC II*, May 30, 1600.

43. *FNC*, Jan. 11, 1590.
44. *FNC*, Jan. 10, 1590.
45. *LAC*, Dec. 19, 1589. Cf. *FNC*, Jan. 10, 1590.
46. *FNC*, Jan. 10, 1590.
47. *IRA*, Mar. 23, 1589.
48. *IRA*, Apr. 24, 1589. Cf. *MNC I*, Jan. 8, 1590.
49. *FNC*, Jan. 11, 1590. For the Fast of Esther, see CC, Dec. 16, 1589 (in *FNC* and *IRA*); *FNC*, Nov. 13, 1589, Jan. 10, 1590; *MNC II*, May 29, May 30, 1600; Lea, *The Inquisition in the Spanish Dependencies*, p. 208.
50. *LCM I*, Aug. 9, 1589 (p. 47); IRA, Nov. 29, 1589 (in *FNC*); *MNC I*, Jan. 8, 1590; *FNC*, Nov. 10, 1589, Jan. 11, Sept. 28, 1590; *ALC*, July 10, 1590.
51. See preceding note, *IRA*, July 5, 1589, and CC, Dec. 16, 1589 (in *FNC*).
52. *LCM I, FNC, MNC I* and *IRA* passim, especially *IRA*, Mar. 16, 1589. See also Francisco Díaz, Feb. 19, 1592 (morning session), in *JA I*, for the possibility of a Sunday service.
53. *IRA*, Nov. 29, 1589; CC, Dec. 23, 1589 (in *FNC* and *MNC I*); *LCM I*, passim; and especially *MNC I*, Jan. 17, 1590.
54. CC, Dec. 16, 1589 (in *FNC* and *MNC I*); *LAC*, Dec. 19, 1589.
55. *LCM I*, Aug. 9, 1589 (pp. 51–52); CC, Dec. 16, 1589 (in *FNC* and *MNC I*); *IRA*, Nov. 27, 1589; *FNC*, Sept. 28, 1589, Jan. 11, 1590; and especially *MNC I*, Jan. 17, 1590.
56. Cf. above, chapter 4, and *LCM I*, Jan. 15, 1590 (pp. 86 ff.).
57. CC, Dec. 4, 11, 22, 23, 1589 (in *LAC*).
58. *IRA*, Nov. 29, 1589. CC, Dec. 4, Dec. 11, 1589 (in *LAC*).
59. Francisco Díaz, Feb. 19, 1592 (in *JA I*).
60. CC, Dec. 4, 11, 16, 20, 22, 23, 1589 (in *LAC, FNC, LCM I*, manuscript only, and *MNC I*); *LAC*, Dec. 19, 1589.
61. CC, Dec. 11, 1589 (in *LCM I*, in the manuscript only, not in the printed text).
62. *IRA*, Mar. 16, July 5, 1589.
63. *LCM I*, Aug. 12, 1589 (p. 69).
64. *LCM I*, Sept. 7, 1589 (p. 76); *IRA*, Nov. 27, 1589; CC, Dec. 22, 1589 (in *FNC*); *LAC*, Dec. 23, 1589.
65. *LAC*, Dec. 23, 1589; *MNC II*, May 30, June 2, 1600. On the declaration between the members of the family and their in-laws, see also *LCM II*, Feb. 14, 1596 (p. 362). See also ALC, Oct. 9, 1600 (in *ADC*). Here Anica, referring to the 1590s, states that Antonio Díaz de Cáceres occasionally did observe the Sabbath.
66. *IRA*, Aug. 29, 1589.
67. Francisco Díaz, Feb. 10, 19, 20, 24, Mar. 6, 1592 (in *JA I*).
68. *LCM I*, Aug. 11, 1589 (pp. 59–60); CC, Dec. 23, 1589 (in *FNC* and *MNC I*); *FNC*, Jan. 15, 1590.

69. *GRC,* Oct. 19, 1589.
70. *LCM-A* (pp. 472–73); *GRC,* Apr. 18, 1589, Feb. 6, 1590. See also *LCM II,* July 27, 1589 (Accusation, section 5). The Gospel quotation is from Matthew 5:17–18, translated from the Spanish in the trial records.
71. *GRC,* Apr. 20, 1589. See Psalms 68:19 (Vulgate 67:19) and 47:6 (Vulgate 46:6).
72. Psalms 147:20.
73. *LCM I,* Aug. 7, 1589 (p. 43).
74. *LCM-A* (p. 473).
75. CC, Dec. 23, 1589 (in *MNC I*).
76. Felipe Núñez, Mar. 7, Mar. 8, 1589, in *IRA* and *LCM I* (pp. 8 ff). Cf. also his testimony on Sept. 22, 1589 (in *IRA*).
77. Felipe Núñez, Mar. 7, 1589 (in *IRA* and *LCM I* [p. 11]).
78. *LCG,* Defense, Oct. 6, 1589 (p. 333).
79. Felipe Núñez, Mar. 7, 1589 (in *IRA* and *LCM I* [p. 11]).
80. *GRC,* Apr. 17, 1589.
81. Ibid.
82. Ibid.
83. *LCM I,* Aug. 11 (p. 61), Aug. 12, 1589 (p. 66).
84. *MNC II,* May 31, 1600.
85. *Expediente de las raciones diarias que recibían los presos de las cárceles secretas del Santo Oficio,* AGN, *ID,* Vol. 213, Dossier 12, Mar. 20, May 4, 1589.
86. Manuel Francisco de Belmonte, May 20, 1596, in *Miguel Hernández,* AGN, *ID,* Vol. 158, Dossier 2.
87. *LAC,* Dec. 23, 1589.
88. *LCM I,* Aug. 12, 1589 (p. 66); *FNC,* Sept. 30, 1589.
89. *LCG,* introduction (*Auto de prisión* and *Prisión,* p. 212).
90. *GRC,* beginning. Cf. ibid., *Accusation,* July 24, 1589.
91. See above, chapter 1, pp. 18–19.

CHAPTER 7

1. Lewin, *El Santo Oficio en América,* pp. 29 ff.; and idem, *La Inquisición en Hispanoamérica,* pp. 174 ff. See E. Pallares, *El procedimiento inquisitorial,* pp. 98 ff., and B. Llorca, *La Inquisición en España,* pp. 91 ff., where the author, a defender of the Holy Office, discusses the organization of the Inquisition.
2. Lewin, *El Santo Oficio en América,* pp. 60 ff.
3. *LCM I,* May 9, 1589 (pp. 7–8).
4. *LCM-A* (p. 475).
5. Ibid. On the secret prison, see Lea, *A History of the Inquisition of Spain,* 2: 507 ff. On life in the cells see M. de la Pinta Llorente, *Las cárceles inquisitoriales españolas,* pp. 149–92.
6. Pallares, *El procedimiento inquisitorial,* p. 154.
7. The Spanish term *auto de fe* is, of course, the equivalent of the more

commonly used *auto-da-fé*, which is Portuguese. On the background of the judicial use of torture, see D. Haek [pseud. Franz Helbing] and M. Bauer, *Die Tortur*, pp. 115–30; P. Fiorelli, *La tortura giudiziaria nel diritto comune*, 1: 99–101, 168–69, and passim; 2: passim; G. Martínez Díez, "La tortura judicial en la legislación histórica española," *Anuario de historia del derecho español* 32 (*Estudios en homenaje a Don Galo Sánchez*): 223–300. See also A. Baião, "O tormento segundo os códigos inquisitoriais," in *Episódios dramáticos da Inquisição portuguesa*, 2: 251–65.

8. *LCM I*, May 12, 1589 (p. 16).
9. Ibid.
10. *LCM I*, May 12, May 13, 1589 (pp. 17 ff.), and notations in his case dated June 2 and Nov. 2, 1589 (p. 19); ML, May 12, 1589 (in *BRC*).
11. *LCM I*, May 13, 1589 (pp. 20 ff.); *BRC, Auto de prisión*, Apr. 20, 1589.
12. *LCM I*, May 15, 1589 (pp. 23–24).
13. *BRC*, Letter of the inquisitorial commissary, Francisco López Rebolledo, May 20, 1589, and his deposition of June 8, 1589; also the declarations of Manuel Gómez de Silvera and Diego Márquez de Andrada and the testimony of Rodrigo de Avila and his brother-in-law, Diego de Espinosa, May 6, 1589.
14. *LCM I*, June 19, 1589 (pp. 24 ff.).
15. *IRA*, Mar. 16, 1589.
16. *IRA*, Mar. 18, 1589.
17. *IRA*, July 20, July 24, Aug. 1, Sept. 7, Dec. 12, 1589. Isabel also stated that her husband was a good Christian. Ibid., Dec. 12, 1589.
18. *IRA*, Mar. 23, Apr. 10, 11, 12, 14, 1589 (= in part *LCG*, pp. 215–20).
19. *LCG, GRC*, beginning of trial records.
20. *GRC*, Apr. 17, 1589. Cf. chapter 2, note 39 above.
21. *GRC*, Apr. 17, 18, 20, 22, Oct. 16, 19, 27, Nov. 8, 1589. The quotation is from Nov. 8.
22. *LCG*, Apr. 17, 1589 (p. 280).
23. Ibid. (pp. 280 ff.).
24. *LCG*, Apr. 19, 1589 (pp. 284 ff.).
25. *LCG*, Apr. 27, 1589 (pp. 291–92).
26. See the interesting note to this effect in Gonzalo Pérez Ferro, July 14, 1597 (in *ADC*) and the advice of the Conesjo de Indias to King Philip II, dated June 29, 1597. In this document, which mentions Lobo Guerrero's appointment to the archbishopric of New Granada, the Consejo stresses the need to appoint in Lobo Guerrero's place not Alonso de Peralta, "que es mozo para gobernar en aquella Inquisición" but rather a "persona de mucha experiencia y buena edad y de quien se tenga grande satisfacion [sic]." The document is found in M. Cuevas's *Documentos inéditos del siglo XVI para la historia de México*, pp. 463–64.
27. *LCM I*, July 27, 1589 (pp. 31 ff.).
28. Ibid (pp. 34 ff.).
29. *LCM I*, July 31, 1589 (p .37).

30. *LCM I*, Aug. 2, 1589 (pp. 37–38. Read "Aug. 2"; the transcript's "July 2" is an error).
31. Pallares, *El procedimiento inquisitorial*, p. 155.
32. *LCM I*, Aug. 7, 1589 (p. 40).
33. *LCM I*, Aug. 7, 9 (morning), 9 (afternoon), 11 (morning), 11 (afternoon), 12, 1589 (pp. 40 ff.).
34. *LCM I*, Aug. 14, Aug. 23, 1589 (pp. 71 ff.).
35. *LCM-A* (p. 475).
36. Ibid. (p. 476). On Francisco Ruiz de Luna, see Medina, *Historia . . . de la Inquisición en México*, pp. 108–9. For the date of his incarceration, see AGN, *ID*, Vol. 213, Documents 12 ff., 156–57.
37. *LCM-A* (p. 477).
38. Ibid. (p. 476).
39. Ibid. (p. 476).
40. *LCM II*, Feb. 15, 1595 (p. 234). It is quite conceivable that the name Lumbroso, a family name used by Jews in Spain, was somehow connected to the ancestry of Luis de Carvajal. We even find a Joseph Lumbroso in the company of Benveniste de la Caballería and Todros Abendauhuet in an Aragonese financial document drawn up after 1391. See I. (F.) Baer, *Die Juden im christlichen Spanien*, 1: 754–55. Baer's documents also record the complaint by a Don Lumbroso in Ciudad Rodrigo in 1492, and a grant by the queen to Lumbroso Abenaso, clearly the same person, of a hundred thousand maravedis for the wedding—probably the dowry—of his daughter "in recognition of the good services you have performed for me." Baer, ibid., 2: 426.
41. Cf. *LCM-A* (p. 477): "Our misfortune and trouble has reached such a state that if anyone professes and affirms it [the Law of Moses], these heretics [the inquisitors] inflict the greatest cruelties upon them and burn them alive."
42. *LCM I*, Sept. 7, Sept. 13, Oct. 21, 1589 (pp. 74 ff.). The testimony of Oct. 21 does not appear in the printed transcript of Luis's trial, but is found in *LCG* (pp. 266–67).
43. *LCM I*, Oct. 20, 1589 (pp. 82–83).
44. On the care exercised by the Inquisition in this regard, see the instruction in Pallares, *El procedimiento inquisitorial*, p. 157.
45. *LCG*, Sept. 18, Sept. 23, Oct. 6, 1589 (pp. 317 ff.). The final quotation is on p. 344.
46. Ibid., p. 346.
47. *FNC*, Nov. 10, 1589. Cf. her audiences prior to July 5, 1589.
48. *IRA*, Nov. 27, Nov. 29, 1589.
49. See testimony of respective trials at dates indicated. See also *LAC*, Dec. 15, Dec. 23, 1589; CC, Dec. 11, Dec. 16, 1589 (in *FNC* and *MNC I*); *MNC I*, Jan. 8, 17, 18, 1590.
50. See FNC, May 12, Nov. 10, 11, 14, 1589; Jan. 10, Jan. 11, 1590 (in *LCM I* [not in printed transcript]), and *LCM I*, Feb. 6, 1590, Sentence [p. 105]. The sentence claims that he even confessed to involvement with Judaizing in Benavente.

51. *LCM-A* (pp. 477–78).
52. Ibid. (pp. 478–79). The psalm in question is probably the thirty-third, which ends with the verse "Let Thy mercy, O Lord, be upon us,/According as we have waited for Thee" (Psalms 33:22). See also Psalms 119:41.
53. E. O'Gorman, ed., *Libro primero de votos de la Inquisición de México, 1573–1600*, pp. 128 ff.
54. Lea, *A History of the Inquisition of Spain*, 3: 72 ff. (cf. Pallares, *El procedimiento inquisitorial*, p. 158).
55. O'Gorman, *Libro primero de votos*, pp. 132, 133, 137–43.
56. Lea, *A History of the Inquisition of Spain*, 3: 215. In his *The Inquisition in the Spanish Dependencies*, p. 208, Lea makes the mistake of following the Inquisition and calling Francisco Rodríguez de Matos a "rabbi" and "dogmatizer." He also incorrectly lists the date of the trial as 1592 and confuses Governor Carvajal with his namesake.
57. Ibid., pp. 93 ff., 135 ff.
58. Lea, *The Inquisition in the Spanish Dependencies*, p. 216. Cf. idem, *A History of the Inquisition of Spain*, 2: 315 ff.
59. Lea, *A History of the Inquisition of Spain*, 3: 123 ff.; Toro, *La familia Carvajal*, 1: 336–37.
60. Lea, *A History of the Inquisition of Spain*, 3: 209 ff.
61. Medina, *La Inquisición en México*, p. 107.
62. Toro, *La familia Carvajal*, 1: 346.
63. See Medina, *La Inquisición en México*, p. 108. (cf. also p. 158) and, for Gonzalo Pérez Ferro, Jr., the sentence in his trial, *ID*, Vol. 126, Dossier 11.
64. O'Gorman, *Libro primero de votos*, p. 131; Medina, *La Inquisición en México*, p. 84.
65. *ALC*, Aug. 31, 1590.
66. O'Gorman, *Libro primero de votos*, pp. 128–29.
67. Lea, *A History of the Inquisition of Spain*, 3: 214 ff. Toro, *La familia Carvajal*, 2: 265. Cf. E. Glaser, "Invitation to Intolerance: A Study of the Portuguese Sermons Preached at Autos-da-fé," *HUCA* 27: 327 ff.
68. *LCM I*, Feb. 6, 1590 (pp. 91–92), and O'Gorman, *Libro primero de votos*, pp. 128, 138, 143.
69. See the respective cases and O'Gorman, *Libro primero de votos*, pp. 128–29, 132–33, 137–41.
70. *LCG*, Feb. 13, 1590 (pp. 362 ff.); O'Gorman, *Libro primero de votos*, pp. 129–30, 133, 143.
71. Cf. above, note 66.
72. Medina, *La Inquisición en México*, p. 109. Cf. Lea, *A History of the Inquisition of Spain*, 4: 95.
73. *GRC*, Aug. 1, Aug. 31, 1590, Aug. 12, 1591.
74. *LCM I*, Feb. 24, 1590 (pp. 108 ff.).
75. *LCG*, Feb. 26, 1590 (p. 372).
76. *ID*, Vol. 213, Dossier 12.
77. See respective cases, end.
78. *LCM I*, Mar. 5, 1590 (p. 111). Cf. Toro, *La familia Carvajal*, 1: 346, 349.

79. Order assigning Luis to the hospital, signed by the Inquisition's secretary, Pedro de los Ríos, on Mar. 5, 1590, and found in *LCM I,* end (p. 111).

CHAPTER 8

1. *LCM-A* (pp. 475, 482 ff.); *LCM II,* Feb. 25, 1595 (p. 242), Feb. 14, 1596 (p. 360), and reconstruction from the above. Rodríguez de Silva's house may have been the one mentioned as belonging to Jorge de Almeida in chapter 1. See chapter 1 above, note 38, and accompanying text.
2. Baltasar's letter (Nov. 15, 1590) in *LCM II,* Mar. 2, 1595 (pp. 252 ff.).
3. Roth, *The History of the Jews of Italy,* pp. 179–80, and, for the period beginning with 1585, pp. 317 ff. Cf. M.J. Benardete, *Hispanic Culture and Character of the Sephardic Jews,* pp. 41, 83–84.
4. Baltasar's letter, loc. cit. (p. 254).
5. Baltasar's letter (p. 257), *LCM II,* Feb. 14, 1596 (p. 364). This Duarte de León is not to be confused with Doña Francisca's grand-uncle of the same name, who was already dead. See *LCG,* Apr. 16, 1589 (p. 279).
6. The popes were Sixtus V and Urban VII. Both died in 1590.
7. These facts and numerous others in the paragraphs below are recorded in the *Libro de Antonio Díaz de Cáceres, maestre de la nao nombrada Nuestra Señora de la Concepción.* The book, better known as the *Libro de rol,* has long been missing from the AGN. See M. A. Cohen, "Antonio Díaz de Cáceres: Marrano Adventurer in Colonial Mexico," *AJHQ* 60 (1970–1971): 169 ff. For a summary and excerpts, see Toro, *La familia Carvajal,* 2: 56 ff.
8. On the Philippines, see A. de Morga, *History of the Philippine Islands,* 2 vols.; W.L. Schurz, *The Manila Galleon,* passim; and for the Philippine trade, P. Chaunu, *Les Philippines et le Pacifique des Ibériques.* See also Vietia Linaje, *The Spanish Rule of Trade to the West Indies,* p. 262. On the relations between New Spain and the Philippines, see L. González, "Expansión de Nueva España en el Lejano Oriente," *HM* 14: 206–26; L. Romero Solano, "La Nueva España y las Filipinas," ibid. 3: 420–31; M. del Cármen Velázquez, "Historia de América y Filipinas," ibid. 15: 638–60; and R. Bernal, "México en Filipinas," ibid. 14: 187–205. On Legazpi, see J.I. Rubio Mañé, "La expedición de Miguel López de Legazpi a Filipinas," *BAGN* (Second Series) 5: 427–798, and C. Quirino, "El primer mexicano en Filipinas," *HM* 14: 250–60.
9. Antonio Bocarro, chronicler in chief of the state of India, made this statement in 1635. It is quoted by C.R. Boxer in *Macau na época da restauração (Macau Three Hundred Years Ago),* p. 27. See also *ADC,* Introductory material; Schurz, *The Manila Galleon,* pp. 130 ff.; and the following additional works by C.R. Boxer: *Fidalgos in the Far East, 1550–1770: Fact and Fancy in the History of Macao,* pp. 29 ff., 40 ff; *The Great Ship from Amacon: Annals of Macao and the Old Japan Trade, 1555–1640,* with important documents, pp. 173 ff.; *Four Cen-*

turies of Portuguese Expansion: A Succinct Survey, especially pp. 16, 37, 41; "Missionaries and Merchants of Macao, 1557–1687," in *III Colóquio internacional de estudos luso-brasileiros: Actas*, 2: 211 ff.; *Portuguese Society in the Tropics: The Municipal Councils of Goa, Macao, Bahia and Luanda, 1510–1800*, pp. 42 ff.; *The Portuguese Seaborne Empire, 1415–1800*, pp. 42 ff.; *The Portuguese Seaborne Empire, 1415–1825*, especially pp. 39 ff. See also T. Chang, *Sino-Portuguese Trade from 1514 to 1644*, recently (1969) reproduced photomechanically, with a few corrections, from the first edition (1934).

10. *LCM-A* (p. 484 ff.); *ADC*, Introductory material.
11. *ADC*, preliminary material in the trial records, especially folios 79, 83. On smuggling and contraband in Acapulco, see Priestley, *The Coming of the White Man*, p. 188.
12. *JA I*, Introductory material; *ID*, Vol. 213, Dossier 2, Mar. 20, 1589.
13. *JA I*, June 17, June 18, 1590.
14. *LCM II*, Feb. 8, 1596 (p. 317); *JA II*, Apr. 14, 1590, and passim.
15. *LCM-A* (p. 484); *JA I*, letter from Morván dated July 10, 1590, and letter from Pedro de Medinilla, sent from the Taxco region on July 15, 1590, to announce "Luis de Morván's misfortune" and received in the capital on July 29. Both are found in the early pages of the trial record.
16. *LCM II*, Feb. 8, 1596 (pp. 316–17).
17. *JA I*, testimony of Julián de Castellanos in audiences of May 15, 25, 30, June 6, June 7, July 14, July 20, 1590.
18. *LCM II*, Feb. 8, 1596 (p. 316).
19. Letter of Jorge de Almeida, July 1595, in *LCM II* (pp. 169 ff.), and *Hector de Fonseca*, especially May 24, July 5, 1596, Feb. 25, 1597.
20. *JA I*, testimony of Francisco Díaz, Feb. 19, 1592 (afternoon hearing).
21. Ibid., Introductory material. The Francisco Rodríguez mentioned here is not identifiable with his namesake, Justa Méndez's husband, despite the latter's dealings with the Carvajal family. See *Francisco Rodríguez*, May 11, 1595, where we do not find Simon Gómez mentioned among his family. See also his testimony against IRA (folios 59–68) and ADC (folio 69) and passim.
22. Gaspar's letter is also found in *JA I*, Introductory material.
23. *LCM II*, Feb. 12, 1596 (pp. 344–45); *DDN*, Jan. 3, Jan. 10, 1601. Toro, *La familia Carvajal*, 2: 119, does not read this evidence correctly. He states that Diego Díez Nieto and his father arrived with the family's writs of liberty at the beginning of October 1594 (the ship arrived on October 2. See Chaunu and Chaunu, *Séville et l'Atlantique*, 3: 530), and that Domingo Cuello, who had arrived on the same ship, came to congratulate the Carvajals at that time. However, from a combination of the trial records of the family, especially *JA III*, and *Diego Díez Nieto*, which Toro does not mention, and the passage in *LCM II*, it is apparent that the Díez Nietos came to the New World in 1592 and had not left as of October 1594, and that Domingo Cuello's congratulations and his later contacts with Luis de Carvajal all took place beginning with the earlier date.

Diego Díez Nieto insisted that the name of Baltasar's wife was

Ana, not Esther, as was stated in the accusation against him (DDN, Jan. 26, 1601, in *JA III*). Mariana recalled her sister-in-law's name as Esther (*MNC II,* June 3, 1600).

In his first trial before the Inquisition, Diego Díez Nieto admitted that he had been born a Christian. Now that he claimed to have always been a Jew, he was subjected to an oath *more judaico* (DDN, Jan. 26, 1601, in *JA III*). But he could not long maintain his disguise as a Jew. For Almeida's letter, see *LCM II* (pp. 169 ff.) and note 19 above.

24. *LCM II,* Feb. 15, Mar. 2, 1595 (p. 234), July 12, 1596 (p. 383); Cf. LD, Feb. 10, 1595, in *LCM II* (pp. 154–55). Cf. also above, chapter 7, note 40.
25. *LCM-A* (pp. 479–80).
26. *ALC,* Feb. 9, 1592. *LCM-A* (p. 485) speaks of a female warden bringing little Ana to visit her family, and some, like Toro, *La familia Carvajal,* 2: 121, therefore assume the girl remained in jail. Since the evidence shows Ana to have been living at the home of Pedro de los Ríos, the "warden" appears to have been Ríos's wife or servant.
27. *LCM II,* Feb. 12, 1596 (pp. 349–50).
28. *LCM-A* (pp. 480–81).
29. *FNC,* Mar. 5, 1590. On the school at Santiago Tlatelolco, see T. Zepeda Rincón, *La instrucción pública en la Nueva España en el siglo XVI,* pp. 69 ff.; A.M. Carreño, "El colegio de Tlatelolco y la educación indígena en el siglo XVI," *Divulgación histórica* 1: 196 ff.; R. Ricard, *The Spiritual Conquest of Mexico,* pp. 221 ff.; and especially F.B. Steck, *El primer colegio en América: Santa Cruz de Tlatelolco.* See also J. Jiménez Rueda, *Historia de la cultura en México: El Virreinato,* pp. 265 ff.; V.G. Quesada, *La vida intelectual en la América española durante los siglos XVI, XVII y XVIII,* pp. 34 ff.
30. *LCM-A* (pp. 480–81).
31. For the life of Sahagún and bibliographical references, see "Sahagún, Fr. Bernardino de," in *Diccionario Porrúa,* pp. 1250–51.
32. *LCM-A* (pp. 478–79).
33. Ibid. (pp. 480–81); LD, Feb. 3, 1595 (in *LCM II,* p. 136).
34. The inventory of the library of the Colegio de Santa Cruz is found in J. García Icazbalceta's *Nueva colección de documentos para la historia de México,* 5: 255 ff. It was taken on or shortly after July 31, 1572.
35. *LCM-A* (pp. 481–82). On Oleaster, see for example, M.A. Cohen, "The Autobiography of Luis de Carvajal, the Younger," *AJHQ* 55: 302, note 110.
36. *LCM-A* (p. 482).
37. Ibid. (p. 486).
38. ML, Jan. 30, 1595 (in *LCM* II, pp. 128–29); *LCM II,* Feb. 15, 1595 (pp. 234 ff.); Feb. 9, 1596 (p. 326); and *Last Will* (p. 415).
39. *LCM II,* Mar. 13 (pp. 260–61), June 10, 1595 (pp. 262 ff.), Feb. 10, 1596 (p. 333).
40. *LCM II,* Feb. 8, (p. 322), Feb. 10, (p. 339), July 13, 1596 (p. 391).
41. *LCM II,* Feb. 9, 1595 (p. 221), July 12, 1596 (p. 387).

42. ML, Jan. 30, 1595 (in *LCM II*, p. 129).
43. ML, Jan. 30, 1595 (in *LCM II*, p. 134); LD, Feb. 3 (in *LCM II*, p. 137), Feb. 9 (ibid., p. 147), Feb. 10, 1595 (ibid. pp. 150, 154); Sebastián Rodríguez, July 6, 1595 (ibid., p. 210); LAC, June 2 (ibid. 201 ff.), Oct. 20, 1595 (in *MNC II*); *JM I*, Feb. 20, 1595; *LCM II*, Mar. 2 (pp. 250–51), June 10, 1595 (p. 278), Feb. 10 (p. 336), Aug. 20, 1596 (p. 402). Contrary to Liebman's assertion (in *The Enlightened*, p. 49), Luis's verse is not found in either J. García Gutiérrez's *La poesía religiosa en México* (the anonymous poems on pp. 33 ff. are not by him) or in A. Méndez Plancarte's *Poetas Novohispanos*.
44. *LCM II*, Feb. 15, 1595 (pp. 235 ff.), and Luis's letters, both those included within the trial (pp. 171 ff.) and those appended to it (pp. 499 ff.), especially the material found on pp. 509, 513, 527 (for messianism), and pp. 507, 515 ff. (for the idea of the divine origin of the family's afflictions).
45. Gaspar de los Reyes Plata, Jan. 10, 1596 (in *LCM II*, p. 184); Alonso Ortiz de Padilla, Jan. 16, 1596 (ibid., p. 212).
46. *LCM II*, Feb. 12, 1596 (pp. 345 ff.). On the importance of the sacrifice of Isaac among the Jews of the Middle Ages, and the various interpretations given it, see S. Spiegel, *The Last Trial*, pp. 17 ff.
47. *LCM-A*, beginning (p. 463). According to Toro, *La familia Carvajal*, 1: 15, the autobiography was in a booklet approximately nine by fifteen centimeters, bound in pasteboard and covered with embossed brown leather. It was written in very small letters, though in a clear, fine hand. Examples of Luis's writing can be seen in his *Last Will*, still attached to his trial records (second trial) and three of his letters, found in *JA II*, Introductory material and that dealing with his brother-in-law's business matters. The full spelling of the words "Adonay Sevaoth" (note that Luis did not apparently know or mark the sound of the Hebrew *tsade* in *Ṣevaot*) is reconstructed from his signature to the document in *LCM II*, Dec. 15, 1595. There, however, the word is spelled "Salvadth," the error most likely attributable to the inquisitorial scribe.
48. *LCM-A* (p. 482).
49. *LCM II*, Feb. 12 (p. 349), Feb. 17, 1596 (p. 372).
50. IRA, July 15, 1596 (in *MNC II*); Medina, *Historia . . . de la Inquisición en México*, pp. 108, 158. For incidents involving Antonio Díaz Márquez and young Carvajal, see ML, Jan. 11, 1595 (in *ADM*); LD, Feb. 3 (in *LCM II*, pp. 139, 143–44), Feb. 9, 1595 (in *LCM II*, p. 145); Pedro de Fonseca, Feb. 20, 1595 (in *LCM II*, p. 169); *LCM II*, Feb. 8 (p. 320), Feb. 9 (pp. 325–26), Feb. 10, 1596 (p. 342); IRA, July 13, 1596 (in *MNC II*); LAC, Aug. 3, 1596 (in *ADM*); FNC, Sept. 14, 1596 (ibid.); *ADM*, Feb. 10, 1597; *ADM, Conclusión*.
51. *LCM II*, Feb. 8 (p. 309), Feb. 9, 1596 (pp. 332–33); LD, Feb. 10, 1595 (in *LCM II*, p. 152). Cf. *Gabriel Enríquez*.
52. *LCM II*, July 13, 1596 (p. 393). Cf. *LCM II*, Feb. 8, 1596 (p. 320); LD, Feb. 10, 1595 (in *LCM II*, pp. 152–53).
53. *LCM II*, July 13, 1596 (p. 391).

54. LD, Feb. 3, 1595 (in *LCM II*, pp. 138, 140, 148–49); *LCM II*, Feb. 8, 1596 (p. 318), and by inference from *LCM-A* (pp. 495–96).

On Manuel de Lucena's visits to Luis de Carvajal the Younger at the *colegio*, see ML, Jan. 30, 1595 (in *LCM II*, pp. 127 ff.). Lucena claimed that these took place in the summer of 1593, but from other evidence it is obvious that the two men were fast friends again as early as 1591.

Other Judaizers of note met by Luis de Carvajal included Andrés Núñez, *LCM II*, Feb. 12, 1596 (pp. 352–53); a young Portuguese named Aillón, *LCM II*, Aug. 20, 1596 (pp. 402–3); Feliciano de Valencia, *LCM II*, Nov. 7, 1596 (pp. 438 ff.); Gaspar Pereyra, *LCM II*, Feb. 14, 1596 (p. 360); the husband of Leonor Díaz, Leonor Díaz herself, and Ana López, *LCM II*, Feb. 14, 1596 (p. 359); Antonio Rodríguez, *LCM II*, Feb. 10, 1596 (pp. 340–41); Simón Rodríguez, *LCM II*, Aug. 14, 1596 (pp. 396–97), LD, Apr. 26, 1596 (in *LCM II*, p. 213) and Diego López, Mar. 3, 1595 (in *LCM II*, p. 215); Pedro Rodríguez Saz, *LCM II*, Feb. 10, 1596 (pp. 330–31); Lucena's circle in Pachuca, *LCM II*, Aug. 20, 1596 (p. 402); and Manuel Díaz and Francisco Vaez, *LCM II*, Feb. 10, 1596 (p. 335); LD, Feb. 9, 1595 (in *LCM II*, p. 142).

55. LD, Feb. 9, 1595 (in *LCM II*, p. 142); Pedro de Fonseca, Feb. 20, 1595 (in *LCM II*, p. 167). *JM I*, Feb. 20, 1595; *LCM II*, Mar. 2, 1595 (p. 258), Oct. 14, 1596 (p. 427); LAC, May 29, 1595 (in *JM I*).

56. *LCM-A* (p. 480). Cf. *LCM II*, June 10, 1595 (pp. 276–77); LAC, June 3, 1595 (in *MNC II*); *MNC II*, June 6, 1600.

57. Susana Galván, Jan. 21, 1595 (in *LCM II*, p. 188). A curious note is found in the depositions of *Manuel Gil de la Guardia* on Oct. 3, 1603. He says that on Friday afternoons Ruy Díez Nieto "swept and washed his floor and put his room in order as if it were some holy temple."

58. *JM I*, Nov. 10, 1595; *LCM II*, Feb. 8, 1596 (p. 303). Cf. ML, Jan. 30, 1595 (in *LCM II*, p. 131); LAC, June 20, 1595 (in *MNC II*).

59. FNC, May 31, Sept. 1, 1595 (in *MNC II*); LAC, June (not July) 2, 1595 (in *LCM II*, p. 199).

60. ML, Jan. 30, 1595 (in *LCM II*, pp. 132–33). LAC, June 3, 1595 (in *MNC II*).

61. ML, Nov. 2, 1594 (in *MNC II*), Jan. 30, 1595 (in *LCM II*, pp. 131–32); LAC, May 29, 1595 (in *LCM II*, pp. 192 ff., and *MNC II*); *LCM II*, Feb. 8, 1596 (p. 319); *LC I*, Dec. 14, Dec. 15, 1600.

62. ML, Nov. 11, 1595 (in *LCM II*, pp. 134–35); FNC, Sept. 1, 1595 (in *MNC II*); LAC, June (not July) 2, 1595 (in *LCM II*, pp. 194 ff.), Oct. 21, 1595 (in *MNC II*); *LC I*, Jan. 2, 1601. In the original the poetic prayers read as follows:

Más quiero ser pregonero
de la casa del Señor
que no ser emperador
deste mundo entero

and

Si con tanto cuidado cada día
cantásemos loores al Señor

como Él tiene de darnos alegría
y en todas nuestras cosas su favor,
no fueran nuestros males tan contínuos,
no durara tan grande adversidad
de sus bienes todos nos haría dignos
y de poblar su santa ciudad. . . .

63. Duarte Rodríguez, May 21, 1596, in *Juan Rodríguez*. Cf. ML, Nov. 11, 1595 (in *LCM II*, p. 135).
64. Duarte Rodríguez, May 21, 1596 (in *Juan Rodríguez*) and ML, Nov. 2, 1594 (in *MNC* II).
65. LAC, June 2, 1595 (in *MNC II*); *LCM II*, Feb. 8, 1596 (pp. 304–5).
66. *LCM II*, Feb. 8, 1596 (p. 304); *JM I*, Nov. 10. 1595.
67. LAC, July 2, 1595 (in *LCM II*, p. 204); *LC I*, Dec. 24, 1600.
68. *MNC II*, June 7, 1600.
69. ML, Nov. 2, 1594 (in *MNC II*) and Jan. 30, 1595 (in *LCM II*, p. 131); LAC, Oct. 23, 1595 (in *MNC II*); *LCM II*, Feb. 8, 1596 (p. 302).
70. LAC, June (not July) 2, 1595 (in *LCM II*, p. 194).
71. LAC, Oct. 25, 1595 (in *MNC II*); *LCM II*, June 10, 1595 (p. 278). Cf. ibid., Feb. 14, 1595 (p. 229).
72. Pedro de Fonseca, Feb. 20, 1595 (in *LCM II*, p. 166), and note 73 below.
73. IRA, July 13, 1596 (in *MNC II*).
74. See, for example, *JM I*, Nov. 10, 1595.
75. *LCM II*, Feb. 8, 1596 (p. 302); IRA, July 13, 1596 (in *MNC II*).
76. Pedro de Fonseca, Feb. 9, 1595 (in *LCM II*, p. 164); ML, Jan. 30, 1595 (in *LCM II*, p. 131); *JM I*, Nov. 10, 1595; and IRA, July 15, 1596 (in *MNC II*).
77. See, for example, LAC, May 29, 1595 (in *JM I*); LAC, June 20, 1595 (in *MNC II*); *MNC II*, June 12, 1600; DDN, Jan. 18, 1601 (in *JA III*).
78. LAC, June 3, 1595 (in *MNC II*).
79. *Información sobre el cumplimiento de su penitencia* [*de Leonor*], Feb. 28, 1591, in *LAC*, concluding material.
80. ML, Nov. 13, 1594 (in *JM I*); *JM I*, Feb. 8, 1595, Apr. 4, 1596. See also *Catalina Enríquez*, wife of ML, and the case of JM's mother, *Clara Enríquez* and *LCM II*, Feb. 10, 1596 (p. 335).
81. *Catalina Enríquez*, Aug. 16, 1596; ML, Sept. 12, 1596 (in *MNC II*); cf. *MNC II*, June 2, 1600, and LAC, Nov. 7, 1595 (in *LCM II*, pp. 206 ff.). For additional information about Justa Méndez's Sabbath and holiday observance, see IRA, July 15, 1595 (in *MNC II*); LAC, Oct. 20, 1595 (in *MNC II*), Nov. 7, 1595 (in *LCM II*, pp. 206 ff.); *LCM II*, Feb. 8, (pp. 307–8), Feb. 9 (p. 324), Feb. 10 (p. 336), Aug. 30, 1596 (p. 409).
82. *LCM II*, Aug. 20, 1596 (p. 404). Querétaro, which did not figure in the Carvajals' journeys in New Spain (see map on p. 88) was already an important city in the sixteenth century. It is located a little less than 195 miles northwest of Mexico City.
83. *JM I*, Feb. 20, 1595.
84. LAC, Oct. 20, 1595 (in *MNC II*); *LCM II*, Feb. 9, 1596 (p. 324).
85. *JM I*, Sept. 1, 1595. Cf. *LCM II*, July 13, 1596 (pp. 388 ff.).

86. *JM I*, Nov. 10, 1595.
87. *JM I*, Feb. 20, 1595.
88. *LCM II*, Feb. 25, 1595 (p. 247); cf. *LCM-Letters* (pp. 173, 500, 507, 516).

CHAPTER 9

1. *ADC*, Mar. 22, 1597; *MNC II*, May 30, 1600. Cf. *LCM II*, Feb. 25, 1595 (p. 247).
2. DDN, Jan. 18, 1600 (in *JA III*); FNC, Sept. 26, 1596 (in *ADC*): "Si no hacía las ceremonias de la dicha ley era por temor de no ser preso por la Inquisición."
3. LAC, Oct. 21, 1595 (in *MNC II*); *LCM II*, Feb. 14, 1596 (p. 362); FNC, Sept. 26, 1596 (in *ADC*); DDN, Jan. 28, 1600 (in *JA III*); *MNC II*, May 30, Oct. 22, 1600; ALC, Oct. 11, 1600 (in *ADC*).
4. *LC I*, Dec. 14, 1600; *MNC II*, Jan. 2, 1601.
5. *MNC II*, June 5, 1600.
6. *MNC II*, June 6, 1600; *LC I*, Dec. 14, 1600.
7. *LC I*, Dec. 14, 1600.
8. ALC, Oct. 9, 1600 (in *ADC*); *MNC II*, Oct. 22, 1600.
9. *LC I*, Dec. 14, 1600; ALC, Oct. 11, 1600 (in *ADC*).
10. DDN, Jan. 18, 1600 (in *JA III*).
11. *ADC*, Feb. 1, 1597; ALC, Oct. 9, 1600 (in *ADC*).
12. DDN, Jan. 10, 1600 (in *JA III*).
13. *LCM-A* (pp. 487–88).
14. *LCM-A* (pp. 489–90).
15. *LCM-A* (p. 490). See above, chapter 8, p. 196.
16. *LCM-A* (pp. 490 ff.). On monasteries in New Spain, their number and architecture, see Kilham, *Mexican Architecture of the Vice-Regal Period*, p. 11, and passim.
17. LD, Feb. 10, 1595 (in *LCM II*, p. 151).
18. *LCM II*, Oct. 14, 1596 (pp. 424 ff.).
19. ML, Nov. 13, 1594 (in *JM I*); Manuel Rodríguez Navarro, Apr. 27, 1595 (in *JM I*); Duarte Rodríguez, May 21, 1596 (in *Juan Rodríguez*).
20. *Catalina Enríquez*, Jan. 31, 1595; *LCM II*, Feb. 14, 1595 (pp. 229–30).
21. *LCM II*, Feb. 10, 1596 (p. 341).
22. *LCM-A* (p. 492).
23. DDN, Jan. 16, 1600 (in *JA III*); *MNC II*, May 31, Oct. 22, 1600.
24. *MNC II*, Jan. 2, 1601.
25. ALC, Oct. 11, 1600 (in *ADC*).
26. LAC, Oct. 23, 1595 (in *ADC*).
27. *LCM-A* (p. 494).
28. *ADC*, Mar. 22, 1597.
29. ALC, Oct. 11, 1600 (in *ADC*).
30. *LCM-A* (p. 494).
31. *ADC*, Mar. 22, 1597.
32. Jorge de León, Mar. 27, 1597 (in *ADC*); Hector de Fonseca, Mar. 27, 1597 (in *ADC*).

33. *ADC*, Mar. 22, 1597.
34. *LCM-A* (p. 493); *LCM II*, Feb. 12, 1596 (p. 345).
35. *LCM-A* (p. 495). Removal of the *hábito* in *LCM I* (pp. 112-13).
36. *LCM-A* (p. 494).
37. Removal of the *hábito*, loc. cit.
38. LD, Feb. 3, 1595 (in *LCM II*, p. 137).
39. Letters from LCM to the Inquisition in *JA II*, pp. 584 ff.; letter from Jorge de Almeida (in *LCM II*, p. 170); *LCM II*, Feb. 9, 1595 (p. 221).
40. LD, Feb. 10, 1595 (in *LCM II*, p. 154).
41. LD, Feb. 3, 1595 (in *LCM II*, pp. 137-38).
42. LD, Feb. 10, 1595 (in *LCM II*, p. 154).
43. *LCM-A* (p. 495).
44. LD, Feb. 10, 1595 (in *LCM II*, pp. 148-49).
45. Ibid.; *LCM-A* (p. 495). See also *Manuel Gómez Navarro*, beginning.
46. *LCM-A* (p. 495).
47. Almeida's letter, loc. cit. Cf. also Chaunu and Chaunu, *Séville et l'Atlantique*, 3: 542 ff.
48. Document of imprisonment, *LCM II* (pp. 124-25); Susana Galván, Jan. 21, 1595 (in *LCM II*, pp. 186 ff.).
49. *LCM-Letters* (p. 500).
50. LD, Feb. 3, 1595 (in *LCM II*, p. 136); *LCM II*, Mar. 13, 1595 (pp. 260-61).
51. LD, Feb. 11, 1595 (in *LCM II*, pp. 159-60). According to Díaz, the roses represented the doctrine taught by Luis.
52. LD, Dec. 19, 1594 (in *ADM*); LD, Feb. 3, Feb. 11, 1595 (in *LCM II*, pp. 139, 157-58). Cf. Medina, *La Inquisición en México*, p. 133.
53. LD, Feb. 3, 1595 (in *LCM II*, pp. 136-37).
54. LD, Feb. 3, 1595 (in *LCM II*, pp. 137 ff.); Pedro de Fonseca, Feb. 9, 1595 (in *LCM II*, p. 162).
55. LD, Feb. 3, 1595 (in *LCM II*, p. 139); cf. the accusation against Luis, June 10, 1595 (p. 269).
56. *LCM-Letters* (pp. 501, 504, 506, 510, 527); *LCM II* (p. 173); LD, Feb. 11, 1595 (in *LCM II*, pp. 160-61).
57. LD, Feb. 11, 1595 (in *LCM II*, p. 156).
58. LD, Feb. 10, 1595 (in *LCM II*, pp. 154-55).
59. LD, Feb. 9, 1595 (in *LCM II*, pp. 145, 148, 151).
60. LD, Feb. 11, 1595 (in *LCM II*, p. 161).
61. Pedro de Fonseca, Feb. 9, 1595 (in *LCM II*, pp. 162 ff.).
62. LD, Feb. 11, 1595 (in *LCM II*, pp. 157-58). Cf. LD, Feb. 3, 1595 (in *LCM II*, p. 141).

CHAPTER 10

1. Report of Fray Alonso de Contreras to the Inquisition, *ID*, Vol. 158, Document 2, and Toro, *La familia Carvajal*, 2: 282-301.
2. *LCM II*, Feb. 11, Feb. 14, 1595 (pp. 221 ff.).
3. *LCM II*, Feb. 15, 1595 (pp. 231-32).

4. *LCM II*, Feb. 15, Feb. 25, Mar. 2, 1595 (pp. 232 ff.).
5. *LCM-Letters* (pp. 173, 501).
6. *LC I*, Dec. 14, 1600.
7. *LCM-Letters*, passim.
8. *LCM-Letters*, presented by Gaspar de los Reyes Plata, May 7, 19, and 20, 1595 (in *LCM II*, pp. 171 ff.).
9. Gaspar de los Reyes Plata, May 22, 1595 (in *LCM II*, p. 178).
10. *LCM-Letters* (pp. 499 ff.).
11. *LCM-Letters* (p. 506). Cf. letters presented by Gaspar de los Reyes Plata (in *LCM II*, pp. 175, 177).
12. *LCM-Letters* (pp. 519 ff.).
13. LD, Feb. 3, Feb. 9, 1595 (in *LCM II*, pp. 140–41); Pedro de Fonseca, Feb. 9, Feb. 20, 1595 (in *LCM II*, pp. 163, 166–67).
14. *LCM II*, June 10, 1595 (p. 284).
15. Ibid. (p. 285).
16. Ibid. (pp. 275 ff.).
17. Ibid. (especially pp. 279 ff.). Cf. González Obregón, *Las calles de México*, 2: 12.
18. *LCM II*, June 10, 1595 (p. 285).
19. *LCM II*, June 14, 1595 (p. 287).
20. *LCM II*, Oct. 30, Oct. 31, Nov. 4, 1595 (pp. 289 ff.).
21. *LCM II*, Dec. 15, 1595 (p. 294). In his *Relación historiada de las exequias funerales de la Magestad Del Rey Philippo Nuestro Señor*, Dionisio (Dionysio) de Ribera Flores (Flórez) claims that in his conversation with the Jesuits Luis affirmed, "Oh, damn the tribunal of the Holy Office. If it did not exist in this kingdom, I could count the Christians in it with these fingers." Ribera Flores goes on to say that Luis accompanied these words by stretching out his hand and adds that he uttered his statement with a devilish gesture, his face transfigured and his eyes ablaze, "like a rabid dog and famished lion who leaves the thicket of the forest . . . in search of prey." In J. García Icazbalceta, *Bibliografía mexicana del siglo XVI*, p. 449.
22. *Votos*, Feb. 6, 1596, in *LCM II* (pp. 297–98).
23. *LCM II*, Feb. 8, 1596 (p. 300).
24. Ibid. (p. 307).
25. *LCM II*, Feb. 8, 9, 10, 1596 (pp. 307 ff.).
26. *LCM II*, Feb. 12, Feb. 14, 1596 (pp. 355 ff.), and *Votos* (ibid., p. 365). See *LCM II* (manuscript) folios 374 recto to 377 verso. (The folio numbers in this case are correct and best identify the passage.)
27. *LCM II*, Feb. 15, 1596 (p. 366).
28. Ibid. (pp. 367–68).
29. See *LCM II*, Feb. 16, 1596 (p. 368).
30. *LCM II*, June 27, 1596 (pp. 380 ff.). Thus, possibly also July 13, 1596 (pp. 588 ff.), or July 14, 1596 (pp. 396 ff.), or Aug. 20, 1596 (pp. 402 ff.), or Sept. 28, 1596 (pp. 419 ff.), or Sept. 30, 1596 (pp. 422 ff.), or Oct. 21, 1596 (pp. 432 ff.), or Nov. 3, 1596 (pp. 436–37), or all of these.
31. IRA, July 13, July 15, Aug. 31, Nov. 12, 1596 (in *MNC II*).

32. *LCM II*, Aug. 24, 1596 (pp. 405–6).
33. In *LCM II*, Sept. 12, 1596 (pp. 412 ff.).
34. Actually, the numbers of paragraphs 5 and 9 are missing. Paragraph 5 is easy to detect between paragraphs 4 and 6, but the ninth section is not easy to detect between paragraphs 8 and 10.
35. Actually, August 1596 still belonged to the Hebrew year 5356. According to the Judaizers' calendar (see chapter 5 above), the year 5357 began on September 1. Perhaps we should read "this sixth month," that is, September, in Luis's date, counting from April, the first month in the biblical calendar.

CHAPTER 11

1. See *LCM II*, end (p. 457); Medina, *La Inquisición en México*, pp. 127 ff., where, however, Medina confuses Luis de Carvajal the Younger with his governor-uncle. For the time of Luis's last march and execution, see the declaration of Fray Alonso de Contreras in *LCM II*, end (pp. 457–58).
2. Medina, *La Inquisición en México*, pp. 109 ff.
3. Ibid., p. 121. See also G. García, ed., *Documentos inéditos o muy raros para la historia de México*, 25: 67 ff.
4. Medina, *La Inquisición en México*, pp. 121 ff.
5. A. de Contreras, "Relación verísima de la conversión y católica muerte de Luis de Carvajal," in Toro, *La familia Carvajal*, 2: 283.
6. Toro, *La familia Carvajal*, 2: 253 ff.; Medina, *La Inquisición en México*, pp. 121 ff.
7. Contreras, "Relación verísima," p. 284.
8. See note 6 above, and Medina, *La Inquisición en México*, pp. 123 ff. On sermons preached at autos-da-fé, see Glaser, "Invitation to Intolerance," pp. 327–85; idem, "Portuguese Sermons at Autos-da-Fé: Introduction and Bibliography," *Studies in Bibliography and Booklore* 2: 53–78, 96; A. Cassuto, "Bibliografia dos sermões de Autos-da-Fé impressos," *Arquivo de bibliografia portuguesa* 1: 293–345. See also above, chapter 7, note 67.
9. Contreras, "Relación verísima," p. 284.
10. *LCM II*, end (p. 456). On the cost and location of the *quemadero*, see Lea, *The Inquisition in the Spanish Dependencies*, p. 206, and *Guía de la Ciudad de México*, pp. 118 ff. For the description of the march and other aspects of an earlier auto-da-fé (1574), see also González Obregón, *México Viejo*, pp. 131 ff.
11. Contreras, "Relación verísima," p. 284; Lea, *The Inquisition in the Spanish Dependencies*, p. 206.
12. *LCM II*, end (p. 457).
13. Cf. note 5 above. See also Contreras's declaration in *LCM II*, end (pp. 457–58).
14. Contreras's written declaration, Dec. 9, 1596, in *LCM II*, end (pp. 458–59). On the sentences meted out to the family see O'Gorman, *Libro primero de votos*, pp. 300 ff. The sentence of Luis de Carvajal the

Younger is reprinted in M. León-Portilla, A. Barrera Vásquez, L. González, E. de la Torre, and María del Carmen Velázquez, eds., *Historia documental de México*, 1: pp. 298–302.

15. Contreras, "Relación verísima," pp. 293 ff.
16. Francisco de Soto Calderón, July 8, 1597, in *Ana de Guillamas*, alias Peralta. See also ibid., *Presentación*, and Manuela Martínez de León, July 19, 1597.
17. *Juan Plata*, June 19, 1600. For earlier background testimony regarding Manuel Tavares see *Juan Plata*, June 16 and 18, 1600.
18. See *MNC II*, end.
19. Bernardino Vázquez de Tapia, June 13, July 23, 1598 (in *MNC II*).
20. Luisa de Castilla, July 23, 1598 (in *MNC II*).
21. Bernardino Vázquez de Tapia, July 23, 1598 (loc. cit.). María de Peralta is called his grandmother here, but this is unlikely. Cf. *MNC II*, May 29, 1600, where she is called his mother.
22. Luisa de Castilla, loc. cit.
23. Ibid.; María de Peralta, July 23, 1598 (in *MNC II*).
24. *MNC II*, June 5, 1600. But cf. *MNC II*, May 29, 1600, where she said, referring to Judaism, that "she decided to withdraw from that blindness in which her soul was beclouded" in 1598.
25. *MNC II*, May 29, 1600.
26. *MNC II*, passim; Riva Palacio, *México a través de los siglos*, 2: 712 ff.
27. Medina, *La Inquisición en México*, pp. 135–36.
28. Ibid., pp. 131–32.
29. *ADC*, Dec. 19, 1596; Jan. 8, Jan. 15, Feb. 1, Feb. 4, Mar. 18, Mar. 22, 1597.
30. *ADC*, Mar. 22, 1597.
31. Testimony of Jorge de León, Catalina de León (wife of Gonzalo Pérez Ferro), Doña Ginebra (wife of Sebastián Rodríguez), Isabel (China), Alonso de Castro, Andrés de Mondragón, Diego Díez Nieto, Lucia (India), Pablo (Chino), and Hector de Fonseca, all on Mar. 27, 1597 (in *ADC*).
32. *ADC*, Apr. 18, 1597.
33. Testimony of witnesses in trial of *ADC*, beginning and passim.
34. Jorge Rodríguez, July 9, July 11, 1600 (in *ADC*).
35. *ADC*, Feb. 18, 1601.
36. *ADC*, Mar. 2, 1601.
37. *ADC, Votos*, Mar. 5, 1601. Cf. also Medina, *La Inquisición en México*, pp. 157. I do not know where Liebman, *The Enlightened*, p. 140, got the information that Díaz de Cáceres received a fine of a thousand duros (instead of ducats) and was sentenced to be exiled to Spain. Such information does not appear in his sentence or in any other document of the time.
38. *JA II*, beginning.
39. Juan Salado, Jan. 23, 1591; Gaspar Delgado, Jan. 24, 1591; Diego Díaz, Jan. 26, 1591; García de Saucedo, Jan. 28, 1591; Ana Núñez, Jan. 29, 1591; Antonio Díaz Márquez, Jan. 30, 1591; Fernando de Vega, Jan. 31, 1591; María Ortiz, Jan. 31, 1591; Cristóbal Gómez, Feb. 5, 1591;

Tomás de Fonseca, Feb. 6, 1591; Gonzalo Pérez Ferro, Feb. 14, 1591; all in *JA II*. Also *ADC*, Jan. 23, 1596 (folio 602 recto).

40. Documents relating to Felipe de Palacios, in *JA II*, folios 612 ff.

41. *JA III*, with sentence near end of case, its pronunciation attested to by the inquisitor Pedro de Mañozca.

42. *LC II*, Feb. 1, 1652. This took place after Leonor's first trial before the Inquisition in 1601. Liebman, *The Enlightened*, p. 140, states incorrectly that "after 1601 the only two lineal descendants of Francisco Rodríguez de Matos and Francisca de Carvajal in Mexico were Anica de Carvajal, daughter, and Leonor de Cáceres, granddaughter."

43. *LCM II*, Mar. 2, 1595 (pp. 258–59).

44. See, for example, G.B. de Rossi, *Historisches Wörterbuch der jüdischen Schriftsteller und ihrer Werke*, pp. 183–84; and "Lombroso, Jacob," *JE*, 8: 154.

45. C.B. Friedberg, ed., *Bet Eked Sefarim*, 2: 393, no. 1282. As a result, statements like those of G. Tibón, *Onomástica hispanoamericana*, p. 106, to the effect that Miguel "llegó a ser un famoso rabino en Salonica" are based on an uncritical acceptance of Luis's statement. In turn Tibón's error has been repeated constantly. The 1588 date for the first edition of the *Heshek Shlomo*, mentioned by Kayserling in his *Biblioteca Española-Portugueza-Judaica* (p. 64) raises certain questions in the mind of I. Sonne about the correctness of the attribution of the book to Jacob Lombroso, "Yaakov Lumbrozo ve-ha-Heshek Shlomo" (Hebrew), *Kiryat Sefer* 11 (1932): 499–506, especially pp. 499–500.

46. *JM I*, making no mention of Justa's marriage, and Luis de Carvajal's reference to her as a "blessed girl" on the day of his death (see above, note 9) indicate clearly that Justa Méndez was not married before her arrest by the Inquisition in February 1595. She probably married shortly after the removal of her penitential garb.

47. See decree in *JM I*, near end. See also *JM II*.

48. Ángel Guillaza, July 6, 1604, in *JM II*.

49. Andrés de Mondragón, Mar. 13, 1606, and Diego de Espinosa, Mar. 14, 1606, in *JM II*. On Clara Enríquez, see Medina, *La Inquisición en México*, pp. 171, 408.

50. Decree of June 4, 1608, implemented Sept. 23, 1608, in *JM I*, near end.

51. *ID*, Vol. 366, Dossier 27, Letter 4, folio 339a. The inquisitorial official communicated his knowledge in a letter dated Mar. 29, 1629.

52. *ID*, Vol. 373, Dossier 28, folios 259–60.

53. Blanca de Rivera, May 19, July 7, Oct. 2, 1642, in *ID*, Vol. 393, Dossier 6. This document has only seven folios, not 71 pages, as stated by S.B. Liebman, *A Guide to Jewish References in the Mexican Colonial Era, 1521–1821*, p. 39. See also testimony against Justa Méndez by Isabel Núñez, arrested for Judaizing in 1642, in *ID*, Vol. 415, Dossier 2, folio 264, and of Felipa de la Cruz in *ID*, Vol. 417, Dossier 16.

54. *JM III* is not available. Perhaps the testimony of Blanca de Rivera (see note 53 above) once formed part of the introductory section of the case. For the disposition of this case and the rest of the auto-da-fé of 1649, see Medina, *La Inquisición en México*, pp. 196 ff., especially p. 409.

55. See *LC II*, Feb. 1, Mar. 21, 1652.
56. See Medina, *La Inquisición en México*, pp. 203–4.
57. *LC I*, Dec. 14, Dec. 15, 1600. Ana's arrest was actually ordered on June 26, 1596. See O'Gorman *Libro primero de votos*, pp. 204, 206. Liebman, *The Enlightened*, p. 140, states that both Anica and young Leonor saw Mariana burned at the stake in 1601. This is incorrect. Reconciled prisoners of the Inquisition were not present at the *quemadero*.
58. *LC I*, Dec. 14, Dec. 15, 1600.
59. *LC II*, Feb. 1, Mar. 21, 1652.
60. Ibid. Cf. *LC II*, May 20, May 27, 1653.
61. *LC II*, Feb. 1, Mar. 21, 1652. Liebman, *The Enlightened*, p. 148, states that Leonor did not mention Luis's name during the hearings of 1652 and 1653. The evidence shows that she mentioned it on Feb. 1, 1652.
62. *LC II*, May 27, 1653.
63. Ibid.
64. *LC II, Votos*, June 25, 1653.
65. Testimony of Tristán de Lara on February 12, 1706, in *Petición de José de la Rosa*, AGN, *ID*, Vol. 560, Dossier 3.
66. Ibid.
67. The petition of José de la Rosa, in the case file marked *Petición de José de la Rosa*, loc. cit.
68. Ibid., passim, especially the testimony of Cristóbal de Fuentes, mestizo, on February 13, 1706, Tomás de Lira, on the same day, and Juana de Alemán, on February 14, 1706, as well as the inquisitorial audiences of May 6 and 7, 1706. On the family, see also M.A. Cohen, "Carvajal," *EJ* 5, cols. 220–22.
69. Medina, *La Inquisición en México*, pp. 243 ff.; Lea, *The Inquisition in the Spanish Dependencies*, pp. 231 ff. Lea's view that the auto-da-fé of 1649 "marks the apogee of the Mexican Inquisition" still stands despite the fact that the *Abecedario de los relajados, reconciliados, y penitenciados* lists numerous later cases. Cf. S.B. Liebman, "The Abecedario and a Check-list of Mexican Inquisition Documents at the Henry E. Huntington Library," *HAHR* 44: 555, and the *Abecedario* itself. See also R. Gómez, "Un auto de fe en el siglo XVII (Algunos datos desconocidos sobre este célebre suceso)," *BAGN* 14: 215–17, dealing with the auto-da-fé of April 11, 1649; and, in general, M.A. Cohen, "Latin America, Colonial Period," *EJ* 10, cols. 1448–49. For seventeenth-century secret Judaism in Europe, see Y.H. Yerushalmi, *From Spanish Court to Italian Ghetto—Isaac Cardoso: A Study in Seventeenth Century Marranism and Jewish Apologetics*.

On the problem of determining the number of Judaizers and the confusion in defining "Jew" and "Judaizers," see M.A. Cohen, "Some Misconceptions about the Crypto-Jews in Colonial Mexico," *AJHQ* 61: 277–93.
70. See, inter alia, León, *Historia de Nuevo León*, pp. 90 ff., and Alessio Robles, *Coahuila y Texas en la época colonial*, pp. 101 ff., 180–81.
71. C. Landis, *Carabajal, the Jew: A Legend of Monterey* (sic), passim.
72. Alessio Robles; *Monterrey en la historia y en la leyenda*, pp. 55 ff.

Bibliography

OF SECONDARY SOURCES

Abecedario de los relajados, reconciliados, y penitenciados, Mexico City, 1561 (with additions to the beginning of the eighteenth century).

Adler, Cyrus. "Trial of Jorge de Almeida by the Inquisition in Mexico." *PAJHS* 4 (1896): 29–79.

Aguirre Beltrán, Gonzalo. *La población negra de México.* Mexico City, 1946.

———. "The Slave Trade in Mexico." *HAHR* 24 (1944): 412–31.

———. "Tribal Origins of Slaves in Mexico." *Journal of Negro History* 31 (1946): 269–352.

Alamán, Lucas, ed. *Diccionario universal de historia y geografía.* 7 vols. Mexico City, 1853–1855, and 3 appendixes, 1855–1856.

Alba, Rafael. *Nuevo León: Reseña Geográfica.* Paris–Mexico City, 1810.

Albanés, Ricardo. *Los judíos a través de los siglos.* Mexico City, 1939.

Alcambar, José. *O Estatismo e a Inquisição.* n.p. [Regua?], [1956].

Alcedo, Antonio de. *Diccionario geográfico-histórico de las Indias occidentales.* 5 vols. Madrid, 1786.

Alessio Robles, Miguel. *La ciudad de Saltillo.* Mexico City, 1932.

———. *Perfiles del Saltillo.* Mexico City, 1937.

Alessio Robles, Vito. *Coahuila y Texas en la época colonial.* Mexico City, 1938.

———. *Monterrey en la historia y en la leyenda.* Mexico City, 1936.

———. *Saltillo en la historia y en la leyenda.* Mexico City, 1934.

Almansa, Javier Ruiz. "La problación de España en el siglo XVI: Estudio sobre los recuentos de vecindario de 1594, llamados comúnmente 'Censo de Tomás González.'" *Revista internacional de sociología* 3 (1945): 114–36.

Altamira y Crevea, Rafael. *Historia de España.* Vol. 2. Madrid, 1928.

Alves, Francisco M. *Memorias arqueológico-históricas do Distrito de Bragança, Os Judeus no Distrito de Bragança.* Bragança, 1925.

Amador, Elías. *Bosquejo histórico sobre Zacatecas.* Zacatecas, 1892.

Amador de los Ríos, José. *Estudios históricos, políticos y literarios sobre los judíos de España*. Madrid, 1848.

————. *Historia social, política y religiosa de los judíos de España y Portugal*. 3 vols. Madrid, 1875.

Ameal, João. *História de Portugal*. Porto, 1940.

Anchel, Robert. *Les Juifs de France*. Paris, 1946.

Apenes, Ola. *Mapas antiguos del Valle de México*. Mexico City, 1947.

Aquinas, Thomas. *Summa Theologica*. Translated by the Fathers of the Dominican Province. 3 vols. New York, 1947–1948.

Arleguí, J. *Crónica de la Provincia de San Francisco de Zacatecas*. Mexico City, 1737.

Arregui, Domingo Lázaro de. *Descripción de la Nueva Galicia*. Edited by François Chevalier. Seville, 1946.

Artíñano y Galdácano, Gervasio de. *La arquitectura naval española*. Madrid, 1914.

————. *Historia del comercio con las Indias durante el dominio de los Austrias*. Barcelona, 1917.

Asensio, Eugenio. "El erasmismo y las corrientes espirituales afines." *Revista de filología española* 36 (1952): 31–99.

Assaf, Simha. *Be-Oholei Yaakov* [Hebrew]. Jerusalem, 1943.

Astraín, Antonio. *Historia de la compañía de Jesús*. 6 vols. Madrid, 1909–1920.

Aydelotte, Frank. "Elizabethan Seamen in Mexico and Ports of the Spanish Main." *AHR* 48 (1942): 1–19.

Azevedo, J. Lúcio d'. *História dos Christãos-Novos portugueses*. Lisbon, 1921.

Bab, Arthur. "Carvajal (Caravajal), Luis de." *Enciclopaedia Judaica* [German]. Vol. 5, cols. 62–63.

————. "Die Juden im Amerika spanischer Zunge (1492–1916)." *Jahrbuch für jüdische Geschichte und Literatur* 26 (1925): 95–146; 28: 139–65.

Baer, Itzhak [Fritz]. *Die Juden im christlichen Spanien*, 2 vols. Berlin, 1929–1936.

————. *Toledot ha-Yehudim bi-Sefarad ha-Noṣrit*. Tel Aviv, 1959. Translated into English by Louis Schoffman as *A History of the Jews in Christian Spain*. 2 vols. Philadelphia, 1961–1966.

Baez Camargo, Gustavo. *Protestantes enjuiciados por la Inquisición en Iberoamérica*. Mexico City, 1960.

Baião, Antonio. *Episódios dramáticos da Inquisição portuguesa*. 3 vols. Porto, 1919; Rio de Janeiro, 1924; Lisbon, 1938.

————. *A Inquisição em Portugal e no Brasil*. Lisbon, 1921.

Bailey, Helen Miller and Nasatir, Abraham P. *Latin America*: *The Development of Its Civilization*. Englewood Cliffs, New Jersey, 1960.

Bakewell, P.J. *Silver Mining and Society in Colonial Mexico, Zacatecas, 1546–1700*. Cambridge, England, 1971.

Balbuena, Bernardo de. *Grandeza Mexicana*. Edited by Francisco Monterde. Mexico City, 1941.

Ballesteros y Beretta, Antonio. *Historia de España y su influencia en la historia universal*. 10 vols. Barcelona, 1941–1958.

Bancroft, Hubert H. *History of Mexico*. 6 vols. San Francisco, 1882–1887.

————. *History of the North Mexican States and Texas*. 2 vols. San Francisco, 1884–1889.

Baron, Salo Wittmayer. *A Social and Religious History of the Jews*. 15 vols. to date. New York, 1952–.

Barros, João de. *Rópica Pnefma*. Edited by I.S. Révah. 2 vols. Lisbon, 1952–1955.

Bataillon, Marcel. *Érasme et l'Espagne: Recherches sur l'histoire spirituelle du XVIe siècle*. Paris, 1937.

————. *Erasmo y España: Estudios sobre la historia espiritual del siglo XVI*. Translated, with corrections and additions, by Antonio Alatorre. Mexico–Buenos Aires, 1966.

Baxter, Sylvester. *Spanish-Colonial Architecture in Mexico*. 10 vols. Boston, 1901.

Bédarride, I. *Les Juifs en France, en Italie et en Espagne*. Paris, 1861.

Beinart, Haim. *Anusim be-Din ha-Inqviziṣia* [Conversos on Trial by the Inquisition] [Hebrew]. Tel Aviv, 1965.

————. "The *Converso* Community in 15th Century Spain." *The Sephardi Heritage*. Edited by R.D. Barnett. London, 1971, pp. 425–56.

————. "The *Converso* Community in 16th and 17th Century Spain." *The Sephardi Heritage*. Edited by R.D. Barnett, London, 1971, pp. 457–78.

————. "La formación del mundo sefardí." *Actas del primer simposio de estudios sefardíes*. Edited by Jacob M. Hassan, with the collaboration of María Teresa Rubiato and Elena Romero. Madrid, 1970, pp. 43–48, and discussion on pp. 371–76.

————. "The Judaizing Movement in the Order of San Jerónimo in Castile." *Scripta Hierosolymitana* 7 (1961): 167–92.

————. *Ha-Mishpatim mi-Ta'am ha-Inqviziṣia be-Toledo neged ha-Mityahadim bi-Tekufat ha-Gerush u-ve-Dorot ha-Rishonim le-aḥar ha-Gerush* [Trials of the Judaizers by the Toledan Inquisition: From Its Establishment till the Beginning of the Sixteenth Century] [Hebrew]. Jerusalem, 1955.

————. "Ha-Nidonim be-Vet-Din ha-Inqviziṣia she be-Toledo" ["The Defendants before the Inquisitorial Court in Toledo"] [Hebrew] *Tarbiz* 26 (1957–1958): 71–86.

————. "The Records of the Inquisition as a Source of Jewish and Converso History." *Proceedings of the Israel Academy of Sciences and Humanities* 2 (1967): 211–27.

————. "Two Documents concerning Confiscated Converso Property." *Sefarad* 17 (1957): 280–313.

Beltrán y Rezpide, Ricardo. "América en tiempo de Felipe II según el cosmógrafo-cronista Juan López de Velasco." *Revista de las Españas* 1 (1926): 187–96.

Benardete, Maír José. *Hispanic Culture and Character of the Sephardic Jews*. New York, 1952.

Benítez, Fernando. *Los primeros mexicanos* [*La vida criolla en el siglo XVI*]. Mexico City, 1962.

Berger, M. "Briev von a Marranen" [Yiddish]. *Annual of the American Branch of the Yiddish Scientific Institute* 1 (1938): 185–216.

Bermúdez Plata, Cristóbal. *Catálogo de pasajeros a Indias durante los siglos XVI, XVII y XVIII.* 3 vols. Seville, 1940–1946.

Bernal, Ignacio. *Mexico before Cortez.* Garden City, New York, 1963.

Bernal, Rafael. "México en Filipinas." *HM* 14 (1964–1965): 187–205.

Bernáldez, Andrés. *Historia de los Reyes Católicos,* 2 vols. Seville, 1870.

Blanco-Fombona, Rufino. *El conquistador español del siglo XVI.* Madrid, 1922.

Boehmer, Eduard. *Bibliotheca Wiffeniana: Spanish Reformers of Two Centuries, from 1520.* 3 vols. London, 1874–1904.

Bolton, Herbert E. *Explorations on the Northern Frontier of New Spain, 1535–1706.* Berkeley, 1915.

———. "The Mission as a Frontier Institution in the Spanish-American Colonies." *AHR* 23 (1917–1918): 42–61.

———. *The Spanish Borderlands.* New Haven, 1921.

Borah, Woodrow Wilson. *New Spain's Century of Depression.* Berkeley, 1951.

Bossom, Alfred C. *An Architectural Pilgrimage in Old Mexico.* New York, 1924.

Bourne, Edward Gaylord. *Spain in America, 1450–1580.* Edited by Benjamin Keen. New York, 1962.

Boxer, Charles R. *Fidalgos in the Far East, 1550–1770: Fact and Fancy in the History of Macao.* The Hague, 1948.

———. *Four Centuries of Portuguese Expansion: A Succinct Survey.* Johannesburg, 1961.

———. *The Great Ship from Amacon: Annals of Macao and the Old Japan Trade, 1555–1640.* Lisbon, 1959.

———. *Macau na época da restauração (Macau Three Hundred Years Ago).* Macao, 1942.

———. "Missionaries and Merchants of Macao, 1557–1687." *Colóquio internacional de estudos luso-brasileiros: Actas.* Vol. 2. Lisbon, 1960, pp. 210–24.

———. *The Portuguese Seaborne Empire, 1415–1825.* London, 1969.

———. *Portuguese Society in the Tropics: The Municipal Councils of Goa, Macao, Bahia and Luanda, 1510–1800.* Madison and Milwaukee, Wisconsin, 1965.

Boyd-Bowman, Peter. "La emigración peninsular a América: 1520 a 1539." *HM* 13 (1963): 165–92.

Braamcamp Freire, Anselmo. "Povoação de Trás os Montes no XVI. século." *Archivo histórico portuguez* 7 (1909): 241–90.

Braden, Charles S. *Religious Aspects of the Conquest of Mexico.* Durham, North Carolina, 1930.

Brandi, Karl. *The Emperor Charles V.* London, 1939.

Braudel, Fernand. *La Méditerranée et le monde méditerranéen à l'époque de Philippe II.* 2 vols. Paris, 1966.

Braunstein, Baruch. *The Chuetas of Majorca.* New York, 1936. (Reprinted with new introduction by the author, New York, 1972.)

Brebner, John Bartlet. *The Explorers of North America, 1492–1806.* London, 1933.

Brondo, Whitt E. *Nuevo León.* Mexico City, 1935.

Cantera Burgos, Francisco. "Fernando de Pulgar y los conversos." *Sefarad* 4 (1944): 295–348.

———. *El poeta Cota y su familia de judíos conversos.* Madrid, 1970.

Carande Thovar, Ramón. *Carlos V y sus banqueros.* 2 vols. Madrid, 1943–1949.

Caro Baroja, Julio. *Los judíos en la España moderna y contemporánea.* 3 vols. Madrid, 1961.

———. *La sociedad criptojudía en la corte de Felipe IV.* Madrid, 1961.

Carreño, Alberto María. "El colegio de Tlatelolco y la educación indígena en el siglo XVI." *Divulgación histórica* 1 (1940): 196–202.

———. "Una desconocida carta de Fray Pedro de Gante." *MAMH* 20 (1961): 14–20.

———. "Luis de Carvajal (El Mozo)." *MAMH* 15 (1956): 87–101.

———. *La vida económica y social de Nueva España al finalizar el siglo XVI.* Mexico City, 1944.

Carrera Stampa, Manuel. "Planos de la ciudad de México." *Boletín de la Sociedad Mexicana de Geografía y Estadística* 67 (1949): 265–431.

Carrillo y Gariel, Abelardo. *El traje en la Nueva España.* Mexico City, 1959.

Casas, Gonzalo de las. *La guerra de los chichimecas.* Edited by José F. Ramírez. Mexico City, 1944.

Caso, Alfonso. "Los barrios antiguos de Tenochtitlán y Tlatelolco." *MAMH* 15 (1956): (7)–63.

Cassuto, Alfonso. "Bibliografia dos sermões de Autos-da-Fé impressos." *Arquivo de bibliografia portuguesa* 1 (1955): 293–345.

Castro, Américo, *España en su historia: Cristianos, moros y judíos.* Buenos Aires, 1948.

———. *La realidad histórica de España.* Mexico City, 1954.

———. *The Structure of Spanish History.* Translated by Edmund L. King (based on *España en su historia: cristanos, moros y judíos*). Princeton, New Jersey, 1954.

Castro y Rossi, Adolfo de. *Historia de los judíos de España.* Cadiz, 1847.

———. *A History of Religious Intolerance in Spain.* London, 1853.

"Catálogo de Pobladores de Nueva España." *BAGN* 13 (1942): 95–197.

Cavo, Andrés. *Los tres siglos de México durante el gobierno español.* 3 vols. and supplement. Mexico City, 1836–1838.

Cervantes de Salazar, Francisco. *México en 1554.* Edited by Joaquín García Icazbalceta. Mexico City, 1939.

Chang, T'ien-tsê. *Sino-Portuguese Trade from 1514 to 1644* (reproduction of Leiden, 1934, edition, with a number of corrections). Leiden, 1969.

Chapman, Charles Edward. *Colonial Hispanic America: A History.* New York, 1933.

Chaunu, Huguette and Chaunu, Pierre, *Séville et l'Atlantique, 1504–1650.* 8 vols. Paris, 1955–1960.

Chaunu, Pierre. *Les Philippines et le Pacifique des Ibériques (XVIᵉ, XVIIᵉ, XVIIIᵉ siècles).* Paris, 1960.

———. "Veracruz en la segunda mitad del siglo XVI y primera del XVII." *HM* 9 (1959–1960): 521–57.

Chávez Orozco, Luis. *Historia de México.* 2 vols. Mexico City, 1934–1940.

Cheetham, Nicolas. *Mexico: A Short History.* New York, 1971.

Chevalier, François. *Land and Society in Colonial Mexico.* Berkeley 1963.

Chueca Goitia, Fernando and Torres Balbás, Leopoldo. *Planos de ciudades iberoamericanas y filipinas existentes en el Archivo de Indias.* 2 vols. Madrid, 1951.

Cirot, Georges. *Recherches sur les Juifs espagnols et portugais à Bordeaux.* Bordeaux, 1908.

Cohen, Martin A. "Antonio Díaz de Cáceres: Marrano Adventurer in Colonial Mexico." *AJHQ* 60 (1970–1971): 169–84.

———. "The Autobiography of Luis de Carvajal, the Younger," *AJHQ* 55 (1965–1966): 277–318.

———. "A Brief Survey of Studies Relating to Luis de Carvajal, the Younger," *The American Sephardi* 3 (1969): 89–90.

———. "Carvajal." *EJ* 5, cols. 220–22.

———. "Don Gregorio López: Friend of the Secret Jew." *HUCA* 38 (1967): 259–84.

———. *The Jewish Experience in Latin America.* 2 vols. Waltham, Massachusetts, 1972.

———. "Latin America, Colonial Period." *EJ* 10, cols. 1448–49.

———. "The Letters and Last Will and Testament of Luis de Carvajal, the Younger," *AJHQ* 55 (1965–1966): 451–520.

———. "Marrano." *EJ* 11, col. 1018.

———. "Marrano Diaspora." *EJ* 11, cols. 1019–25.

———. "New Christians." *EJ* 12, col. 1022.

———. "The Religion of Luis Rodríguez Carvajal." *AJA* 20 (1968): 33–62.

———. "Some Misconceptions about the Crypto-Jews in Colonial Mexico." *AJHQ* 61 (1971–1972): 277–93.

———. "Treviño de Sobremonte, Tomás." *EJ* 15, cols. 1379–80.

Colby, Charles C. *Source Book for the Economic Geography of North America.* Chicago, 1921.

Colección de documentos inéditos para la historia de Hispano-América. Vol. 11. *Publicaciones del Instituto Hispano-Cubano de Historia de America (Sevilla); Catálogo de los fondos americanos del archivo de protocolos de Sevilla, Tomo 2—Siglo XVI.* Madrid–Barcelona–Buenos Aires, [1930].

Conway, G.R.G. *An Englishman and the Mexican Inquisition, 1556–1560.* Mexico City, 1927.

———. "Hernando Alonso, a Jewish Conquistador with Cortes in Mexico." *PAJHS* 31 (1928): 9–31.

———. "List of the Sanbenitos of the Condemned Jews Placed in the Cathedral Church of Mexico between 1528 and 1603." *PAJHS* 21 (1928): 26–31.

Cook, Sherburne F. and Simpson, Lesley Byrd. *The Population of Central Mexico in the Sixteenth Century.* Berkeley, 1948.

Corominas, Juan. *Diccionario crítico etimológico de la lengua castellana.* 4 vols. Bern, 1954–1957.

Cortés, Hernán. *Cartas y documentos.* Edited by Mario Hernández Sánchez-Barba. Mexico City, 1963.

Cossío, David Alberto. *Historia de Nuevo León*. 6 vols. Monterrey, 1926–1933.

Cossío, José L. *Del México Viejo*. Mexico City, 1934.

Coulton, George G. *The Death Penalty for Heresy from 1184 to 1917 A.D. Medieval Studies,* Second Series, No. 18. London, 1924.

———. *Inquisition and Liberty*. Boston, 1959.

Cuevas, Mariano. *Documentos inéditos del siglo XVI para la historia de México*. Mexico City, 1914.

———. *Historia de la iglesia en México*. 5 vols. Mexico City, 1921–1928.

———. *Historia de la nación mexicana*. Mexico City, 1940.

Cuevas Aguirre y Espinosa, José Francisco de. *Extracto de los autos de diligencias y reconocimientos de los ríos, lagunas, vertientes y desagües de la capital México y su valle*. Mexico City, 1748. Reproduced in facsimile, Mexico City, 1907.

Cumberland, Charles C. *Mexico: The Struggle for Modernity*. New York, 1968.

Dahlgren, Charles B. *Historic Mines of Mexico*. New York, 1883.

Davidson, Basil. *The African Slave Trade: Precolonial History, 1450–1850*. Boston, 1961.

Davies, R. Trevor. *The Golden Century of Spain, 1501–1621*. New York, 1965.

Davis, David Brion. *The Problem of Slavery in Western Culture*. Ithaca, New York, 1966.

Del Hoyo, Eugenio. "Don Martín de Zavala y la minería en el Nuevo Reino de León," *Humanitas. Anuario del Centro de estudios humanísticos* (of the University of Nuevo Leon), 4 (1963): 411–26.

Della-Pergola, Sergio. "Pisa." *EJ* 13, cols. 561–63.

Diário de Lisboa. (Controversy regarding the Inquisition and the New Christians.) May 6, 13, 27; June 3, 17; July 15, 22, 29; August 5, 12, 19, 26; September 2, 1971.

Dias, Manuel Nunes. *O capitalismo monárquico português (1415–1549): Contribuição para o estudo do capitalismo moderno*. 2 vols. Coimbra, 1963–1964.

Díaz del Castillo, Bernal. *Historia verdadera de la conquista de la Nueva España*. Edited by J. Ramírez Cabañas. 2 vols. Mexico City, 1960.

———. *The True History and Conquest of Mexico*. Translated by Maurice Keatinge. 2 vols. New York, 1927.

Diccionario Porrúa de historia, biografía y geografía de México. Mexico City, 1964.

Domínguez Ortiz, Antonio. "Los conversos de origen judío después de la expulsión," *Estudios de historia social de España* 3 (1955): 223–345. Published separately also, Madrid, 1957.

———. *La clase social de los conversos en Castilla en la Edad Moderna*. Madrid, 1955.

———. "Los *cristianos nuevos*: Notas para el estudio de una clase social," *Boletín de la Universidad de Granada* 21 (1949): 249–97.

———. *The Golden Age of Spain 1516–1659*. Translated by James Casey. London, 1971.

———. "Historical Research on Spanish Conversos in the Last 15 Years," in *Collected Studies in Honour of Americo Castro's Eightieth Year.* Edited by Michael P. Hornik. Oxford, 1965, pp. 63–82.

———. *Los judeoconversos en España y América.* Madrid, [1970].

Douais, Célestin. *L'Inquisition: Ses orignes, sa procédure.* Paris, 1906.

Dubnow, Simon. *Divre Yeme Am Olam* [Hebrew]. 10 vols. Tel Aviv, 1948.

Durán, Diego. *The Aztecs: The History of the Indies of New Spain.* Translated with notes by Doris Heyden and Fernando Horcasitas. New York, 1964.

———. *Historia de las Indias de Nueva España e islas de la tierra firme.* Edited by Ángel María Garibay. 2 vols. Mexico City, 1967.

Elliott, J.H. *Imperial Spain, 1469–1716.* London, 1963.

Encinas, Diego de. *Cedulario Indiano.* Madrid, 1596. Reproduced in facsimile, ed. A. García Gallo. 4 vols. Madrid, 1945.

Enciclopedia Judaica Castellana, s.v. "Carvajal y de la Cueva, Luis de" (2:576–79); "Carvajal (El Mozo), Luis de" (2:571–76).

Enciclopedia Universal Ilustrada Europeo-Americana. 70 volumes and additional volumes of appendixes and supplements. Madrid, 1958– .

Escriche, Joaquín. *Diccionario razonado de legislación y jurisprudencia.* 4 vols. Madrid, 1874–1876.

Espejo, Cristóbal and Paz, Julián. *Las antiguas ferias de Medina del Campo.* Valladolid, 1912.

Farinelli, Arturo. *Marrano: Storia di un vituperio.* Geneva, 1925.

Fernández del Castillo, Francisco. *Libros y libreros en el siglo XVI.* Mexico City, 1914.

Fernández Duro, Cesáreo. *La armada española desde la unión de las coronas de Castilla y León.* 9 vols. Madrid, 1895–1903.

———. *Disquisiciones náuticas.* 6 vols. Madrid, 1876–1881.

Fiorelli, Piero. *La tortura guidiziaria nel diritto comune.* 2 vols. Milan, 1953–1954.

Fisher, Lillian E. *Viceregal Administration in the Spanish-American Colonies.* Berkeley, 1926.

Forteza y Pinya, Miquel. *Els descendents dels jueus conversos de Mallorca. Quatre mots de la veritat.* Palma, 1966.

Friedberg, C.B., ed. *Bet Eked Sefarim* [Hebrew]. 4 vols. Tel Aviv, 1951–1956.

Friede, Juan. "Algunas observaciones sobre la realidad de la emigración española a América en la primera mitad del siglo XVI." *Revista de Indias* 12 (1952): 467–96.

———. "The *Catálogo de Pasajeros* and Spanish Emigration to America to 1550." *HAHR* 31 (1951): 333–48.

Füllöp-Miller, René. *The Jesuits: A History of the Society of Jesus.* New York, 1956.

Gage, Thomas. *A New Survey of the West Indies, 1648.* New York, 1929.

Gama Barros, Henrique de. "Judeus e Mouros em Portugal em tempos passados." *Revista Lusitana* 34 (1936): 165–265; 35 (1937): 161–238.

García, Genaro and Pereyra, Carlos, eds. *Autos de fe de la Inquisición de México . . . 1646–48 (Documentos inéditos o muy raros para la historia de México.* Vol. 28). Mexico City, 1910.

————. *El clero de México durante la dominación española (Documentos inéditos o muy raros para la historia de México.* Vol. 15.) Mexico City, 1907.

————. *La Inquisición de México (Documentos inéditos o muy raros para la historia de México.* Vol. 5). Mexico City, 1906.

García, Trinidad. *Los mineros mexicanos.* Mexico City, 1895.

García Cubas, Antonio. *Diccionario geográfico, histórico y biográfico de los Estados Unidos Mexicanos.* 5 vols. Mexico City, 1888-1891.

García Gutiérrez, Jesús. *La poésia religiosa en México (siglos XVI a XIX).* Mexico City, 1919.

García Icazbalceta, Joaquín. *Bibliografía mexicana del siglo XVI.* Edited by Agustín Millares Carló. Mexico City, 1954.

————. *Colección de documentos inéditos para la historia de México.* 2 vols. Mexico City, 1858–1866.

————. *Don Fray Juan de Zumárraga, primer obispo y arzobispo de México.* New ed. Revised by Rafael Aguayo Spencer and Antonio Castro Leal. Madrid, 1929.

————. "Education in the City of Mexico during the Sixteenth Century." Translated by Walter J. O'Donnell. *Texas Catholic Historical Society, Preliminary Studies* 1 (1931), no. 7: 1–61.

————. *La instrucción pública en la ciudad de México durante el siglo XVI.* Mexico City, 1893.

————. *Nueva colección de documentos para la historia de México.* 5 vols. Mexico City, 1886–1892.

García de Proodián, Lucia. *Los judíos en América.* Madrid, 1966.

García Pimentel, Luis. *Descripción del arzobispado de México hecha en 1570 y otros documentos.* Mexico City, 1897.

————. *Relación de los obispados de Tlaxcala, Michoacán, Oaxaca y otros lugares en el siglo XVI.* Mexico City, 1904.

Gardiner, C. Harvey. *Naval Power in the Conquest of Mexico.* Austin, 1956.

Gibson, Charles. *The Aztecs under Spanish Rule: A History of the Indians of the Valley of Mexico, 1519–1810.* Stanford, California, 1964.

————. *Spain in America.* New York, 1966.

————. *Tlaxcala in the Sixteenth Century.* New Haven, 1952.

Gilman, Stephen. *The Spain of Fernando de Rojas: The Intellectual and Social Landscape of LA CELESTINA.* Princeton, 1972.

Girard, Albert. *Le commerce français à Séville et Cadix au temps des Hapsbourg.* Paris, 1932.

Glaser, Edward. "Invitation to Intolerance: A Study of the Portuguese Sermons Preached at Autos-da-fé." *HUCA* 27 (1957): 327–85.

————. "Portuguese Sermons at Autos-da-fé: Introduction and Bibliography." *Studies in Bibliography and Booklore* 2 (1955): 53–78, 96.

————. "Referencias antisemitas en la literatura peninsular de la Edad de Oro." *Nueva Revista de Filología Hispánica* 8 (1954): 39–62.

Glick, Thomas F. Review of Miquel Forteza y Pinya's *Els descendents dels jueus conversos de Mallorca. Quatre mots de la veritat,* in *Jewish Social Studies* 33 (1971): 230–32.

Goldmann, Jack. "The Tragic Square of Don Luis de Carvajal y de la Cueva." *The Historian*. Autumn 1946, pp. 69–82.

Gómez, Rodolfo. "Un auto de fe en el siglo XVII (Algunos datos desconocidos sobre este célebre suceso)." *BAGN* 14 (1943): 215–17.

———. "Dos documentos relativos a Luis de Carvajal, el Viejo." *BAGN* 22 (1951): 551–58.

Gómez de Cervantes, Gonzalo. *La vida económica y social de Nueva España al finalizar el siglo XVI*. Edited by Alberto María Carreño. Mexico City, 1944.

González, J. Eleuterio. *Colección de noticias y documentos para la historia del Estado de Nuevo León*. Monterrey, 1867.

González, Luis. "Expansión de Nueva España en el Lejano Oriente." *HM* 14 (1964–1965): 206–26.

González Obregón, Luis. *Las calles de México*. 2 vols. Mexico City, 1941.

———. *México Viejo*. 2 vols. Mexico City, 1891–1895.

———. *México viejo y anecdótico*. Paris, 1909.

———. *Rebeliones indígenas y precursores de la independencia mexicana en los siglos XVI, XVII, XVIII*. Mexico City, 1952.

———. *The Streets of Mexico*. Translated by Blanche Collet Wagner. San Francisco, 1937.

González Peña, Carlos. *Historia de la literatura mexicana*. Mexico City, 1966.

Gosse, Philip. *The Pirates' Who's Who*. London, 1924.

Gratianus (Gratian, the Canonist). *Decretum Magistri Gratiani*. Edited by Aemilius Friedberg. Leipzig, 1959.

Green, Otis Howard. *Spain and the Western Tradition: The Castilian Mind in Literature from El Cid to Calderón*. 4 vols. Madison, Wisconsin, 1963–1966.

——— and Leonard, Irving A. "On the Mexican Book Trade in 1600: A Chapter in Cultural History." *HR* 9 (1941): 1–40.

Greenleaf, Richard E. *Zumarraga and the Mexican Inquisition*. Washington, D.C., 1961.

———. *The Mexican Inquisition of the Sixteenth Century*. Albuquerque, 1969.

Griffin, Charles C. and Warren, J. Benedict, *Latin America: A Guide to the Historical Literature*. Austin, Texas, 1971.

Gringoire, Pedro. "Protestantes enjuiciados por la Inquisición." *HM* 11 (1961–1962): 161–79.

Grunebaum-Ballin, P. *Joseph Naci, duc de Naxos*. Paris, 1968.

Grünwald, Max. "Note sur les Marranes à Rouen et ailleurs." *REJ* 89 (1930): 381–84.

Guerra, Santos. *Terras da Guiné e Cabo Verde*. Lisbon, 1956.

Guía de la Ciudad de México. Mexico City, 1964.

Guiraud, Jean. *Histoire de l'Inquisition au moyen âge*. 2 vols. Paris, 1935–1938.

Guttmann, Heinrich. "Marranen und Apostaten unter den spanischen Juden." In *Jewish Studies in Memory of Michael Guttmann*, edited by Samuel Löwinger. Budapest, 1946, pp. 129–74.

Haek, David [pseud. Franz Helbing] and Bauer, Max. *Die Tortur: Geschichte der Folter in Kriminalverfahren aller Zeiten und Völker.* Berlin, 1926.

Hakluyt, Richard. *The Principal Navigations, Voyages, Traffiques and Discoveries of the English Nation.* 12 vols. Glasgow, 1903–1905.

Hamilton, Earl. *American Treasure and the Price Revolution in Spain, 1501–1650.* Cambridge, Massachusetts, 1934.

Hammond, George P. *Don Juan de Oñate and the Founding of New Mexico.* Santa Fe, 1927.

——— and Rey, Agapito. *Don Juan de Oñate, Colonizer of New Mexico.* 2 vols. Albuquerque, 1953.

———, eds. *Expedition into New Mexico Made by Antonio de Espejo 1582–1583, as Revealed in the Journal of Diego Pérez de Luxán, a Member of the Party.* Los Angeles, 1929.

Hanke, Lewis. *The Spanish Struggle for Justice in the Conquest of America.* Philadelphia, 1949.

Haring, Clarence H. *The Spanish Empire in America.* New York, 1947.

———. *Trade and Navigation between Spain and the Indies in the Time of the Hapsburgs.* Cambridge, Massachusetts, 1918.

———. "Trade and Navigation between Spain and the Indies: A Review, 1918–1948." *HAHR* 40 (1960): 53–62.

Hefter, Joseph et al. *Crónica del traje militar en México del siglo XVI al XX. Artes de Mexico,* Vol. 15 (1968): 3–114.

Helps, Arthur. *The Spanish Conquest in America.* Edited by M. Oppenheim. 4 vols. London, 1900–1904.

Henríquez Ureña, Pedro. *A Concise History of Latin American Culture.* Translated with a supplementary chapter by Gilbert Chase. New York, 1966.

Herculano, Alexandre. *História da origem e estabelecimento da Inquisição em Portugal.* 3 vols. Lisbon, 1896–1897.

———. *History of the Origin and Establishment of the Inquisition in Portugal.* Translated by John C. Branner. Stanford, 1926 (This edition has been reprinted twice, New York, 1968, and, with an introduction by Y. H. Yerushalmi, New York, 1972.)

Hermann, Paul. *The Great Age of Discovery.* Translated by Arnold J. Pomerans. New York, 1958.

Hernández, Francisco. *Antigüedades de la Nueva España.* Translated from the Latin by Joaquín García Pimentel. Mexico City, 1945.

Hernández Millares, Jorge and Carrillo Escribano, Alejandro. *Atlas Porrúa de la República Mexicana.* Mexico City, 1966.

Herrera y Tordesillas, Antonio de. *Historia general de los hechos de los castellanos en las islas y tierra firme del mar Océano.* Vol. 2. Madrid, 1934.

Hurtado, Juan and González-Palencia, Ángel. *Historia de la literatura española.* Madrid, 1949.

Instrucciones que los virreyes de Nueva Epsaña dejaron a sus sucesores. Mexico City, 1867.

Jacobs, Joseph. *An Inquiry into the Sources of the History of the Jews in Spain.* London, 1894.

Jiménez Moreno, Wigberto. *Estudios de historia colonial.* Mexico City, 1958.

———. "El noreste de México y su cultura." *MAMH* 19 (1960): 176–87.

Jiménez Rueda, Julio. *Corsarios franceses e ingleses en la Inquisición de la Nueva España.* Mexico City, 1945.

———. *Herejías y supersticiones en la Nueva España.* Mexico City, 1946.

———. *Historia de la cultura en México: El Virreinato.* Mexico City, 1960.

———. "Proceso contra Francisco de Sayavedra, por erasmista 1539." *BAGN* 18 (1947): 1–15.

———. "La secta de los alumbrados en la Nueva España." *BAGN* 16 (1945): 5–31.

Kahane, Henry and Kahane, Renée. "Christian and Un-Christian Etymologies." *Harvard Theological Review* 57 (1964): 23–38.

Kamen, Henry. "Confiscations in the Economy of the Spanish Inquisition." *The Economic History Review, Second Series,* 18 (1965): 511–25.

———. *The Spanish Inquisition.* New York, 1965.

Kayserling, Meyer [Moritz]. *Biblioteca Española-Portugueza-Judaica.* Strasbourg. 1890. New ed., with additional material and prologomenon, by Yosef H. Yerushalmi. New York, 1971.

———. *Ein Feiertag in Madrid.* Berlin, 1859.

———. *Geschichte der Juden in Portugal.* Leipzig, 1867. (Translated into Portuguese with the title *História dos Judeus em Portugal,* by Gabriele Borchardt Corrêa da Silva and Anita Novinsky, with introduction, updated bibliography, and notes by Anita Novinsky, São Paulo, 1971.)

Kellenbenz, Hermann. *Sephardim an der Unteren Elbe: Ihre Wirtschaftliche und Politische Bedeutung vom Ende des 16. bis zum Beginn des 18. Jahrhunderts.* Wiesbaden, 1958.

Kilham, Walter H. *Mexican Architecture of the Vice-Regal Period.* Toronto, 1927.

Kirkpatrick, F.A. *The Spanish Conquistadores.* London, 1934.

Kohut, George A. "Caceres." *JE* 3: 480–81.

———. "Jewish Heretics in the Philippines in the Sixteenth and Seventeenth Century." *PAJHS* 12 (1904): 149–56.

———. "Jewish Martyrs of the Inquisition in South America." *PAJHS* 4 (1896): 101–87.

———. "The Martyrdom of the Carabajal Family in Mexico, 1590–1601." *The Jewish Tribune* (Portland, Oregon), March 25, 1904.

Konetzke, Richard. *Colección de documentos para la historia de la formación social de Hispanoamérica, 1493–1810.* Vol. 1. Madrid, 1953.

———. "Grundzüge der spanischen Gesetzgebung über die Auswanderung nach dem amerikanischen Kolonialreich." *Festschrift Percy Ernst Schramm.* Vol. 2. Wiesbaden, 1964, pp. 105–13.

Kubler, George. *Mexican Architecture of the Sixteenth Century.* New Haven, 1948.

———. "Population Movements in Mexico." *HAHR* 22 (1942): 606–43.

Lafuente Machaín, Ricardo de. *Los portugueses en Buenos Aires (siglo XVII).* Madrid, 1931.

Lafuente y Zamalloa, Modesto. *Historia general de España.* 6 vols. Barcelona, 1879–1885.

Landis, Charles K. *Carabajal, the Jew: A Legend of Monterey.* Vineland, New Jersey, 1894.

Lang, M.F. "La búsqueda de azogue en el México colonial." *HM* 18 (1968–1969): 473–84.

Lea, Henry C. *Chapters from the Religious History of Spain Connected with the Inquisition.* Philadelphia, 1890.

———. *Ferrand Martinez and the Massacres of 1391.* New York, 1896.

———. *A History of the Inquisition in the Middle Ages.* 3 vols. London, 1888.

———. *A History of the Inquisition of Spain.* 4 vols. New York, 1906–1907.

———. *The Inquisition in the Spanish Dependencies.* New York, 1908.

León, Alonso de. *Historia de Nuevo León* (with additions by an anonymous author and General Fernando Sánchez de Zamora). Edited by Genaro García (*Documentos inéditos o muy raros para la historia de México,* Vol. 25). Mexico City, 1909.

———. *Historia de Nuevo León.* Edited by Israel Cavazos Garza. Monterrey, 1961.

Léon, Henry. *Histoire des Juifs de Bayonne.* Paris, 1893.

Leonard, Irving A. *Books of the Brave.* Cambridge, Massachusetts, 1949.

———. "On the Mexican Book Trade, 1576." *HR* 17 (1949): 18–34.

León-Portilla, Miguel; Barrera Vásquez, Alfredo; González, Luis; de la Torre, Ernesto; Velázquez, María del Carmen. *Historia documental de México.* Vol. 1. Mexico City, 1944.

Lewin, Boleslao. *La Inquisición en Hispanoamérica (Judíos, protestantes, patriotas).* Buenos Aires, 1962.

———. *Mártires y conquistadores judíos en la América Hispana.* Buenos Aires, 1954.

———. *El Santo Oficio en América y el más grande proceso inquistorial.* Buenos Aires, 1950.

Liebman, Seymour B. "The Abecedario and a Check-list of Mexican Inquisition Documents at the Henry E. Huntington Library." *HAHR* 44 (1964): 554–67.

———. *The Enlightened.* Coral Gables, Florida, 1967.

———. "Fuentes desconocidas de la historia mexicano-judía." *HM* 14 (1964–1965): 707–19.

———. *A Guide to Jewish References in the Mexican Colonial Era 1521–1821.* Philadelphia, 1964.

———. "The Jews of Colonial Mexico." *HAHR* 43 (1963): 95–108.

———. *The Jews of New Spain.* Coral Gables, Florida, 1970. Translated into Spanish as *Los judíos en México y América Central,* by Elsa Cecilia Frost. Mexico–Madrid–Buenos Aires, 1971.

———. "Los judíos en la historia de México." *Cuadernos Americanos* 26 (1967): 145–56.

———. "The Long Night of the Inquisition." *The Jewish Quarterly* 12 (1965): 28–32.

———. "They Came with Cortes: Notes on Mexican-Jewish History." *Judaism* 18 (1969): 91–102.

Livermore, Harold V. *A History of Portugal.* Cambridge, England, 1947.

————. *A New History of Portugal.* Cambridge, England, 1969.

Llorca, Bernardino. *La Inquisición en España.* Barcelona, 1954.

————. "La Inquisición española y los conversos judíos o *'marranos.'* " *Sefarad* 2 (1942): 113–51.

————. *Die Spanische Inquisition und die "Alumbrados" (1509–1667).* Berlin, 1934.

Llorente, Juan Antonio. *A Critical History of the Inquisition in Spain.* (The English edition published in 1823, republished Williamstown, Massachusetts, 1967.)

————. *Historia crítica de la Inquisición en España.* 10 vols. Madrid, 1822.

Loeb, Isidore. *Le sac des juiveries de Valence et de Madrid en 1391.* Paris, 1886.

Longhurst, John E. *Erasmus and the Spanish Inquisition: The Case of Juan de Valdes.* Albuquerque, 1950.

————. *Luther and the Spanish Inquisition: The Case of Diego de Uceda, 1528–1529.* Albuquerque, 1953.

López, Rodolfo. "Correspondencia de Luis de Carvajal con su familia." *BAGN* 4 (1933): 697–733.

López de Velasco, Juan. *Geografía y descripición universal de las Indias* [1571–1574]. Madrid, 1894.

López Martínez, Nicolás. *Los judaizantes castellanos y la Inquisición en tiempo de Isabel la Católica.* Burgos, 1954.

Loth, David. *Philip II of Spain.* New York, 1932.

Lumbroso, Jacob. *Melo Kaf Nahath* [Hebrew]. Venice, 1638–1639.

Lynch, John. *Spain under the Habsburgs.* 2 vols. New York, 1964, 1969.

MacNutt, Francis A., trans. and ed. *The Letters of Cortes.* 2 vols. New York, 1909.

Madariaga, Salvador de. *The Rise of the Spanish American Empire.* New York, 1947.

Maeso, David G. "Sobre la etimología de la voz *marrano* (criptojudío)." *Sefarad* 15 (1955): 373–85.

Mahler, Eduard. *Handbuch der Jüdischen Chronologie.* Leipzig, 1916.

Maillet, Henri. *L'Église et la répression sanglante de l'hérésie.* Edited by Karl Hanquet. Liège–Paris, 1909.

Maisonneuve, Henri. *Études sur les origines de l'Inquisition.* Paris, 1960.

Malkiel, Yakov. "Hispano-Arabic Marrano and Its Hispano-Latin Homophone." *JAOS* 68 (1948): 175–84.

Malvézin, Théophile. *Histoire des Juifs à Bordeaux.* Bordeaux, 1875.

Mariel de Ibáñez, Yolanda. *La Inquisición en México durante el siglo XVI.* Mexico City, 1946.

Markham, Clements R., ed. *The Hawkins' Voyages during the Reigns of Henry VIII, Queen Elizabeth and James I.* London, 1878.

Martínez del Río, Pablo. *Alumbrado.* Mexico City, 1937.

————. "La aventura mexicana de Sir John Hawkins." *MAMH* 2 (1943): 241–95.

Martínez Díez, Gonzalo. "La tortura judicial en la legislación histórica española." *Anuario de historia del derecho español* 32 (*Estudios en homenaje a Don Galo Sánchez*): 223–300.

Matos, Luis de. *Les Portugais en France au XVIe siècle: Études et documents.* Coimbra, 1952.

——. *Les Portugais à l'Université de Paris entre 1500 et 1550.* Coimbra, 1950.

Maynard, Theodore. *Saint Ignatius and the Jesuits.* New York, 1956.

Means, Philip Ainsworth. *The Spanish Main, Focus of Envy, 1492–1700.* New York, 1935.

Mecham, J. Lloyd. "Antonio de Espejo and His Journey to New Mexico." *Southwestern Historical Quarterly* 30 (1926): 114–38.

——. "The Northern Expansion of New Spain, 1552–1822. A Selected Descriptive Bibliographical List." *HAHR* 7 (1927): 233–76.

Medina, José Toribio. *Historia del tribunal del Santo Oficio de la Inquisición en México.* Santiago, Chile, 1905. Second ed., with notes and additions, by Julio Jiménez Rueda, Mexico City, 1952.

——. *La imprenta en México (1539–1581).* 8 vols. Santiago, Chile, 1907–1912.

——. *La primitiva inquisición americana (1493–1569).* 2 vols. Santiago, Chile, 1914.

Mendes dos Remédios, Joaquim. *Os Judeos em Portugal.* 2 vols. Coimbra, 1895–1928.

Méndez Plancarte, Alfonso. *Poetas Novohispanos.* 3 vols. Mexico City, 1942–1947.

Mendieta, Gerónimo de. *Historia eclesiástica indiana.* Edited by Joan de Domayquía. 4 vols. Mexico City, 1945.

Mendizábal, Miguel Othón de. "Carácter de la conquista y colonización de Zacatecas." *Obras Completas.* 6 vols. Mexico City, 1946–1947. Vol. 5: 73–82.

——. "Compendio histórico de Zacatecas." *Obras Completas,* 5: 83–271.

——. "Demografía mexicana: Época colonial, 1519–1810," *Boletín de la Sociedad Mexicana de Geografía y Estadística* 48 (1939): pp. 301–41.

—— *La evolución del noroeste de México.* Mexico City, 1930.

——. "La minería y la metalurgia mexicanas, 1520–1943." *Obras Completas,* 5: 25–72.

Merriman, Roger Bigelow. *The Rise of the Spanish Empire in the Old World and in the New.* 4 vols. New York, 1962.

Milano, Attilio. "Ferrara." *EJ* 6, cols. 1231–33.

——. *Storia degli ebrei in Italia.* Turin, 1963.

Miranda, José. *España y Nueva España en la época de Felipe II.* Mexico City, 1962.

——. *El tributo indígena en la Nueva España durante el siglo XVI.* Mexico City, 1952.

——. *Las ideas y las instituciones políticas mexicanas. Primera parte, 1521–1580.* Mexico, 1952.

Monterde, Francisco. *Perfiles de Taxco.* Mexico City, 1932.

Montúfar, Alonso de. *Descripción del arzobispado de México hecha en 1570.* Edited by L. García Pimentel. Mexico City, 1897.

Morga, Antonio de. *History of the Philippine Islands.* 2 vols. Cleveland, 1907.

Morissey, Richard J. "The Northward Advance of Cattle Ranching in New Spain, 1550–1600." *Agricultural History* 25 (1951): 115–21.

Moses, Bernard. *The Establishment of Spanish Rule in America.* London, 1898.

———. *Spanish Colonial Literature in South America.* London–New York, 1922.

———. *The Spanish Dependencies in South America.* 2 vols. London, 1914.

Mota y Escobar, Alonso de la. *Descripción geográfica de los reinos de Nueva Galicia, Nueva Vizcaya y Nuevo León.* Edited by Joaquín Ramírez Cabañas. Mexico City, 1940.

Motolinía, Toribio de. *History of the Indians of New Spain.* Translated by Elizabeth Andros Foster. Berkeley, 1950.

———. *Motolinia's History of the Indians of New Spain.* Edited by Francis Borgia Steck. Washington, D.C., 1951.

Neasham, V. Aubrey. "Spain's Emigrants to the New World." *HAHR* 19 (1939): 147–60.

Netanyahu, Benzion. *Don Isaac Abravanel: Statesman and Philosopher.* Philadelphia, 1968.

———. *The Marranos of Spain.* New York, 1966.

Neuman, Abraham A. *The Jews in Spain: Their Social, Political and Cultural Life during the Middle Ages.* 2 vols. Philadelphia, 1942.

"Nómina del tribunal de la Inquisición de Nueva España, 1571–1646." *BAGN* 26 (1955): 53–90; 293–313; 487–518; 687–707; 27 (1956): 315–61, 495–559; 703–48.

Novinsky, Anita. *Cristãos Novos na Bahia.* São Paulo, 1972.

Obregón, Balthasar de. *Historia de los descubrimientos antiguos y modernos* [1584]. Mexico City, 1924.

O'Gorman, Edmundo. *Historia de las divisiones territoriales de México.* Mexico City, 1966.

———. ed. *Libro primero de votos de la Inquisición de México, 1573–1600.* Mexico City, 1949.

Oleaster, Jerome [Hieronymus ab Oleastro]. *Commentaria in Mosi Pentateuchum.* Antwerp, 1569.

Oliveira Marques, A. H. de. *History of Portugal.* 2 vols. New York, 1972.

Oliveira Martins, Joaquim Pedro. *História de Portugal.* Porto, 1886.

Orozco y Berra, Manuel. *Historia antigua de la conquista de México.* Edited by Miguel León Portilla. 4 vols. Mexico City, 1960.

———. *Historia de la dominación española en México.* Vol. 2 (in *Biblioteca histórica mexicana de obras inéditas,* Vol. 9). Mexico City, 1938.

———. *Memoria para el plano de la ciudad de México.* Mexico City, 1867.

Ots Capdequí, José María. *España en América: El régimen de tierras en la época colonial.* Mexico City–Buenos Aires, 1959.

———. *El estado español en las Indias.* Mexico City, 1941.

———. *Instituciones sociales de la América española en el período colonial.* La Plata, Argentina, 1934.

Pallares, Eduardo. *El procedimiento inquisitorial.* Mexico City, 1951.

Paramo, Ludovicus. *De origine et progressu Officii Sanctae Inquisitionis.* Madrid, 1598.

Parkes, Henry Bamford. *A History of Mexico*. Boston, 1960.

Parry, J.H. *The Spanish Seaborne Empire*. New York, 1966.

———. *The Spanish Theory of Empire in the Sixteenth Century*. Cambridge, England, 1940.

Paso y Troncoso, Francisco del. *Epistolario de Nueva España. Biblioteca histórica mexicana de obras inéditas*. Second series. Vols. 10 and 11. Mexico, 1940.

Paulo, Amílcar. *Os Judeus em Trás-os-Montes*. N.p., 1965.

———. "Os Marranos nas Beiras." *Beira Alta* 19 (1960): 109–21, 191–203, 443–62; 20 (1961): 101–14, 295–314.

———. *Os Marranos em Portugal. Reminiscências judio-portuguesas*. Porto, 1971.

Peers, E. Allison. *Spain: A Companion to Spanish Studies*. New York–London, 1956.

Peres, Damião et al. *História de Portugal*. 8 vols. Barcelos, 1928–1938.

Pérez Bustamante, Ciríaco. "La población de Nueva España en el siglo XVI." *Boletín de la biblioteca Menéndez y Pelayo* 10 (1928), pp. 58–73.

Pérez Castro, Federico. "España y los judíos españoles: Interpretación de algunos aspectos de su cultura." In *The Sephardi Heritage*. Edited by R.D. Barnett. London, 1971, pp. 275–322.

Pérez de Tudela Bueso, J. *Las armadas de Indias y los orígenes de la política de colonización*. Madrid, 1956.

Peterson, Frederick A. *Ancient Mexico: An Introduction to the Pre-Hispanic Cultures*. New York, 1959.

Phelan, John L. *The Millennial Kingdom of the Franciscans in the New World*. Berkeley, 1956.

Philips, Miles. *Relación*. Edited by Joaquín García Icazbalceta, in his *Obras*, Vol. 7 (1898; 2d. ed. 1968), pp. 151–296.

Picón-Salas, Mariano. *A Cultural History of Spanish America*. Translated from the Spanish by Irving A. Leonard. Berkeley, 1962.

Pike, Ruth. "Seville in the Sixteenth Century." *HAHR* 41 (1961): 1–30.

Pimenta Ferro, Maria José. *Os Judeus em Portugal no século XIV*. Lisbon, 1970.

Piñera, Humberto. *El pensamiento español de los siglos XVI y XVII*. New York, 1970.

Pinta Llorente, Miguel de la. *Las cárceles inquisitoriales españolas*. Madrid, 1949.

———. *La Inquisición española*. Madrid, 1948.

———. *La Inquisición española y los problemas de la cultura ye de la intolerancia*. 2 vols. Madrid, 1953.

———. *Proceso criminal contra el hebraista salmantino Martín Martínez de Cantalapiedra*. Madrid, 1946.

———, ed. *Procesos inquisitoriales contra Francisco Sánchez de las Brozas*. Madrid, 1941.

Pi-Sunyer, Oriol. "Historical Background to the Negro in Mexico." *The Journal of Negro History* 42 (1957): 237–46.

Portillo, Estéban L. *Apuntes para la historia de Coahuila y Téxas*. Saltillo, [1886].

Powell, Philip Wayne. "The Chichimecas: Scourge of the Silver Frontier in Sixteenth Century Mexico." *HAHR* 25 (1945): 315–38.

——. "Presidios and Towns on the Silver Frontier of New Spain, 1550–1590." *HAHR* 24 (1944): 179–200.

——. *Soldiers, Indians and Silver: The Northward Advance of New Spain, 1550–1600*. Berkeley, 1952.

——. "Spanish Warfare against the Chichimecas in the 1570s." *HAHR* 24 (1944): 580–604.

Prescott, William H. *History of the Conquest of Mexico and History of the Conquest of Peru*. New York, 1936.

——. *History of the Reign of Ferdinand and Isabella, the Catholic*. 3 vols. Philadelphia, 1872.

Priestley, Herbert Ingram. *The Coming of the White Man, 1492–1848*. New York, 1929.

——. *The Mexican Nation: A History*. New York, 1923.

Quesada, Vicente G. *La vida intelectual en la América española durante los siglos XVI, XVII y XVIII*. Buenos Aires, 1910.

Quirino, Carlos. "El primer mexicano en Filipinas." *HM* 14 (1964–1965): 250–60.

Ramírez Aparicio, Manuel. *Los conventos suprimidos de México*. Mexico City, 1861.

Recopilación de leyes de los reynos de las Indias. 4 vols. Madrid, 1756.

Révah, I.S. "Autobiographie d'un Marrane, édition partielle d'un manuscrit de João (Moseh) Pinto Delgado." *REJ* 119 (1961): 41–130.

——. "La controverse sur les statuts de pureté de sang: Un document inédit: 'Relación y consulta del Cardenal Guevara sobre el negocio de Fray Agustín Saluzio' (Madrid, 13 août 1600)," *Bulletin Hispanique* 73 (1971): 263–306.

——. "Fundo de manuscritos pour l'histoire des nouveaux chrétiens portugais." *Boletim internacional de bibliografia luso-brasileira* 2 (1961): 276–312.

——. "Les Marranes." *REJ* 108 (1959–1960): 29–77.

——. "Les Marranes portugais et l'Inquisition au XVIe siècle." In *The Sephardi Heritage*. Edited by R.D. Barnett. London, 1971, pp. 479–526.

——. "La religion d'Uriel da Costa, Marrane de Porto." *Revue de l'histoire des religions* 161 (1962): 42–76.

Ricard, Robert. *La conquête spirituelle du Mexique*. Paris, 1933. Translated as *The Spiritual Conquest of Mexico*, by Lesley Byrd Simpson. Berkeley, 1966.

——. "Pour une étude du judaisme portugais au Mexique pendant la période coloniale." *Revue d'histoire moderne* 14 (1939): pp. 516–24. Reprinted in his *Études sur l'histoire morale et religieuse du Portugal*. Paris, 1970, pp. 196–204.

Riva Palacio, Vicente. *México a través de los siglos*. 5 vols. Mexico City, 1887–1889.

——, and Payno, Rafael. *El libro rojo, 1520–1867*. Mexico City, 1870.

Rivera Cambas, Manuel. *Los gobernantes de México*. 2 vols. Mexico City, 1872–1873.

————. *México pintoresco, artístico y monumental.* 3 vols. Mexico City, 1880–1883.

Rivkin, Ellis. "The Utilization of Non-Jewish Sources for the Reconstruction of Jewish History," *JQR (N.S.)* 48 (1957–1958): 183–203.

Roel, Santiago. *Nuevo León: Apuntes históricos.* Monterrey, 1938.

Romero Solano, Luis. "La Nueva España y las Filipinas." *HM* 3 (1953–1954): 420–31.

Rosenblat, Ángel. *La problación de América en 1492: viejos y nuevos cálculos.* Mexico City, 1967.

————. *La población indígena de América desde 1492 hasta la actualidad.* Buenos Aires, 1945.

Rossi, Giovanni Bernardo de. *Historisches Wörterbuch der jüdischen Schriftsteller und ihrer Werke.* Translated by C.H. Hamberger from *Dizionario storico degli autori ebrei e delle loro opere.* Leipzig, 1839.

Rotbaum, Iṭic Croitoru. *Documentos coloniales originados en el Santo Oficio del Tribunal de la Inquisición de Cartagena de Indias (Contribución a la Historia de Colombia).* Bogotá, 1971.

Roth, Cecil. *The History of the Jews of Italy.* Philadelphia, 1946.

————. *A History of the Marranos.* Philadelphia, 1932.

————. "Jews, Conversos and the Blood-Accustation in Fifteenth-Century Spain." *The Dublin Review* 383 (1932): 219–31.

————. "The Religion of the Marranos." *JQR (N.S.)* 22 (1931–1932): 1–33. Reprinted in his *Gleanings: Essays in Jewish History, Letters and Art.* New York, 1967, pp. 119–51.

————. *The Spanish Inquisition.* London, 1937.

————. *Venice (History of the Jews in Venice).* Philadelphia, 1930.

Rubio Mañé, J. Ignacio. *Introducción al estudio de los virreyes de Nueva España, 1535–1746.* 3 vols. Mexico City, 1959–1963.

————. "La expedición de Miguel López de Legazpi a Filipinas." *BAGN* (Second Series) 5 (1964): 427–798.

————. *D. Luis de Velasco, El Virrey Popular.* Mexico City, 1946.

————. *Movimiento marítimo entre Veracruz y Campeche, 1801–1810.* Mexico City, 1954.

————. "Ordenanzas para la limpieza de la ciudad de México." *BAGN* 27 (1956): 19–24.

Rubio y Moreno, Luis. *Pasajeros a Indias (Colección de documentos inéditos para la historia de hispano-américa,* Vols. 9 and 13). 2 vols. Madrid, 1917.

Ruiz Almansa, Javier. "La población de España en el siglo XVI: Estudio sobre los recuentos de vecindario de 1594, llamados comúnmente 'Censo de Tomás González.'" *Revista internacional de sociología* 3: (1945) 114–36.

Rumeu de Armas, Antonio. *Los viajes de John Hawkins a América (1562–1595).* Seville, 1947.

Saco, José Antonio. *Historia de la esclavitud de los indios en el Nuevo Mundo.* 2 vols. Havana, 1932.

————. *Historia de la esclavitud de la raza africana en el Nuevo Mundo.* 3 vols. Havana, 1938.

Sahagún, Bernardino de. *Historia general de las cosas de Nueva España.* Edited by Ángel María Garibay. Mexico City, 1956.

Salomon, Herman P. "The Portuguese Inquisition and Its Victims in the Light of Recent Polemics." *The Journal of the American Portuguese Cultural Society* 5 (1971): 19–28, 50–55.

———. Review of Seymour B. Liebman, *The Jews of New Spain, AJHQ* 62 (1972–1973): 190–201.

Sámano, Juan de. *Relación de la conquista de los teules chichimecas que dió Juan de Sámano.* In Joaquín García Icazbalceta, *Colección de documentos inéditos para la historia de México.* Vol. 2. Mexico City, 1866, pp. 262–87.

Sanceau, Elaine. *The Reign of the Fortunate King 1495–1521.* Hamden, Connecticut, 1969.

Sanz Arizmendi, Claudio. "Cuatro expediciones de Juan Haquinés." *Boletín del Instituto de Estudios Americanistas de Sevilla* 1 (1913): 59–69.

Saraiva, António José. *História da cultura em Portugal.* 3 vols. Lisbon, 1950–1962.

———. *Inquisição e Cristãos-Novos.* Porto, 1959.

Scelle, Georges. *La traite négrière aux Indes de Castille.* Vol. 1. Paris, 1906.

Schäfer, Ernst. *Beiträge zur Geschichte des spanischen Protestantismus und der Inquisition im sechzehnten Jahrhundert.* 3 vols. Gütersloh, 1902.

———. *El consejo real y supremo de las Indias.* 2 vols. Seville, 1935–1947.

Schurz, William Lytle. *The Manila Galleon.* New York, 1939.

Selke, Ángela. *Los chuetas y la Inquisición.* Madrid, 1972.

Serrão, Joel, ed. *Dicionário de história de Portugal.* 4 vols. Lisbon, 1963–1971.

Seville. *Catálogo de los fondos americanos del Archivo de protocolos de Sevilla.* 5 vols. Madrid, 1930–1937.

Sicroff, Albert A. "Clandestine Judaism in the Hieronymite Monastery of Nuestra Señora de Guadalupe." *Studies in Honor of M.J. Benardete.* New York, 1965, pp. 89–125.

———. *Les controverses des statuts de "pureté de sang" en Espagne du XVe au XVIIe siècle.* Paris, 1960.

———. "Limpieza de sangre." *EJ* 11, cols. 255–56.

Sigüenza, José de. *Historia de la orden de San Jerónimo.* In *Nueva biblioteca de autores españoles.* Vol. 8. Madrid, 1907.

Simpson, Lesley Byrd. *The Encomienda in New Spain: The Beginning of Spanish Mexico.* Berkeley, 1950.

———. *Many Mexicos.* Berkeley, 1966.

———. *The Repartimiento System of Native Labor in New Spain and Guatemala.* Berkeley, 1938.

Solórzano Pereira, Juan de. *Política Indiana.* Madrid, 1736.

Sonne, Isaiah. "Yaakov Lumbrozo ve-ha-Ḥeshek Shlomo" (Hebrew). *Kiryat Sefer* 11 (1932): 499–506.

Soustelle, Jacques. *Daily Life of the Aztecs on the Eve of the Spanish Conquest.* Translated from the French by Patrick O'Brian. New York, 1961.

Spiegel, Shalom. *The Last Trial.* New York, 1967.
Steck, Francis Borgia. *El primer colegio en América: Santa Cruz de Tlatelolco.* Mexico City, 1944.
Stephens, Henry M. *Portugal.* New York–London, 1893.
Szajkowski, Zosa. "Trade Relations of Marranos in France with the Iberian Peninsula in the Sixteenth and Seventeenth Centuries." *JQR* 50 (1959–1960): 69–78.
Tamayo, Jorge L. *Geografía general de México.* 2 vols. Mexico City, 1949.
Thompson, J. Eric. *Mexico before Cortez.* New York–London, 1933.
Tibón, Gutierre. *Onomástica hispanoamericana.* Mexico City, 1961.
Toro, Alfonso. *La familia Carvajal.* 2 vols. Mexico City, 1944.
———, ed. *Los judíos en la Nueva España* (Vol. 20 of the *Publicaciones del Archivo General de la Nación*). Mexico City, 1932.
Torquemada, Juan de. *Tractatus contra madianitas et ismaelitas.* Edited by Nicolás López Martínez and Vicente Proaño Gil. Burgos, 1957.
Torquemada, Tomás de. *Compilación de las instrucciones del Oficio de la Santa Inquisición.* Madrid, 1630.
Torre, Antonio de la and Suárez Fernández, Luis. *Documentos referentes a las relaciones con Portugal durante el reinado de los Reyes Católicos.* 3 vols. (*Consejo Superior de Investigaciones Científicas, Patronato Menéndez Pelayo, Biblioteca "Reyes Católicos," Documentos y Textos,* Numbers 7, 8, and 10). Valladolid, 1958–1963.
Torres-Ríoseco, Arturo. *The Epic of Latin American Literature.* Berkeley, 1967.
Toussaint, Manuel. *Tasco.* Mexico City, 1931.
Trens, Manuel B. "Apuntes históricos sobre el nordeste de México." *BAGN* 28 (1957): 323–34.
———. "La legislación española de Indias en la Nueva España." *BAGN* 23 (1952): 415–51.
Universal Jewish Encyclopedia, s. v. "Caceres (or Cacerez), Antonio Diaz de" (2:621); "Carabajal, Luis de (Governor)" (3:36); "Carabajal (Caravajal), Francisca Nuñez de" (3:36).
Uribe de Fernández de Córdoba, Susana. "Bibliografía histórica mexicana." *HM* 15 (1965–1966): 132–54.
Usque, Samuel. *Consolaçam as tribulaçoens de Israel.* Translated by Martin A. Cohen as *Consolation for the Tribulations of Israel.* Philadelphia, 1965.
Vacandard, E. *The Inquisition: A Critical and Historical Study of the Coercive Power of the Church.* Translated by Bertrand L. Conway. London, 1908.
Vaillant, George C. and Vaillant, Suzannah B. *The Aztecs of Mexico.* Garden City, New York, 1962.
Valdeón Baruque, Julio. *Enrigue II de Castilla: La guerra civil y la consolidación del régimen (1366–1371).* Valladolid, 1966.
———. *Los judíos de Castilla y la revolución trastamara.* Valladolid, 1968.
Valle-Arizpe, Artemio de. *Historia de la ciudad de México según los relatos de sus cronistas.* Mexico City, 1946.
Van der Vekené, E. *Bibliographie der Inquisition.* Hildesheim, 1963.

Van Horne, John. *La "Grandeza Mexicana" de Bernardo de Balbuena.* Urbana, Ill., 1930.

Vázquez de Espinosa, Antonio. *Compendium and Description of the West Indies.* Translated by Charles Upson Clark. Washington, D.C., 1942.

———. *Descripción de la Nueva España en el siglo XVII.* Mexico City, 1944.

Veitía Linaje, José de. *Norte de la contratación de las Indias occidentales.* Seville, 1672.

———. *The Spanish Rule of Trade to the West Indies.* Translated by John Stevens. London, 1720.

Velázquez, María del Cármen. "Historia de América y Filipinas." *HM* 15 (1965–1966): 638–60.

Vetancourt, Agustín de. *Teatro Mexicano.* 4 vols. Mexico City, 1870–1871.

Vicens Vives, Jaime, ed. *Historia social y económica de España y América.* 5 vols. Barcelona, 1957–1959.

Villaseñor y Villaseñor, Alejandro. *Gobernantes de México y formas de gobierno.* Mexico City, 1910.

Vivó, Jorge A. *Geografía de México.* Mexico City–Buenos Aires, [1948].

Von Hagen, Victor. *The Aztec: Man and Tribe.* New York, 1961.

Walsh, William T. *Characters of the Inquisition.* New York, 1930.

———. *Isabella of Spain, the Last Crusader.* New York, 1930.

West, Robert C. *The Mining Community in Northern New Spain. The Parral Mining District.* Berkeley, 1949.

Williams, C. S.v. "Conversion, Theology of." *New Catholic Encyclopedia,* 4: 288–89.

Williams, Schaefer. "The G.R.G. Conway Collection in the Library of Congress: A Checklist." *HAHR* 35 (1955): 386–97.

Williamson, James A. *Hawkins of Plymouth.* London, 1949.

Wischnitzer, W. "Caceres." *Enciclopaedia Judaica* [German], Vol. 4, col. 1244.

Wiznitzer, Arnold. "Crypto-Jews in Mexico during the Sixteenth Century." *AJHQ* 51 (1961–1962): 168–213.

———. "Crypto-Jews in Mexico during the Seventeenth Century." *AJHQ* 51 (1961–1962): 222–68.

Wolf, Eric R. *Sons of the Shaking Earth.* Chicago, 1959.

Wright, I.A. *Spanish Documents concerning English Voyages to the Caribbean, 1527–1568.* London, 1929.

Yerushalmi, Yosef H. *From Spanish Court to Italian Ghetto—Isaac Cardoso: A Study in Seventeenth Century Marranism and Jewish Apologetics.* New York, 1971.

Zamacois, Niceto. *Historia de México desde sus tiempos más remotos hasta nuestros días.* 18 vols. Barcelona, 1878–1888.

Zavala, Silvio. "La amalgama en la minería de Nueva España." *HM* 11 (1961–1962): 416–421.

———. *La encomienda indiana.* Madrid, 1935.

———. *Los esclavos indios en Nueva España.* Mexico City, 1968.

———. *La filosofía política en la conquista de América.* Mexico City, 1947.

———. *Las instituciones jurídicas en la conquista de América.* Madrid, 1935.

————. *New Viewpoints on the Spanish Colonization of America.* Phila-delphia–London, 1943.

Zepeda Rincón, Tomás. *La instrucción pública en la Nueva España en el siglo XVI.* Mexico City, 1933.

Zimmels, H.J. *Ashkenazim and Sephardim: Their Relations, Differences and Problems as Reflected in the Rabbinical Responsa.* London, 1958.

————. *Die Marranen in der Rabbinischen Literatur.* Berlin, 1932.

Zuckerman, B. *Anleitung und Tabellen zur Vergleichung jüdischer und christlicher Zeitangaben.* Breslau, 1893.

Zurita, Alonso de. *Life and Labor in Ancient Mexico: The Brief and Summary Relation of the Lords of New Spain.* Translated by Benjamin Keen. New Brunswick, New Jersey, 1963.

Index

This index follows English alphabetization; hence Spanish *ch*, *ll*, and *rr* are not treated as separate letters. The *ñ*, however, will follow *n*. As in the text, accent marks appear on capital letters as a pronunciation aide.

The index derives primarily from the text. Names, places, and concepts found in the notes are usually mentioned only if they also appear in the text or supplement it. Page numbers in italics refer to the notes.

The names of the members of the Carvajal family listed on pages 277 and 278 are alphabetized according to the first surname found there.